Women
Pulitzer Playwrights

Women Pulitzer Playwrights

Biographical Profiles and Analyses of the Plays

CAROLYN CASEY CRAIG

McFarland & Company, Inc., Publishers
Jefferson, North Carolina, and London

LIBRARY OF CONGRESS CATALOGUING-IN-PUBLICATION DATA

Craig, Carolyn Casey, 1947–
  Women Pulitzer playwrights : biographical profiles and analyses of the plays / Carolyn Casey Craig.
    p.   cm.
  Includes bibliographical references and index.

  ISBN-13: 978-0-7864-1881-7
  softcover : 50# alkaline paper ∞

  1. American drama—Women authors—History and criticism.
  2. Women and literature—United States—History—20th century.
  3. American drama—20th century—History and criticism.
  4. Dramatists, American—20th century—Biography.   5. Women dramatists, American—Biography.   6. Pulitzer Prizes.   I. Title.
  PS338.W6C73   2004
  812'.5099287—dc22
                                            2004020165

British Library cataloguing data are available

©2004 Carolyn Casey Craig. All rights reserved

No part of this book may be reproduced or transmitted in any form or by any means, electronic or mechanical, including photocopying or recording, or by any information storage and retrieval system, without permission in writing from the publisher.

Cover images ©2004 Comstock, Inc.

Manufactured in the United States of America

McFarland & Company, Inc., Publishers
  Box 611, Jefferson, North Carolina 28640
  www.mcfarlandpub.com

To the women in my family,
for being so caring and patient while I worked on this—
my sister Bev, my daughter Wendi, and my niece Becky.

And in memory of my mother, Elaine Ruth,
who would have been the first to read my manuscript.

Acknowledgments

My endless thanks to all the playwrights who gave their time and generous cooperation toward this project—especially Beth Henley, Maggie Edson, Wendy Wasserstein and Paula Vogel, who gave help on repeated occasions. A special note of thanks to Pearl Cleage and LisaGay Hamilton for their assistance and insights, which helped to shape the chapter on the legacy of black women playwrights. To all these women artists, I send my sincere appreciation and my admiration for their work.

Thanks also to the following for special permissions granted: Sherry Green Fisher and the Beah Richards Estate for permission to use lines from Beah Richards, *A Black Woman Speaks* (all rights reserved by the estate); and to Tom Lisanti and the New York Public Library Performing Arts Archives, Billy Rose Collection, for permission to use archival photographs of playwrights.

Contents

Acknowledgments	vi
Introduction. "Take, for Example...": A Brief Retrospect on Women, Theatre, and Prizes	1
Prologue. Family Ties—A Troublesome Knot?	13
PART I. FAMILY LIES AND THE UNWED WOMAN: GALE, GLASPELL, AND AKINS	17
1. The 1920s: Those Not-So-Good Old Days	18
2. Zona Gale and the Real Village Tale	25
3. Susan Glaspell: From Iowa Village to Greenwich Village	44
4. The Depression Years: Gaining Despite the Losses	61
5. Zoe Akins, Escape Artist	66
PART II. DOMESTIC WARS: CHASE AND FRINGS	83
6. The 1940s: Women in a World at War	84
7. Mary Chase and Her Wartime Rabbit	89
8. The 1950s: An Uncomfortable Homecoming	108
9. Ketti Frings and Her Stageworthy Angel	113

PART III. WHOSE WOMAN IS SHE? HENLEY, NORMAN, AND WASSERSTEIN ... 127

10. Being Female in the 1950s, '60s and '70s ... 129
11. Beth Henley's Funny-Terrible World View ... 140
12. The 1980s: Backlash and Beyond ... 160
13. Marsha Norman: Getting Out the Truth about Family and Self ... 166
14. Wendy Wasserstein: Lola's Well-Rounded Daughter ... 184

PART IV. LESSONS DRIVEN HOME: VOGEL AND EDSON ... 207

15. The 1990s: Gender Crisis at the Crossroads (Or, Wrong Turn at the Men's Movement) ... 208
16. Paula Vogel's Winding Road to Victory ... 213
17. Margaret Edson's Advanced Course in *Wit* ... 232

PART V. HISTORY IN THE STAGING? SUZAN-LORI PARKS AND THE SISTERHOOD OF BLACK PLAYWRIGHTS ... 249

18. The Early 2000s: "Bang, Bang—You're American" ... 251
19. Suzan-Lori Parks: Putting Dirt and Deadly Games Onstage ... 259
20. "Also in the Winner's Circle" (The Legacy of Black Women Playwrights) ... 279

Epilogue: Parting Thoughts on Family Flux and Cultural Flummery ... 291
Chapter Notes ... 297
Selected Bibliography ... 319
Index ... 331

Introduction.
"Take, for Example...":
A Brief Retrospect on Women, Theatre, and Prizes

Imagine the sound of a grand fanfare. A sudden flourish of trumpets. The number of trumpets is exactly eleven: one for each woman who has won the Pulitzer Prize for Drama to date. From the 1917 launching of the Drama Pulitzer—the oldest and most prestigious of America's playwriting awards—through 2004, the list of winners has included only these plays by women:

- *Miss Lulu Bett* by Zona Gale (1921)
- *Alison's House* by Susan Glaspell (1931)
- *The Old Maid* by Zoe Akins (1935)
- *Harvey* by Mary Coyle Chase (1945)
- *Look Homeward, Angel* by Ketti Frings (1958)
- *Crimes of the Heart* by Beth Henley (1981)
- *'Night, Mother* by Marsha Norman (1983)
- *The Heidi Chronicles* by Wendy Wasserstein (1989)
- *How I Learned to Drive* by Paula Vogel (1998)
- *Wit* by Margaret Edson (1999)
- *Topdog/Underdog* by Suzan-Lori Parks (2002)

Playwright Arthur Miller once scoffed that, "Like most good luck, the Pulitzer Prize usually comes to those who don't need it."[1] That was easy for

Miller to say—a man who, by the early 1950s, had won a Pulitzer Prize, a Tony Award, and a slew of other awards and grants. But these eleven playwrights have categorically needed the good luck of the Pulitzer Prize, simply because they are women. And, because they are women, they probably deserve more fanfare than male winners: They've tackled much bigger, more forbidding obstacles to make their marks in the blatantly male-dominated world of theatre production. (You may already know that theatre was an exclusive men's club for more than 2,000 years. But did you know that, even now, plays by women make up a scant 8 percent of the total produced on Broadway? Or that, at last report, only 7 percent of the nation's federally funded theatres produce plays by women?[2])

These eleven Pulitzer playwrights have been given scattered fanfares in books and articles. But someone needed to write a book about all of them: to collect the stories of all these remarkable women and their Pulitzer triumphs. Somehow, that someone became me. I had already done in-person interviews with Beth Henley, Marsha Norman and Wendy Wasserstein for my doctoral dissertation. And when two more women took the prize at the century's end—Paula Vogel and Maggie Edson—I arranged to do interviews with them and to see productions of their prize plays. Time crunches prevented a personal interview with the newest winner, Suzan-Lori Parks: She was starting an 11-week book tour for her first novel, but I acquired transcripts and videos of existing interviews with Parks and communicated with her reps and agents. The chapter on Parks also gives a fanfare for other notable black women playwrights, and chunks of my phone interview with playwright-novelist Pearl Cleage are woven into that section. To bring to life the stories of the first five winners, I raided special archives of theatres and arts libraries and the playwrights' home towns for first-hand material. As much as possible, I have used the words and insights of the playwrights themselves to tell the stories of their lives and art.

A strong thread of feminist history was built into this book by its very nature, but I have enlarged it: I set the stage for each playwright and play with a quick sketch of what the decade was like, highlighting the big strokes of women's experiences—in the culture, society, the family. In doing so, I found new, vivid meaning in the truism that art reflects life. On many levels, these playwrights and their plays reflect the journey of women through the last century. To trace this journey, I start with Zona Gale, who barged her way into news journalism when women were barely tolerated in the field, and battled for women's rights in her life and writing. Her Pulitzer play, *Miss Lulu Bett*, championed the unmarried woman who was forced to live as a workhorse in the home of a married relative. It was Gale's prime example of what a few critics called "feminist propaganda."

Tracing this journey through the 1950s leads to the indomitable Ketti Frings. Luckily, while a 1956 issue of *Life* magazine was declaring the career woman "that fatal mistake that feminism propagated,"[3] Ketti was too busy being a career woman to take note. That was the year she crafted *Look Homeward, Angel*, her stunning play based on Wolfe's autobiographical novel. In her diverse career, Ketti wrote acclaimed scripts for both stage and screen.

Wendy Wasserstein's own experiences during and after the women's movement compelled her to write her 1989 winner, *The Heidi Chronicles*. Her title character, feminist art historian Heidi Holland, flounders in the wake of the movement, but now has the power to make choices, including her choice to become the single parent of an adopted baby daughter.

As Gloria Steinem remarked about Wendy's play, "To have a play on Broadway about the change that a woman goes through in her life ... this is a revolution in itself."[4] Against all odds, five of these plays by women opened on Broadway; a few others were moved there after they garnered Pulitzer Prizes. Another story behind the crafting and production of these plays is a bold account of the diverse and surprising ways in which women have gained ground in the theatrical strongholds of men.

To get an idea of how strong those holds have been, imagine how the history of theatre from a woman's perspective might be reduced to one paragraph: In the classic Greek theatre, on which our Western theatre is based, heavily funded state festivals mounted plays written by men, produced by men, performed only by men, in huge competitions honoring the fantastically male god Dionysus. (The plays were even preceded by lush parades with tree-sized phallus "floats.") This gender bias was still in place two thousand years later in the theatre of Shakespeare's day, when all producers, playwrights, managers and actors were, predictably, men, men, and more men. In the seventeenth century, women were finally invited to participate as actresses—but then were not respected for it in the morning. However, over time, actresses did gain respect and a foothold, and paved the way for women in other areas of this "reflection of life" known as theatre.

The theatre artist who selects which aspect of life to reflect from the stage has always been the playwright. Another hard fact of theatre history is that competition and awards have always played a crucial part in determining which plays and playwrights endure to become examples for other writers. If Aeschylus and Sophocles had not walked away with the top prizes from the Festivals of Dionysus, their surviving scripts would not continue to be read and produced. And Eugene O'Neill would not have turned out a trilogy of plays called *Mourning Becomes Electra*—or, perhaps, any plays.

Because what budding playwrights have desperately needed, throughout history, is role models.

Even one hundred years ago, a male would-be playwright could reflect on millenniums of role models and decide that writing for the stage might be worth a try. The wealth of examples open to him has not been limited to the glory that was Greece or Rome. Its bounty has reached across centuries and continents: from Sophocles to Zeami; Kyd to Calderon; Congreve to Chekhov—the list goes on and on.

Meanwhile, what did the budding woman playwright find if she searched across time for some role model or validation? If she dug deep, she might find one determined woman per century; but only the most self-effacing closet dramatist could take heart from such examples as:

- The tenth-century German nun Hrosvitha, who managed to churn out six plays about the terrible torments of virgin martyrs, despite the drawbacks of the Dark Ages;
- The seventeenth-century writer Aphra Behn, who does get a mention in some theatre texts for her comedy of intrigue, *The Rover*. However, Mrs. Behn initially had the "guile" to pass off her writing as the work of a man[5];
- Mercy Otis Warren, who was the Hrosvitha of the American Revolution, turning out never-produced playlets about the terrible torments of Patriot soldiers;
- Lady Gregory, of nineteenth-century Irish theatre, who began playwriting as a widow of fifty. Her years of helping William Yeats with his verse plays were not reciprocated: About her efforts on one play, she wrote, "If I had listened to Mr. Yeats' advice, I should have given it up"[6];
- Anna Cora Mowatt, the first professional American woman playwright. About her 1845 comedy of manners *Fashion*, a local paper announced: "We have little confidence in female dramatic productions ... but we wish the lady a happy debut."[7] (*Fashion* set a record of twenty performances at New York's Park Theatre; yet Anna soon relinquished playwriting for acting);
- Any one of the dozen "Women Who Have Written Successful Plays," whose works are altogether unknown to us, listed in a 1906 article by Virginia Frame.[8]

Greeted with this legacy of obscurity, emerging modern women playwrights have been heroic in managing to emerge at all. Unlike men, they have not had copious role models replete with visibility and validation in their society and beyond. Throughout history, that validation of the (male) playwright has meant valorization through established competitions and awards. Certainly, the "big daddy" of all competitions was the Festival of Dionysus, which accounted for the plays of Aeschylus surviving to reach the twentieth century and the hands of Eugene O'Neill. And surely the immortality of O'Neill as a playwright has been given an incalculable boost by his gain of four Pulitzer Prizes (and a Nobel Prize to boot).

Even benefactors and prize-givers are inspired by example. In 1902, the aging Hungarian immigrant Joseph Pulitzer, who had built a multi-million-dollar newspaper empire, was struck with the idea for a grand scheme that would make an ongoing contribution to journalism. Just the year before, the first prizes of worldwide significance had been bestowed through the beneficence of Alfred Nobel, the Swedish inventor of dynamite. Taking this as his philanthropic cue, Pulitzer aligned himself with Columbia University, and endowed a trust fund from which an array of journalism prizes would be awarded annually. Pulitzer never lived to see his scheme implemented: Mired in disagreements between the benefactor and Columbia's President Butler, the project was shelved for years. It was not until 1917, using guidelines set down in Pulitzer's will, that Columbia introduced the awards that bear his name.

Since the first Pulitzer jury conferred the first Drama Pulitzer in 1918, the prize has been both warmly received and hotly contended. Detractors grumble that the only plays given a shot at a Pulitzer are those that have succeeded on Broadway. But they could aim the same complaint at the other major theatre awards: The New York Drama Critics' Circle Award, launched in 1936 to protest the Pulitzer jury's neglect of Lillian Hellman's controversial *The Children's Hour*; and the annual Tony Awards, given by the League of New York Theatres (only to Broadway plays) since the mid-1940s. New York—and mainly Broadway—still represents the country's biggest capital investment in theatre. So, for better or worse, it remains the prime crucible of theatrical success: America's version of the Festival of Dionysus.

The Pulitzer Prize commands respect for reasons beyond its nine decades of endurance. The prize carries a "heavy weight," as Wendy Wasserstein puts it. (So much so that Wendy quips, "I *never* thought it would happen to me.") The original wording of the Drama Award Citation was perhaps too weighty, in its ponderous Victorian phrasing. That first Drama jury in 1917 could not find a play that would "best represent the educational value and power of the stage in raising the standard of good morals, good taste, and good manners."[9]

The spirit of the award would have to change—and did, when the theatre company of Susan Glaspell and her husband Jig Cook (founders of the Provincetown Players) produced Eugene O'Neill's first full-length play. The play, *Beyond the Horizon*, was lauded by the *New York Telegram* as "a masterpiece" of the 1920 season.[10] The bad news for the Pulitzer jury was that O'Neill's masterpiece was quite devoid of any depiction of high moral standards. The play was a brutal look at the wasted lives of two brothers in love with the same woman. One Pulitzer juror wrote in his report, "I wish this play did not go quite so far in its depressing delineation of a decaying family." Nonetheless, the jurors opted for high merit over high morals, changing the philosophy behind the citation and, eventually, its wording.[11]

The award made to O'Neill's "delineation of a decaying family" was only the second Drama Pulitzer that Columbia managed to give away: In 1919, it had again passed over the theatre season. In 1918 the first Pulitzer had gone to Jesse Williams' *Why Marry?*, a comedy focused on what the playwright called "our most ancient and necessary institution."[12] But as Williams' play and succeeding plays depict, marriage has only been thought necessary for women.

The idea that, for women, almost any marriage is better than none has enjoyed a very long run in American drama. As Jane Bonin noted in her book *Major Themes in Prize-Winning American Drama*, "That marriage (for women) represents the lesser of two evils was to become one of the most pervasive themes in prize-winning American plays."[13] Ironically, the one theme which has become more pervasive in the Pulitzer plays has been that of family dysfunction—and, yes, decay—which O'Neill introduced in *Beyond the Horizon* (and which Zona Gale continued with her 1921 winner, *Miss Lulu Bett*). These two themes run point-counterpoint throughout prize drama, reflecting an ambivalence about marriage and the family. "In drama as in life," states Bonin, "marriage is usually ... the pivotal event in a woman's life."[14] Yet, post-marriage family life is portrayed as demoralizing and even devastating to the individual. This trend inspired Tom Scanlon's book *Family, Drama, and American Dreams*, which argues that "American drama in the twentieth century has been strikingly preoccupied with problems of family life."[15] (Three-fourths of all prize-winning American plays have centered on family problems.)

Skeptics might ask whether these prize-winning plays are truly representative. An emphatic "yes" is given by Jane Bonin, as well as by Thomas Adler in his book *Mirror on the Stage: The Pulitzer Plays as an Approach to American Drama*. Adler takes the Pulitzer plays as our primary index of "representative plays."[16] Bonin hails prize-winning drama as "a sensitive barometer ... to the public taste [and] its general concerns and attitudes"—a "useful index to the American value system."[17]

The dispersal of the Pulitzer plays, throughout the country and beyond, argues for their wide appeal and influence. Besides enjoying runs in far-flung theatres, the bulk of the Pulitzer plays have been translated into films (including such early winners as Gale's *Miss Lulu Bett* in 1921, and Akins' *The Old Maid*, 1935). And surely, a remarkably common theme running through them is what Adler calls the "deromanticizing of the American family." Adler cites Zona Gale's *Miss Lulu Bett* as the wellspring for this theme: "Gale ... begins in *Lulu Bett* a deromanticizing of the family that will continue in much of American drama; what should be a nourishing fount for its members is often awash in selfishness and recrimination."[18]

So, the main themes found in these Pulitzer plays by women come as no big surprise. Nine of them are focused on family members in turmoil, if not crisis; a tenth centers on an alternative form of family. These eleven playwrights help to prove the rule that American drama has been, as Tom Scanlon claimed, "strikingly preoccupied with problems of family life."[19] What sets apart the plays of these eleven Pulitzer winners is that their reflections of family problems are filtered through the visions and experiences of women.

By the examples of their plays and lives, these women have made me think about family in new ways, perplexing ways, creative ways. The personal family stories of these women are as fascinating as the stories they've crafted for the stage—from Zona Gale, who married at 54, after she had already adopted her daughter, Leslyn—to Wendy Wasserstein, who gave birth to her baby Lucy at age 48—to Maggie Edson, who shares a home and two sons with her partner, art-curator Linda Merrill—to Suzan-Lori Parks, who is the first black woman to take the prize, and the wife of Paul Oscher, the first white musician to play with Muddy Waters.

Exploring the background of each playwright and play helps to illuminate the whole sweep of plays and the near-century of life they have spanned.

Now, to begin this tribute to a century of Pulitzer-Prize women playwrights, their plays, and the life they've reflected, I start with a quick introductory fanfare (minus trumpets) for each of these eleven winning women:

Zona Gale, the 1921 winner for *Miss Lulu Bett*, was a petite but stubborn Wisconsin writer who pestered her way into news reporting before her triumphs as a best-selling novelist and playwright. The thrust behind her play and book version of *Miss Lulu Bett*, both written in the year women won the vote, was how much more was needed in terms of women winning true independence. Zona was a relentless feminist and social activist, whose public stands and writing could have landed her in prison.

Susan Glaspell, the 1931 winner for *Alison's House*, took the Pulitzer with the last play in her wide-ranging career. Co-founder of the seminal Provincetown Players (with her husband George Cram Cook), Susan introduced Eugene O'Neill to the Players, which led to O'Neill's huge success but also to the unjust overshadowing of Glaspell's own contributions: a dozen play scripts, her acting and directing talents, and her shaping influence on the work of O'Neill and others.

In Glaspell's *Alison's House*, the family of an acclaimed poet (patterned after Emily Dickinson) clashes over a sheaf of poems that expressed her love for a married man. Glaspell wrote the play from a most personal vantage point, having begun her relationship with George Cook while he was still married to another.

Zoe Akins, 1935 winner for *The Old Maid*, enjoyed a phenomenal career on both coasts, writing and adapting a string of plays and screenplays that starred the biggest talents in New York and Hollywood. Despite the devastations of the Depression and World War II, Akins' lush melodramas flourished, providing much-needed escape for the era's audiences. But her scripts—*The Old Maid* in particular—also challenged the family and social restraints that were stifling women.

Mary Coyle Chase, the 1945 winner for *Harvey*, began as a brazen news reporter who disguised herself as a man to cover stories off-limits to women. However, it was her family's Irish tales of charms and "pookas" that would inform Mary's stage comedy featuring a giant invisible rabbit. In Mary's play the family of Elwood Dowd is torn apart, then brought together, by the antics of Elwood's rabbit pooka. Labeled a play with "a spiritual message in farce terms," Mary's script questioned social assumptions while it provided comic relief in the closing months of war.

Like Zoe Akins, Ketti Frings (winner for *Look Homeward, Angel*, 1958) wrote for both stage and screen. In paring down Thomas Wolfe's epic novel for her play, Frings made the work her own. She distilled the conflict into two crucial weeks leading up to protagonist Eugene's break from his destructive family. Critics cheered the play as a work of "splendid artistic creation."

Beth Henley, 1981 winner for *Crimes of the Heart*, was the first woman to win the Drama Pulitzer in 23 years, and first woman to win the New York Drama Critics' Award in 21 years. And, she won them both with her first full-length play. In what is now her canon of plays, typically set in Southern families, *Crimes* was the first to plumb the virtues and vices of marriage and family life, especially as they affect the self-image of women. The play's MaGrath sisters rally together to overcome family myths and scandals, and do so with Henley's quirky blend of heartbreak and hilarity. Like most of Henley's women, they struggle to break free of what Beth calls "the traps of other people's definitions."

For Marsha Norman, the 1983 winner for 'Night, Mother, feeling alien in her own family helped to produce her exquisite sympathy for a character whose break from family becomes a matter of life and death. Like her character Jessie, Marsha was "born into a family to which I did not belong." However, Marsha forged a sustaining second family—a matriarchy—which her character Jessie could not. The way Jessie escapes family, and takes ultimate control of her life, is through her well-planned suicide. Marsha's drama details the last two hours of Jessie's life, spent with her mother Thelma who, as Marsha puts it, "does not know enough about Jessie to save her life if she had to."[20]

After taking the Pulitzer Prize for 'Night, Mother, Marsha garnered a Tony Award for *The Secret Garden*, the hit Broadway musical created by an unprecedented matriarchy of women artists.

Wendy Wasserstein, 1989 winner for *The Heidi Chronicles*, tends to center her plays around bright, ambitious women. For her script that took the Pulitzer, Tony, and New York Drama Critics' Awards, Wendy started with the question, "What's happened to feminism ... to all that political commitment?" Her play follows the title character through twenty years of the rise and demise of the women's movement. It also depicts a "generation for whom friends are their family"; a generation in which Wendy includes herself. (She explains that her own family provided "different kinds of role models ... but my nurturing has always come from my friends.... They really are my family."[21])

Paula Vogel, the 1998 winner for *How I Learned to Drive*, crafts plays that are overtly theatrical and political. Her subjects push hot buttons, and her plays promote a dialogue, if not a debate, among viewers. (They're often followed by an audience "talk back.") The hot topic behind her Pulitzer winner is pedophilia. The play is the episodic, disturbing story of a young girl's coming of age at the hands of her Uncle Peck, hands both mentoring and molesting. But Vogel mitigates her dark topics with her deft comedy and her wildly theatrical devices. Hallmarks of her plays include voice-overs, projections, black-outs, and multiple-character "Greek chorus" roles.

Margaret (Maggie) Edson, winner for *Wit* (1999), is first and foremost an elementary school teacher. But the protagonist in her play is a very different teacher—a smug, cerebral college professor who learns through her impending death what is essential in life. In the play's layered ironies, the aloof and powerful Dr. Bearing, professor of John Donne's complex poetry, becomes the scrutinized subject, the impotent lab rat. Yet Vivien Bearing's Waterloo of cancer is what teaches her a most vital lesson in compassion.

At first glance, it seems that family is hardly apparent in Maggie's script. However, she points out that "you don't *see* family, with mom and dad and the kids. But there is a definite generational structure, of teachers and students, [with] a lot of the characteristics of family."[22]

Suzan-Lori Parks made history in 2002 as the first black woman to take the Drama Pulitzer, with *Topdog/Underdog*. (Three black male playwrights had already claimed the prize: August Wilson, Charles Fuller Jr., and Charles Gordone.) For Parks, the stage is the ideal place to make and remake history, because both theatre and history are rife with what she calls "Rep and Rev"—repetition and revision. Her repeated, revised stagings of Lincoln's assassination are a case in point. Her script *The America Play* features a black Abe Lincoln "Faux Father" who takes shots from sideshow patrons in the "Great Hole of History." In *Topdog/Underdog*, Parks pairs another black Lincoln with his blood brother, Booth, whose resentment of Lincoln's top-dog status leads to the play's final, fatal climax.

Suzan-Lori Parks has enjoyed advantages only dreamed of by women playwrights (of any color) a few decades ago. She attended Yale School of Drama's prestigious playwriting program, studied acting in London, and has had an aggressive, high-powered supporter in George C. Wolfe, the influential black director of the Public Theater in New York.

These eleven playwrights have been the stars of my research for this book. My interviews with the extant winners (with the exception of Ms. Parks) have been in person and extensive: The ones with Marsha Norman, Wendy Wasserstein, and Maggie Edson took place in New York and were at least two hours, as was the one with Paula Vogel, done at Arena Stage in Washington, D.C. My briefer Chicago interview with Beth Henley—wedged in during Beth's playwrights' workshop at Center Theater—was supplemented by my audio and audiotaping of that three-day workshop, and a follow-up phone call in spring 2003. For the non-extant playwrights, I've rounded up similar firsthand material from preserved interview transcripts, journal entries, and personal correspondence.

I have traveled the country to view various productions of these Pulitzer plays by women. Not coincidentally, I have also included these playwrights and their work in teaching my theatre and women's studies courses in Chicago and elsewhere.

The very fact that there exists a women's studies program at scores of universities reminds me of writer-editor Rachel Koenig's words:

> Though women make up half the human race, women's words do not exist in equal numbers.... If women's words were, or ever had been cherished, encouraged, or revered, we can be certain they would not have been lost to us, and those few fragments which did

survive time and the elements ... would need no special excavation.²³

This also reminds me of what Marsha Norman said about the still-palpable need for women to prove themselves in and outside of theatre. I interviewed her over lunch after her Tony-winning triumph with *The Secret Garden* (a musical created by five women):

> The understanding of women has been historically so narrow that women have needed to hit particular things that will mark them, you know? Jane Goodall says, "We can talk to apes." Margaret Mead says, "We can understand primitive societies." Lillian Hellman comes along and says, "We can write really nasty plays." Jean Kerr comes along and says, "We can write really funny plays." Beth Henley has said, "We can write these Southern gothics better than anybody ... and now, for once (with *The Secret Garden*), we can make gigantic wonderful musicals all by ourselves."
>
> It seems to be necessary to be ... adding to the list of what we can do. It's almost like, maybe in Times Square, there's some kind of big billboard that says "Women Can...," then there's a list. See, what I hope is that ... this list, once it gets longer and longer ... the sheets roll off and it finally rolls on into the Midwest and on into the mountains ... and finally someone will say, "What the hell do we need this list for? It's perfectly obvious that women can do anything."²⁴

These eleven Pulitzer winners clearly prove that women can hold their own with the best of men in playwriting. And by their examples, these playwrights have encouraged what Paula Vogel calls an "exponential growth of younger women writers." Paula cheerfully comments, "It feels like every woman playwright of the 1960s had two or three children; and if I'm one of them, I've got now—I don't know—twenty kids, probably, in terms of women playwrights."²⁵

After talking to the contemporary winners, I came away with a strong sense of a growing family of American women playwrights. (Marsha Norman might call it a matriarchy.) There is an acknowledged comradery among them; and about that comradery, Paula Vogel adds very aptly: "We always write in a community. We have to create our own community. This goes back to the notion of family."²⁶

Prologue. Family Ties— A Troublesome Knot?

> Family is just accident, Jessie... It's nothing personal...
> They don't mean to get on your nerves. They don't even
> mean to be your family; they just are.
> —Thelma in *'Night Mother*, by
> Marsha Norman[1]

Drama must have conflict. This is an accepted truism, as time honored as "art reflects life." Still, the spotlight on family conflict is so bright in the plays of these eleven women—and in most prize plays—it prompts this question: If the playwright's art does mirror life, why is family life so marked by discord? The reasons given by sociologists and psychologists are not far from the answers offered by these playwrights. Marsha Norman (quoted above) was right on target.

The fact is that in its scrutiny of human behavior and interaction, the art of the playwright clearly reflects the behavioral sciences. So much so, that the main explanations for family conflict offered by art and science are, essentially, the same. I list here what I've found to be the main explanations, to set up a few parameters for the discussions of family problems—onstage and off—that follow in the book:

• Birth families can be accidents of nature; offspring can be strangers to their parents and each other. This irony, captured in the above quote from *'Night, Mother*, applies to all of the troubled families that people these Pulitzer plays. About this problem, of feeling alien within one's own family, much has been published by Nancy Napier, an acclaimed New York family therapist. A main reason "it is amazing we survive growing up in families," as Napier declares, is found in the power behind family myths—false beliefs upheld for the sake of conformity and the appearance of unity.[2]

- Every family creates and perpetuates myths about itself and the world. As Nancy Napier describes it, myths operate "to cover up things the family judges to be unacceptable.... They control family members through loyalty, guilt, humiliation, or punishment" when values are transgressed.[3] Seven of these plays involve the family cover-up or punishment of some secret or scandal. In Gale's play, the dark secret involves bigamy, and Lulu is made the scapegoat. In Akins' play, her old maid character, Charlotte, pays a life-long penance for a brief affair that produces a child. In Henley's play, various crimes of the heart have been committed by the MaGrath sisters since their mother's scandalous suicide gave control of their lives to Old Granddaddy. The disastrous society marriage that Granddaddy contrived for Babe has led to the current family scandal: Babe shooting her smug lawyer husband "slap in the gut."

Faulty marriages are such a common focus of stage art (and behavioral science) that they warrant their own heading:

- Marriages are often initiated for the wrong reasons altogether. An example of this family problem is found in nine of these plays. An extreme example is the accidental marriage of Lulu Bett in the course of a parlor game. Yet calculated marriages can be just as faulty, when the motive is wrong. In at least four of these plays, a wrong motive for marriage is the pursuit of money and status, the result of another long-running myth: Self-worth depends on net worth. This skewed belief is seen and challenged in the plays of Glaspell, Akins, Chase and Frings. But the most glaring example is found in members of Akins' stage family, who admit to marrying for the same reason their ancestors came to this country: to ensure "living for a bank account instead of dying for a creed." The upper-class marriages in these plays do not fare well. But the middle-class family takes its lumps, too, reflecting its actual rough ride through the twentieth century. The compelling explanation for this is found in history:

- The family just isn't what it used to be—literally. Before the Industrial Revolution changed everything, the family was a unit of production, the center of both the private sphere and public sphere. When the Industrial Revolution hit, the household's men went off to work, and the family ceased to work as a unit. As the authors of *Families in Flux* put it, "This divided the sexes and the generations ... keeping women and children in the private domain of the home."[4] What is arguably true is that these changes have had the most resounding impact on women. But all family members have sustained aftershocks. Tom Scanlon claims in *Family, Drama, and American Dreams*, that the family has become "a source of great hopes and of great disappointment.... We demand much of the family, making it the focus of our dreams of harmony and ... the nightmare to be escaped. Our thoughts and dreams are ambiguous.... We strive for freedom and are appalled by loneliness; we reject family structure and yearn for its security."[5]

Scanlon's point about ambiguity supports a common theme found in these plays, and what is perhaps the most universal cause for anxiety about family:

- Our feelings about family *must* be ambiguous, because of the paradox of human need: We all harbor a strong need for connection—and a strong pull for independence. Most of the playwrights in this series speak to this dilemma of "needing to go versus longing to stay." For now, a quote from Marsha Norman nicely sums it up:

> The problem of having people around ... being committed, being whatever you want to call it, is that, when you want them there, you want them there, and when you don't want them there, you want them to vanish.... Most of us manage to not say that out loud. Right? This is our accommodation to family.[6]

Despite this internal conflict, breaking ties with family can be extremely hard, especially for women. As Carol Gilligan has so eloquently documented (in her book *In a Different Voice* and elsewhere), women share a special capacity for connection. They "tend to see the world comprised of relationships rather than of people standing alone. ... Women not only define themselves in the context of human relationship, but also judge themselves in terms of their ability to care."[7]

Playwright Marsha Norman echoes Carol Gilligan, in talking about the depth of women's connections: "That's just how we do it. That's the great strength of women.... It has been perceived and sort of put down as 'Well, this is a silly, stupid weakness.' But in fact, it's this ability to maintain connections over a whole lifetime.... This is a great and difficult thing."[8]

In their work and lives, these women playwrights have also documented and celebrated another parameter of family connection:

- Virtually every person has two kinds of family: A birth or "given" family; and a second "created" family formed of friends and significant others. This created family can be the more nurturing one; it can offset a birth family of strangers and allow for a circle of friends who are indeed family. This "created family" phenomenon is at work in several plays, especially *The Heidi Chronicles*, in which the created family is clearly the paramount form.

For the following treatments of these eleven Pulitzer playwrights, plays, and their settings, I've divided the text into five parts. Part I, "Family Lies and the Unwed Woman," includes the three earliest winners, *Miss Lulu Bett*, *Alison's House*, and *The Old Maid*. The two mid-century winners, *Harvey* and *Look Homeward, Angel*, are paired in Part II under the heading "Domestic Wars." The three winners from the 1980s, *Crimes of the Heart*, *'Night, Mother*, and *The Heidi Chronicles*, form a trio for Part III entitled "Whose Woman Is She?" The two end-of-the-century winners, *How I Learned to Drive* and *Wit*, are paired in Part IV, titled "Lessons Driven Home." *Topdog/Underdog* is featured in Part V, "History in the Staging?" which gives a fanfare for Suzan-Lori Parks as well as a tribute to other black women playwrights who have helped to pave the way for Parks' win.

To give a better gauge of how art has reflected life, I precede the discussion of each playwright and play with a quick colorful recap of the period (to "set the stage"), giving most focus to what was happening to women. This is followed by a profile of the respective playwright, enlivened by direct quotes from her. Next comes a short synopsis of her Pulitzer play, and some conclusions about its reflection of life—especially family life.

The brief epilogue offers a few notions (of mine and other women) about the state of American family and culture, along with a postscript on women playwrights.

Wherever possible in this book, the words and insights of the playwrights themselves are used. Often, these include the playwright's insights about her own experiences of family, both given and created.

PART I

Family Lies and the Unwed Woman: Gale, Glaspell, and Akins

The first two of these playwrights wrote their Pulitzer plays during that notorious post-war decade known for its roar: Zona Gale wrote *Miss Lulu Bett* in 1920; Susan Glaspell completed *Alison's House* in 1929. The Roaring Twenties embraced a decade of bewildering changes.

Almost overnight, the magic of the radio broadcast and the mass-produced automobile put Americans in the know and on the go, vastly changing family life. The mood of the whole nation shifted, from an abiding idealism to reckless materialism, fostered by the "buy now, pay later" plan. And pay—to a devastating degree—is precisely what Americans would do, beginning on a Black Thursday in 1929.

The twenties brought in what historian Bruce Catton called "a strange new world both gaudy and sad." Gaudy because of its restless vitality; sad because it was an "empty place between two eras, with old familiar certainties and hopes drifting off like mist and new ones not yet formulated."[1]

Zona Gale and Susan Glaspell were at the height of their careers during this restless era of cross-currents. In plays and novels, both of them portrayed the struggle between traditional values and new attitudes. Typically, they presented this struggle in the family setting. But their themes extend beyond the family and into society, where families form and function.

To show how Gale and Glaspell were model spokeswomen for this era and its women, what follows is a brief look at these postwar years. This backward glance gives a quick feel for the climate of the decade, then focuses on the circumstances of women.

1

The 1920s: Those Not-So-Good Old Days

"The Roaring Twenties" was an apt description, but another might have been "more lies than ties." Behind the gaudy facade of film stars and hot jazz, there lurked a growing distrust and disillusionment. The idealism rallied for the war effort had been spent, and people were feeling cheated. What would transpire during the decade would enlarge that feeling. And, for women, it would magnify their discontent in a world not of their making.

Consider the red-letter events of the 1920s: Prohibition created a vast underworld of crime that would flourish long after the Act's repeal. A "Red Scare" caused the arrests of 6,000 suspected Communists, and the seizing of books and letters as supposed evidence. (Zona Gale's book version of *Miss Lulu Bett* had just shared the honor of best-selling novel of 1920 with Sinclair Lewis' *Main Street*, when Lewis' book was banned for creating "a distaste for the conventional good life of the American people."[1]) *Harper's* magazine declared that this was "no longer a free country ... on every hand, free speech is choked off."[2]

President Warren Harding brought to Washington what political writer Bruce Bliven denounced as "one of the most astonishing collections of crooks, grafters, and blackmailers ever assembled."[3] Harding's "Ohio Gang" were among the decade's worst lawbreakers. According to Bliven, "[they] eagerly solicited bribes.... In graft and waste, this group cost the country about two billion dollars."[4] More erosion of the public trust would come with the trial of Sacco and Vanzetti, two Italian radicals accused of a payroll heist and murder. Despite weak evidence and bias among jurors, Sacco and Vanzetti were electrocuted. An explosive response arose from people who felt that "the test of a nation's integrity rests in its scrupulous protection of the rights of minorities."[5] Zona Gale was one of those people.

The rights of minorities were attacked on local fronts by a rising Ku Klux Klan. Hiding behind their hooded capes and flaming crosses, Klansmen pursued their racist goal: "To unite white male persons [and] maintain forever white supremacy." The Klan's numbers soared to four million by 1924, despite a federal investigation.[6]

With its leadership steeped in corruption, much of post-war society—women and youth in particular—saw the American Dream as an inherited nightmare. One youth grumbled in *Atlantic Monthly* about inheriting a world "knocked to pieces, leaky, red hot."[7] The rosy ideals of the old order had failed, so why should its moral code be maintained? That code, as outlined in Frederick Lewis Allen's book *Only Yesterday* (his history of the 1920s), held that:

> Young girls must look forward in innocence to a romantic love match which would lead them to the altar and (until then), they must allow no male to kiss them. It was expected that some men would succumb to the temptations of sex, but only with a special class of outlawed women.[8]

A fed-up young generation launched a moral revolt that spread like wildfire. Girls were indeed being kissed; they were also defiantly smoking and dancing the body-to-body foxtrot. Parents were alerted by F. Scott Fitzgerald's eye-opening book *This Side of Paradise*. Its brash heroine, Rosalind, was the prototype Flapper: "pretty, impudent ... briefly clad ... a once-in-a-century blend."[9] Frederick Allen recalled that "families were torn with dissension over cigarettes and gin and all-night automobile rides."[10] How could "flaming youth" be expected to resist basic urges in back seats (when Freud's new theories on sex suggested they couldn't)?

A flurry of laws were passed, mainly dress codes for women. One state bill forbade any female over fourteen to wear a skirt that did not reach "that part of the foot known as the instep."[11] These were futile straws in the wind of a moral revolt.

The youth revolution got the best publicity, but the more indelible one involved middle-class women. Historical writer-editor Bruce Catton wrote that "the big change in American mores from 1920 to 1929 might conceivably be charted just in terms of what happened to women":

> They entered the new era with long hair, long skirts and—whenever any deviation from Victorian moral codes was suggested—long faces; they left it with short hair, short skirts, and short shrift for anyone who denied them more or less equal privileges with men.[12]

In her book *Women and the American Experience*, Nancy Woloch concurred that "clearly, women's roles ... were undergoing the most change."[13]

Breaking Ties That Bind— Only Womankind

In 1920, a Los Angeles barber filed for divorce because of "evidence of indiscretion" in his wife, Marsha. For instance, her new bathing suit seemed designed for "exhibiting ... the shape and form of her body."[14] Another disgruntled spouse sought divorce because his wife now "went to business all week and did her housework on Saturday and Sundays and it was not to my satisfaction."[15] Court records vividly preserved the showdown between old standards and the new.

Most of the old standards were double standards: constraints that applied only to women. Feminists (including Zona Gale) were publicly denouncing laws that gave men the right to their wives' earnings and guardianship over their children[16]—throwbacks to an archaic mandate whereby the very "legal existence of the woman is ... consolidated into that of her husband."[17] Even after they gained the right to vote, women held no sway in the public sphere, or in its fast-growing industries.

Women could get work, but mainly in positions with dismal pay and conditions. Typical were the garment factories, where women could put in ten-hour days, be charged for needles and thread, and find exit doors locked to prevent them from stealing fabric. Little had changed, even in the wake of such tragedies as the Triangle Factory fire, in which 146 women died because exit doors were locked.[18] (Zona Gale would condemn the conditions behind this tragedy in her book *A Daughter of the Morning*.)

In the twenties, the goal of the women's movement was independent status. For Margaret Sanger, the key was a woman's right "to control her own body." As a public health nurse, Sanger witnessed the horrid plight of women who were chronically pregnant, or maimed or dead from desperate abortions. Sanger was arrested after opening her first birth control clinic, but her trial brought publicity and funds to her fight. By the time she opened her new clinic in 1923, physicians were dispensing contraceptives.[19] For Suzanne LaFollette, the key was economic independence—which would mean invading fields considered "the special province of men."[20] (Zona Gale and Susan Glaspell had already barged into news journalism.) A nervous medical profession started banning women as students and interns. In a reversal of previous gains, by 1930 the number of women doctors had shrunk from six percent of the total to less than four and one-half.[21]

Despite all obstacles, the married career woman became a New Woman, featured in *Nation* magazine as wanting "work of her own ... some means of self-expression," but also wanting "a home, husband, and children, too."[22] One article lamented that marriage "lops off a woman's life as an individual;" yet renouncing marriage caused a lopping off, too—a choice between "the frying pan and the fire."[23]

The frying pan of marriage remained the choice of most women, even those who also boldly pursued the fire of a career. Examples who took headlines were pilot Amelia Earhart and anthropologist Margaret Mead, who firmly held the conviction that she "could establish and hold her place ... with men."[24]

In most areas, individualism for the twenties woman came down to that: holding her place with men. The bobbed hair and dangling cigarette of the Flapper were the trappings of her change into man's sporting pal. And the popular image of wife became that of "sexual partner and agreeable companion."[25]

Despite the new egalitarian marriage ideal, companionship still involved unequal effort. As Nancy Woloch summed it up:

> The responsibility of being an amiable companion fell on the wife ... she had to be able to propose enjoyable joint activities and [be] attractive, agreeable, and available. Such goals were not achieved without effort.... [She] would have to work at it.[26]

No matter how hard wives worked at it, discord worked its way into marriage. Inflated expectations produced inflated discontent, which led to inflated spending—a fleeting distraction. "Both men and women became preoccupied with material goods," reported *A History of Private Life*. Spending for personal consumption nearly tripled within ten years.[27] But consumerism could not deliver the married "good life" it promised: By the decade's end, America had the world's highest divorce rate.[28] Those who blamed the emancipation of women were, as *A History of Private Life* noted, "simply wrong ...":

> The income women earned was meager [and] few rejected the ideal of marriage that rested on a breadwinner and a full-time homemaker.... Men also demonstrated ambivalence. They may have been attracted to the youthful and exciting "new women," but they also wanted domestic, frugal, and virtuous wives who would keep house and tend to the children.[29]

Clearly, much remained to be reconciled between old values and new roles. What left women confused was the speed of change more than its scope. Women had gained more control over their lives, thanks to everything from contraceptives to canned soups. But most of the limits on their participation in the world were still in place. Psychologist Lorine Pruette lamented that most women were still living "contingent lives," continuing to "work through another person [because] it appears to be the easier way."[30]

As Emily Blair suggested, it may have been easier because "the best man continued to win" anyway. A Democratic Committee leader, Blair reflected in 1931 that women—even the best women—still worked "for and under men.... All standards, all methods, all values, continued to be set by men."[31]

In that same year, 1931, the men who set standards for the American theatre nonetheless chose to honor Susan Glaspell's *Alison's House* as the season's best play. The choice was debated, but one Pulitzer juror firmly defended this play, "which plumbed the deep American love of home and family."[32]

Glaspell's play not only plumbed America's abiding link to family; like Zona Gale's winner (*Miss Lulu Bett*), *Alison's House* questioned and challenged the standing prejudices about marriage and family, and women's roles in them. Both plays offer a window on the struggle to reconcile an older generation's myths with a newer one's values. True to the adage about writers and their material, clearly Gale and Glaspell were writing about what they knew.

THE COMMON GROUND OF GALE AND GLASPELL

The work and lives of Zona Gale and Susan Glaspell held striking parallels: Both grew up in small Midwestern towns, started out as news reporters, and wrote notable fiction before they attempted playwriting. Both of them were married, in middle age, to sons of their towns' leading families, after those sons' first marriages were dissolved. And both of them died, from bouts of pneumonia, in their sixties.

Gale's lifelong ties to Portage, Wisconsin, were echoed in Glaspell's enduring link to Davenport, Iowa. Both women brought their home towns into their fiction—slightly disguised. Both became acknowledged writers of local color, focused on the details of everyday living. In the simplest rituals and objects, they found a wellspring for the real drama of life, and keys to its deeper meaning.

In fact, a strong mystical bent marked their lives and work. They spoke and wrote about life existing on other planes, and about breaking through barriers to some higher form of life and self. Gale wrote of "Something More" and of climbing beyond "the present mechanistic wall."[33] Glaspell drew characters on the verge of life, trying to break through to "The Outside"—to "otherness."[34]

Dualities abound in their writing, reflecting the ambivalence of the period. While outworn ideals are smashed, lost values are also lamented. The family is drawn as an arena of cross-currents. And often, one member's welfare is squared off against the family's rules and traditions.

In their work and lives, Gale and Glaspell raised the call for women to lead self-governing and fulfilling lives. Gale was an avid social activist and feminist, championing better working conditions and rights for women. Glaspell was much less the activist in person; but in her writing, as in Gale's, political flags were waved. Both women produced a few works that were risky for the time. For instance, Gale's wartime novel *Heart's Kindred* was blatant pacifism; so was Glaspell's play *The Inheritors*. Both works defied the Sedition Act and could have sent their writers to jail for disloyalty to the country's war efforts.

Gale's best-selling novel *A Daughter of the Morning* was a loud cry for social action: It exposed the horrors of the sweatshop, where the machines were insured but the lives of the girls working at them were not. ("The top story where the fire had been ... That was where they had jumped from ... smashed or burned to death."[35])

In much of their work, both writers explore and test the dividing line between individualism and isolation. They turn it into a dramatic device, using a central character who stands apart. Glaspell often centers her action around a character who never even appears. A prime example is her one-act play *Trifles*, which editor Judith Barlow hailed as "near-perfect short play construction."[36] *Trifles* is set in the crude kitchen of a farm wife being held for the murder of her husband. When the wives of two men investigating the crime are left alone among the kitchen's "trifles," they uncover the grim facts of the accused woman's life and the evidence needed for a motive. In a silent moment of compassion, they conceal it from the men.

In Gale's *Faint Perfume*, as in *Miss Lulu Bett*, the outsider is a single woman forced to live with smug relatives. Yet within the outsider, Miss Leda, there stirs a spirit attuned to the faint perfume of spring. (The title sprang from Gale's concept of God as "an influence, less a force than a fragrance."[37])

Despite the threads of spirituality in their work, Gale and Glaspell were accomplished writers of realism. Their work suggests that the spiritual abides in the mundane; that those who lead simple lives apart are the most attuned to spiritual vibrations.

In various ways, Gale and Glaspell stood apart as their characters did. They tested the boundaries of individuality; they assaulted the barriers that were hampering women. Their contributions to American theatre are discussed in their profiles that follow. However, the broad strokes of their innovations are these: Along with their contemporary Eugene O'Neill, they deserve credit for the creation and popularization of a native dramatic realism, one centered on regionalism and the family. They also helped to bring the experiences of women to mainstream stages, in plays that challenged the prevailing attitudes about women. And by their own examples, they became role models for women overcoming obstacles to do what they loved.

Both Gale and Glaspell would have been more comfortable if their greatest mark in theatre could have been made outside the concerns of box office or Broadway. (Ironically, when Glaspell brought Eugene O'Neill to the Provincetown Players—which she cofounded—she charted a course that led to the commercial channels she had condemned.)

Zona Gale's contributions to the Little Theatre movement were tied to her support of community theatre. A typical Gale gesture was the offering of her play *Neighbors* royalty-free to any theatre group that would plant a tree. Against her publisher's protests, she waived her royalty rights to allow amateur groups to stage *Miss Lulu Bett*.

Zona Gale's personality merged a chronic soft touch with an iron will, a combination that would appear onstage in her character of Lulu Bett.

2

Zona Gale and the Real Village Tale

Zona Gale was quite proud of how she had elbowed her way into news journalism: She secured her first reporting job by relentless pestering. "I presented myself every morning at the desk of the city editor to ask for an assignment." When she was finally assigned a flower show, Gale was ecstatic: "I never shall forget my thrill at the phrase 'cover it.'[1] A month later, Gale joined the staff of *The Evening Wisconsin*. When she was handed her first pay envelope, she drew a happy picture of herself on it and mailed it, contents and all, to her parents.

This small reminiscence is a good introduction to Zona Gale—the woman, the writer, and the daughter. Described by interviewers as a small and delicate brunette with remarkably tiny hands, she displayed an incongruously fierce will. She was a determined individualist, yet she gave her parents almost slavish devotion.

Zona seemed obsessed with matters of family. She realized how difficult, even destructive, family could be. Divorce and family discord abound in her plots and themes. But her life and writing conjure up images of family as a potent agent for the bestowal of blessings or curses.

Her own family loomed large, always. Growing up in picturesque Portage, Wisconsin, she was an only child, much adored by her parents. Her mother Eliza was a Victorian ex-teacher and religious zealot. Her father Charles was quite a contrast: a liberal-minded railroad engineer from whom Zona absorbed a keen social consciousness. Their tight family triumvirate was jealously guarded by Mrs. Gale.

As a child, Zona made two pronouncements: One, that she would become a writer; and two, that she would someday marry Will Breese, a boy who gave her a sled ride and was the son of a leading Portage family. Both predictions came true, although her marriage to Breese did not take place until Gale was 54 and had an adopted daughter (Leslyn), and Breese was a widower with an adopted daughter of his own.

Zona's love of books and dialogue came from her parents. Her mother habitually read aloud, including the works of Shakespeare. Zona later recalled that the "give me the dagger" speech provided material "excellent for acting out on the way to bed."[2] A cherished eighth-birthday gift from her father was a copy of *Paradise Lost*.

Early in life, Zona decided that she was "different ... from the whole world."[3] She felt things, and saw things—like the lady in an apple tree who appeared to her while playing with best friend Edith Rogers. "Such *lies*," Edith insisted. "You'll never write a book.... You've got to tell the truth to write books."[4] The advice was worth taking. For years, Zona turned out romantic, exotic tales that met with a stream of rejection slips. Even her stint at reporting did not cure her of this penchant.

Two awakenings finally caused a shift in her writing toward the simple and familiar. The first came while she was living in New York, walking through Central Park in early spring. She got the idea for a story about the joy of spring as it might be experienced, not by young lovers, but by "old lovers, in whom the years had not dulled their sense of perfect companionship."[5]

She sold forty stories about these aging lovers, "Pelleas and Etarre"; stories still tinged with romance, but a step closer to realism. (Gale would never lose her love of fanciful names, however, and bemoaned that they were "wasted on medicines and spices."[6])

Gale's second awakening came on a return visit to Portage. She overheard two women talking over tea and suddenly realized, "Why this is wonderful! This is the sort of thing people talk about ... everywhere." From that day on, she wrote "only of people living the everyday life."[7]

Making such a discovery was what Zona called "stepping over a threshold." One was her "sense of social consciousness ... the knowledge that we rise, and fall together." In an interview with Keene Sumner, she added:

> Another threshold was the other consciousness that life is something better than this which we believe it to be.... But none of these impressions [was] more vivid than the sudden perception of the interest of commonplace things that came to me that afternoon as I listened to these women talking.[8]

This threshold crossed, Gale sold 100 stories about the people of Friendship Village, her fictionalized Portage. In a range of magazines and then five book volumes, Gale's account of everyday life was narrated by Calliope Marsh, a woman whose stories celebrated the innate kindness in people. Readers and critics alike shouted "hallelujahs for Friendship Village," and Zona Gale was called "one of the foremost writers of our time."[9] Talking to a journalist over lunch in Manhattan, Zona shared her recipe for successful writing:

> People want human nature, [which] is the same here in a New York restaurant as it is in Friendship Village. Here they may be talking about the opera, a dinner-dance, a scandal.... In the little town they may be talking about the school entertainment, the church supper, the newest piece of gossip.... The things we talk about don't matter.... [What] does count is that when we talk about anything, we unconsciously tell something about ourselves....[10]

Her fortunes rapidly growing, Gale continued to send her parents two-thirds of her earnings, despite the scolding of friends who felt "she was starving herself to do so."[11] Her letters urged her parents to buy a farm like the sprawling homesteads of her friends, Mabel Wright or Mark Twain. ("We were to have driven over to Mark Twain's yesterday ... but for the rain," one letter related.[12]) But her parents were not thinking of farms. On one of Zona's visits to Portage, her father pointed out a site on the Wisconsin river. Zona promptly had a lovely riverside home built for the Gales, with a study for herself, and a living room mantle inlaid with her father's favorite sayings: "Everything is a thought first"; and "Nothing is as fine as the Temple that love builds."[13]

A few years later, questions and rumors abounded as to why Zona moved back from New York to her parents' Portage temple. Did she need to return to the source of her characters? Or did her parents miss her too much? One widespread rumor pointed to Zona's broken affair with poet Ridgely Torrence, an engagement ended at the urging of her mother, Eliza.

In two main areas of her life, Zona's activities met with heated protest from her rigid Victorian mother. The first of these was her involvement with the promising poet, Ridgely Torrence. There could be no doubt that Zona loved him. The stream of letters that she wrote to him, numbering more than 150, clearly chart their relationship and her feelings. (The letters were bequeathed by Torrence to Princeton University.) Decades after their breakup, Zona wrote to Torrence, "I do so hope that in our next incarnation, we can fall in love all over again—and *that* time, have enough more star-dust, in me, to carry it off."[14] Hefty amounts of stardust would have been required to offset the protests of Mother Gale. She wrote to Zona:

He is not old enough yet to have a wife.... As far as your perfect companionship about books is concerned, all lovers who like books read them before marriage.... After marriage it fades away.... I am quite sure he will lay back, read his Poetry and let you do the bread winning (if there is any bread).... So, little girl, don't marry him.[15]

In his casual biography of Zona Gale, *Still Small Voice*, August Derleth wrote that, undeniably, "Mrs. Gale was jealous of any man who might marry Zona; she did everything in her power to keep intact the little domestic triangle of parents and daughter."[16] Zona allowed the Torrence affair to die a slow death, and made the move back to her parents. (It was not until after her mother's death that Zona married Will Breese, her childhood crush.)

A second area where her mother intervened, although with mixed results, was in Zona's social activism. In this, Mrs. Gale had something of a foe in her own husband. Charles Gale was an outspoken humanitarian who understood Zona's impulses, even if her activities also worried him. Zona pursued her causes wherever she went. At a summer fair with her old friend Edith Rogers, Zona spent the day at a women's-suffrage tent. Called back to work in New York, Zona received and ignored the advice from her mother: "I would let that mess of women alone!"[17]

Unfortunately, Mrs. Gale did hold sway over Zona with her fanatic support of Prohibition. "The drinks belong to Satan," she wrote Zona, "... and, little girl, don't, I pray, be a party to this thing."[18] Despite her own doubts, Zona took the side of the "drys." As Derleth noted, "Zona's background was too strong ... to break away enough to see [the greater] dangers of Prohibition."[19] Nothing blinded Zona to the dangers of war, however, and it was her avid pacifism that most distressed her mother. Mailing a peace appeal back to Zona, Mrs. Gale warned: "I send this peace thing on. You stick to your job—let others tend to this.... It will lessen your influence with your books and you can reach more people with them."[20]

Mrs. Gale's advice backfired and encouraged a new book. Already Zona had jotted notes for a novel upholding pacifism and an array of human rights. Enlarging on these, she wrote *Heart's Kindred*, the tale of a brutish man, the Inger, who revels in killing creatures until he is converted by a pacifist woman and the death of his own father. The book featured Jane Addams as a character, to voice Gale's ideals: "It is the mind of love ... beside it, governments are nothing.... The people are heart's kindred, met here together for their world-work.... Nations must cease to interrupt."[21] The book might have landed Zona in jail for voicing criticism of the wartime government. As it was, Zona's anti-war statements made her subject to surveillance by federal agents. Fearing for her safety, her father secretly bought

Liberty Bonds in her name, in hopes they might help her case if she were arrested.²²

In her next novel, *A Daughter of the Morning*, Zona had another axe to grind, this one about working conditions for women. Her character Cosma fought for fire escapes, sanitation, and fairer wages, the very reforms that Gale championed. Another character in the best-selling book was a writer who claimed, as Gale might, "I travel for the human race.... I shall always be a philanthropist. The commodity is books."²³

As attached to the Midwest as she was, Zona still loved the vibrant life of New York. She adapted to hotel living, since she hated and avoided housework. (She also championed housewives: one of her characters cried: "They're all prostituted to housework—every woman in Katytown!"²⁴) The forces that pulled her back to Portage would not keep Zona from spending two months of every winter in her usual Gotham Hotel room.

Zona Gale (Wisconsin Historical Society, ©Hi-11760)

When Zona moved back to Portage, she did so as a well-known writer, ready to cross over other thresholds. Her first attempt at playwriting had been carelessly discarded by a hotel maid. That threshold would come a bit later. What came first was her most acclaimed novel, based on her renewed view of Portage. Entitled *Birth*—despite publisher Macmillan's concern that it sounded "like a treatise by Sanger"—the book struck a new, somber note of realism.²⁵

The change reflected a change in Zona and her trust in people. Being observed by the Secret Service had been sobering. But worse was the scrutiny of people she knew, who regarded her pacifism with suspicion or disdain. Zona emerged wounded, but wiser. The effects on her writing were salutary: Creating the town of Burage in her novel *Birth*, Gale now showed "both sides of the village street." As August Derleth described it,

> The doubt cast upon her motives by the people she knew and trusted ... served only to establish in her a firm balance.... If before this time Zona Gale's villages were credible, recognizable, true, Burage lived, Burage breathed.... It is Burage, and not Friendship Village, which is Zona Gale's Spoon River.[26]

Critics gave the book high praise, but it was neglected by readers who missed the cheerful tone of Friendship Village. Zona knew that she had turned in the right direction, however, and was not about to turn back. She followed *Birth* with her sharply realistic bestseller, *Miss Lulu Bett*. The book was what critical biographer Harold Simonson called Gale's "most successful treatment of ... the duty-bound, domestically enslaved woman of her day."[27] The action of *Lulu Bett* covered six months in the Deacon family household, with chapters titled "April" through "September." The writing style was spare and direct: "The Deacons were at supper. In the middle of the table was a small, appealing tulip plant, looking as anything would look whose sun was a gas jet."[28]

Gale's simplicity made her bitter theme hit home. The simple story of Lulu's maltreatment in her married sister's house was the ironic story of all women reduced to marginal living in the homes of relatives: "There emerged from the fringe of things, where she perpetually hovered, Mrs. Deacon's older sister, Lulu Bett, who was 'making her home with us.' And that was precisely the case. *They* were not making her a home, goodness knows. Lulu was the family beast of burden."[29]

Miss Lulu Bett shared with Sinclair Lewis' *Main Street* the honor of "best-selling novel of 1920." Reviews of Gale's book were glowing. "Great" was the adjective applied to it for so long that critic Robert Benchley apologized for merely hailing it as a "great book": "But I can't do anything else. I'm very sorry."[30] The book was cheered by Edith Wharton, who commended Gale on the "hard little picture" she drew.[31] (And in a note to Zona, Fannie Hurst likened the story of Lulu to "a nice new shining star reflected in ... dishwater full of greasy reality."[32])

The *Chicago Tribune*'s review struck a prophetic note: "The technique makes the book almost as clear cut as a play. Indeed, when Miss Gale settles down to the dramatization of her story, as she undoubtedly will, her task will be a singularly easy one."[33] As much as Zona wanted to adapt the book herself, she was afraid to. But that summer, after Broadway producer Brock Pemberton optioned *Miss Lulu Bett*, he wrote to Zona: "The more I consider the matter the more convinced I am that you are the one to make 'Lulu Bett' into a play. I am so afraid that anyone else would miss the flavor of the book.... When you have finished, if there is any need [for] changes, we can call in a play carpenter."[34]

Zona promptly sat down and turned her novel into a play. In an interview, she confessed, "I'm almost ashamed to say how quickly it was done...." I finished it in a week, but as I wasn't satisfied with the last act, I held it over from Saturday till Monday, to revise it. So I can say that it took me ten days, and that doesn't sound quite so bad."[35]

In his return letter to Zona, Brock Pemberton's response to the script was unqualified praise: "I am thrilled with the play. It is the kind of thing I hoped to get and ... was sure I wouldn't—If I had to call in an outsider.... It cuts to the quick and lays bare the lives of the characters. In its simplicity, sincerity and reality, it strikes a new note in the theatre."[36]

Zona came to New York to watch and advise in rehearsals. Before its opening at the Belmont, *Lulu Bett* had two unorthodox previews. Zona coaxed Pemberton into allowing a preview by the Wisconsin Players; then a second preview made *Miss Lulu Bett* "the only play in history that ever opened in Sing-Sing." (David Belasco had just presented the prison with his new folding stage; and for his premier of *Lulu Bett*, a wife-murderer and a bigamist were "pressed into service as stage hands."[37])

The following night, Zona's mother was seated in the Belmont's second row, and heard the thunderous applause for her daughter at the curtain call. The *Evening World*'s review claimed that the whole town was "likely to fall in love with and want to marry Miss Lulu Bett." Robert Benchley (in *Life*) called the play "great because of its pitiless fidelity to everyday people" and life.[38] The review that pleased Zona the most was the one in *The New Republic*: "Miss Gale has done what perhaps only a feminist, and certainly what only an artist can do. She has shown, in perfect American terms, the serious comedy of an emancipation."[39]

A week after its Broadway opening, however, the play had a new ending, prompted not by critics, but by letters from audience members. The play's original ending was different than that of the novel. In the book, Lulu's accidental marriage to a houseguest—through some role-playing that is witnessed by her magistrate brother-in-law—is proved invalid. (The estranged first wife of the houseguest, Ninian, is reported to be alive.) The book still allowed an apparently happy ending for Lulu, by having her marry a good-hearted neighbor, Cornish.

The time span in the book was six months. In the play, it was six weeks; but the literal time of the action was, of course, two hours. Convinced that Lulu could not marry two men in such a short time "no matter how vehemently the program announced that time had elapsed,"[40] Gale had changed the ending for the stage. Her original play ending had Lulu respond to Cornish's marriage proposal with "Sometime, maybe.... But first I want to see out of my own eyes."[41] As she left the Deacon household, she called, "I'm going I know not where ... But I'm going from choice."⁴²

However, after the play's opening, Gale and Pemberton received hundreds of letters questioning the play's "disappointing" ending. "These cheated theatre goers wanted Lulu to get her man," wrote John Toohey, "so Miss Gale obligingly saw that she did."⁴³ In the altered stage ending, Lulu's marriage to Ninian is proved valid: As she departs the Deacon household, Ninian returns with proof that his first wife is dead, and Lulu gladly takes him back.

The audiences who saw as happier an ending that leaves Lulu married to a virtual stranger were viewing it through the contemporary prejudice: that, for a woman, any marriage was better than none.

Several critics objected; they preferred the old ending, Lulu setting off alone. At heart, Zona agreed; but she dearly wanted to please her audience and producer. Pemberton still had great reason to be pleased thirty weeks into the play's run: *Variety* reported its box office at $5,000 to $6,000 weekly—"Should run well into June."⁴⁴ Meanwhile, the debate over the play's ending grew. Finally, Pemberton sent this telegram to Zona:

> PLEASE SEND ME FOURTEEN HUNDRED WORDS ON DRAMATIZING LULU HAPPY ENDING FOR TIMES MAGAZINE / PLAY GOING FAMOUSLY TODAY ... GIVING TEA PARTY FOR YOU FRIDAY SO PLEASE BE HERE / YOU ARE AN IMPORTANT PERSONAGE IN THIS HOUSEHOLD LULU⁴⁵

The press release from Zona declared, "If a play is to represent life— it must not always end an episode unhappily.... It is true that the ironic, the tragic ... must constitute many a curtain. But not all."⁴⁶

By this time, Zona was glad to escape to Portage and focus on her writing. She was working at home, and could enjoy her parents' reaction, when the telegram came to announce that she had won the Pulitzer Prize. August Derleth noted that she could also enjoy the critics' debate about the choice, a debate that "has become almost traditional to manifest."⁴⁷ That year's runner-up had been Frank Craven's domestic comedy *The First Year*. However, the jury agreed that "it would be a handsome thing to give the prize to a woman ... and Miss Gale is a woman to whom such an honor can go with justice."⁴⁸ So Zona stepped across another threshold. (Paramount's film of *Lulu Bett*, with a screenplay by Clara Beranger, appeared in late 1921.)

Zona's next project was her novel *Faint Perfume*. In its story of a writer who returns from New York to start her life again in Prospect, it held hints of autobiography. Zona was more self-assured than her character,

Leda Perrin. But Leda was infused with Zona's sense of mysticism, which soon became enlarged. The year that *Faint Perfume* became another bestseller (1923) was the year in which Zona's mother died. The family triumvirate was finally broken. Zona became closer to her father and shared with him her sense of Eliza's spirit. "The most heavenly things are happening," she wrote to him, "in waking with a sense of mother ... her nearness."[49]

It was no coincidence, however, that Zona increased her political activities after her mother's death. She spoke out for progressive politics, and for Wisconsin senator Robert LaFollette as independent candidate for president. Her feminism clearly colored her politics:

> I would say that [progressive policies] are politics socialized.... They regard human life and its right to grow as more important than property rights.... Broadly speaking, these are the principles and the faith of most women, outside politics.[50]

From the campaign trail, Zona wrote, "I tell LaFollette's story ... at the national convention, and a little at Washington."[51] LaFollette took more votes than any independent ever had; but a year after his defeat, he was dead. Zona wrote a memorial for her politician friend (who had led investigations into the graft of the Ohio Gang).

Her relentless activism took Zona in far-flung directions: She joined the Save Sacco and Vanzetti cause when ethnic bias obscured justice in their trial. She organized women's groups to tackle everything from child labor to prison reform. Her article in *Nation* magazine took a piercing look at "What Women Won" through suffrage, and still needed to win. It denounced state laws that barred women from civil service and married women from teaching posts. Its long roll call of offending states included:

DELAWARE: Fathers could will children away from mothers.
LOUISIANA: Married women were classified with children and the insane as unable to contract on their own.
VERMONT: The earnings of a married woman belonged to her husband.[52]

In her home state, Gale helped write the pioneering Wisconsin Equal Rights Law, which erased these old inequities. At her alma mater, she became the first woman on the University of Wisconsin's Board of Regents (and later decried their first meeting, when they spent the morning "discussing whether somebody should be engaged as football coach").[53]

Always striving to balance her public concerns with her writing, Zona began a stage adaptation of her novel *Birth*. Its story was more complex than that of Lulu Bett, with a Greek chorus effect provided by the town gossips of Burage. Brock Pemberton put the resulting play into production, but this time he did call in a script carpenter. Even though most critics praised the play, public response was mild, and it closed in six weeks.

Taking this in stride, Zona resumed her life and causes in Portage. Her longing for family was taking odd routes: For the Indian family who turned up on her doorstep, she provided a rented house, beds and linens. Zona and her father had themselves been taken under the wings of their good friends, the Batty family, with whom they spent Christmases. Zona loved acting out Anderson's fairy tales with the Battys' daughters.

"I think that Hans Christian Andersen gave me ... the feel of Somewhere Else," Zona wrote in a letter. He understood "the child's sense that this is not our home but that there is something lovely where we indisputably belong."[54] Zona believed children were closer to a spiritual Something More, and that their personification of objects was mystical. She used this idea in her novel *Preface to a Life*, about a character who becomes a madman in the eyes of his neighbors. But his madness is the childlike grasping for Something More. His sense of universal motion reflected Gale's:

> Young Bernard Mead leaned from the window of his room, and met the darkness, not as space, emptied of light, but as a powerful positive—black, breathing, packed with shapes.... Through his room floated the light of his lamp, acting on every small object.... These things seemed to have been caught doing their duty. Chairs looked busy, washstand preoccupied, carpet patient....[55]

Through her character Mead, Zona even voiced her belief that our key to the spirit world lay in vibrations, like radio waves: "Maybe the unknown isn't so unknown.... There's radio ... maybe the unseen isn't so unseen as we've tried to make out."[56]

Zona's readers and critics did not know what to make of *Preface to a Life*. Harold Simonson later defined it as "the author's psychological pilgrimage to her mother's spirit world."[57]

Spending time with children made Zona long for a child of her own. In the year she turned fifty-three, Zona "assumed the care of a baby," a girl she named Leslyn.[58] (No biographical material on Gale explains the details, but August Derleth and several Gale papers in the Wisconsin Historical Society confirm that Zona did acquire, then adopt, this baby girl.) The event thrilled Zona but vastly complicated her life. Her aging father did not want a child around, so she rented a house and hired a nurse. Zona kept profuse records of the baby's progress.

Still, she found time to put together a collection of essays. Her closing essay on "Allotropes" merged her ideas about the artist-writer with her mysticism. (An allotrope is one form of an element that can take other forms, a diamond being an allotrope of coal.) Zona urged artists to work toward a "finer, fairer allotrope" of humanity by revealing the "spiritual treasures" hidden within the ordinary.[59]

About this time, Zona happily renewed her acquaintance with her childhood crush, Will Breese. She and the widowed Breese met by chance in California, at Frank Miller's Mission Inn. Back in Portage, their new friendship flourished. After an evening out, when Breese stopped his car and proposed to her, Zona quietly replied, "Will, I've always adored you."[60] The next day, Zona's father heartily approved: "Now I can feel that Zona will have someone [to] keep her from landing either in the poorhouse or in jail."[61] His jest was sincere, since Zona was always handing out her opinions, and her earnings. Her charities filled a solid page.[62]

With Zona's marriage to Will Breese in 1928, her second childhood prediction came true. She moved into his almost block-long house, bringing Leslyn, who was more formally adopted by both of them. Breese built his bride a "richly carved oak-paneled study." Like her former study, it held no telephone or typewriter. Zona chose to do her writing by hand.[63]

In many ways, Gale's marriage was highly unorthodox. She wore no wedding ring and continued to sign "Zona Gale" in the Gotham Hotel register, despite Will's objection that, if he were along, this might cause "an embarrassing moment."[64] Zona never did housework or learned to cook. But she was fully aware that few women had her good fortune or choices. Few wives ever write as many letters to their husbands as she wrote to Will. They both traveled, so contact by mail was vital. To one letter, Zona added a playful postscript: "Mr. Breese—dear Mr. Breese, this is to let you know that I had a very nice time on my visit with you. I liked your home, your food ... and above all, I liked my host. In fact, I loved him."[65]

Zona's joy in her marriage was short-lived, however. The following year, her father died. "We lost father, to the eye of earth," she wrote a friend.[66] Zona never truly recovered from the loss. Her grief inspired her melancholy novel *Papa La Fleur*, which was set in Portage—with no disguises, this time, for the town.

She turned over to the Portage Women's Club the lovely riverside home, and renewed activities away from Portage. She helped Phillip LaFollette (son of her old friend Robert) become governor of Wisconsin. Her lectures took her to campuses across the nation and brought her four honorary doctorates. When Columbia offered her a post as professor of journalism, she declined. However, in 1933 she accepted an appointment to Chicago's International Congress of Women, where she discussed women's issues along with Jane Addams and Eleanor Roosevelt.

In the Depression years, Zona's Friendship Village stories resurfaced as radio plays for NBC. The old stories helped people cope and were some comfort to Zona. But her malaise toward the end of her life was compounded by an ugly political scandal. At its center was Glenn Frank, whom Gale had helped select as president of the University of Wisconsin. Later accused of shifting his liberal policies to gain political favor, Frank was dismissed by governor Phillip LaFollette. Forced to take sides, Zona finally broke ties with her lifelong friends, the LaFollettes.

Depleted in health and spirit, she accepted a long-standing invitation from Japan. She set off as a cultural ambassador, but also to renew her "center of old energy." Between rounds of receptions, Zona lingered in the countryside near the tiled roofs of peasants, the mossy hills, and waterfalls. ("It is all here," she exclaimed to Pearl Buck. "All is now a window where once had been a wall."[67]) Her news-reporter side absorbed other images, however: The status of women was even more alarming in Japan. She came home, intending to write a book about Japan and begin "the inevitable autobiography."[68] But her California stop-over at Frank Miller's Mission Inn sparked her interest in the Wisconsin-born Miller, and she resolved to write Miller's biography.

During Zona's absence, her novel *Light Woman* was published, taken from a magazine serial. Her main character, Mitty, was essentially a Flapper in pursuit of fun. When Mitty and her lover make a visit to his father's farm, she pretends that they are married "in the same holy bonds which bind—and gag—all of them." After the pretense is exposed, and the old father is indignant, Mitty rails, "You're all so sure, so sure of marriage, so sure of rules, rules, rules! ... And where has it got us? ... That old world—I do not call it orderly. But there is a new world and I live in that world. I hate your rules! I do what I think!"[69]

Reviews were mixed for *Light Woman*, but a few critics agreed that it was "perfectly suited to the purpose of stage or screen."[70] Gale's theatre ally, Brock Pemberton, agreed: "If we get it on as a play, the movie price will be far [greater] ... Remembering that *Ah, Wilderness* was the home life of this type of family and knowing that you can write rings around Mr. O'Neill when it comes to [this], I am looking forward to another Pulitzer Prize winner."[71]

Battling ill health, Zona pushed herself to finish the script of *Light Woman*. Near the end of the year, she scrawled a letter to Pemberton:

> The last act [went] to you yesterday.... I have been in bed for ten days with bronchial trouble.... I'm reading the Noel Coward plays.... Coward uses the simplest means—suspense, just by somebody starting again and again to change; laughter—by a telephone cord handling—a grand handling of properties always. And speed.

> As you know so well ... casting and handling of properties and speed are three magics. Played very fast, with a George Chew kind of father (for Belden) and a heavenly Billly and Mitty, and—she said modestly—the lines, this ought to be a show. I'll come to see it![72]

But it never happened. Pemberton delayed production and finally allowed his option to lapse. He may have felt that audiences supporting *Tobacco Road* and *Of Mice and Men* would not sustain such a contrast. Zona was deeply disappointed. As August Derleth observed, "She had enjoyed the life of the stage ... she wanted more of it."[73]

A sad but telling comment on Gale's unselfishness was the fact that her impulse to complete Frank Miller's biography prevented her from finishing her own. Six months after *Frank Miller of Mission Inn* appeared, Zona Gale was dead at 64. (The fragment of her autobiography is appended to August Derleth's book about Gale, *Still Small Voice*.) Having stubbornly neglected her bronchial trouble, Zona succumbed to pneumonia during the Christmas holidays of 1938. Despite sub-zero temperatures, the funeral church overflowed with state dignitaries and local residents; and among the mourners outside the door were three Winnebago women.

Knowing it would please Zona, Will Breese arranged for their home to become the Portage Public Library, with the provision that Zona's study would remain exactly the same.

The published writings of Zona Gale take up a three-foot bookshelf. She is a legend in her home state of Wisconsin, whose Historical Society holds 30 boxes of Gale papers and memorabilia, including her Pulitzer Prize. Why she is not better known elsewhere is a hard question to answer. Harold Simonson wrote that it was "true that neither Zona Gale's fame nor sensationalism equaled that of many other realists.... But it is well to remember that her widely read novel *Miss Lulu Bett*, exactly contemporaneous with Lewis' *Main Street*, was hardly less influential in establishing the new direction in provincial realism."[74]

Gale's influence toward a new realism was brought to the theatre with her play of *Miss Lulu Bett*, and that influence was given a significant boost with her Pulitzer Prize. The honor made her a more visible role model throughout America and beyond. Zona Gale the artist was inseparable from Zona Gale the feminist and activist. Decades later, Harold Simonson noted that "her reformist activities ... would put her in the vanguard even today.... In a country where national issues find too few feminine leaders, Zona Gale's example is worth imitating."[75]

By any standards, Zona Gale's accomplishments were remarkable. Her work is still poignant, since the substance of her writing is the theme that every person has dignity that no other person, or group, has a right to deny or abuse.

Clearly, Zona saw the potential of family to be a force for nurturing individual self-worth. However, she also condemned the power of family to strip away the dignity of its members—especially the woman whose powers are already compromised in a world not of her making. Such a woman provided the main character and theme of *Miss Lulu Bett*, which launched Zona Gale's feminism, and her reflections of life, into the decade of the 1920s.

THE PLAY—THE "RESCUE" OF *MISS LULU*

At the start of Zona Gale's *Miss Lulu Bett*, we are introduced to members of the Deacon household as they convene for supper. First, the petulant child Monona comes to the dinner table, sneaks a cookie, and begins her tuneless "terrible little chant." Her parents Dwight and Ina enter next, with Ina complaining that her sister Lulu has failed to call them for supper, and "looks so bad" if company should call. Lulu Bett, who has prepared the supper and tried to brighten the table with a potted tulip, enters with muffins and is taken to task by Dwight for her twenty-five cent purchase of the tulip plant. He snaps that his professions—of magistrate and dentist—"do not warrant" the purchase of spring flowers.

Asked by Ina to fix a special supper for the picky Monona, Lulu goes off to fix milk toast. But on her way, Lulu stops, unnoticed, and tosses the tulip out the window; a small foreshadowing of her later rebellion.

Dwight is the smug dictatorial keeper of two other women in the house as well: The widowed mother of Ina and Lulu, Mrs. Bett; and the Deacons' teenaged daughter Diana. Like Lulu, both of these women are weary victims of Dwight's pontificating and patronizing treatment.

(It's already clear that Lulu is the beast of burden who runs the household. Through her interactions with visitors, starting with a mild-mannered neighbor, Cornish, we discover that Lulu is a marvelous cook and seamstress, can play the piano and sing, and has a quick and low-key humor, mostly about herself. Yet her skills are seen as valueless in a world of Dwight Deacons.)

Dwight gives Lulu a second scolding for not telling him about a letter he finds on the mantle, but is distracted by its contents. Dwight's world-traveling brother, Ninian, whom he hasn't seen in 20 years, will be paying them a visit next week. Dwight embarrasses Lulu by joking that Ninian will "take one look at her and want to settle down here."[76] While he and Ina prepare to go to their study club, they leave Lulu to get the shrieking

Monona off to bed. Then Lulu watches as the teenaged Diana begins a flirtation with Bobby Larkin, a boy from the neighborhood.

When Ninian arrives, he does take a liking to Lulu, and quickly sees that her lot in the household is too hard—they "make a slave" of her. He urges Lulu to leave and find work that she likes; but she responds that the trouble is "women like me can't do any other work." Besides, all she would like to do is "take care of folks that needed me ... have them want me."

After Ninian tells Monona a tall tale about growing diamonds, a fabrication he calls drama, he gets inspired to take the whole family, including Lulu, to the theatre. The rattled Lulu who, according to Ina, "never goes anywhere" (because they don't invite her) finally consents.

While preparing to leave, Ninian is still in a play-acting mood and cajoles Lulu into reciting the marriage vows with him. As soon as they've said their impromptu "I wills," Dwight realizes that, since he is a magistrate, they are now married according to law.

Ninian shocks them all by convincing Lulu to let it stand and to make this theatre night their send-off. Moreover, his planned trip to Savannah can now become their honeymoon. Off they all go in a flurry, leaving Mrs. Bett with Monona, who keeps chanting, "I was to a wedding..."

Act Two opens on the porch, a month later, with Ina pointing out a neglected window screen to Dwight. She also points out the new neighbors' limousine. They start bemoaning the lack of Lulu to leave in charge of the house while they visit Dwight's aunt, when Lulu suddenly comes up the front walk. She painfully explains that Ninian was married long ago to a woman he thinks is now dead, but he's not sure. He wanted Lulu to know the truth; she left because she couldn't live with the uncertainty.

All Dwight can think of is the gossip that Lulu's return will promote, and the threat of a bigamy scandal. He seizes the chance to make Lulu the scapegoat. She can come back "on the old terms" on one condition: The townspeople will be led to believe that Ninian was displeased with Lulu, and sent her back. Dwight plants in the dejected Lulu the thought that Ninian invented a former wife, just to be rid of her. Meanwhile, in the play's subplot, Diana conspires to run away by eloping with Bobby Larkin. When Lulu discovers the plan (which fails because the two are underage), Diana wails to her aunt that she hates her father's taunts and contempt, and is ready to "love almost anybody" who's nice to her. Lulu is amazed that Di's feelings are so like her own.

When proof arrives in the mail that Ninian was married before (and did not invent a wife to be rid of Lulu), Lulu is still sad, but relieved. The situation prompts from the sympathetic neighbor Cornish an awkward marriage proposal, which Lulu gently rejects. But Dwight again uses the news to turn the tables against Lulu. Now it's clear that Lulu was with Ninian for a month with no legal marriage. She can't be so selfish as to make this shameful news known and bring disgrace to her family. When Lulu finally erupts in a furious flow of words about Dwight being the selfish one, who would sacrifice anyone for his own self image, Dwight pulls a last card from his deck of tricks: It's Ninian he's thinking of. Does Lulu want to send Ninian to jail, for the crime of bigamy? This defeats the cornered Lulu; but she defiantly rejects Ina's fatuous pity for her and all women not lucky enough to "be so protected, so loved" by a "good kind husband."

Act Three opens on the porch, where Mother Bett is tidying up. Lulu comes out carrying a suitcase, and emotionally explains to her mother that she must go: She can't bear another day in Dwight's house or this town. In one of her lucid moments, Mrs. Bett says, "I often wondered why you didn't go before." After Lulu goes off toward the station and others emerge clamoring after a breakfast that Lulu has not fixed, Mother Bett reveals what has happened.

Amid the confusion, Ninian comes up the walk. He has come, he says, with proof that his first wife is dead after all. He wants to tell Lulu. Informed that she's gone off to catch the train, Ninian takes off after her. Monona erupts from the house, to report Ina's trials with making breakfast: she's "burned all over" and "so cross."

Minutes later, Lulu returns, having heard at the station that Ninian is back in town. When Dwight emerges to yell at Lulu for upsetting his household and neglecting breakfast, Lulu announces that she has left his house for good; she's going elsewhere to get work. Ina is aghast: What will people think of them if they allow Lulu to do that?

Ninian returns to the fracas, and Dwight advises him not to sacrifice himself for Lulu's sake since she is well enough off with them. "You hypocrites!" Ninian snarls, to the glee of Mrs. Bett, who is glad to hear plain talk at last. Ninian says that if she will forgive him, he has come back for Lulu—his only wife. As Lulu assures him that she has already forgiven him, the curtain falls.

(Note that this was the amended ending, written after Gale was flooded with letters from audience members wanting Lulu to get her man. In Gale's original ending, there is no proof that Ninian's first wife is dead: Lulu simply gets the gumption to pull free, and goes off to "call my soul my own." The first ending was more in line with feminist ideals. But in the altered ending, Lulu's acceptance of Ninian is by choice; and individual choice is the point.)

In light of Zona Gale's social activism and feminism, the most striking feature about her play is not surprising: *Miss Lulu Bett* puts center stage all the social assumptions that were stifling women, that would fuel the women's movement. Gale uses the Deacon household to condemn the myths surrounding women's roles:

- that rules of behavior are different for women than for men;
- that a woman's inherent role is to serve;
- that men's pursuits in the public sphere are of value while women's activities in the private sphere are not—and that a woman's place *is* the private sphere;
- that the pivotal event in a woman's life must therefore be her marriage.

In their small town, Lulu is stifled by another myth: that a family member's welfare is secondary to the image of the family within its social circle.

While Gale's characters take their part within the play, they also take part in her portrayal of the larger human drama being played out in American households. As critical biographer Harold Simonson declared, "*Miss Lulu Bett* ... reinforced the current hue and cry over women's rights."[77] There were Lulus everywhere, living economically dependent lives in homes of those who had, in effect, captured them. Editor Judith Barlow wrote that women like Lulu were "without husbands or money, hence valueless in the eyes of the world."[78]

Trapped and exploited by her given family, Lulu is badly in need of rescuing by outsiders, and of a chance for created family. Since she rarely treads past the porch, help must come to her, or she must reach the point of breaking bonds, come what may. Gale provides both possibilities: While Lulu grows in determination to break free, two outsiders encourage her to do so. Her alliances with Cornish and Ninian give her a taste of freedom and of a kinder, created family.

Ina Deacon is as much the antithesis of her sister as Dwight is of his brother. Ina bears traits of the modern woman in her aloofness to housework and her longing for limousines. But Ina is rooted in the past. She harks of the anti-feminist woman who feared losing what Barbara Ehrenreich decried as the "one great 'privilege' that rests on difference; the right to be supported by a man."[79] Dwight Deacon is a composite captor, a smug little man-about-town and man-of-the-house. Making Dwight a magistrate as well as a dentist is a useful device for Gale. It creates a more literal sense of Dwight sitting in judgment of Lulu; but it also sets up humor. Dwight flusters Bobby with his joke: "What's this? Came to see the justice about getting married, did you? Or the dentist to have your tooth pulled ... Same thing—eh?"

The play was billed a "domestic comedy"; but its humor is sharp-edged and satirical. The marriage of Dwight and Ina smacks of parody, a cartoon of the era's so-called companionate marriage. Dwight and Ina embrace the vogue for study clubs; yet their conversations never go deeper than what the neighbors are up to. They give lip service to affection with their inane endearments: "my little puss ... my darling little dictionary." But marriage is merely part of an image they project.

Instead of ties of affection, what binds the Deacon family is the mesh of pretense and myths that Dwight uses to keep his charges in check. The intent behind his myths is exactly that defined by Nancy Napier and outlined in the Prologue: "to control family members through loyalty, guilt, humiliation, and punishment."[80] Dwight's appeal to family ties is pretentious and self-serving: "The family bond is the strongest bond in the world. Family. Tribe ... the family reputation is the highest nobility." What his reputation boils down to, for Dwight, is a selfish bid for social approval. His management of Lulu exposes his "family bond" for the cruel trap it really is. Dwight and Ina do not know the true meaning of family—or friendship.

The play's outside characters, Cornish and Ninian, display the redeeming qualities that Dwight and Ina lack. Cornish is an awkward but caring figure, whose admiration for Lulu is heartfelt: "I guess you can do most anything you set your hand to, Miss Lulu." He assures her, "It don't make any difference to your friends what people say," a sentiment that shows how unfriendly Lulu's own family is. The generous Cornish would have Lulu take his money, even if she won't take him. Clearly, Ninian's generosity is more flamboyant: His hosting of the theatre party is to show off, and he admits it. Still, Ninian is a fair and sympathetic listener, who truly wants to know what Lulu feels. In drawing both Cornish and Ninian as better men than Dwight, Gale drew them as more progressive men, ready to view women as worthy equals. They see the irony of Lulu's situation in this house: She, who is most dependent, is actually most capable.

The whole Deacon family is a haphazard, discordant group. The two daughters chafe at their attachment as much as Lulu. In one outburst, the restless Monona wails, "I hate the whole family." The teenaged Diana bears traces of the Flapper: she's willful and sexual and longing for romance. Yet even she yields to the bias that marriage will be her main destiny. Already remote from her parents, Di would escape them altogether, as Lulu would.

Lulu's revolt grows with the confidence planted in her by outsiders; but the seeds are already in her (her tossing of the tulip plant foreshadows her transformation). Small doses of approval and freedom nurture the Lulu who finally stands up to Dwight and his skewed beliefs.

Better late than never, Lulu takes her leave, albeit as Mrs. Ninian Deacon. An important point is that, before Ninian's return, Lulu is already on her way to the train. Her return from the station implies that her link to Ninian may have begun by chance, but it will continue by choice. The final curtain can be taken, not necessarily as a happy ending for Lulu, but as a happier starting-over point.

Despite the years since its creation, *Miss Lulu Bett* still holds merit. It boldly illustrates the issues that gave rise to the women's movement. And Gale's main argument—respect for the inner worth of every person—is poignant in a society grown even more preoccupied with status and externals. Gale also condemns a form of hypocrisy that still flourishes in family and society: the use of control in the guise of protection. But Gale's playfulness mitigates her criticism, in bits of dialogue and business. Every time Monona is told to "run around and play," Gale has the child do just that—dash about in circles. When Mrs. Bett is invited along to the theatre, she declines with, "No, I'm fooled enough without fooling myself on purpose" (the response of Zona's father when he "refused to change the clocks for daylight saving").[81] Some stylistic elements of *Lulu Bett* give the play a modern feel. Its staccato, repetitious dialogue and its fidelity to everyday banality put the play ahead of its time—especially in Gale's device of starting two scenes with characters having the same conversation. But above all, *Miss Lulu Bett* holds merit and interest as the work of a woman who was vitally connected to her world and deeply committed to improving the status of women.

3

Susan Glaspell: From Iowa Village to Greenwich Village

Susan Glaspell was born a few years after Zona Gale and led a remarkably parallel life.[1] Like Gale, she grew up in a Midwestern river town, lost her heart quite early to a boy from the town's leading family, and married him in middle age after his prior marriage was dissolved. As a writer, she also moved from news journalism to local-color fiction, and from a sentimental style to a socially-conscious realism that was tinged with mysticism. Susan, however, ventured into surrealism, and she enjoyed more success as a playwright in New York. But like Zona Gale, she won the Pulitzer for a play involving crisis and scandal in a small-town family. Susan Glaspell even resembled Zona Gale; she, too, was a small, fragile-looking woman. And, at the age of 65, her life ended as Gale's had (at 64), in a fatal attack of pneumonia.

Susan Glaspell's river town was Davenport, Iowa, where her pioneer grandparents had settled to raise fruit crops. Susan learned, as soon as she could read, what an important name "Cook" was in her thriving town: She checked out countless books from the Cook Memorial Library, attended services at Cook Memorial Church, and walked past the imposing Cook Home for elderly women. She also passed the big boxlike mansions that belonged to descendants of these enterprising Cooks. In one of these mansions, George "Jig" Cram Cook had been born—an event of great import in the life of Susan Glaspell.

Susan grew up knowing all about Jig Cook, born nine years before she was. She had often heard stories of the cabin where the Cooks spent their summers. Jig's mother, Ellen, had decided to move the old log cabin built by her parents, out from the backwoods and to a place of honor by the river. Since "Iowa people with money for new houses were not bothering with log cabins," this was startling news. So was the report that this freshly chinked cabin was stocked with volumes of Plato, and Greek urns, of all things. And conversations around the fireplace might include "the mystic rites of India or the music of Beethoven."[2] When Susan finally made a trip to the cabin, she found it to be all that she had heard and more. Ellen Cook was warm and gracious, inviting guests to read or wander along the river bank.

The day of Susan's first visit, Jig Cook happened to be home from teaching at the University of Iowa. A scholar of the classics, the tall, athletic Jig had a classic physique and a shock of gray-streaked hair. When Jig came into the room to retrieve a copy of Renan's *Life of Jesus* Susan blurted out, "Oh, you read it in French." He gave her a surprised but simple "yes," and went out.[3] (Years later, Susan would tease Jig about his initial indifference to her, when she was so enthralled with him.) Their paths would cross again, but not for several years.

After graduating from Drake University, Susan worked her way through graduate school in Chicago. Here, she was fascinated by what she saw and absorbed: the new Socialism, outbursts of feminism, and the worlds revealed by the dramas of Ibsen and Chekhov. With her English degree and widened horizons, Susan returned to Iowa and wangled a job on the Des Moines *Daily News*—"the first paper in Iowa to employ women as reporters."[4]

After two years that included a stint as "The News Girl" with her own column, Glaspell quit the *Daily News*. "I boldly gave up my job and went home to Davenport to give all my time to my own writing. I say boldly, because I had to earn my living."[5]

Glaspell's critical biographer, Arthur Waterman, divided her life and work into three periods: The first launched her career as a short-story writer and novelist, and ended with her marriage to Jig Cook. In the middle period, from 1913 until the mid-twenties, her life centered on her relationship with Cook and their theatre, the Provincetown Players. The third period began with Cook's death, and marked the final stage in Susan's writing—a biographical tribute to Cook, her Pulitzer play, and a few more novels defining "the particular values the Midwest has for the Modern World."[6]

During the first period, Susan churned out enough magazine stories to become the leading writer of Davenport (which became "Freeport" in her fiction). While supplying the sentiment craved by her readers, she also hit upon the themes that would define her later writing. Typical was "Unveiling Brenda," in which she romantically paired an elite English professor with his best student (a farm girl), then depicted their fight to overcome the disapproval of others.

Her first novel, *The Glory of the Conquered*, traced a love story between an artist, Ernestine, and a scientist, Karl, and was high romance. (Karl goes blind and dies, leaving Ernestine to paint the world they loved.) It did have its voice of realism, in Karl's news-reporter cousin, Georgia. But Susan was still working against her own reporter instincts, not writing about "real people living real lives."[7] It would take something of an awakening—akin to that of Zona Gale—to bring her to the realistic style that would make her mark. Susan's awakening was a slow one, involving a journey to Europe, and a journey back to George Cram Cook.

In the years that Susan spent in Chicago, Jig Cook had given up teaching to become a philosopher-farmer and writer at the cabin. After his political novel *The Chasm* was published, Jig became friends with the liberal Floyd Dell, whose writings Jig admired. From their friendship, which paired Cook's idealism with Dell's socialism, there sprang a Monist Society—Davenport's first and only.

Word of this excited Susan. She stopped going to church with her parents and began attending these new Sunday sessions. She was thrilled to hear Jig speak, "welding universalist religion with Greek philosophy and the principles of a socialist economy."[8] As Jean Gould noted in *Modern American Playwrights*, "Susan saw during these early days how contagious his enthusiasm could be; she was to witness it again, when they formed the Provincetown Players."[9]

Later, Floyd Dell would recall the first impressions he and Jig had of Susan: "slight, gentle, sweet ... a little ethereal ... but evidently a person of great energy, and brimful of talent."[10] Both men found Susan's early writing voice too "medieval-romantic," and urged her to change it.

Susan and Jig became close friends outside the Monist Society, going for long walks and talking. They stopped short of romance, because each had other commitments. Jig was already engaged to a Chicago girl; Susan had agreed to a job on a New York paper, to be followed by a year abroad with her friend Lucy. Still, she and Jig had a strange understanding, a sense that their lives would somehow, someday, merge.

Meanwhile, Jig's impact on Susan's viewpoint and art was already taking effect. Jig avidly stressed art's social responsibility: "Our fiction is juvenile," he grumbled, "written for people who ... have never grown up."[11] Cook's example, coupled with a world view widened by her travels—made the vital change in Susan's outlook and writing. Her next novel, appropriately titled *The Visioning*, held all that her first one lacked: realistic background and characters, and a sharp reflection of life. Again, Susan wove her story around a woman. As Arthur Waterman later observed, she typically made her central character "a woman whose experiences form the plot and whose emotions determine the meaning."[12]

In *The Visioning*, Kate Wayneworth Jones is the daughter of a respected military family on an Iowa post. Kate's first action in the book is to save a girl from drowning herself. Protected by her family's privilege, Kate can't understand why anyone would want "to die on a sunny day." But the

Susan Glaspell

girl, Ann Forest, prevails upon Kate that "nothing can be as bad as sunshine."[13] This begins Kate's enlightenment about class struggle in an unjust world. When Ann runs away to Chicago, Kate follows her, to a life that shatters her illusions of privilege. After Kate embraces women's rights and socialism, she ends up with a socialist husband and rejects the political order of her old life.

The transformation of Glaspell's character reflected her own awakening to the vision of social equality—to a world "without exploitation of the poor [and] with the army left out."[14]

While Susan was away from the Midwest, George Cook was having his own revelation: His marriage to the Chicago girl had been a mistake. They had two children, however, so their break would not be simple. In Chicago, Cook had become a reviewer for the *Chicago Evening Post* literary magazine, and had embraced the artists' renaissance that fostered such talents as Carl Sandburg and Ring Lardner. The Chicago renaissance now attracted Susan Glaspell. This time, when their paths crossed, Jig Cook realized that "there could be no one else" but Susan.[15] She began her inevitable love affair with the still-married Cook, raising eyebrows in Davenport and signaling the end of Jig's troubled marriage.

Jig's growing love of theatre was shared by Susan; they rejoiced at productions by the Irish Players who visited Chicago's Little Theatre. Years later, Susan would write: "What we saw done for Irish life [Jig] wanted for American life—no stage conventions in the way of ... true feeling."[16]

While Jig Cook's divorce became final, he and Susan traveled east. On April 14, 1913, they stood before the mayor of Weehawken, New Jersey, and were married. They honeymooned in Provincetown.

During that first summer (in the second period of Susan Glaspell's life), they took long lazy walks around Cape Cod. She wrote a little, he gardened a little, they dreamed a lot. They became friends with other writers getting away from New York, including the radical Jack Reed and Max Eastman. In the following spring, with the help of these friends, Susan and Jig remodeled an old house they bought. The men knocked out walls, opened up the staircase, but "the house stood in spite of their violence."[17] When Susan was forbidden to climb stairs because of sudden heart trouble, Jig contrived a small elevator for her, with silver weights that looked like organ pipes. "A strange sight indeed..." said Susan, "to see me midway between kitchen ceiling and floor."[18]

In the winter, they lived in Manhattan's Greenwich Village, where rents and shopkeepers were kinder to struggling artists. They saw the first stagings of the Washington Square Players, begun in a bookstore and moved to the Band Box Theatre. When their budget allowed a Broadway ticket, they "came away wishing we had gone somewhere else."[19] But their discontent stirred a desire to create a "native theatre"—some hybrid between the Irish theatre and that of the classic Greeks. (Jig longed for "something which was in Greek life ... [that] we are terribly in need of."[20])

In Greenwich Village at that time, Freud and psychoanalysis were the rage. "You could not go out to buy a bun without hearing of someone's complex," Susan later recalled.[21] She and Jig concocted a one-act comedy, spoofing this obsession with Freud. When even the little theatres thought *Suppressed Desires* was too specialized to produce, the two of them resolved to put it on themselves, that summer in Provincetown. The play became half of a double bill with a script by their friend, Neith Boyce. In Boyce's large living room, a set of sorts was provided by Robert Edmond Jones—a "candle here and a lamp there."[22] The evening was such a hit that they had to repeat it for neighbors who felt left out. So they arranged to use an old fish house on the wharf as their theatre, and Jig wrote another play for a second bill. "Thus ended the first season of the Provincetown Players, who closed without knowing they were the Provincetown Players."[23]

The next spring, they returned with big plans: They overhauled their "Wharf Theatre" to hold ninety people ("sitting closely together").[24] They divided the 12-foot stage into fourths to permit levels; and if they opened the sliding doors behind it, the whole sea was their backdrop.

They gave a first bill, then needed a second one. Two Irishmen had taken a shack up the road. Susan asked the older one, "Terry, haven't you a play to read to us?" "No," was the firm reply. "I don't write, I just think.... But Mr. O'Neill has got a whole trunk full of plays."[25] So, from his trunk, Eugene O'Neill took *Bound East For Cardiff*. That night, it was read at Jig and Susan's house, while O'Neill stayed in the dining room. From that moment, "we knew what we were for," Susan would remark.[26]

Two weeks later, a play by Eugene O'Neill was produced for the first time in a Cape Cod fish house. Cook played the dying sailor, Yank; O'Neill was the Second Mate. An obliging fog rolled in on cue. "The sea has been good to O'Neill," Susan wrote years later. "It was there for his opening."[27]

Letters went out to the audience: Associate members were wanted for the Provincetown Players, whose goal was "to give American playwrights of sincere purpose a chance to work out their ideas in freedom." Would they like to subscribe? ("One dollar for three remaining bills."[28])

From the response came real seats and simple sets. When Jig announced a play by Susan for the next bill, she protested; she didn't have one. Jig replied, "You've got a stage, haven't you?"[29] Susan went out to the wharf and sat, staring hard at their bare stage:

> After a time, the stage became a kitchen. I saw where the stove was, the table ... Then the door at the back opened, and people all bundled up came in—two or three men, I wasn't sure which; but sure enough about the two women, who hung back.... When I was a newspaper reporter out in Iowa, I was sent down-state to do a murder trial, and I never forgot going into the kitchen of a woman locked up in town.[30]

Ten days later, the resulting play, *Trifles*, went into rehearsal. Susan's first solo play would endure as one of America's most anthologized one-acts plays. Its simple theme and structure prompted Judith Barlow to comment, 70 years later, that *Trifles* is a "classic example of near-perfect short play construction." In Susan's first use of an offstage protagonist, she created a Minnie Wright who could be "all women trapped in loveless marriages to harsh men."[31] Susan played one of the neighbors who sift through the trifles of Minnie's grim life. So, Susan Glaspell's debut—as playwright and actor—closely followed that of O'Neill.

Of the rest of that "great summer," Susan wrote, "We would lie on the beach and talk about plays—everyone writing, or acting, or producing. Life was all of a piece."[32] That winter, when the group returned to New York, their theatre came with them.

Jig Cook returned to Greenwich Village first and found a theatre: the parlor floor of a brownstone on MacDougal Street. In the joint effort to transform the space, the Players became a motley extended family. Jig virtually lived in the space, overseeing the work. His dauntless mother came to pitch in, tackling every job from costume mistress to scene shifting. Known as "Ma-mie" to all, Ellen Cook would work until midnight and quip, "I want to die with my boots on."[33] Besides the Cooks, the core of the Provincetown Players still included Jack Reed, Floyd Dell, Neith Boyce, and Eugene O'Neill. Now, their Playwrights Theatre on MacDougal Street also gave stage to such artists as Edna St. Vincent Millay and Edna Ferber. The Players' stance was paradoxical: They shunned box-office concerns, but survival depended on building a following. In that first vital New York season, the *Tribune*'s powerful critic Heywood Broun sang praises for their "most efficient experimental theatre," especially "the work of O'Neill and Glaspell."[34] John Corbin of the *Times* hailed the "tense and heartfelt realism of Eugene O'Neill" and "the sensitive feminine perceptions of Susan Glaspell."[35] (In this same season, the French theatre innovator Jacques Copeau visited the Players and admitted to being "touched to the depth of my soul" by Glaspell's acting in her own play, *The People*.[36])

In the seven-year run of the seminal Provincetown Players, Glaspell would contribute eleven scripts—only three less than O'Neill—and continue to excel as both playwright and actress. In his history of the Provincetown Players, Robert Sarlos wrote that for the women characters in Glaspell's play *The Outside*, "the group's best actresses, Ida Rauh and Susan Glaspell, took the roles."[37] Set in an old converted lifeguard station (which in real life became occupied by O'Neill), *The Outside* centers on two women, Mrs. Patrick and her maid Allie, who have withdrawn from life after losing their husbands. To their doorstep, where the forces of sea and sand confront each other, two lifeguards have brought a drowned man. While efforts to revive the man fail, Allie's efforts to re-enter life, and to pull Mrs. Patrick with her, are finally successful.

The play was a departure from Susan's usual Midwest context; but it featured a new hallmark of her work: the intent to break limits of convention. As editor C.W.E. Bigsby wrote in a collection of Glaspell's plays:

"Outside of O'Neill, it is hard to think of anyone in American theatre who would have been prepared to take the risks which Glaspell does in *The Outside*."[38] The play was a fitting metaphor for what Susan and Jig were trying to do with their theatre.

Only the dual driving forces of Cook and Glaspell could keep the Players going despite the clashes of personality that rocked the group from year to year. Cook's maniacal energy and inspired imagination (often manifest in alcoholism) was offset by Susan's ability to remain the calm, detached observer. Each season, as veteran Players dropped away—tired of hard work with little pay—new recruits came on board. While O'Neill did continue to supply scripts, he was "otherwise withdrawn," defying the group's collaborative spirit and its "crucial production principle" that playwrights direct their own work.[39]

Susan Glaspell's play *Bernice* featured her in another lead role and garnered raves. Heywood Broun called it "notable among the dramas of the season," and likened it to *Trifles*, "in that the acts of a dead woman [are] gradually revealed ... through the combined memories of her friends."[40] In the *Times*, Corbin called the play "perfect in each of its ... characterizations," and added: "If the Provincetown Players had done nothing more than give us the delicately humorous and sensitive plays of Susan Glaspell, they would have amply justified their existence."[41]

Like her theatre, Susan was "nothing if not experimental." C.W.E. Bigsby wrote that "each play offered her an opportunity to explore different problems, to test her own abilities."[42] Her next full-length play, *The Inheritors*, drew mixed responses, but James Agate of the *Times* ranked it with Ibsen's *The Master Builder*.[43] The plot reflected Susan's politics: her outrage at the cost of war in human loss, and at the loss (in America) of the right to protest.

The Inheritors centered on the three-generation family of Silas Morton, founder of a college for "the children of the corn fields." The founder's ideals are put on the line when the school is threatened with the denial of state funds unless it expels a radical teacher for being a pacifist. The play's real radical is Madeline, the outspoken granddaughter of Morton, who condemns the greed that has replaced human concerns. She denounces her own father for hoarding the secret of his new strain of corn, and rejoices when the wind blows his gains to the soil of neighbors. In a *New York World* article on Glaspell, Eugene Solow wrote: "Susan Glaspell's heroines are among the most distinguished achievements in the entire range of American drama. They are rebels, every one of them—idealistic rebels."[44]

In 1921 Glaspell's most rebellious heroine, Claire Archer, appeared in *The Verge*, one of the first expressionistic plays on any American stage. Susan directed the play, and essentially designed it by fully detailing Claire's experimental greenhouse and the tower in which Claire later goes insane. *The Verge* opens eerily in the greenhouse, with "patterns of sound" from the wind, frost patterns on the glass, and a light on Claire's new Edge Vine, a plant both "repellent and significant."[45] Into this setting Glaspell thrust a comedy of manners that quickly turns into a psychological drama. Claire's diverting of the household heat to her plants has forced into her greenhouse the three men in her life—Tom, Dick, and Harry (respectively her lover, friend, and husband). Tom Edgeworthy is closest to Claire and her mutant Edge Vine. He understands her urge to break confining patterns of life and seek some higher plane of otherness. But Tom also knows that it lies "on the far side of destruction," and tries to hold Claire back.[46] As she struggles to reach for "otherness," Claire's mind and language break down. Violently rejecting her husband and child—everything familiar—she ultimately strangles Tom and achieves a kind of liberation in her madness. Almost 50 years after her creation, Arthur Waterman referred to Claire Archer as "the most radical woman every presented on the American stage."[47]

The Theatre Guild was intrigued enough with *The Verge* to bring it uptown to the Garrick, to play in matinee.[48] Scripts by Glaspell and O'Neill had already been in demand at uptown theatres. A few had been restaged by the Washington Square Players; when critics mistakenly gave them credit for introducing the talents of Glaspell and O'Neill, Jig set the record straight with a quick letter to the *Times*.[49]

However, when O'Neill's *The Emperor Jones* was moved to Broadway, it created the rift that led to the breakup of the Players. That fatal rift was the divide between members who cherished their experimental status and those who favored a move toward the commercial.

Jig Cook had considered *The Emperor Jones* as O'Neill's best play yet. For its staging, Jig had even built the huge reflective dome he had dreamed up, to enhance effects of lighting and stage depth. The production was cheered by a chorus of critics for script, acting, and "such illusion of distance and the wide outdoors as few of their uptown rivals can achieve."[50] Record crowds streamed to MacDougal Street. Broadway interests entered the picture, and O'Neill's Brutus Jones continued his run at the Selwyn Theatre.

The Provincetown Players mounted one more season after that death blow to group spirit, a farewell bill that offered Eugene O'Neill's expressionistic play *The Hairy Ape*. In form and theme, the play was more influenced by Susan Glaspell and *The Verge* than O'Neill or theatre history have ever acknowledged.

The protagonist of O'Neill's expressionistic play is Yank, a coal-stoking seaman imprisoned by his filthy, dehumanizing job. Realizing how much he is like a caged animal, Yank escapes to seek a higher meaning in life. His experiences with religion and socialism only provoke him to a violent rage. Deranged and disillusioned, he wanders to the zoo where he talks to the gorilla, with whom he feels kinship. Yank frees the beast, to get back at all his oppressors. But the gorilla crushes Yank and leaves him to die behind the bars, "the one and only—Hairy Ape." (O'Neill included a script notation suggesting that perhaps Yank "at last belongs.")

In an article on Susan Glaspell's contributions to playwriting, Linda Ben-Zvie describes Susan's influence on O'Neill and *The Hairy Ape*:

> At the time he was composing his play, O'Neill was meeting his neighbor Glaspell every afternoon after working on his manuscript, his wife Agnes reports. As an indication of how completely O'Neill critics ignore Glaspell and her influence on O'Neill, it is interesting to note that not one has ever mentioned the striking similarities between the two plays and the fact that O'Neill was in such close association with her during its composition.[51]

Before he had even completed the script, O'Neill was privately arranging for its staging by Broadway producers. Director Arthur Hopkins took control of the production early on; but at O'Neill's request, he agreed "to let the Players have it for a few weeks."[52]

Jig Cook wrote a valediction for the Players: "We give this theatre good death; the Provincetown Players end their story here." Days later, Susan found him sitting alone in the theatre, a blue light on his beloved dome ceiling. "It is time to go to Greece," he told her.[53]

They set sail in March, before the opening of *The Hairy Ape*, which they never saw. In Greece they settled in a mountain village, where the peasants came to regard Jig with great love and respect. He built them an amphitheater, and told them stories of their own past. He and Susan raised a little mongrel dog who became victim of a deadly disease. Hours after they buried "ToPuppy," Jig fell ill with the same disease. Days later, Susan allowed the peasants who had loved "Kyrios Kook" to perform the burial rites at Old Delphi. A great stone from the Temple of Apollo was used as Jig's headstone, "a tribute never paid to anyone in Greece before."[54]

A stunned Susan Glaspell returned to New York and began period three of her life—without George Cook. Her pain at losing Jig was compounded on discovering that O'Neill had revamped the Provincetown Players along commercial lines, with Kenneth MacGowan and Robert Edmond Jones. The memorial plaque to Jig on the theatre's facade did nothing to diminish her outrage.

Susan returned to their old house in Provincetown and wrote her own heartfelt tribute to Jig and his gifts to theatre. The theme of her affectionate biography *The Road to the Temple* was the ongoing conflict between the artist and his world. Intrigued by the idea of framing this conflict in a play, she kept turning to the story of Emily Dickinson. Susan wondered how she could bring to life the shocking discovery of Dickinson's "Letter to the World" and the conflict it caused within her staid New England family— And do it without using the Dickinson name.

Susan set her play in the Midwest, calling her poet Alison Stanhope; and again, by the device of keeping her pivotal character offstage, she found an effective way to suggest Emily Dickinson onstage. When *Alison's House* was completed, Glaspell began searching for a producer, refusing to turn to O'Neill and MacGowan.

(An interesting side-note is that, by this time, Kenneth MacGowan was soliciting scripts from Zona Gale. In the Gale archives is a letter from Mac-Gowan which includes these lines: "I'm going to direct the Provincetown Players this year, with ... Bobby Jones and Eugene O'Neill.... By chance, has Brock [Pemberton] sent back one of your plays? I know he's not fool enough to do that, but I hope. We hope to send a play or two uptown after they have been tested."[55])

Glaspell's search for a producer ended on 14th Street with the new experimental Civic Repertory led by Eva Le Gallienne, who both staged and starred in *Alison's House*. Response was favorable enough to extend the run for two additional weeks. And just as the 1931 season was ending, word came that *Alison's House* had won the Pulitzer Prize. The acclaim prompted the Shuberts to move the production to the Ritz Theatre—uptown. This was an ironic yet fitting destiny for the final play of Susan Glaspell. Like Jig Cook, Susan had shunned commercialism. Yet this tribute was evidence that her art had indeed made an impact on mainstream theatre. Jig's faith in her writing abilities was vindicated by the award.

Susan Glaspell's last theatre venture came when she was made the Midwest Director of the Federal Theatre Project (1936–1938). She concluded her writing career as a novelist; her final book, *Judd Rankin's Daughter*, appeared in 1945. In it, her last idealistic heroine sought for meaning and order in the chaos of a world at war. But it was on the landscape of American theatre that Susan Glaspell made her unique and significant mark. In his introduction to a collection of her plays, C.W.E. Bigsby wrote:

> Without her there must be some doubt as to whether the Provincetown Players would ever have been established and certainly whether that crucial organization would have been able to sustain

itself as it did. She was, without doubt, one of its two greatest discoveries.... She chanced more than most of her contemporaries and achieved more than many of them. She deserves more than a footnote in the history of drama. Susan Glaspell died of viral pneumonia on July 27, 1948, having written some of the most original plays ever to have come out of America.[56]

The Pulitzer Prize that Susan garnered for her last play, *Alison's House*, was perhaps a salute to her whole canon of plays, to her creative and remarkable life in the theatre.

The Play—The "Showdown" in *Alison's House*

The action in Glaspell's play begins on the last morning of the nineteenth century: December 31, 1899. Its setting is the Stanhope homestead in Iowa, now up for sale. In this house where the late Alison Stanhope lived and wrote her poetry, and where her feeble surviving sister Agatha still resides, their brother John and his sons are packing up the house's contents. John Stanhope intends to take Agatha back to live with him.

But the central figures of the first scene are John's young secretary, Ann, and a news reporter named Knowles, a great fan of the late Alison who wants to do a story on this closing of her home. Knowles gains Ann's sympathy and interest, and shows her one of his own poems. He tells Ann that Alison "belongs to the world. But the family doesn't know it."[57]

John Stanhope's younger son, Ted, comes in. The irresponsible Ted is always trying to trade on his late aunt's fame. He thinks he can cajole his English professor into a passing grade if he turns in private information about Alison. To the outrage of John and Agatha, Ted has already traded on Alison's affair with a married man, an old taboo family secret.

Also taboo is Alison's old room, yet Ted defiantly shows it to Knowles, who asks to see it "to hold it in memory." When Agatha finds out, she rages that "Alison belongs to us" and so does her room. To placate Agatha, Ann packs up her good tea set, using straw and a basket. Refusing to leave yet for John's house, Agatha vows that she will be "the last to step from the door."

John Stanhope's older son, Eben, arrives from the family law firm (which Eben has joined only to please his father). Eben's respect for his late Aunt Alison puts him at odds with his conniving brother Ted and with his own wife, Louise, a nagging woman who disdains the scandal that Alison brought on the family. When Ted asks, "Was Alison a virgin?" Eben throttles him, and John must break them apart. Louise berates Eben for his raving.

Into this tense situation comes John's prodigal daughter, Elsa, who long ago followed her heart and ran off with a married man. Her reverence for Alison's spirit has brought her here, to ask to spend this last night in the house. Mixed responses to her request are interrupted by word of a fire in a closet upstairs. While the men rush to put it out, Elsa is approached by the shaking Agatha, who mutters about the "burning, all burning." When John and Eben re-enter, they conjecture about how the fire was set—intentionally—using oil and straw. Agatha collapses moaning, "Why couldn't you let it burn.... Couldn't take them away—couldn't."

Act Two opens that afternoon, with Ann typing, John going through papers. An old carriage receipt reminds him that he used to take Ann's mother riding in that carriage. She has been dead for nine years now; but obviously he still holds feelings for her (which he never felt for his wife). When John hears that the reporter Knowles is still about, walking by the river, he threatens Ted with cutoff of his allowance if he talks to Knowles about the fire or the family. The prospective buyers of the house, the Hodges, drop in for another look. After they drone on about how they'll modernize the place for boarders, Eben laments that they will destroy it. But his father "wants it destroyed." He can't bear it going to someone else, unaltered.

John regrets the confusion this causes Agatha, and now Elsa is added to the confusion. When Eben claims that Elsa "doesn't harm anyone," John counters that she harmed them all; she disgraced them. To Eben's reply that "maybe she couldn't help it," John responds, "Alison helped it." To himself, he adds "So did I."

When Louise enters and huffs that, if Elsa is staying the night, she is leaving, John agrees that she should go. The weary Eben sides with his father, much to Louise's chagrin. At the Hodges' reappearance, Louise takes charge and fatuously compliments their plans to remodel. The Hodges finally give John a check, set a date for signing the deed, and go out.

The reporter Knowles returns, claiming he has felt Alison's presence along the river. "It's crazy," he says, but if Ann will walk there with him now, it might seem that "she wouldn't be gone." Ann is surprised and pleased at Knowles' request. John observes that Ann is attracted to the reporter, and softens toward Knowles. He gives him a book of Emerson poems that Alison loved.

Elsa enters and says that Agatha wants to come down. While John goes off to deal with this, Eben asks his sister why she ran off without telling him. She says that he might have stopped her, and she had to go:

That is the way she "loved this man," and still does. Eben quietly wishes that he loved someone that way.

Agatha comes in, clutching a bag. As Elsa helps her to a chair, Agatha takes a portfolio from the bag and thrusts it at her niece, crying "For—Elsa." Agatha collapses, but not in the faint that Elsa assumes it is. John enters and makes the sad determination that Agatha has died.

Act Three begins late that night in Alison's old room, which holds a bed, a desk, a fireplace, and mementoes. Elsa is spending the night here, with John's permission. She is about to open the portfolio from Agatha when Ann comes in to talk with her. Both women are affected by the room; but Ann finally blurts the question, "Can you fall in love all at once, with someone you hardly know?" Ann is already in love with Knowles. Elsa reveals that her own love was "all at once," too, even though she and Bill had known each other since childhood.

After Eben and John enter, and the portfolio is finally opened, they are all stunned by its contents. Here are poems they've never seen, almost as many as were published. These are poems about the beauty and anguish of Alison's love. They are "Alison—at her best." Ted barges in, having heard about the poems, and Eben convinces him to leave, for now.

(Here, the "lights dim to indicate the passage of time.")

After a shocked silence at reading the poems, John haltingly admits that if he'd known Alison's love was this great, he would not have induced her to stay. But still, the poems will never leave this room; he will burn them. Ted rushes back in, bent on reading the poems, and grabs at them, ready to fight. His father takes violent hold of him, threatening to kill Ted if he doesn't drop them. As Eben leaps into the furor, Elsa restrains them all and compels Ted to leave.

Ann returns with Knowles, and makes her own heartfelt plea to John: She knows that he loved her mother; that he denied his love because of Ann and his children, who now urge him to let Alison's words live as "a gift to all love." She urges John to leave the poems to Elsa—"To a woman. Because Alison said it, for women."

At last, all leave the room except for John and his daughter, Elsa. She did not know, she says, that he "had gone through it, too." He denied his love because of what others would think. Elsa insists that what "our little town" thinks cannot matter, when weighed against Alison's words. John struggles with his conscience; and as the clock strikes the turn of the century, he concedes. Allison's words will become one more of her gifts—"from her century to this one."

Alison's House was written from a highly personal vantage point. Susan Glaspell knew what it was like to love a married man: Her relationship with Jig Cook began well before his divorce. And her love for him seemed to be the inexplicable instantaneous love described by her character Elsa. The link between love and art was a vital one for Glaspell: Her love for Cook and her artistic expression were closely woven, making life and work "all of a piece," as she said. In her play, she binds love and art together by suggesting that both are specially ordained, and must stand outside normal rules or understanding. Like Zona Gale, Glaspell saw the artist as a spiritual singer for society: A person of rare perception called to point the way toward a higher level of life and thought.

The play's conflict springs from the fact that artists sing their eloquent best from personal experience. What if the artist's freely interpreted personal experience confronts group censure—here, family censure—from fear of gossip or scandal? The artist's best song may never reach the world to enlarge its understanding, if the family's understanding is too narrow to allow it.

Glaspell's criticism of family strikes a chord already struck by Gale. Like Gale, she condemns the sacrifice of personal well-being to family image. She turns a harsh spotlight on the controls used to keep members in line, serving the family group. What Glaspell does, in effect, is to stage a showdown—between those whose prime concern is for the group and its traditions, and those who would put individual need above group concerns.

At first glance, this seems to translate into a squaring-off between generations. But the division is not that clear-cut. For instance, Eben's wife Louise is of the younger generation, but seems as old and cold as Agatha in her rigid reserve. Conversely, the Hodges are of the older generation, but their pursuit of the modern and their consumer values align them with the new. On Glaspell's battlefield, she does not lump all of one generation in one camp, or depict the members of either camp as all good guys, or bad. She displays sympathy and criticism for both sides. And her strongest criticism is aimed at the extremists in either camp, those most limited in understanding and tolerance.

As the controlling patriarch of this family, John Stanhope is a paler shade of Dwight Deacon in Gale's play. But John harbors a redeeming empathy and undergoes a last-minute conversion that Dwight does not. In an attempt to control his family, John has also used a mesh of family myths. When Alison would have gone off with her married lover, he walled her in with guilt about family disgrace. In theory, his ploy worked: Alison remained, and died a spinster. However, in practice, it backfired badly. Alison channeled her longing into the cache of poems that trigger the family's lethal tug-of-war. Agatha would even burn the house to destroy the intimate poems.

John ultimately threatens to kill his son Ted over control of the poems. John would cover up the poems as he covered up his own illicit love, his own chance for happiness. He has clung to his past love (for Ann's mother) through his ties to Ann, a vestige of created family for John.

John's wielding of family myths has had other sad impacts. He tells his errant son Ted, "You will go into your father's [law] office, which was his father's before him, and you will try to show more interest in the business than your brother does." Ted is hopelessly unsuited for law practice, and Eben is miserable being in it. But Ted's impudence and Eben's glimmer of revolt suggest that the myth that "Stanhope men are lawyers" may finally fade with the century.

What redeems John is that he exhibits doubts about family and his role in it. He confides to Ann, "Sometimes I wish I weren't the head of a family....I wish there weren't any family." His lament is sparked by a run-in with Louise, whose babble about family image makes her an echo of Gale's characters (Dwight and Ina). Louise carps, "I think family should stick together," yet she would bar the door from Elsa.

Louise, John, and Agatha are the extremists in one camp – far too concerned with the past and its codes. The extreme examples in the other camp are Ted and the Hodges, and not the impulsive Elsa, who is most aligned with her late Aunt Alison. Elsa knows that concerns about family image are petty, when weighed against the universal beauty of Alison's art. Elsa puts the spiritual ties of love above family ties, but she also heeds the pull back to family and the past.

On the other hand, Ted and the Hodges, who are preoccupied with personal gain, all seem to mock or desecrate the past. The Hodges will destroy the history of the house, with a make-over into a bright yellow boarding house and their plan to cut down the majestic old trees. John's insensitive son Ted profanes the past at all turns. Ted's probing questions about Alison are crude, his motives always base. When he confronts his father over the poems, Ted swaggers: "I'll be alive when the rest of you are dead. Then I'm the one to look after [the poems].... Knock me down. Try it.... I've sense enough to know the value of things." John threatens to kill Ted rather than let the poems go into Ted's vulgar world.

Glaspell does seem to use Ted as an example of what is most vulgar in the new generation. But she also upholds through Ted's siblings what is worthwhile: Elsa and Eben display compassion and understanding and, until the play's final moments, the only genuine family ties.

Like Zona Gale, Glaspell salutes the idea that kin may not be kindred spirits, that stronger ties may be formed with outsiders in an instant. Glaspell's abrupt match of Ann with the roving reporter Knowles is a mirror of Zona Gale's match-up of Lulu with the visiting Ninian. Ann is a much luckier single woman (whose options make her more typical of the 1930s than of the play's time setting). Pretty, bright, and educated, Ann is not caught in a grim trap, so her attachment to Knowles is clearly by choice. Along with Elsa, Ann and Knowles are the playwright's voice: They appeal for a greater understanding of art and love. Not coincidentally, these three stand apart—on the edge—where Glaspell places the most vital concerns of life. They are most in tune with Glaspell's unseen catalyst, Alison.

In the last moments of the play, there is peace and connection within the Stanhope family. Compelled by Alison's anguished poems of love, and by the fervent pleas of the youths whose love he envies, John allows the poems to live on. The understanding that Alison has evoked in her family can now be passed on "to the world."

Glaspell's play is not without flaws and contrivances: The last day in Alison's house coincides too neatly with the last day of the century, and the last day of Agatha's life. Yet the play is intriguing and suspenseful. Critical biographer Arthur Waterman praised its "overt conflict ... the unbroken dramatic line" and Glaspell's "ability to create a sustained mood."[58] Glaspell's suspense is deftly sustained, and heightened by the hovering presence of Alison. A fire in some form is ever-present, threatening to be the fate of the precious poems up to the final moments.

In an overview of Glaspell's work, John Chamberlain praised the play, adding that "Miss Glaspell is the best person in the world to act as mediator between the idealist and the rest of humanity."[59] Writing in 1966, Arthur Waterman upheld *Alison's House* as "one of the highlights of the American theatre in the 1930's," and a "a fitting close" to the career of Susan Glaspell.[60]

Susan Glaspell wrote twice as many plays as Zona Gale, but even she could not be considered a "prolific" playwright. Zoe Akins was unquestionably a prolific playwright, crafting more stage scripts than Gale and Glaspell combined. Her career straddled Broadway and Hollywood in the 1930s, when American theatre, like life itself, was shaped by the Great Depression.

4

The Depression Years: Gaining Despite the Losses

Not many success stories emerged from the Great Depression, but the career of Zoe Akins was a resounding one. Throughout the Depression and World War II, Zoe enjoyed a thriving career on both coasts, writing and adapting a stream of popular successes that starred the biggest talents in New York and Hollywood. Her characters were brought to life on stage and screen by such stars as Ethel Barrymore, Claudette Colbert, Katharine Hepburn and Bette Davis.

In a period synonymous with staggering losses, Akins prospered as few writers—male or female—ever have. Her extreme success reflected an extreme need for escape from the era's hardships. Her lavish melodramas offered a retreat from life, through characters whose woes were more devastating than those raining down on Depression households. A far cry from the commonplace world of Gale or Glaspell, the setting for an Akins drama was typically high society or low society. Her exaggerated characters were caught in exaggerated dilemmas.

Akins' popularity was a clear sign of her times. Despite the Depression, the popular media flourished by offering entertainment and escape. Neighborhood movie marquees blazed the titles of Fred Astaire and Ginger Rogers films—along with those from Zoe Akins. (Her *Morning Glory*, starring Katharine Hepburn, was one.) But escape was also sought, and found, at home: in Depression households, the number of radio sets quickly doubled. The air waves became ruled by a new type of broadcast that captured, and gave release to, the masses of "home-bound families, but mainly home-bound women": the radio soap opera. A rash of emotional radio serials gathered such momentum and audience that, by 1938, there were thirty-eight to choose from.[1]

In this perspective, the 1935 choice for the Drama Pulitzer—Zoe Akins' melodramatic *The Old Maid*—was not the misguided choice that some detractors grumbled it was. The jurors' unanimous decision aptly reflected the mood of the day and the play's undeniable impact on audiences. After its Broadway opening, *The Old Maid* ran for two years and generated several touring companies. Burns Mantle called it "unquestionably a great women's play," but also conceded that most men would "revel in [its] emotional sweeps as completely as do women."[2]

In its focus on the plight of an unmarried woman living with and dependent upon a manipulative relative, *The Old Maid* is a cousin to Gale's *Miss Lulu Bett*. But the scope and style of *The Old Maid* are distinctly different. Set among high society of Old New York, and spanning 20 years in the life of a woman destroyed by a secret, Akins' reworking of the Edith Wharton story is, essentially, a soap opera. As such, it was at once a throwback to the sentimental dramas of past decades and as current as that week's choice of radio serials.

The formula for a 1930s radio soap opera required that "each episode begin and end with severe troubles."[3] The identical formula seemed to apply to the whole decade, which began with the financial collapse of the nation and ended with rumbles of another world war. Ironically enough, women made some significant gains during the troubled, turbulent decade.

The stock market crash in late 1929 was followed by the collapse of scores of banks. The powerful Bank of the United States folded in December of 1930, causing the domino-like toppling of businesses and farms. Rampant unemployment led to rampant hardship and panic.[4]

Countless Americans faced starvation while Herbert Hoover's administration withheld aid, determined to "hold [government] expenditures within our income." Fortunately, Franklin D. Roosevelt saw things differently. His "new deal for the American people" set up relief agencies almost overnight and put $500 million into the pockets of the jobless. Banks reopened by way of the FDIC, and the WPA (Works Progress Administration) put nearly nine million people to work for the public good. Grateful households cheered for Roosevelt and his string of "alphabet agencies."[5]

In those Depression households, families took giant steps back from all the modern consumerism that had marked the twenties. The streams of families moving from farm areas into the cities halted, as urban areas became "pits of unemployment" rather than places of opportunity.[6] The marriage rate plunged to an all-time low, while extended families pulled together for survival.[7] Housewives revived home businesses: sewing, hairdressing, renting out rooms. Home management took on a whole new meaning and value, giving women new roles and status. Despite the crisis, women forged some surprising new footholds in both private and public life. Much of this change was due to radical changes on Capitol Hill.

Into the White House with Franklin D. Roosevelt came a very avid, outspoken feminist. Eleanor Roosevelt's "First Hundred Days" were as bold and innovative as those of her husband. Immediately after the inauguration, she served tea to 3,000 guests and gave interviews to two women press reporters. This was a startling precedent since most First Ladies, like Mrs. Hoover, granted one interview in four years.[8]

More startling was the news that Mrs. Roosevelt would hold her own press conferences—for women only. In these Red Room Conferences, she planned to cover subjects "of special interest and value to the women of the country" but to exclude politics.[9] By the year's end, however, the First Lady was defending low-cost housing, jobs for women, and equal pay for equal work. She gave reporters newsworthy stories each week, and created new jobs, higher pay, higher status—in short, a "New Deal for Newswomen."[10]

Mrs. Roosevelt introduced her reporters to special guests who were also women. One honored guest was Frances Perkins, the New Deal's secretary of labor and the first woman cabinet member. Under Perkins' leadership, the Labor Department would create the Social Security and Fair Labor Standards Acts, measures that women reformers had been advocating for decades. Perkins had become devoted to labor reform after witnessing the burning of the Triangle Factory, in which 146 women died. She brought her fight against "conditions that would permit such a tragedy" into her role in the New Deal.[11] (Perkins later recalled that "those of us who ... put together the New Deal are bound by spiritual ties that no one else can understand."[12])

Mrs. Roosevelt insisted on women's appointments to high-level posts in what was, essentially, her "women's movement on Capitol Hill." When programs like the Civil Conservation Corps excluded women, she launched programs for them that provided 100,000 jobs. But she felt much more was needed, since four times that many women had lost their jobs.[13]

Predictably, women had been urged to stay home and "leave what jobs there were for male 'breadwinners.'" As Nancy Woloch claimed, the emergency state renewed the assumption that "in the best of times, as in the worst of times, woman's place was in the home."[14] Women in the professions were hardest hit, since men began taking jobs in education and social work. In business, men even took clerical jobs, in hopes of "rising to a semi-executive post."[15]

With mass media and popular culture being among the areas that fared the best, women in these fields were among the most fortunate. They were also among the most visible and became "New Women" of the thirties. In *Women and the American Experience*, Woloch wrote:

> During the media blitz of the 1930s, women emerged in assertive roles—the ambitious career girl, the gutsy entertainer, the sophisticated socialite, the blonde seductress, and leading the list, the worldly-wise reporter. Though hardly cut from a single mold, women in mass culture were distinguished by their vitality. Dynamic, aggressive, even flamboyant, they provided a respite from the apathy or panic that seemed to characterize real life.[16]

These headstrong heroines overran popular culture. An indelible example was Scarlett O'Hara from *Gone with the Wind*, which took the Fiction Pulitzer in 1937 (before becoming a film). If readers winced at Margaret Mitchell's 1,000 pages, they could cheer a few bold heroines among the heroes in comic books, which made their debut telling grown-up tales, not adventures for kids.[17] The newspaper comic strip was also born, to offset dire Depression news. In his book *Fads*, Peter Skolnik noted that:

> The Depression made for a strange assortment of culture heroes and heroines: Scarlett O'Hara, King Kong, Shirley Temple, and legions of bank robbers and parachute jumpers who won our admiration with their reckless daring. We cheered on John Dillinger and Bonnie and Clyde until they dropped.[18]

(Other bright distractions included the on-screen antics of the Marx Brothers and three wolf-taunting "Little Pigs." The pigs were such a rousing metaphor for thwarting the depression wolf at the door that they won an Academy Award for creator Disney.[19])

But the most popular, ever-present escape continued to be the radio broadcast. Listeners later reminisced, "When our pockets were empty, there was still an easy chair and the radio."[20] Needed laughs were tuned in with Bob Hope, or Burns and Allen; upbeat music with the swing sounds of Goodman or Miller. Twice a week, Hedda Hopper revealed the "Inside Story" of Hollywood stars. And soap opera heroines loved and languished daily. (When the characters of radio's first day-time serial, *Clara Lu 'n' Em*, pushed the sponsor's product, Super Suds, the name "soap opera" was coined—and stuck.[21]) The most popular soaps featured women characters who "had recently moved, upward or downward, to a new status." *Backstage*

Wife married a Broadway idol. *Our Gal Sunday* posed the question, "Can a girl from a little mining town in the West find happiness as the wife of a wealthy and titled Englishman?"[22]

Even Eleanor Roosevelt used the radio to enhance her link to the American public. She started "a media blitz of her own," as Nancy Woloch phrased it, becoming "a radio personality in major-network commercially sponsored talks."[23] She also spoke out in print: her publication *It's Up to the Women* counseled women on domestic and civic issues and gave them a voice. The First Lady stressed that a woman needed employment—"to do something which expresses her personality even though she may be a wife and mother."[24]

By 1936, Mrs. Roosevelt's syndicated column "My Day" was appearing in 62 newspapers. Its appeal was such that, by the end of the decade, 136 newspapers ran it. Nancy Woloch claimed "newspaper readers of the 1930s were likely to know more about Eleanor Roosevelt than about any other figure in public life."[25] When Americans voted at mid-decade to keep Franklin D. Roosevelt in the White House, they were also endorsing Eleanor, whose concern for the "one-third of the nation" that was still "ill-housed, ill-clad, ill-nourished," was also apparent. As Woloch noted, the First Lady "steadily took stands to the left of FDR" in social reform.[26]

Of all the benefits Mrs. Roosevelt brought to bear on American society, none was greater than the hand-up she provided for women. Thanks to the example which filtered down from her and scores of other vibrant, aggressive role models—and a growing media network that made them visible—the decade of the thirties became an ironic shining hour for women. It marked an era of their participation in the public sphere that has perhaps never been surpassed.

No woman typified the ambitious, assertive New Woman of the thirties better than Zoe Akins. She was a successful and visible example of a woman who gave a hand-up to others but was clearly the central figure in her own life.

5

Zoe Akins, Escape Artist

Long before 16 of her plays were produced on Broadway and her name was attached to a host of lavish Hollywood films, Zoe Akins was a girl "fully determined to go on the stage." Opposed to the notion, and hoping she would outgrow it, her father finally consented to let her "try the thing until she gets tired of it."[1]

She never did. Although her acting career did not go far beyond her debut as a page in *Romeo and Juliet*, Zoe Akins never got over being "wild about" the stage.[2]

Akins was born in the small town of Humansville, Missouri ("a pretty little place, founded by a Frenchman").[3] But she grew up in St. Louis where her father, Thomas, was postmaster and a Republican National Committee member. Her early experiences of the Midwest were therefore quite cosmopolitan and different from those of Zona Gale or Susan Glaspell. As a member of the "young society set," Akins' first stage appearance—as the humble Shakespearean page—warranted a two-column story and photo in a St. Louis newspaper.[4]

There is, however, an unfortunate and puzzling lack of any significant biographical work on Zoe Akins, so her personal life must be pieced together from bits and pieces of surviving news clips and a rare interview or two.

Of her childhood and adolescence, this much is known: She was educated at home until she was thirteen, then spent two years studying at Monticello Seminary in Godfrey, Illinois, and two more at Hosmer Hall in St. Louis. She loved going to the theatre with her parents and was well trained in literature, especially the classics. As a teen-ager Zoe exclaimed, "I just adore Shakespeare," and she was thrilled to make her debut in a play of his, even as a page.⁵ Later, Shakespearean plots and bits of dialogue would be woven into her plays and titles.

In her teens, Akins was already contributing feature stories and criticism for a publication called *Reedy's Mirror*. For Zoe, the best part of the job was having access to the actors from touring stage companies that played St. Louis. Her favorite among these was the beautiful Shakespearean actress Julia Marlowe. Zoe would never forget the night she went to Marlowe's dressing room after a play, to interview the actress over supper. "She asked for bread and milk, and I got the same thing," Zoe recalled, happy to share in the simple life that she felt an actor should embrace.⁶

Another early and instant stage idol for Akins was Ethel Barrymore. At age 14, before ever seeing the actress on stage, Akins was so struck by Barrymore's face in a Sargent portrait that she was moved to write a poem. Years later after seeing her idol on stage, Akins resolved to someday write a play for her. The eventual result would be *Declassée*, a triumph for both Barrymore and Akins (which would net the playwright three hundred thousand dollars).⁷

Zoe Akins

Zoe Akins was 18 when she did her earnest stint as the page in the Odeon Stock company's *Romeo and Juliet*. Her performance was probably less notable than her comments, quoted in the news item heralding her stage debut: "I have a different idea of the stage than most people, as I think that its object is neither to amuse or educate, but to satisfy the dramatic instincts of people."⁸

Her quotes revealed some of her own dramatic instincts, one of which was "visions of marrying King Alphonso of Spain," the one man she "had designs upon." Another was to play Ibsen's dramas, which Zoe felt contained "the intellectual element" that should mark professional theatre. The news item ended with a fleeting self-appraisal in which young Zoe Akins confided: "I am not what you would call pretty, but I have been told by artists that I have a green skin and a pagan face, and I think that will offset the advantages of beauty or red hair."[9]

Photos of Akins confirm that she would have been considered a character actress, if she had persisted in her original career choice. But after she moved to New York to try her luck with acting or playwriting, the playwriting ultimately won out.

A few other kinds of writing came first. During her first years in New York, Akins supported herself by writing magazine articles and poetry. In those days, Willa Cather was editor of *McClure's Magazine* (before her great success with *O Pioneers!*). Cather took a "friendly interest" in Zoe Akins' work and printed some of her writing in *McClure's*.[10]

Akins' first published book was *Interpretations* (1911), a collection of poetry that was popular enough in England to go into three editions and was later published in New York.[11] Reviewers placed Akins in "that small group of writers—among them Sara Teasdale, Edgar Lee Masters and Carl Sandburg—who contributed largely to the Renaissance of American poetry just preceding the First World War."[12] However, Akins' primary love, and goal, was the theatre.

The Washington Square Players, who had staged Zona Gale's play *Neighbors* (and remounted a few of Glaspell's early plays), were the first to do a professional production of a Zoe Akins play. They staged her one-act *The Magical City*, "a free-verse tragedy" which won the honor of best play in a bill of four plays at the Bandbox, in March of 1916.[13]

Akins' first full-length play, *Papa*, was published in the Modern Drama series before it was staged in Los Angeles in 1916 and New York in 1919. Akins called *Papa* an "Amorality in Three Acts," and critics praised her new twist on social satire. *Town and Country*'s review described an "amorality" as a play in which the characters are "unaware of the moral decencies of the real world." It conceded that Restoration playwrights wrote in a similar genre, but pointed out that their characters were well aware of the moral codes they defied. Truly amoral characters simply "live in a world of their own." *Town and Country* hailed *Papa* as "the most brilliant [and] successful amorality we have ever read."[14]

The title character of *Papa* is a gentleman-scoundrel whose debts require that his two daughters marry quickly and marry well. One of them has a four-year-old girl, fathered by an Italian tenor. To hide this family skeleton from the mother's fiancé, the child's aunt claims maternity, and is generously forgiven by her own fiancé. During a prolonged foursome honeymoon on the Riviera, the child's Italian father shows up. He is charmed by the child—in fact, everyone is. When an "impressive grand dame" decides to marry the grandfather, she does so quite convinced that he is the child's father rather than grandfather. The illegitimate child proves an asset, used to advantage by the adults, whose only moral standard is that of charm.

Papa was a hit in Los Angeles, but closed after only 12 performances in New York. Akins blamed the rushed production it received. Still, George Jean Nathan described *Papa* as "perhaps the best thing of its eccentric kind," surpassing in "imagination, fancy, style ... nine-tenths of the plays written by Americans."[15]

Akins claimed that she wrote *Papa* as a "protest against the drabness of St. Louis in particular and literature in general." Whatever her motives, *Papa* established some hallmarks for plays that would follow. Above all, Akins would try to create her style anew with each play. As she put it, "When I conceive a play, its theme always suggests to me a style, not a story. The style is a kind of music for the play."[16] Another Akins hallmark arose from her fascination with reversals of fortune:

> What interests me as dramatic material is change of fortune.... If someone points out a billionaire who has lost his billions and become a pauper, or a pauper who has become rich, my interest is aroused. Changes work their own drama.[17]

(Such reversals of fortune became the basic formula for the period's radio soap operas.)

A drastic reversal of fortune drove the plot of *Declassée*, Akins' vehicle for Barrymore and her first solid success. A *Herald Tribune* article later reported that "when Ethel Barrymore spoke the romantic lines of Lady Helen Haden in 'Declassée,' the critics agreed that Miss Akins of Missouri had arrived."[18]

Akins' plot traced an elite Englishwoman's fall from grace and wealth. Lady Helen Haden forces her husband to apologize for the charge of card-cheating he has placed against one of their guests, a young man whom she secretly loves. When she learns that the young man, Ned, is indeed a cheat, Helen realizes that she must expose him, despite the scandal it means for her. Divorced and chastised, she comes to America, where she keeps up a bold front by selling off her pearls. Her engagement to an American millionaire is undone when her former lover, Ned, shows up again. In an ambiguous ending, she takes a fatal misstep in front of a taxi, leaving the audience to judge whether her death was a careless or deliberate one.[19]

Most critics, like Burns Mantle, highly praised both vehicle and star: "It is a pleasure to record their joint triumph," wrote Mantle.[20] In the 16 years following the advent of *Declassée*, Zoe Akins would have 15 plays produced on Broadway. Most of them were popular hits, if not artistic successes. Virtually all of them called for elaborate staging: "My plays have been, for the most part, extravagant productions, haven't they?" she commented in a 1941 interview.[21]

Although known for her high drama and extravagance, Akins could and did craft realistic scenes and characters. Her 1921 play *Daddy's Gone A-Hunting* impressed critics with its intense realism. The play depicted the demise of a marriage which the wife, Edith, thinks is fine, but which the husband, Julian, believes is stifling them both. Edith abides by Julian's proposal of an open marriage, and even withstands a confrontation with his lover. But when Edith pretends to have received jewelry from a rich lover, and Julian is indifferent, she realizes his love for her is dead, and she leaves him. Much changed by her new life and an alliance with a wealthy man, Edith still longs and hopes for Julian's love. When her daughter dies, and the loss does not bring Julian back to her, Edith is devastated.

Theatre Magazine raved that "again, Zoe Akins has scored a triumph ... and has retold an old story with an art, a simple beauty, and many deft twists of a vivid imagination."[22] Writing about the play 60 years later, Patricia Yongue praised its "quiet repudiation of women's considerable dependence on men," and pointed up Edith's "horror when she realizes that she cannot expect men or children to provide meaning and identity for her."[23]

The tour-de-force roles that Zoe Akins created for women became another hallmark of her plays. Since the star system was, as she put it, "the only insurance producers used to have against loss," Akins tailored her plays for female stars.[24] John Chapman described how busy—and employed—this kept all concerned (even during the Depression):

> In case any enterprising investigator wants to know who is the busiest person in New York, he doesn't have to look any further than the next sentence. Zoe Akins is that person—for not only does she keep herself as busy as an energetic young Western woman can, but also she makes a huge business for several of our leading actresses, as many box-office managers and head ushers, to say nothing of critics and publishers and bank tellers....
>
> Miss Akins, in spite of the fact that her "Declassée," with Miss Barrymore, is merrily shattering records as it gambols along the transcontinental circuit, and that her other two current productions are more than mediocre successes, is not content to sit in front of a little grate fire and play all day with her fox terrier puppy.[25]

No one could accuse Zoe Akins of resting on her laurels. However, since she did all her writing in bed, a few columnists had fun with this peculiarity. James Reston quelled some of the wilder stories by writing, "She has been trying for years to write her plays at a desk, but can't do it. So there!"[26] Clearly, the habit worked for Akins, who was able to write two or three plays at a time and finish an act in 12 hours. But she was adamant in saying, "I have made it a rule not to rewrite a play."[27] The one concession she made was in changing the order of the acts in her three-act play *The Varying Shore*.

Akins' original concept for *The Varying Shore* was to "turn time backward in flight, so that what normally would have been Act I became Act III." The play was effectively done this way in its Newark tryout. However, when some viewers objected to seeing "a woman middle-aged in the first act, mature in the second, and young in the third," Akins normalized the sequence, despite her preference for the original novel presentation. Akins wrote *The Varying Shore* around its title: "I always admired that line of Shakespeare's, 'Darkling stands the varying shore o' the world,' and conceived the idea of writing a play about the varying shore of a woman's life."[28]

Akins' penchant for Shakespeare was flamboyantly put to use in her murder mystery *The Furies*, starring Laurette Taylor. Despite a title that evoked Greek drama, the storyline of *The Furies* actually recalled the plot of *Hamlet*: John Sands is found dead in his study with a bullet in his heart. His wife was with him just moments before. Her lover, Owen, was also in the house. The dead man's son is sick with suspicion. "Mother," he wails at the discovery, "you have my father much offended." The plot takes a sharp and perverse turn, however. The two likely suspects are absolved, and the wife finds herself locked in a forty-second-floor penthouse with the madman who killed her husband out of love for her. In his review of *The Furies*, Alexander Woollcott wrote that "the ever surprising Zoe Akins has taken a murder mystery and bestowed upon it the sheen of a curious and inverted beauty."[29]

By 1931, Zoe Akins was living on both coasts and was under contract to Paramount studios. She felt at home in her suite at the Ritz-Carlton, but she also loved her Pasadena house. Zoe was in California, adapting Edna Ferber's *Showboat* for the screen, when she became romantically linked with Captain Hugo Rumbold. A British producer and designer, Rumbold had staged scores of Covent Garden and Drury Lane productions, and had "personally mounted *Arms and the Man* for Bernard Shaw."[30] While his stage designs were being exhibited in California, Zoe became involved with him, and they announced their wedding plans. In 1932, at the age of 45, Zoe Akins was married in her Pasadena home. Among guests who witnessed the informal ceremony were Tallulah Bankhead and Noel Coward.[31]

Seven months after her wedding, Zoe Akins was a widow: Hugh

Rumbold died from new complications of old war maladies. This sudden reversal in her own fortunes was one explanation for Akins' three-year absence from Broadway. Another reason was the critics' harsh response to her play *The Greeks Had a Word for It*. Akins "read the terrible notices [and] went to California—in a hurry."[32] Even though *The Greeks* had netted her $115,000 before closing, "it was too sad to have a play withdrawn, its life ended, before the people who might have liked it had a chance to see it."[33] In an article later written for the *New York Times*, Akins added,

> I am not complaining; on the whole, I have fared well ... but I am glad I went to Hollywood and learned what I have learned there. First of all, one learns that he must tell a story. The old woman who sat by the tribal fire and told the tales of her people's heroes, the minstrels who wandered from castle to castle, the town gossip ... the story-teller has always had his special place.... And it is the best purpose of the movies to tell the whole world good stories.[34]

One of the good stories that Akins told—or retold—for the screen was the *Camille* she crafted for Greta Garbo and Robert Taylor. Another highlight among her Depression-era films was *Morning Glory*, the third film of Katharine Hepburn. Adapted from an Akins play about a stage-struck young lady, *Morning Glory* provided Hepburn with her first Oscar-winning role.

Akins could not resist the pull of New York forever. When she fled to Hollywood, she had taken her adaptation of *The Old Maid* with her. A few years elapsed before she dusted off the script and showed it to Harry Moses, who put it into production. Akins felt compelled to adapt Wharton's novel, she said, because "such a task gives the greatest pleasure ... the greatest challenge" when the original work is of a nature "so precious that it must not be injured in the process." She believed that a writer could see "a play in a story which stirs him almost as if it were his very own."[35]

Such had been the case when Zoe read Edith Wharton's *The Old Maid*, the story of an unmarried woman who sacrifices everything to remain near her illegitimate daughter. Akins felt she had adapted the story "with theatrical effectiveness and without destroying the integrity of the original work."[36] Wharton herself had such "perfect trust" in Akins' abilities that she "never even asked to see the completed manuscript."[37]

The Old Maid opened in January 1935 at the Empire Theatre, where Akins' first triumph, *Declassée*, had its run. Helen Mencken played the hapless old maid Charlotte Lovell, and Judith Anderson portrayed her scheming cousin, Delia. Reviewers were invited to a special matinee (to avoid conflict with the opening of Leslie Howard in *The Petrified Forest*), and sat among 1,200 eager matinee ladies. The women loved it; the critics were extremely divided.[38]

Some critics soundly endorsed the play. The *World Telegram* called it a "deeply touching" play.[39] *Cue* magazine said the play's theme made it "ripe for the season's finest cry," predicting that women would "lead the way to *The Old Maid*. Where women go, men follow."[40]

The escapist value of the play was underscored by Arthur Ruhl of the *Herald Tribune*. He wrote, "So plausibly is the old–New York atmosphere, both material and mental, built up, that [viewers] accept for the time, the mood and customs of the day."[41] But dissenters condemned the same features, complaining that the play followed "the older form of emotional drama."[42]

When *The Old Maid* took the Pulitzer Prize, it produced more heated controversy. Some critics felt that the choice reflected a tacit "censorship that eliminated consideration of a genuine American classic"—Lillian Hellman's *The Children's Hour*—because of its allusion to lesbianism.[43] The upshot of the conflict was the creation of the New York Drama Critics' Circle, to rival the Pulitzer juries. The Critics' Circle promised to "do a lot better" in handing out awards.[44] (Nevertheless, their choices over the years have run quite parallel to those of the Pulitzer juries.)

The appeal of *The Old Maid*, already undeniable, was enhanced by the Pulitzer Prize. By the end of 1935 it was playing internationally, having been translated for the Italian, French, and Swedish stages. Peggy Wood and Ina Claire were lined up for the British production. In 1939, the emotional story of Charlotte Lovell was played out on movie screens across America and abroad. The film version was, of course, written by Zoe Akins, and starred Bette Davis as the conniving Delia Lovell.[45]

Akins' success with *The Old Maid* rekindled her love of live theatre. While *The Old Maid* was still on tour, Akins was back in New York with three new plays. Columnist James Reston quipped, in reference to Akins' choice of writing posture, "Zoe Akins, the playwright, has been spending a lot of time in bed lately." Reston added that "every hour she spends away from her job in Hollywood costs her money. Her stay here to help with the play [*O Evening Star*] will cost her approximately $26,000."[46] But Akins had her priorities: In an article titled "The Playwriting Passion," she swore, "I ... really and truly care more for the theatre than anything else in the world."[47]

O Evening Star centered on a woman who finds success in Hollywood in her later years. Although Akins denied any personal link to the facts of Marie Dressler's life, audiences loved making the comparison. (And while Akins shunned the idea of a collaborator, for this script she had help from

George S. Kaufman. When she offered to use his name as collaborator, he declined.[48])

Of the remaining scripts which Akins tackled in her career, a noteworthy one is her translation of a French play, *The Happy Days* by Claude-Andre Puget. (Akins translated plays from both French and Hungarian.[49]) Of special interest is not the script itself, which dealt with the discovery of love in five adolescents, but a circumstance of the play's production: Leading the young cast, in her second Broadway appearance, was Diana Barrymore. Twenty-two years earlier, her aunt Ethel had appeared in Akins' play *Declassée*, which had revived the career of Ethel Barrymore and marked the arrival of playwright Zoe Akins from Missouri.

Her conquest of Broadway must count among Zoe Akins' contributions to the status of women in American theatre. Besides the example of her own success as an encouraging role model, Akins provided vehicles that enhanced the status of the era's top actresses. She also brought about more interest and acceptance regarding women's issues as subjects for the stage.

There is a dismaying lack of any mention of Zoe Akins in the gamut of theatre history books. She is not even a footnote in the generally-used texts. She fares not much better in film history volumes. This seems an unfair dismissal of a writer who was such a prolific contributor to our popular culture for more than three decades.

In her own era, Zoe Akins was well-known and respected in America, Britain and parts of Europe. The finest directors of the day were eager to stage her scripts, George Cukor and Guthrie McClintic among them. (Cukor directed Akins scripts for both stage and screen.[50]) Although critics sometimes disparaged the emotional excesses of her work, Akins also had abiding fans in the top-string critics. The mischievous Alexander Woollcott once wrote a spoof of an Akins scenario and titled it "Zowie: or the Curse of an Akins Heart" (printed in *Vanity Fair*), but it was the sincerest form of flattery. He was fascinated by her work. Woollcott wrote of Akins, "Whatever she may write for the stage, whatever the perversities of her viewpoint and the caprices of her ever restless and curious imagination, you may be sure of one thing—it will be the play that will count."[51]

In *Our American Theatre*, Oliver Saylor called Zoe Akins "the chief romancer of our stage ... mistress of sentiment held in leash by sophistication."[52] As Zoe Akins herself liked to think of it, "I write from the heart, for the great collective heart."[53]

Unfortunately, Zoe Akins had only begun work on her memoirs when she died in Los Angeles in 1958, at the age of 72. Of the surviving published interviews with Akins, the one that best conveys a sense of the playwright's personality is the casual interview done in her Ritz-Carlton suite by Ward Morehouse in May 1941. Morehouse quickly sets the hectic mood of the room, introduces the reader to the "ample and exuberant" Zoe Akins, then wisely allows the playwright's amusing and jumbled thoughts to speak for themselves. Here are a few highlights:

> A pigeon fluttered to the window ledge, and Mrs. Johnson (the maid) to the phone, which was forever ringing. The room was in indescribable clutter—trunks, bundles, hat boxes, overflowing flower vases, room service trays. A copy of her novel (her first), "Forever Young" lay upon a table ... her Pomeranian was at her feet, coyly. Miss Akins tossed off a milk and whiskey punch, lit a cigarette, answered the phone, turned to me and said: "Don't mind the disorder and everything—I'm rushing off to the races. My first holiday in years ... My mother is a wonderful race track fan, even though she's eighty-six.... My mind is unstable. I have no character. But if I'm alone enough I can find out what I personally want to say and say it.... I've got a lot to write and I'm never at a loss for ideas.... George Jean Nathan used to be wonderful to me.... I think I've disappointed many people as a playwright—my early fans ... George Nathan used to say of me that I wrote weakly but never cheaply ...
>
> I think Lillian Hellman has one of the finest talents in the theatre, but I personally feel shy about introducing politics into a play.... I'm very much too fat but I'm good at badminton and I love gardening.... I loved Ethel Barrymore in "The Corn is Green." She gave me my start with "Declassée"....
>
> The critics panned the pants off "The Greeks Had a Word for It," didn't they? ... I simply loved getting the Pulitzer Prize with 'The Old Maid.'"[54]

THE PLAY—HOW SHE BECAME *THE OLD MAID*

Zoe Akins reveals the ironic and emotional story of Charlotte Lovell in five episodes. The first opens in June 1833 at the country estate of the Lovell family. In her room, Delia Lovell is preparing for her wedding to James Ralston, a match Delia is making for status and security. She is also making this match to forget her love for Clem Spender, an artist whose bohemian lifestyle she refused to share. But now to her door comes her cousin Charlotte (a poor relation) with news that Clem is here, now, for the wedding. He has sent with Charlotte a gift for Delia: a lovely blue cameo. The shaken Delia tucks the necklace into her bodice as a bride's "something blue," and faces the wedding march. She entreats Cousin Chatty to "watch Clem ... be kind to him"—an easy request for Charlotte since she, too, has secretly loved Clem.[55]

The second episode opens six years later, at Charlotte's day nursery (for the poor working class). The children are teasing a shy five-year-old, Tina, until Charlotte steps in to scold them. Tina is an orphan who lives with a black caretaker, and this is the subject of their taunts. The chastised children sing a good-bye song for Miss Charlotte, who will be going away for a while on her wedding trip. Chatty is engaged to Joe Ralston, the brother of Delia's husband James.

After all the children leave, except Tina, two visitors arrive at the school: Mrs. Mingott, the widowed aunt of James and Joe Ralston; and Dr. Lanskell, a family friend and physician. While Dr. Lanskell goes off to check Tina, Mrs. Mingott gives Chatty a pre-wedding gift of money. She knows how much a modest sum, "say five hundred dollars—means to any girl, even when she's marrying a rich man." Chatty is thrilled; she will use the funds to keep her nursery going.

Three more guests arrive: Charlotte's cousin Delia with her husband James, and James' brother Joseph (Chatty's fiancé). The surprised Chatty says that if they've come to see the children, all have left except Tina, who is delicate and always has her supper here. The word "delicate" alarms James, since he and Delia have a child, little Dee, at home. And Joseph, too, has concerns for Charlotte, since diphtheria is now an epidemic. But Delia is charmed by Tina, and takes the child on her lap, unconcerned that Mrs. Mingott has realized who Tina is: She is the "hundred-dollar-baby," left years ago at one of those "disgraceful shanties" on Broadway, with money pinned to its bib. Delia lets Tina try on her necklace, the blue cameo; Charlotte pointedly hands the necklace back.

Left alone together, Chatty and Joe embrace. She tells him about the gift from his aunt, and her plans for it. His response shatters her: He will gladly pay for someone to run the nursery; but Chatty cannot go on with it. They quarrel, both stunned by the other's stubbornness; and Joe leaves, saying that he'll be waiting for word that Chatty agrees with him.

Episode three opens that night, in the Ralston drawing room. Delia is by the fireplace with Mrs. Mingott, who leafs through a family album. She recalls the family's first stubborn Englishman, who came to America set on "living for a bank account instead of dying for a creed." After Dr. Lanskell calls Mrs. Mingott to the music room to sing, Delia is alone only a moment. Charlotte rushes in, very distraught. She gasps that she needs help, or her wedding plans may be ruined. Delia must help Chatty convince Joe to let her keep her nursery. When Delia responds that Charlotte will have her own babies to care for, Chatty blurts out, "That's just it ... How can I give up my own baby?" Between sobs, Charlotte pours out her story: Tina is her own child, born of a brief love for a man who loved someone else. Chatty's long trip south, with Dr. Lanskell's help, had been for this pregnancy, not for an alleged lung ailment. She refuses to give the father's name; but Delia finally guesses it—Clem Spender, who turned to Chatty after Delia's wedding. Delia's sympathy now turns to cold efficiency. She needs time to think, she says, but promises that Clem's child will not remain where she is. This gives Chatty hope, and she goes to await word.

Delia is pacing, upset and jealous, when Joe comes in to talk with her. He is convinced that Chatty won't give up her nursery, and is resigned to letting her continue it, if he can just be sure there is no health hazard. Delia evades Joe's questions, until he decides to give in—to go tell Chatty she can have her way. "No!" Delia counters, then quickly tosses off the lie that Chatty cannot be married; she is already ill, has even been coughing blood. This news devastates Joe, and he leaves. Now, Delia completes her plans by evoking a promise from her husband: James will set up a house for Chatty and that "little girl she's so fond of." Delia sends for Chatty and informs her that she "*had* to break off the engagement," to keep Chatty and Tina together. Chatty is incensed, and threatens to tell Joe the truth. But Delia subdues her with the thought of "making a home" for Tina, and Chatty is defeated. Crying softly, she takes off Joe's ring.

The fourth episode is in the drawing room, 14 years later. Dr. Lanskell is telling Chatty (now the "typical old maid") that she must be pleased at having managed a nice home for Tina, that Delia has "done her best." Charlotte scoffs, "her best to spoil her." Since Delia brought Chatty and Tina into this house—after James' death 12 years ago—Delia has indulged Tina. And it's worse, now that Delia's own child Dee is married.

Delia comes in, along with four youths: her daughter Dee and son-in-law John Halsey; Tina and John's cousin, Lanning. They talk about the ball the four are going to, and the fact that Tina always returns late. When Charlotte criticizes this, Tina tells Delia—now her "momma"—to make Cousin Chatty stop finding fault. Tina snaps at Charlotte, "momma knows what it is to be young" and popular. She huffs that Cousin Chatty should not wait up for her again. But as usual, Charlotte takes up her vigil in a chair.

Hours later, a closing door awakens Chatty. She withdraws to the next room to hear Tina enter with Lanning and flirt with him. As the two kiss, and are about to kiss again, Delia appears and says a brisk good-bye to Lanning, who thanks her for not scolding him. But Charlotte emerges to say it's not Lanning who should be scolded. The boy takes his awkward leave, and Tina rages at Chatty for driving him away and for being an old maid who "has never known love."

Alone with Delia, Charlotte claims that she will end her mistake now; she will take Tina away, to where they can live plainly and unknown. Delia recoils, then counters that only she can give Tina a respectable life. She proposes now to adopt Tina, legally—to give her the Ralston name and all that Chatty claims she wants for Tina. Slowly and painfully, Charlotte concedes.

For the fifth episode, the drawing room is decorated for tomorrow's wedding, that of Tina to Lanning Halsey. Charlotte listens from the stairs as Tina thanks Delia for everything and for being the only mother she would want. Delia reminds Tina of how generous Chatty has been, giving Tina all of her grandmother's jewels and the veil that Chatty almost wore. Tina dismisses the thought that any man could want to marry Cousin Chatty. As soon as Tina goes off to bed, Chatty shocks Delia with the notion that tonight, for once, Tina should be spoken to about the facts of life—by her true mother. Delia is alarmed, but too weary to argue as Chatty goes off to Tina's room. But Charlotte soon returns, looking somehow at peace. She says she could not, after all, tell Tina; perhaps because neither Tina nor her father "really belonged" to her.

With relief, Delia takes Chatty's hand and says "We'll go together." But Tina suddenly enters, and Chatty breaks away to the garden. Delia urges Tina to go after Chatty, and to remember that Chatty "didn't marry a man who loved her very much" because she would not give up Tina. When Tina asks why no one has ever told her this, Delia replies, "sometimes people are selfish." Delia adds that tomorrow, after Tina says her good-byes to everyone else, she should save her last kiss for Cousin Chatty. Tina vows, "I won't forget," and goes off to find Charlotte.

Zoe Akins made the story of *The Old Maid* her own. She began her play with the wedding of Delia (which received a two-line reference in the book), changed the dynamics of Wharton's characters, and invented new ones. And her omission of Delia's second child—a son—made for a better balance of two mothers and two daughters. Akins crafted a more tense and vivid conflict than that of Wharton's novel.

By its very title, *The Old Maid* evokes the bias that marriage is the essential event in a woman's life. To punctuate the point, Akins places a wedding at the beginning and end of her play, and begins the main conflict with the demise of Chatty's wedding plans. A fourth marriage, between

Dee and John Halsey, takes place between episodes. Aside from Chatty's endeavors with her nursery, the play's women are wholly defined by, and concerned with, their ties to men and hopes for marriage. In Akins' setting, even more than Gale's, the single woman is bereft of identity and value, looked upon with suspicion or contempt.

An old maid has never been sketched as desirable. Mary Anne Ferguson wrote the following about unmarried women in all literature, but it aptly describes Akins' "old maid" image: "With very few exceptions the old maid ... has been either pitied or ridiculed in literature ... frequently [seen as] thin and emaciated to symbolize withdrawal from life.... The term 'old maid' is always pejorative in our society."[56]

Stereotypically, the old maid is presented as a virgin. Charlotte is a stark exception. She has known sexual love, and has even mothered a child, which makes her old-maid status all the more ironic and compromised. Delia is the obvious agent in casting Chatty as the trapped spinster, but her manipulations only work because of the myths that bind their family and society.

The most blatant feature about family and society, in this setting, is the degree to which they overlap: Almost everyone is related. Besides the match-up of the Lovell cousins with the Ralston brothers, there are the ultimate matches of two pairs of cousins: Dee and Tina with John and Lanning Halsey. (And report comes that Clem Spender forsakes his art to marry a rich cousin.) The upshot is that all of higher society becomes one's extended family, and supplies not extensive support but intensive control. To make matters worse for the lone woman, the chances for rescue by a caring outsider are almost nil. Charlotte has no prospects for a created family beyond her nursery children, for whom she is the rescuer.

In this too-tight society, personal need is more pressed to conform to standards. And here, those standards are extremely material ones. As Mrs. Mingott flatly states and James demonstrates, the Ralston motto is "to live for a bank account instead of dying for a creed." On a past occasion, when James Ralston's banks stopped loan payments, the hungry working class demanded bread by dumping flour in the streets. James snarls that they "should have been shot down like mad dogs." The reflex response of the Ralston society is contempt, not compassion, for any have-nots. While this can have a stifling effect on some men (Clem Spender is scorned for pursuing art), women are the most controlled and confined.

What happens to the woman who is clever and willful, longing to wield some control in such a society? The character of Delia presents one possibility. Thwarted in choosing and controlling her own destiny, she takes ruthless charge of Chatty and Tina.

Chatty is a have-not relation who comes close to having it all: her child by a man she loved, her work in her nursery, and marriage to a wealthy and relatively fair-minded man. This is more good fortune than Delia is willing to allow: She uses Chatty's dark secret to control her, and to acquire the child of Clem Spender. She plunges Charlotte into the role of the old maid—something Delia "couldn't bear to be" herself. But Delia does become a widow, a much more respectable position. The death of James actually aids her scheme: It allows her to move Chatty and Tina under her roof, and eventually leads to Delia's full-out adoption of Tina. Tina becomes a carbon copy of Delia, down to the cameo that she will wear as a bride, never knowing it came from her father (the blue cameo was an Akins device).

The real drama of the story may start at the play's ending. Until now, Delia and Chatty have been locked together as family by their tug-of-war over Tina. The curtain drops with the question of whether they will now be forced to connect as family in some other, positive way.

In this series of plays, Delia is not the only character who mistreats another woman. (Others include Ina in *Lulu Bett*, and Chick in *Crimes of the Heart*.) Akins intends not to excuse Delia's behavior, but rather to explain it and examine the setting that fosters her behavior.

In many ways, Akins' Pulitzer play echoes those of Gale and Glaspell. All three plays attack the myths that have limited the lives of women, and they share other striking features. While their social circles are vastly different, both Miss Lulu and Cousin Chatty are resigned to being unmarried poor relations. Then, in a Cinderella turnabout, each of them is presented with a rescuer who happens to be an in-law's brother. Each woman seems to suddenly catch up with the fortunes of her luckier married relative, then lose it all just as suddenly. For both women, their loss is compounded by emotional blackmail at the hands of a selfish relative. At least Lulu escapes her trap, to a kinder keeper. Charlotte is not only more trapped by her family and society, she is also bound by ties—and lies—to her illegitimate child.

These first three Pulitzer plays offer grim images of life for the unmarried woman. Yet, like most prize plays, they also paint dismal pictures of married life. These playwrights do not flat-out condemn the whole idea of marriage, but they do condemn an abuse of power in the family setting. All three suggest that women have been subject to controls that are not only unjust but counter-productive to family and society as a whole. They lament the loss of feminine expression in both settings. A society that can't value a Lulu for her homespun gifts, an Alison for her heartfelt poetry, a Charlotte for her loyalty and ideals (or a Clem Spender for his impulse to paint) will engender humans with a paucity of spirit amid a wealth of material riches.

This was not a frivolous message for Zoe Akins to convey during the Great Depression. While she gave audiences escapism into an old world of luxury, she also reminded them that material ease is no substitute for ease of spirit.

PART II

Domestic Wars: Chase and Frings

In a way, the next two plays in this series are polar opposites. Mary Coyle Chase's *Harvey* is the most farcical play in the group. Ketti Frings' *Look Homeward, Angel* is one of the most serious, almost tragic in its depiction of the needless death of a young man. Yet these plays share some surprising common ground—or battle ground.

The family in each play contains extreme examples of dreamer-idealists pitted against dream-crushing realists. While both playwrights use the family as their arena for the dreamer-vs.-realist conflict, their themes extend to the society beyond. (The struggle between idealism and stark realism has surfaced in the earlier plays, but it takes center stage in these two.)

Because *Harvey* is a farce, the dreamer of its plot (Elwood) gets to keep his dream, and even makes converts of some dream crushers by the play's end. He does so with the help of a peculiar ally—his big invisible rabbit friend who, in the end, becomes part of the play's Dowd family. In *Harvey*, the dreamer wins all.

On the more earnest battlefield of the Gant family in *Look Homeward, Angel*, three dreamers wage desperate fights for their lives: One dies (Ben), one remains a prisoner (W.O. Gant), and the dreamer-protagonist Eugene escapes to carry on his fight in the world beyond.

In the literal world beyond, battles and wars both actual and figurative were a grim part of life in the forties and fifties, the decades in which these plays were created.

6

The 1940s: Women in a World at War

The year was 1942. Obviously, the world had not been made "safe for democracy" by the Allied Forces in the First World War. Hitler's lightning war on Poland had ignited a more devastating Second World War, and America had been pulled into it by Japanese aggression in December of 1941. While Japanese diplomats were in Washington, meeting for the "preservation of peace," Japan staged a sneak attack on the U.S. naval base in Pearl Harbor. In a radio broadcast the next day, President Roosevelt gave the solemn declaration of war.

Mothers whose sons were too young to serve were torn between relief and empathy. (Mary Chase was among them.) Their hearts went out to those whose sons were called. Meanwhile, World War II raged on, forcing American families—barely recovered from the blows of the Depression—to sustain another round of shocks and adjustments.

Since the number of men called to fight was seven times the number called for World War I, the impact on everyday life was immense. The instant need for workers thrust women into job positions never before open to them, in both business and government. During the war, "there was no job that a woman could not fill."[1]

The war became a massive industry that brought a perverse end to Depression-era unemployment.[2] It became the patriotic duty of women to go to work. "The More Women at War—the Sooner We'll Win," read one appeal of the War Advertising Council. "Women by the millions must work in war plants—carry on vital civilian services—release men for combat by joining the WAVES, WACS, SPARS, and Marines."[3]

For years, women's branches of the military had been urged by prominent women like Mrs. Roosevelt and pilot Jacqueline Cochran (Cochran was the star aviatrix of the era, breaking all-time flight records for speed and altitude). In 1941, Congresswoman Edith Rogers introduced a bill to launch a Women's Army Auxiliary Corps. While the bill was being "dissected, bisected, stalled ... sandbagged," women were already training and serving in auxiliary posts. After the December attacks on Hawaii (where 82 Army nurses were serving), a government policy shift brought about women's service corps. Women's duties were noncombatant, but dangerous nonetheless. Pilots of the Women's Airforce Service Pilots corps (WASPS) tested airplanes, ferried bombers to airbases, and towed targets for gunnery practice.[4]

But Rosie the Riveter became the familiar icon of the wartime womanpower worker. Clad in overalls and armed with her acetylene torch, Rosie was everywhere, including Norman Rockwell's cover for the *Saturday Evening Post* of May 29, 1943. She was even the topic of a hit song that sold 3.5 million records in a year and gave Sinatra, "the Voice," some competition.[5]

In some defense plants, women took shifts as disc jockeys to send piped music to fellow workers. (Such tunes as "Whistle While You Work" helped pass the time and provided a rhythm for the riveting of airplane seams.[6]) A bigger appeal of the defense plant was the pay: it averaged 40 percent higher than work in consumer industries.[7] Men were still earning more than women, and Congress failed to pass an Equal Pay Bill; but women appreciated the relatively higher pay.

New industries suddenly emerged—plastics and synthetic rubber among them—and existing ones were overhauled. Automobile plants converted to making tanks and planes; some producers of printer's type turned out bullets. Emotional appeals were attached to production goals: As one flyer proclaimed, each bullet that the war worker produced might "avenge her son."[8] Hollywood joined in the propaganda by showing stars in a range of war-effort jobs: Lucille Ball in a defense plant, Claudette Colbert as a welder. Meanwhile, an army photographer discovered Marilyn Monroe (Norma Jean Dougherty) on an assembly line.[9]

The new workforce of women embraced a wider age range than ever. For the first time, the majority of women workers were married, and over thirty-five. Of these, one-third had young children at home,[10] which prompted a whole new teenage enterprise: babysitting. In Peter Skolnik's book on American fads, he wrote that the term "teen-ager" was coined during wartime, "dignifying the adolescents who had become invaluable in the scarce labor market."[11] Teenagers became a new consumer market, eager to buy phonograph records and to sink nickels into jukeboxes. At pajama parties, high school girls wrote "V-Mail" letters to boyfriends overseas, or knitted socks for "Bundles for Britain."[12] High school students helped to harvest farm crops, and virtually every family planted its backyard "Victory Garden." (Few could afford the rationing point-value of canned produce anyway.)

As shortages were felt on every level, bicycles came out of garages while cars remained in them. Writer-historian Ruth Corbett reminisced:

> We were asked to save many things that had before been waste material. Boy scouts came to our doors to collect flattened, de-labeled tin cans.... We turned in paper [and] kept rolls of foil by adding every scrap we found on packaging or even along the street.[13]

Peter Skolnik also recalled the big drives "for the bacon grease that went into explosives, for the nylon stockings that went into gunpowder bags and parachutes."[14]

Inevitably, the situation and shortages were exploited by some: "There were hoarders, cheaters, profiteers and those who wanted the continuance of war because they'd never earned so much money," Ruth Corbett wrote. "People still had the vices and virtues intact."[15]

Women were affected by the war in wildly diverse ways. The experience of the factory welder was much different from that of the Women's Army Corps cadet. Different still was the harrowing experience of the 50,000 Japanese-American women kept in West Coast internment camps (where they lived much like prisoners, guarded by armed sentries).[16] Of course, women with a loved one at the front shared a different, harrowing connection to the war.

A curious contradiction marked the impact of war on marriage and the family. Despite its disruption of home life, World War II caused an explosive increase in marriage and the birth rate, creating the now-famous "baby boom" phenomenon. Editors of *History of Private Life* and historian Nancy Woloch give similar reasons for this wartime marriage paradox.

Many marriages were spurred by the possibility of draft deferments for married men in the first years of the war. Others were hastened by the groom's imminent departure for overseas. Lack of money stopped being a barrier to marriage or starting a family. And certainly, war on the heels of the Depression fostered a longing to forge ties that were stable. A return to normalcy became equated with commitment to family.

There were other faces to this marriage paradox, however: While it was true that the war "removed men from the home front, demonstrating that women could manage without them," the scarcity of men also increased "male value." With the ratio at two women for each man in the age range of 20 to 24, young women were struck with "urgency regarding marital prospects."[17]

But the question that would haunt feminists for decades, and prompt a stream of studies and books, was this: Why, in this heyday of Rosie the Riveter—when most women were enjoying newfound independence and income—was there also such a madding rush into marriage and parenthood?

One explanation was that Rosie represented a temporary phenomenon: The same patriotic spirit that urged her to work for the war effort was supposed to compel her to return home when it was over. Her job would end, or a veteran would need it. The war may have brought her "unprecedented employment opportunities; higher wages [and] public recognition," but it also carried strong forces that put checks on her ambitions. Nancy Woloch stressed that "during World War II, behavior changed more than convictions ... about family life and woman's place."[18]

As noted in *History of Private Life*, the "ideal of the nuclear family [was] promoted as the centerpiece of the war effort." Men were, after all, "fighting to protect their families back home."[19] A sample of the pervasive appeal to family values was the film *This Is the Army*, which starred a uniformed Ronald Reagan. Sponsored by the government (as many wartime films were), its plot centered on the attempts of the soldier's girlfriend to persuade him to marry her despite the war. The film culminated in their wedding just before he was shipped abroad—and became the most successful film of the decade.[20]

Women were given mixed signals, even by other women. Psychiatrist Marynia Farnham warned against the "psychological purgatory" set up by the opposing demands of marriage and career. A career required much "drive, self-assertion, competition," while marriage and mothering meant being "protective ... passive or receptive."[21] Writer Agnes Meyers told *Atlantic* readers, "God protect us from the efficient go-getter business woman whose feminine instincts have been stifled." But other women, like Frieda Miller of the Women's Bureau, avidly defended women's ambitions and their "need to make a contribution to society." The war had proved women's capacities, Miller argued, and they should not be forced back to the kitchen.[22] Typical of how quickly the careers of women ended was the case of the corps of WASPS: They were abruptly dismissed with no military status or veterans' benefits, an injustice not corrected until 1979.[23]

On the whole, women of the forties had no unified voice, no vanguard of feminism to fight what Nancy Woloch saw as the post-war mindset:

"Once the war was over, the woman worker was no longer a symbol of patriotic ardor but rather a threat to social and economic security."[24]

Of women who took their first jobs during World War II, three-fourths wanted to keep them. Granted, this desire was strongest among older, married workers who had already raised their children. But across the board, women workers were barraged by post-war media that blazed the slogan, "Isn't a Woman's Place in the Home?"[25]

As quickly as legions of women had left home to take up the tools of a trade, they returned to the utensils of housekeeping. The window of opportunity that showed them a glimpse of a new model of marriage—with shared roles—was, once again, slammed shut. The editors of *History of Private Life* gave this brief summary of the return to family status quo:

> The potential for a new model family, with two equal partners who shared bread-winning and homemaking tasks, never gained widespread support.... In spite of the opportunities opened up by the Depression and the war, neither policy makers nor the creators of the popular culture encouraged that potential. Instead, they pointed to traditional gender roles as the best means for Americans to achieve the happiness and security they desired.[26]

Among the legacies left by war were economic recovery, a market bursting with goods and services, and a host of technical advances. But these were bought at a tremendous price of human misery and loss, and through the rise of powers of destruction that were unfathomable. The use of the A-bomb at Hiroshima ended the war; it also unleashed the threat of worldwide devastation. So, post-war peace was very conditional, at best.

America could be thankful that it was never occupied and was barely touched by shelling. However, the families of the more than 300,000 Americans killed in the war could not feel that they had been spared.[27] How were these people supposed to put their lives back together, and take any pleasure in living? This was the question that formed in the mind of Mary Coyle Chase, and never left her.

7

Mary Chase and Her Wartime Rabbit

If Mary Coyle Chase had not had four Irish uncles, she might never have become a writer, much less the author of *Harvey*. Her mother's brothers filled Mary's mind with tales of leprechauns and banshees and pookas. From her childhood love of these folktales, Mary would shape her model for a six-foot rabbit who was invisible but still managed to become a national image, and something of a national treasure, during the 1940s.

Mary was born in Denver because Colorado was where her four uncles had settled, lured from Ireland by the promise of the gold rush. The luck of the Irish apparently was not with them, since nothing panned out—quite literally—and they went broke. Badly in need of a housekeeper, the four McDonough boys welcomed the arrival of their young sister, Mary, then 16 years old. Mary McDonough took up the post of housekeeper while she attended a Denver school. There, she met Frank Coyle, who had turned up with nothing from the Oklahoma land rush. The two impoverished lovers married and somehow scraped together a $50 down payment for a west-Denver home.[1]

After three children in a row, nine years elapsed before the Coyles' last child and second daughter was born. "Little Mary" became the family pet, lavished with attention and story-telling.[2]

Between their tales of supernatural characters, Mary's uncles would also argue Irish politics and statesmen. So lively were their debates about Oliver Cromwell that Mary was shocked when she learned that the man had been dead for hundreds of years. "I always thought he was someone my uncles had just left on a street corner downtown."[3]

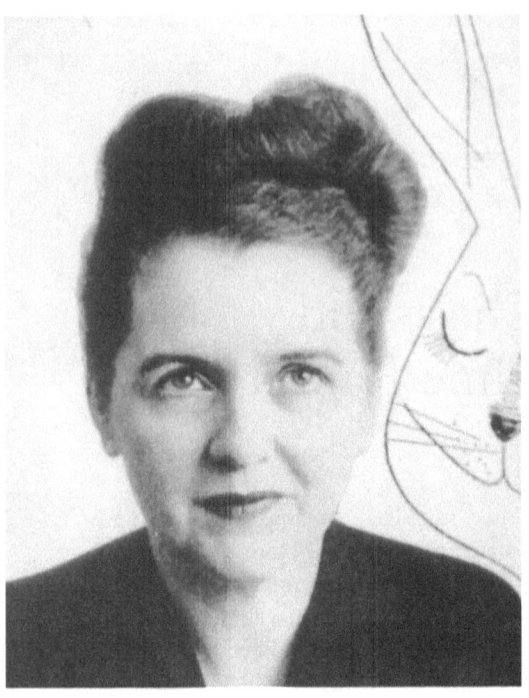

Mary Coyle Chase

Mary's mother was a humanitarian with a clairvoyant intuition. Her vision of her own father's death, as it was happening back in Ireland, proved to be true and exact.[4] Mary took to heart her mother's humane counsel, especially one piece of advice: "Never be unkind or indifferent to a person others say is crazy. Often they have a deep wisdom. We pay them a great respect in the old country, and we call them fairy people, and it could be they are sometimes."[5]

The comment had been prompted by Mrs. Coyle's rescue of a tiny old woman who was the target of boys with snowballs. The act was typical of Mary's mother, who practiced the compassion she preached. The Coyles were a poor family themselves, but had great dignity. Mary's underwear was made from flour sacks, with the result that her backside often bore the imprint, "Pride of the Rockies." But alongside that slogan would be the loving touch of Mrs. Coyle's embroidery. Mary's mother was quick to help families who were even needier than hers. As a child, Mary sometimes went with her mother to take "food to people when they were hungry [or] things to people who had a sorrow in the family."[6]

Mary was not an unkind child but was, admittedly, mischievous: "I got the highest grades for studies and the lowest for deportment."[7] She had a tomboy "reputation for physical daring," but could remain absorbed in a book for hours. After reading Dicken's *A Tale of Two Cities*, she wrote inside the book's jacket: "My name is Mary Coyle. I am eight years old. I have just read this book. Don't you think that I am smart?"[8]

An incident involving her brother Charlie cast a shadow over Mary's childhood and left a lasting mark. When the high-spirited Charlie ran away from home, he and two other boys were found by a policemen as they were shaking a gum machine. When the boys tried to run, the policeman fired his gun and wounded Charlie. The story ran in the Sunday papers; and although the policeman was later fired, the Coyle children were ostracized. Mary became an outcast at school, and the resulting hurt and anger never really left her.[9]

Charlie recovered and later went into show business as a circus clown. Lights and crowds also attracted Mary, who found herself—at age 11—outside the Denham Theatre in a sea of people pouring in for a matinee of *Macbeth*. Mary went in and was spellbound. From then on, she was "drawn to the theatre, as a camel is drawn to a water hole."[10] She would skip school to attend other matinees, walking everywhere to save carfare for tickets. Denver was a great theatre town, since the theatre that followed the gold diggers had taken hold there and flourished. Besides the Denham company's stagings, Mary could see a different show each week at the Broadway, have her pick of three melodrama houses on Curtis Street, or see vaudeville at the Orpheum or the Pantages. Mary had no desire to act, but a powerful desire to write plays.

The family's years of scrimping allowed some money for college, and Mary entered the University of Denver at age 16. After two years there and two more at the University of Colorado, she took a job on the *Rocky Mountain News*. Mary had already worked for the *News* in summer, just for carfare: "I figured that on the *News* I would meet *Life*."[11]

Her first paying position on the *News* was writing sob-sister features, but she pushed her way into covering nitty-gritty news. Mary was remembered by a fellow reporter as "curious, dressed in the flapper style of the period, [with] good looking legs and a fine face, and ... the bland, amoral effrontery of a good, aggressive, cityside reporter."[12] She was top-notch at stealing photographs of controversial figures, was not above disguising herself as a man to cover stories where women were banned, and displayed the daring-do of her tomboy days. Among her exploits: Hiding out in the Moffat Tunnel to cover the blasting of its final section; riding in a small injured aircraft; and hooking a ride on the side of a truck to deliver a story in time. Once, while phoning in from a murder trial she was covering, she was told to go home, where a fire had broken out in her closet. "All right," she replied, "but let me finish my story first."[13]

When the *Rocky Mountain News* merged with a rival paper, the *Denver Express*, the result was a pivotal merger for Mary: It brought *Express* reporter Robert Chase into the newsroom with her. Liking what she saw, Mary nudged a friend and said, "I'm going to marry that fellow." She kept her word. Borrowing her friend's car, Mary always managed to pass by just as Chase was leaving work, so she could give him a lift home.[14]

The two were point-counterpoint, in that the level Chase had a knack for "keeping his head when everyone else is pacing the ceiling." But they were both dedicated news writers. When the two were married in 1928, fellow news reporters spread "the persistent legend that Bob and Mary were married on their lunch hour, while waiting for a jury to come in."[15]

The Depression was at its worst when Mary became pregnant with the first of their three sons. From home, she tried to supplement Bob's modest salary by doing the freelance writing she had always wanted to do. She sold a few stories to Eastern papers, but concentrated on a novel that evolved into her first play. *The Banshee* harked back to the stories of her uncles, but was a serious drama bordering on melodrama. Her central character, Margaret, hears the wail of a banshee and mistakenly concludes that the death it forewarns will be that of her older son, the lover of a married woman. Margaret's meddling to prevent one son from being killed results in the ironic death of her other son. The play did not sell (and would not until 15 years later), and Mary Chase made a quick, enduring shift to writing comedy.[16]

As an ardent admirer of President Roosevelt, Mary was pleased when the New Deal brought her first comedy to the stage and Depression-era audiences. As part of the Federal Theatre Project, the old Baker Theatre of Denver was refurbished, and a group of actors were hired in hopes of launching a self-supporting company. By fall of 1936, the Baker was off and running; and its second offering was the new play *Me, Third* by Denver's own Mary Chase.[17]

By now, Mary had two small sons and was pregnant with her third. The inspiration for *Me, Third* came from her own situation: To ease her household duties on a tight budget, Mary hired a maid who was an inmate of a home for delinquent girls. This, added to Mary's knowledge of Denver political scandals, gave rise to her script *Me, Third*—titled after the campaign slogan of its main character ("God First, the People Second, Me, Third").[18] The character, a lawyer named Hazlett, is running for office on a sparse budget. He and his wife pretend to be rich by hiring a maid who is on parole, and an errant yard man who falls in love with Mrs. Hazlett. The Baker's director grabbed up the comedy-satire, and Federal Theatres elsewhere followed suit.[19]

The play was a hit with audiences and the press, which generally shared the *Denver Post*'s opinion that *Me, Third* was "hilariously funny, packing laugh upon laugh."[20] Encouraged by this sweet taste of success, Mary was seized by an idea. Recalling that Antoinette Perry, one of New York's leading directors, was a Denver native, she mailed Miss Perry a copy of *Me, Third*. Perhaps some New York producer would be interested in it.

Antoinette Perry (whose name would be given to Broadway's Tony Awards) had relinquished her acting career to marry a businessman and raise two children. Then, as a widow, Tony returned to the stage and acted in Brock Pemberton's productions, until she became his co-producer and director in 1928. Tony Perry passed on the copy of Mary's play to Pemberton.[21]

By then, Brock Pemberton was a balding curmudgeon known for being innovative and harboring a soft spot for new playwrights. In his list of credits was the production of Zona Gale's *Miss Lulu Bett*, and his wise decision to buy the rights to Luigi Pirandello's *Six Characters in Search of an Author*. But Pemberton also had had his failures of note; in 1936, he had not produced a play in two years.

Me, Third had just closed in Denver when Pemberton called Mary to say that he wanted to produce her play: Could she come to New York immediately? She had given birth only five weeks before and had no money to cover the trip; but the chance seemed golden, so she and Bob borrowed the funds. Mary left for New York just before Christmas of 1936, leaving her infant son in the hands of his father and two brothers.

Locking herself in her hotel room, Mary worked through the holidays, doing rewrites on *Me, Third*, which Pemberton for some reason had renamed *Now You've Done It*. Tony Perry was directing; her daughter was playing the part of the maid on parole. Pemberton predicted a hit, and the signs were good. From rehearsals alone, offers for movie rights had been made, but Pemberton advised waiting until after the play opened.[22]

On opening night in February, the audience loved it; someone logged the number of laughs at 220. But almost all the reviews were brutal. In the middle of his pan, one critic even conceded, "I must admit, however, that the audience on opening night seemed to adore it."[23] The reviews killed the play before it had a chance; and Pemberton had to close after 43 performances. (He later fumed in an interview, "Why must we let the critics in?"[24])

Pemberton could better afford his loss of $15,000 than Mary and Bob could afford what the venture cost them. Instead of returning from New York with a hoped-for nest egg, Mary came home badly in debt. Selling the family car barely made a dent in the bills:

> We went for three years without an automobile to get out of debt.... The whole thing was ... a disaster ... a terrific blow. I don't think I ever would have tried it again if Mr. Chase hadn't said to me, "Write another play immediately. When a pilot crashes, they make him take up another plane before he leaves the field."[25]

Mary Chase resumed her life with this resolution: "I would never write for Broadway again. I thought the song, 'There's a Broken Heart for Every

Light on Broadway,' had been written especially for me."²⁶ Keeping her sights on the local front, Mary set up her old typewriter again. She also set up a model stage made from boxes, with wooden spools to chart character moves.

In the next three years, she turned out three full-length plays and a one-act comedy. The first, *Sorority House*, was drawn from her college days, when she was snubbed as a pledge because of her poverty and social class. Mary wrote her experience into the character of a hard-working girl named Alice, who arrives on campus during rush week and becomes an unwitting pawn in a Greek society trade-off. The *Denver Post* said Mary had followed *Me, Third* with "another bulls-eye" and was "on her way to recognition as one of the foremost ... writers for the theatre." The *Rocky Mountain News* called the play "brilliant satire," and *Variety* said it held "plenty of laughs and not a few tears."²⁷ Mary was again faced with tempting offers—one from a noted stage producer, and another from R.K.O. Films. Fearing that lightning might strike twice if she chose the stage route, Mary sold the rights to R.K.O. for $2,500. The amount and the success of the film were both modest. But at least the Chases were able to replace their car.²⁸

While Mary's next script, *Colorado Dateline*, was never published or fully produced, it refined her technique and her knack for drawing on her background. The plot centered on a rookie reporter who loses her objectivity and becomes involved with the accused in a murder trial.

Her first one-act play, *Too Much Business*, came next and was set in a movie house full of raucous kids. Staged at the University of Denver, the play featured audience participation: viewers were used as the raucous movie crowd. (With three irrepressible boys at home, Mary had ample role models for this and her future writings about children.²⁹)

By now, World War II was a bleak and constant intrusion on life. Mary decided she had to be of help, somehow, through her writing. She started by writing a play to lighten the spirits of the trainees at nearby Camp Hale. The result was her musical comedy *A Slip of a Girl*, which was produced through the USO in 1941.

Mary's social activism took several forms in those years. She did publicity for the National Youth Association; helped form a chapter of the Newspaper Guild; and wrote a radio program for the Teamsters. Always sympathetic to labor, she marched in picket lines, incongruously dressed in the big hats that were her penchant. She pitched in with the strike of Mexican sugar-beet workers, and became secretary for Spanish workers in their paper-plant strike. Whatever it took—supplying food, carrying signs, or bullying the police—Mary was in the thick of it; and her support made a difference. One strike that she championed led to "the first industrial contract for this minority group in Colorado," a fact that made her proud.[30]

Meanwhile, the war kept coming closer to home for Mary. Although her own sons were too young to serve, she could imagine the dreadful loss of a son. She felt stabbing empathy for the neighbor across the street, when she received the black-bordered telegram about her only son. Already a widow, the woman was now alone, still going off to her job after years of hard work to put her boy through school. Mary wondered how the woman withstood it; and what it might take to make her laugh again:[31]

> I used to stand ... and watch her walk swiftly out her door to catch an 8:30 A.M. streetcar. I always walked to school with my own sons, and I would see her just after I had left them safely at school. I not only felt sympathy and grief for this woman ... but I was amazed at how she could go on living and working.... Finally I began to wonder if this woman ever would be able to laugh again ... what kind of thing would make her laugh. I thought if I could contrive something like this—for her—then it would make thousands of other mothers who had received those black-bordered telegrams laugh again.[32]

For many months, Mary Chase was "haunted day and night" by this thought.[33] She made start after start, bent on creating some kind of comic relief for those who suffered most from the war.

To Mary, laughter was one of the three ingredients vital to life. At age 17, she had firmly decided that "love, laughter, and beauty" were the qualities "worth living for." These were qualities that Mary hoped to put into her writing—especially now, for this woman and others like her.[34] "I did some praying about it, and one morning when I was only half awake, I saw a big white rabbit following a psychiatrist."[35] An odd vision to most, but not Mary. Many of the legends she grew up with described the antics of a pooka: a "large benign Irish Fairy" in animal shape. Mary decided that the animal in her vision was a pooka, attached to one of the doctor's patients.[36]

From this seed of an idea, it took two years for the full-fledged *Harvey* script to grow. "I don't like to cry about it," Mary later recalled, "but none of it came easy.... I wrote three versions of *Harvey*: I tried it with a man-sized canary instead of a rabbit, and I tried it, too, with a woman for the central character instead of a man."[37]

For a while, Mary wrote with Tallulah Bankhead in mind. But her protagonist switched back to being a man, and remained a man. Elwood P. Dowd combined qualities of various men in her life: an old newspaper buddy; her uncles; but especially her brother Charlie, who sought his escape from reality, as Elwood did.[38]

Mary developed her own tricks for escaping into her writing. One was to wait until the house was quiet, which meant until the boys were in bed and her husband was at work. (Bob was now a city editor at the *Rocky Mountain News*, working from 5:00 P.M. to 1:00 A.M.) A better trick was the trance-like state of concentration she achieved; it blocked out everything. Her son Jerry once recalled that "she always worked at home, but during her strong sessions, she was no more accessible than if she were holed up somewhere else."[39] Still, the boys saw her as "a marvelous parent" and felt "well taken care of." Of course, they found their own uses for Mary's writing trances. "My children made cunning use of this [writing] period," Mary remembered. "Ask her now," they conspired. "*Now* she'll say yes."[40]

Often, working on the script was Mary's own escape from the war. "When I am in one of my writing trances," she explained, "I am cushioned against the sadness and griefs of the world.... I worked with the radio blaring the news of Dunkirk, through the casualties of Bastogne."[41] What kept Mary most on track, however, were her thoughts of the woman across the street: "I would look out the window at her as I was writing scenes for the play and I always used this test—would it amuse her? Would this device divert her? Would this line strike home to her?"[42]

Mary completed her final reworking of the script in spring of 1944. She wrote to Brock Pemberton, expressing her hopes that she had created a play in which "the laughs are deep and rooted in the truth."[43] Pemberton had never stopped believing in Mary Chase's "instinct for theatre." Nor had he stopped judging scripts by his two criteria: first, "Do I like the play?" and second, "Has it a chance of success?" Mary Chase's new script passed his tests and Pemberton phoned her to say he was putting *The Pooka*, as it was then titled, into production.[44]

Mary knew that there were risks to her family finances (again), but she knew that she had to go. She felt there was some larger purpose to it all. Her sons went to live with friends for two months; Bob was left to his own resources. Mary went to New York on her advance from Pemberton.

While Mary made some changes requested by Pemberton, he went casting about for a cast. The role of the dreamy, affable Elwood was the biggest challenge. Pemberton's attempts to induce Harold Lloyd (the silent film comic) to do the role were to no avail. And Jack Haley, the Tin Man of *Oz*, also declined the role. No one else seemed right. Frank Fay, who had gone from vaudeville to nightclub entertaining, was now a reformed alcoholic and almost a recluse in California. Pemberton was skeptical, but gave Frank Fay a shot at the role. The rest was theatrical history: "From the moment he read the part, there was no doubt in my mind, and now it seems impossible to imagine anyone else in his place." (Brock Pemberton nonetheless put himself into the role, years later, in regional productions. Mary Chase felt he was unsuited for the part, but he loved it.[45])

Equally perfect for the role of Elwood's sister Veta Louise was Josephine Hull, who had triumphed in *You Can't Take It with You* and *Arsenic and Old Lace*. Tony Perry directed *The Pooka*, with all her comedy instincts in high gear.

Not until a week before its pre–Broadway tryouts in Boston, did *The Pooka* acquire the title of *Harvey*, for the name of its invisible character. At that point, too, the invisibility of Harvey was still in question. Mary Chase felt the pooka should appear at least once; Pemberton did not. It took a rabbit-suited stage manager appearing in a preview, to convince Mary to leave Harvey to the audience's imagination. However, to make Harvey's presence more palpable, Mary made a last-minute line addition: To Wilson's reading of the definition of a pooka at the end of Act One, she added "and how are you, Mr. Wilson?"—as a greeting from Harvey. (In New York, a further touch of Harvey was introduced by the mysterious opening and closing of doors at the end of Act Two.[46])

Mary went to the Boston opening of *Harvey* in a borrowed dress, carrying a purse that contained only a few good-luck tokens: a four-leaf clover from Josephine Hull; a two-dollar bill from another cast member; and a note from her husband which read: "Don't be unhappy if the play does not succeed. You still have your husband and your three boys, and they all love you."[47]

Despite the audience's laughter, Mary did not realize she had succeeded. It took Frank Fay's call the next day ("Kid, you have got a hit") and the all-out praise of the Boston critics to make it sink in. The *Boston Globe* proclaimed that Elwood P. Dowd was "one of the earth's most beautiful people," and it cheered for Mary's "deft parrying of realism with logic carried to its ultimate fantasy."[48] The *Boston Herald* applauded Chase's fantasy, "stated in so sweetly reasonable a fashion that you emerge from the theatre ... nearly convinced that it all happened."[49] Mary's favorite comment came from the *Record* critic, who best expressed what she was trying to do: "*Harvey* is a play with a spiritual meaning in farce terms."[50]

The Boston triumph made Mary all the more afraid of a letdown after the New York opening. This time, she had more than a note to remind her of Bob's support. He was sitting beside her; and he could share her relief at the audience's response that night—as well as her astonishment over the glowing reviews the next day. John Chapman of the *News* extolled *Harvey* as the "most delightful, droll, endearing, funny and touching piece of stage whimsy I ever saw."[51]

Time magazine summed up *Harvey* as the "funniest and most likeable fantasy that Broadway has seen in years,"[52] and Joseph Wood Krutch wrote in *The Nation* that "here is, indeed, one of those miracles which still occasionally occur just when theatergoers have reason to doubt that miracles happen."[53] Six weeks later, a columnist indicated what a sell-out hit *Harvey* had become: "I met Harvey the other night. Frank Fay introduced us in a play called *Harvey*, dreamed up by Mary Chase and enshrined ... at the 48th Street Theatre. Try to get in between now and the Fourth of July. I was quite comfortable on the left prong of a chandelier."[54]

Of all the acclaim that *Harvey* collected over the years, no comment meant more to Mary Chase than the one she overheard one night in the lobby:

> I could stand, anonymous as a ghost ... and see the smiling faces of people whose names I would never know ... enjoying the play.... One night I heard a man say to a friend, "The first time Mother laughed since Joe was killed." Even though the path was thorny, I felt I had kept my bargain with the woman across the street.[55]

The success of *Harvey* was much more than Mary ever bargained for, or was prepared for. "I was fortified against failure but not against success."[56] She and Bob were overwhelmed by the "wrecking crews" which now paraded through their lives:

> On the first wrecking crews are the people who have known you always and thought they had you pegged.... They coax you to confess you really didn't write that play, did you? Wasn't it a brother in California, a cousin twice removed—removed to Leavenworth? ... And then there was the wrecking crew [that] discussed you with authority in other houses: "That dame! When I first knew her she was eating canned soup without peeling off the tin.... Don't tell *me* about *her!*"
>
> At such times your few truly fond friends stay away ... They don't want to seem to be celebrity chasing. Then began years of commuting between Denver and New York and Europe ... shuttling back and forth between my three sons and the comics who were playing *Harvey* ... my role with one group helped me with the other. One of my boys would say, "That Bill Smith took my ball bat." One of my comics would tell me ... "That ham actor who plays the attendant is ruining my second act exit." The answer in both cases is the same: "I will not let him do this thing to you."[57]

On May 7 of the spring following *Harvey*'s opening, Mary had just gotten home from the seeing a movie—the film version of *You Can't Take It with You* starring Josephine Hull (who had played Veta in *Harvey*). The telephone rang. It was Bob, at work, with the news that *Harvey* had won the Pulitzer Prize: "I just yelled when he told me. I had wanted to win the Pulitzer Prize all my life ... and I had no idea I'd ever get it."[58]

The tribute of a Pulitzer Prize offset some of the damage of the "wrecking crews"; but Mary gave much credit to support from her family—most of all, Bob, her Rock of Gibraltar: "The Pulitzer Prize should come in two sections, one for the winner and one for the winner's mate. I have survived it, but it took all I had and then some. I had to borrow a little—from Bob and the Bible."[59]

Harvey was no exception to the rule that a Pulitzer Prize play suddenly meets with opposition, even if it had none before. Some critics upheld *The Glass Menagerie* as the worthier season offering. A few detractors grumbled about *Harvey*'s apparent advocacy of drinking. At these implications, that Elwood was a lush who saw the Pooka because he drank, Mary recoiled. "It's not a play about a drunk," she insisted. Elwood would see Harvey anyway. "The liquor was inserted to keep it from being a preachment."[60]

Even if *The Glass Menagerie* had opened before the last day of the Pulitzer season, chances are the jury still would have awarded the prize to *Harvey* without dissent. John Hohenberg, the award's administrator for 20 years, made no apologies for the selection. *Harvey* was just what Americans needed and wanted: "Laughter and relief from anxiety ... in the closing months of World War II."[61]

In 1950, Universal Pictures bought the screen rights to *Harvey* for the unprecedented sum of one million dollars. Once more, Mary argued her point, that Harvey should be seen once, just "walking arm-in-arm with Elwood at the fade-out.... I don't want anybody to go out ... thinking Elwood is a lush." Once again, she lost. But Jimmy Stewart's sensitive and gracious Elwood made Harvey profoundly real, and was anything but a "lush."[62]

Ironically, Mary began to battle a drinking habit herself, as a result of her quick and overwhelming success. She jested that, for her, money had "never been anything you made," rather "something you owed."[63] But she had been deeply hurt by what she saw in "the flare of sudden fame"—"the glittering eye of Greed, the distorted faces of her sisters Envy and Malice."[64]

Mary recovered and helped found a Denver House of Hope for female alcoholics. Then she retrenched herself in work. While she never again achieved the special combination that was *Harvey*, she did create a few other notable works:

In 1952, her play *Mrs. McThing* opened on Broadway, starring Helen

Hayes and introducing Fred Gwynne. A child's fantasy, it featured a witch who substitutes a changeling for a widow's bad little boy. Reviews were mixed and compared the play to *Peter Pan*.

Mrs. McThing was still running when Mary's new play *Bernardine* opened in October of 1953. The city temporarily renamed Shubert Alley "Mary Chase Alley," with signs directing theatergoers to her two plays. Guthrie McClintic—who had directed plays by Zoe Akins—was the director of *Bernardine*, which was a sensitive look at the sexual fantasies and foibles of teenaged boys. Again, reviews were mixed, but Brooks Atkinson called it "wonderfully artless and fresh." (A film version followed, starring Pat Boone; but Hollywood weakened the charm of the story and Mary Chase's main character, Beau.[65])

Most of Mary Chase's final creations were for children—either stories, or locally-produced plays. In the last year of her life, she relented and permitted something she had long resisted as unsuitable: a musical version of *Harvey*. Having turned down offers from the likes of Rogers and Hammerstein, Leonard Bernstein and Danny Kaye, she finally allowed an Irish-American producer to arrange a Canadian staging of *Say Hello to Harvey*. Donald O'Conner played the affable singing Elwood; Leslie Bricusse (of *Stop the World* fame) wrote the script and music. Mary Chase's son Michael served as a production stage manager.

Despite the opening sellout crowds and standing ovation, Mary shared the critics' verdict that the show was too long and the music interfered with the story. No plans were made to re-stage it elsewhere, and a worn-out Mary Chase flew home to Denver. After helping to close the show, her son Michael followed a few weeks later. Arriving home, he was stunned by the news that his mother had died of a heart attack that day. Mary Chase was 74 years old. Her obituary in the *Rocky Mountain News* stressed the fact that Mary Coyle Chase's play *Harvey* had "made the woman across the street laugh."[66]

Mary Chase once said, "I wanted to be a great playwright, and I never made it." Sometimes she did write with greatness, however; and most of her creations bear the marks of "laughter, love, and beauty." In a bittersweet recollection, she confessed, "I never regretted *Harvey*, but I shouldn't have spent as many years as I did trying to surpass it."[67]

Harvey was Mary Chase's shining hour, and it gave a few shining hours of escape during the end of World War II and its aftermath. But Mary Chase's legacy of Harvey is still alive, reaching new generations of theatregoers and viewers of television and videos. (In the 1990s, the play was staged three times in Chicago alone, once by the prestigious Steppenwolf Company.) In its gentle exercise of audience imagination and its universal message about faith in intangibles, Mary Chase's farce "with a spiritual meaning" remains unique.

THE PLAY—*HARVEY*: REVERSING REALITY WITH RABBIT TRICKS

The setting is the faded grandeur of the Dowd family home, now the household of Elwood P. Dowd, his widowed sister Veta Louise, and her daughter Myrtle Mae. As Act One lights come up on the library, off-key singing is heard from the adjacent parlor, where Veta is hosting a Wednesday "program tea" in hopes of securing a society entree for her daughter. When Veta and Myrtle emerge from the parlor to tend to a phone call and the arrival of Mrs. Chauvenet, Veta tells Myrtle, "the point of this whole party is to get you started." Mrs. Chauvenet, for one, has a grandson the right age for Myrtle Mae. But Myrtle is not enthused: How can they have a social life around Uncle Elwood and his invisible six-foot rabbit pooka—Harvey? The party today was only possible because Elwood was playing cards at the firehouse.[68]

However, Elwood makes an untimely return; and when he earnestly tries to introduce Harvey to Mrs. Chauvenet, the society matron flees in alarm. Myrtle is mortified and wants to flee, too; but Veta vows that Elwood has disgraced them "for the last time in this house"—she's going to do something. Elwood cheerfully accepts Veta's request that he sit out the party in the library. He pulls a bottle from behind a book, and starts reading to Harvey from *Jane Austen*.

Scene Two opens in "an office in Chumley's Rest," with Veta explaining to Nurse Kelly her decision to commit Elwood. Kelly has their strong-armed attendant Wilson collect Elwood from a waiting taxi. Veta continues stating her case to Chumley's young assistant, Dr. Sanderson (who has a love-hate relationship with the attractive Nurse Kelly). Assured that what she says is confidential, Veta bewails Elwood's habit of dropping into pubs, "sitting around with riffraff ... inviting them to the house." And worst of all is his comradery with his six-foot rabbit pal. She eventually even confides, "every once in a while, I see that big white rabbit myself." This tidbit convinces Sanderson that Veta must be the loony one, and he sets about correcting what he believes to be the error of Nurse Kelly, whom he instructs to send for Elwood so amends can be made. Meanwhile, Wilson has hauled Veta upstairs, and she's now in room 13, "screamin' and kickin' like hell."

Elwood is a cordial gentleman to Kelly and Sanderson. When Sanderson blurts that "Miss Kelly and I have made a mistake here this afternoon,"

Elwood construes this to mean that they've been sexually indiscreet. Double entendres follow, until Sanderson stuns Elwood with his opinion that Veta has a drinking problem. Elwood dismisses the notion and starts to introduce Harvey, but Sanderson keeps pressing to have Veta committed. Elwood finally replies, "Only if she liked it ... and wanted to stay." But he will confer with Judge Gaffney (their family friend and lawyer). After Sanderson and Kelly consent to have a drink with Elwood at Charlie's that night, Elwood leaves.

Kelly and Sanderson are having a tiff when Chumley enters to check that this matter of the woman with the big rabbit has been "smoothed over." (He notices a hat left behind, and assumes that the two holes in it are a new fad.) When all three run off to see about Veta, whom Wilson has wrestled into the hydro-tub, Elwood returns and encounters Chumley's wife, Betty. She has come to collect her husband for a cocktail party. Elwood asks Betty if she has seen his friend around. She says no, but offers to give his friend a lift into town if they do see him. After Elwood leaves, Chumley returns, and Betty relays the offer she made regarding Elwood's friend—"Harvey." At the name, Chumley goes berserk, and fires Sanderson for his mistake.

Act Two, Scene One, opens again in the Dowd library, an hour later. Myrtle Mae has been showing the house to a prospective buyer, to the dismay of Judge Gaffney, who reminds her that the house belongs to Elwood. Veta storms in looking disheveled, and rants at Judge Gaffney to sue them at Chumley's Rest. She goes upstairs, and Myrtle goes off to get something to show the judge—something Elwood once brought home.

Wilson and Chumley arrive, having searched 17 bars without finding Elwood. However, Chumley now wants to handle Elwood's case personally; it "interests" him. While Gaffney takes Chumley up to Veta, Wilson flirts with Myrtle Mae and gets her to fix him a sandwich. They go off, and Elwood enters briefly, long enough to phone Chumley's Rest and hear that Harvey is not there. But Elwood spots the parcel that Myrtle has brought in, and he places its contents—a portrait of himself and Harvey—on the mantle, on top of his mother's portrait. He leaves, unseen by Veta and Chumley who re-enter, Veta still fuming. The changed portrait evokes a scream and near-faint from Veta. But a phone call from Elwood, who reports that Harvey has just walked in at his end, sends Chumley chasing off to catch Elwood at Charlie's Place.

Scene Two is back at Chumley's Rest. Chumley has been missing for hours; the fired Sanderson has been packing his things. He now taunts Nurse Kelly about the date he saw her with; she counters with insults about Sanderson's date. Elwood arrives, to keep his invitation for a drink with them, and Sanderson questions him about Chumley. Elwood explains that after a long evening with Harvey and Chumley, the two of them left without him. Elwood wistfully describes bar-hopping with his pooka: "Harvey and I warm ourselves in these golden moments. We have entered as strangers, and soon we have friends." While Sanderson takes Elwood upstairs, Chumley sneaks in and tells Wilson to lock the door—he's being followed. Chumley goes into his inner office and locks that door, too. But while the lights dim, doors open and close as Harvey enters Chumley's office, despite locks.

Act Three is set in Chumley's Rest, a few minutes later. Myrtle and Judge Gaffney arrive, and Gaffney concedes to Chumley that there actually might be a Harvey. (The rattled Chumley knows he exists, but can't admit it.) Chumley tells Sanderson that he's not fired; Chumley wants such an "astute young man" on his staff. This turn of events swiftly unites Sanderson and Nurse Kelly: her "Oh, Lyman" is met with his "Oh, baby." Veta arrives with Elwood's robe, since the plan to admit him is on again. Sanderson suggests that they give Elwood a "formula 977" injection, used in psychopathic cases. Veta is outraged; she knows that Elwood is not a psychopath. But she consents to the "reality shot" for the sake of normalcy.

When Elwood is brought in, Chumley learns that Harvey can not only predict the future, he can stop clocks. "You can go away as long as you like ... not one minute will have ticked by." Chumley mutters to himself, "To hell with decency! I've got to have that rabbit!" He joins the others in pressing Elwood to accept the shot and be rid of Harvey. Elwood sadly agrees, to make Veta happy. Chumley takes Elwood inside to prepare the injection.

Meanwhile, a cab driver comes in, looking for his fare from Veta. She can't find her coin purse, but assures him that she'll get the money from her brother as soon as he gets his injection. But the cabby insists, to the point that Veta interrupts the injection to get Elwood. Elwood gives the cabby his fare, along with a warm invitation to their house, and goes back inside. The cabby regrets that such a "sweet guy" will be changed by the injection. He knows, because he has seen plenty of the "before and after" on his route. After the shot, they become "perfectly normal" men—and he knows what bastards they are. Veta knows, too, and not wanting Elwood to become that, she bellows "Stop it ... Elwood come out of there." In her enlightened turnabout, Veta now comes to the defense of Elwood and Harvey (and is grateful that the rabbit hid her coin purse). Chumley's office door unlocks and slowly opens as Harvey emerges; Elwood happily goes off with his pooka and the rest of his family.

Mary Chase's *Harvey* was lasting proof of the credence she gave to her mother's counsel, "Never be unkind or indifferent to a person others say is crazy. Often they have a deep wisdom."[69] The play was also Chase's most successful blend of the three ingredients she felt were vital to life: love, laughter, and beauty. There is beauty and love in Elwood's crazy wisdom and his innate kindness to others. Laughter abounds in the chaos that he innocently unleashes in the supposedly sane society bent on converting him to what they consider normal reality.

Chase's play holds features obviously different from the three previous Pulitzer plays discussed. Hers is a full-out comedy with elements of farce and fantasy, and its main female character is antagonist to a male protagonist. However, it strikes a few chords that are echoes of the earlier plays: Chase's device of using an unseen title character as the catalyst for action harks back to the technique of Susan Glaspell. And in the first scene, the social assumptions about women which Chase ridicules are the same assumptions that are challenged (more seriously) in the foregoing plays: That the main goal of a woman's life is to marry and to marry well, and that a family's younger generation should play out the patterns set by previous generations. The action and conflict of *Harvey* spring from Veta's frantic ploys to find a proper husband for Myrtle Mae.

Veta is desperately trying to debut Myrtle for women whose sons and grandsons are blue-blooded bachelors. She does this through the Wednesday Forum tea—a pretentious social ritual launched by her "lantern-jawed" mother, who scaled the social ladder from pioneer oxcart to cultural leader. However, all this culture is now represented by an aging soprano whose voice is fading, "but not fast enough." Chase wisely leaves to the imagination Miss Tewksbury, warbling offstage and off-key. In Chase's cartoon of high society, she does allow a glimpse of one symbol of the 75 ladies ensconced in the parlor: Mrs. Chauvenet, dressed in the clichés of "gold and plush, and mink scarf even though it is a spring day."

Veta's entire party is a social cliché, and her belief in her own matchmaking scheme is shaky. At one point she even says, "Oh Myrtle—you've got so much to offer ... there's something sweet about every young girl. And a man takes that sweetness and look what he does with it!" Still, it is the way of the world in her context, so she is quick to add, "But you've got to meet somebody, Myrtle. That's all there is to it." (Whether the war-era shortage of men figured into Veta's urgency is not implicit in Chase's script, but audiences might have made the connection.)

The huge obstacles to a society entree for Myrtle are Elwood and his unacceptable, invisible pal. Realizing this, Myrtle is ready for a disaster to strike Elwood—a hit-and-run truck, perhaps. But Veta stops short of such cruel thoughts. For one thing, she cares about her brother; for another, she knows that Elwood is not deliberately inventing Harvey. Still, to dispel Harvey from the house, Elwood must go; she must take action.

One catch is that Elwood owns the house, having inherited it from their mother. This normally would make Elwood the household head, the patriarch and liaison between his family and society, if this were a normal household of the era, and Elwood a conventional middle-aged man.

But Elwood has, in effect, taken leave of his normal family and their social context. His outsider status is wonderfully conveyed in his first entrance: Into the caricature of stuffy society set up for Veta's party comes the light step of the benign Elwood, with his battered felt hat and his unorthodox sidekick. The antithesis to Veta's club ladies, Elwood is as socially unconcerned and free wheeling in his attachments as anyone could be.

Elwood has not only formed a unique created family with Harvey (to whom he "tells everything" and with whom he "goes everywhere"). He spends most of his time creating satellite families with whom he and Harvey have "golden moments," tumbling from bar to bar to firehouse. They do have a home base at Charlie's Place, where both are unconditionally accepted and understood. Elwood longs to have his given family merge with his created family. It seems that Harvey is willing; he would do anything for Elwood. To Betty Chumley, Elwood laments, "Harvey is fond of my sister, Veta. That's because he is fond of me, and Veta and I come from the same family. Now, you'd think that feeling would be mutual, wouldn't you? But Veta doesn't seem to care for Harvey."

Elwood leaps at every chance to meet others and introduce them to Harvey. He blithely crashes Veta's party, and when Betty inadvertently gives him the address of the McClure cocktail party, he crashes that, too. Clearly, people hold a stronger appeal for Elwood than alcohol. What insulates him from reality is not liquor, but his own belief system (which evoked Harvey). Elwood happily claims that he "wrestled with reality for forty years [and] finally won out over it."

When Veta attempts to commit Elwood, and the play's action moves to Chumley's Rest, Chase introduces her extreme versions of the archetypal Patriarch: Doctors Chumley and Sanderson, serious professionals who presume to set the standards for behavior. These frantic high-key men make an instant, comedic contrast to the unhurried, unassuming Elwood. Chase pokes fun at them even before Elwood enters: Nurse Kelly boasts to Veta that "whenever people have mental breakdowns they at once think of Dr. Chumley."

The image of authority attached to these white-coated professionals begins toppling with Sanderson's bungle of Elwood's admission. Chumley rails at him, "Doctor—the function of a psychiatrist is to tell the difference between those who are reasonable, and those who merely talk and act reasonably." This is a distinction which Chase bids her audience to make. She challenges—and ridicules—the right and ability of these (or any) professionals to decide what is reasonable. She also suggests that what they deem reasonable is not a desirable state of being.

In Chase's turnabout, the innocent and oblivious Elwood gets the best of everyone else. And he does so while displaying more kindness, humanity, and even social graces than the lot of them. His gallant treatment of Nurse Kelly is the antithesis of Sanderson's insulting, chauvinistic stance. And he genuinely tries to befriend the nurse and doctor, inviting them to his second home, Charlie's Place: "When I enjoy people I like to stay right with them."

By Act Two, Chase has the audience rooting for Elwood to escape with his ideals and rabbit intact. Here, reality looms first in the person of Myrtle, attempting to sell the house out from under Elwood. Judge Gaffney, another arbiter of what is "real," wants Elwood returned to reality; but at least he upholds Elwood's property rights. Gaffney lends more credence to Harvey, since he has "had that rabbit in [his] office many's the time."

The bedraggled Veta comes home outraged and ready to sue Chumley. But Myrtle remains ruthlessly set on banishing Elwood. In her absolute denial of Harvey, Myrtle is an agent of reality who gives reality a bad name. (Chase hints at a match between her and the brutish sanitarium attendant, a hint that these two insensitives deserve each other.) However, Myrtle is instrumental in another win for Elwood's side. She retrieves the oil portrait of Elwood and Harvey that was stashed in the garage. When Elwood places the portrait on the mantle, covering the one of his late iron-jawed mother, he is, in essence, usurping his given family with his created one.

Harvey goes beyond being friend or family to Elwood. He is something of an earth angel who protects Elwood, and who has powers that Elwood has never utilized.

By Act Three, Harvey has been made real to the audience in many ways. Others besides Elwood have seen him; Chumley has spent an evening with him; and doors have mysteriously opened and closed. (Critics who interpreted Harvey as a figment of Elwood's boozing somehow overlooked all this.) The play reaches a crossroads in the crossfire between the real and ideal when Chumley sees Harvey: when the alleged arbiter of sanity begins to see the very thing that defines Elwood as crazy. Even Chumley concludes that Harvey is a miracle, and regrets spending his life "among fly-specks while miracles have been leaning on lamp-posts" (where Elwood met Harvey). Elwood has never made use of Harvey's power to alter time and place: "I always have a wonderful time just where I am, whomever I'm with," he tells Chumley. But the doctor envies and wants this power, and decides "I've got to have that rabbit."

Chumley's motives for wanting to return Elwood to reality with an injection of "formula 977" are different from the others.' Still, the final scene has everyone pitted against Elwood. And while he could resist the rest of them, Elwood cannot resist the plea from Veta, since he feels that "Veta should have everything she wants." He sadly agrees to the injection, which will replace his vision of Harvey with a clear view of his responsibilities.

At this final hour, Mary Chase brings in an outside rescuer for Elwood in the person of the cab driver, who knows too well the effects of this reality injection: People subjected to it are "no fun," "they got no faith" and "they crab, crab, crab." Vita realizes, almost too late, that this is just what her father and husband were like. She does not "want Elwood that way."

Calling a halt to the shot in the nick of time, Veta rallies to the other side and "throws herself weepingly" on Elwood. To the others she rants, "and what's wrong with Harvey? If Elwood and Myrtle and I want to live with Harvey, it's nothing to you! You don't even have to come around." Elwood's created family is merged, at last, with his real family—one that is now accepting of his gentle, soft-focused view of reality.

When theatre audiences of the 1940s sat down to watch *Harvey*, they were wrestling with their own grim realities of war. Through Chase's work, many not only escaped for a while, but left with renewed faith in the human spirit and the hope that they might find the equivalent of Harvey in their own lives. Mary Chase's comedic battle between the real and the ideal holds this timeless lesson: The open-hearted dreamer can perceive much beauty and wonder that is denied to the closed-minded realist.

8

The 1950s: An Uncomfortable Homecoming

Of all the diversions that technology offered Americans after World War II, the most welcome and quickly assimilated was television. It had made a spectacular public debut at the 1939 World's Fair in New York. However, few families had been in a position to purchase the luxury of a television set before the war. And broadcasts by RCA or its rival networks (CBS and Dumont) were still sparse. By 1950, television sets and broadcasts were catching on like wildfire, forever changing family life (much more than the radio had in the twenties).[1]

Movies, newspapers and magazines all had to fight for survival. Radio gave up competing in comedy and drama, and offered round-the-clock music and news. A few hit radio shows, like *Dragnet* with Jack Webb, made successful transitions from radio to the small screen. As most of the program titles suggested—*The Kraft Television Theatre, Gillette Cavalcade of Sports, Texaco Star Theatre*—early programs were sponsored by individual companies. By the mid-fifties, production costs had risen so high that sponsors were forced to share time slots.[2]

The social impact of television was staggering and almost impossible to assess. Communications specialist Marshall McLuhan phrased it this way: "Ours is a brand new all-at-once-ness. 'Time' has ceased, 'space' has vanished. We now live in a *global* village ... a simultaneous happening."[3]

American families could now tune into what was happening in that global village, and found most of it deeply disturbing. The hot war in Europe had been followed by a Cold War that thwarted peace efforts by the new United Nations. Churchill warned that a sinister Iron Curtain had been drawn across Europe. Russia had quickly gone from being an ally to being a threat, and had tested its own A-bomb in 1949. A third world war of atomic proportions seemed possible enough for the Civil Defense Act to provide public fallout shelters. Families built and stocked their own bomb shelters. School children crouched in hallways for air raid drills.[4]

Another hunt for "Communists among us" reached obsessive levels. One sensational trial followed Julius and Ethel Rosenberg to the electric chair, despite flimsy evidence. (Two halves of a Jello box were produced as "spy-to-spy identification.") The House Un-American Affairs Committee cornered informants into pointing fingers at scores of unlikely subversives, including Hollywood writers, actors, and college professors.[5] Wisconsin's Republican senator Joseph McCarthy launched a four-year smear campaign to further his political career. He attacked a host of public figures, including Presidents Eisenhower and Truman. When McCarthy made the U.S. Army his target, the resulting televised Army-McCarthy hearings led to his public downfall and a Senate vote of condemnation against him.[6]

Government agents and private citizens who scanned the skies for Russian aircraft did not see what they were looking for, but they sighted impressive numbers of UFOs (unidentified flying objects). The paranoia of some Americans came to include fear of other worlds as well as other nations. Meanwhile, the U.N. intervened in South Korea against North Korean Communist forces; 90 percent of the non–Korean soldiers under the U.N. flag were American.[7]

Thanks to television, Americans could now witness the harsh realities of war at home. They could also watch highlights of the campaign for one of the most popular presidents in U.S. history. General Eisenhower was elected in 1952 and reelected in 1956, by landslides.

Post-war prosperity had brought middle-class status within reach of more Americans than ever before. This new material security, jostling with a mood of fear and paranoia, produced a strange crop of expectations about home and family.

The suburbs became a new mecca in the 1950s. A housing crunch caused by the baby boom made enterprising investors buy up lots outside city limits and sprinkle them with prefabricated houses. The prototype for this was Levittown, the Long Island potato field converted by William Levitt. Its tract houses were "as alike as the potatoes had been," but "for $60 a month and no money down, $7990 bought you four rooms and an [expansion] attic, a washing machine, outdoor barbecue, and a 12" TV set built into the living room wall."[8]

The years of financial struggle and war made Americans retreat to the familiarity of the traditional family. But having weathered such hardships themselves, baby-boom parents became dead-set on giving their children all the comforts that they had missed. This led to what *Private Life* editors called the "rise of a powerful ideology that placed children at the center of family happiness."[9] Popular culture was overrun with images of wholesome child-centered families. Television proffered "the least objectionable [family] programming," featuring whitewashed families like the Cleavers of *Leave It to Beaver*, and the Andersons of *Father Knows Best*.[10]

The new-again blatant message from the media was that a woman's place was in the home, and her headquarters was the kitchen. *A History of Private Life* detailed the post-war "polarized gender roles": "The distinct roles for male breadwinners and female homemakers reflected a separation of the sexes more reminiscent of the Victorian era than anything in the 20th century."[11]

The vigorous economy meant more jobs for women, but the range of possible jobs "narrowed into largely clerical and service jobs with low pay and little opportunity for advancement."[12] Women's jobs were, therefore, just that—jobs. Middle-class women defined their "careers" in terms of homemaking and child-raising. As *History of Private Life* noted:

> Given the lack of prestigious and rewarding work for women outside the home ... many women in the 1950s gave up occupational ambitions to become career homemakers. They described their choice by using the word "career," something for which they sacrificed and worked hard. Often the pursuit of that goal required tolerating a less-than ideal marriage, scaling down expectations, and resigning oneself to a great deal of unhappiness.[13]

As the decade of the fifties wore on, 60 percent of women college students dropped out to marry.[14] Those who remained in college were bucking a powerful social myth, that further education for women was superfluous if not harmful. In *Life* magazine's 1956 Christmas issue, the new American career woman was "that fatal error that feminism propagated"; she was described as suffering from a "serious disease" and needing help from a therapist.[15]

Look magazine said that "The American woman is winning the battle of the sexes":

> No longer a psychological immigrant to man's world, she works, rather casually ... as a way of filling a hope chest or buying a new home freezer. She gracefully concedes the top jobs to men. This wondrous creature also marries younger than ever, bears more babies and looks and acts far more feminine than the "emancipated" girl of the 1920s and '30s.[16]

8. *The 1950s: An Uncomfortable Homecoming* 111

If women of the fifties chafed at their home labors, they were bombarded with the message that better equipment was the remedy. Typical was the advertisement in the October 1954 *House and Garden*, which showed an apron-clad housewife in a chair, her feet up on a stool. The caption read: "Can you relax for Woman's Hour with a clear conscience, because you have worked well in a kitchen designed to your needs?"[17] In a General Electric ad, a wife washed a stack of dishes while her husband and child looked on. The husband complained, "Seems you spend more time with the dishpan than you do with us!" The wife replied, "I wouldn't *have* to if we had a General Electric Dishwasher!"[18]

In her book *Woman: Her Changing Image*, Ann Shearer described how intensely the homemaker myth prevailed in the fifties. But she also stressed that, even then, women were asking themselves, "What's wrong with this picture?"

> So hard have the fifties been stamped with the image of woman as wife, as mother, as household drudge, that it's perhaps difficult to recognize that then, too, just as now, women were seeking the answer for themselves.[19]

Women were not the only ones wrestling with the forces of conformity. As the uniformity of tract housing seemed to generate tract marriages, tract families and tract culture, teenagers sought alternative lifestyles. But often, the results were still conformity: Teenaged boys aped the example of Elvis Presley; the tougher ones mimicked James Dean, the "rebel without a cause."

In the fifties, the strongest outcry for rights came from black Americans, who found their hero in Martin Luther King, Jr. They found a heroine too, in Rosa Parks, the seamstress who refused to give up her seat on a Montgomery bus. Triumphs in federal rulings ended segregation in schools and transportation. But those resistant to integration drew lines and turned some urban areas into battlefields.[20]

While social pressures were simmering close to the surface of American life, the surface itself continued to bear the collective stamp, however counterfeit, of an adjusted society replete with contended families. After the fifties ended, while some looked back with fond nostalgia, many Americans regretted the somnambulance that had allowed them to feel complacent. Women wondered what had happened, and why it had seemed so right to embrace the homemaker myth. Betty Friedan, who would become the oracle of the women's movement in the following decade, gave this explanation:

> What happened to women is part of what happened to all of us in the years after the war. We found excuses for not facing the problems we once had the courage to face. The American spirit fell into a strange sleep.... The five babies, the movement to suburbia do-it-yourself ... took the place of those larger needs with which the most spirited in this nation were once concerned. The family and its loves and problems—this, at least, was good and true.[21]

The family, which was already a prevailing topic for drama, became an even more popular stage subject during the fifties. But the families depicted on stage were some of the most troubled ever to take the spotlight. The decade's Pulitzer winners included Joseph Kramm's *The Shrike*, Tennessee Williams' *Cat on a Hot Tin Roof*, O'Neill's *Long Day's Journey into Night*, and of course, Ketti Frings' *Look Homeward, Angel*. Their turbulent family settings were a far cry from the sugar-coated child-centered families of the era's television series.

On the whole, theatre was battling with television to survive. The free entertainment of television came just as production costs in the theatre were soaring. The result was that, between 1944 and 1960, the price of tickets doubled. Producers made every effort to stage plays with the broadest appeal.[22]

The competition from television was fierce: By mid-decade, home audiences could even opt for serious drama from *Matinee Theatre* or *Masterpiece Playhouse*.[23] However, in bringing theatre to those who had never experienced it, albeit on a screen, television also made some converts on behalf of theatre. When *Hallmark Hall of Fame* presented *Hamlet* in 1953, it was estimated that more people saw it that night than during its 350 years of stage history.[24]

For playwrights, television did provide the benefit of another venue, to keep them working, eating, and reaching an audience. It was a venue with a magic ability to recycle for new generations the works of writers such as Mary Coyle Chase—and Ketti Frings.

9

Ketti Frings and Her Stageworthy Angel

Luckily for Ketti Frings and American theatre, while a 1956 issue of *Life* magazine was declaring the career woman "that fatal mistake that feminism propagated," Ketti Frings was too busy being a career woman to pay attention. That was the year Ketti conquered the mammoth task of adapting Thomas Wolfe's autobiographical novel for the stage.

Ketti had set her heart and sites on a writing career early in life. Her first triumph came as a child in Dayton, when she won a newspaper contest with her essay on "What Santa Claus Really Means." Looking back, she commented, "I knew right then that I was going to be a writer; so I just made it my business to be as good a writer as I could be." There was something prophetic about Ketti's prize for her essay: two tickets to a movie theatre. She became a top-notch writer and adaptor for the screen, as well as an award-winning playwright. Ketti later quipped that, to become a writer, "All you have to know is what Santa Claus really means—and you're on your way." Her path from Santa Claus essay to successful stage and screen plays was not quite as simple as that, however.[1]

Twenty-two years before her husband gave her the nickname "Ketti" (which stuck), Katherine Hartley was born in Columbus, Ohio, to the wife of a traveling paper-box salesman. Guy Hartley took his wife and three daughters on the road with him; by the time she reached her teens, Katherine had lived in 13 different cities, ranging from Portland, Oregon, to Brooklyn, New York.[2]

After her mother died, she and her two sisters were left with an aunt in Milwaukee, where she attended a school for girls. "When I was in school,"

Ketti Frings

she recalled, "I wrote plays so that I could write myself the best parts."[3] She had visions of becoming a "glamorous actress," but she "desperately wanted to write for the stage." After a year of college in St. Louis, she headed for New York to be closer to her dream.[4]

While writing advertising copy in New York and for Bamberger's department store in New Jersey, she tried to crash Broadway as an actress. A producer gave her a new script to read for an audition. After studying it overnight, she returned it to the producer, saying she didn't think she wanted to be in that show because it was not very good. "He threw me out, of course."[5]

Her judgment was confirmed when the play closed after seven performances. By then, she had decided to move to California to give Hollywood a try. For a while, the closest she came to writing for the movies was writing about them, and about their stars. Under the assumed name of Anita Kilgore, she wrote for fan magazines, "describing Claudette Colbert's new home for the fans, asking Robert Taylor his thoughts on marriage and the like."[6]

This was not the creative writing she had set out to do, so she took off for Europe with plans to write a novel. At the St. Moritz, in the south of France, she met a charming German ex-prize fighter and ski instructor named Kurt Frings. Her ski lessons with Frings turned into a romance; her novel-writing was put on hold, and the two of them were married. She became his little "Ketti"—a diminutive for Katherine—even though she was a slender 5' 7" tall.

Two long and difficult years would pass before Kurt Frings was allowed to enter the United States. While they waited for his immigration quota number to come up, Kurt lived in a Tijuana community of war refugees, and Ketti lived in a tiny Hollywood apartment. On weekends, she made the long drive south to Mexico, and stayed with Kurt among the European hopefuls—men and women praying and plotting to get into the United States.

Ketti put all of these experiences into her first novel, Hold Back the Dawn. In a Tijuana setting, a German man anxiously awaits entry into America. His wife commutes between his immigrant colony and her one-room Hollywood apartment, where she writes the fan-magazine articles that support them.

Even before the book was published in 1940, Ketti had started translating her story into a screenplay, and scheming ways to get a producer's attention. "I had an idea which now seems a little silly. Instead of titling the story in the usual way ... I called it Memo to a Movie Producer. A printer set those words for me in impressive type." Having interviewed a Paramount producer for a magazine, she was able to wangle a 15-minute appointment with him. She decided to use only 15 seconds of it. "Naturally, he was surprised when I laid the manuscript on his desk, said 'thank you,' and walked out." Her hope was that he would use the remaining 14 minutes and 45 seconds to look through her script.[7]

Her ploy worked. Within 48 hours, her story had been bought by the studio. The film of Hold Back the Dawn was released in 1941 and starred Charles Boyer and Olivia de Haviland.

By then, Ketti and Kurt were together and settled in Hollywood, where he became an actors' agent. The money from Hold Back the Dawn was "enough to keep the Frings in patios for a year," as one columnist put it.[8] Ketti could now indulge her passion for playwriting and the theatre. Her first Broadway play, Mr. Sycamore, was a fantasy (based on a Robert Ayre story) in which a disgruntled postman turns into a tree. Critics were kinder to its star, Lillian Gish, than they were to the script; but Brooks Atkinson wrote, "Give Mrs. Frings credit for having tried something original."[9] The dauntless Ketti was "not too bruised by its lack of success.... You can only learn from your mistakes."[10]

When the war began to dominate the news, Ketti Frings—like Mary Chase—wondered how she might help through her writing. In her book God's Front Porch, she tried "to dispel some of the world's gloom, to make those who are frightened a little less frightened." She wove a fantasy in which a young corporal killed in Africa makes his way to Heavenly Bend Junction. To her touching picture of how God might welcome those who had unwillingly left the earth and their families, she added a hint of how He might work a small miracle for a war-torn world.[11]

By the late 1940s, Ketti Frings was a busy, established screen writer. She had already turned out several of the two dozen screen stories that she would craft in her career. Some of her films, such as The Accused featuring

Loretta Young, became popular successes. But her first surefire hit, combining popular appeal with resounding critical success, came with her film adaptation of *Come Back, Little Sheba*. The play by William Inge had just been a hit on Broadway with Shirley Booth as Lola, the housewife awash in delusions and denial. For Ketti Frings' powerful screen version of the drama, Burt Lancaster played Doc, the tormented alcoholic husband, and Shirley Booth recreated the role of Lola, a performance which garnered the Oscar for best actress.

Ketti Frings "hit the bulls-eye again" with her screenplay of Joseph Kramm's Pulitzer-Prize play, *The Shrike*. José Ferrer had both staged and starred in the Broadway run of the play, about a suicidal down-trodden theatre producer trapped in a loveless marriage. Ferrer repeated his dual capacities when Universal bought the film rights. During the shooting of Ketti Frings' script, Ketti served as "a second pair of eyes for director José Ferrer." She viewed all of Ferrer's scenes from the camera position, since, as Ferrer claimed, "Ketti knows exactly how I feel about every word in the script."[12]

When she sat down to adapt Thomas Wolfe's autobiographical novel *Look Homeward, Angel*, Ketti was already well known for her superb adaptations and her skillful handling of domestic drama. Her interest in the idea of adapting the novel began in 1950, although she had long been something of a "Wolfe idolater."[13] Having read his novels and finding them "full of dramatic materials," she finally read his play *Mannerhouse*. "I hadn't known until then that Wolfe had wanted to be a playwright."[14]

This was an understatement. Wolfe tried everything humanly possible to create a viable play. He studied playwriting at the University of North Carolina, acted with Carolina Playmakers, and became a member of George Pierce Baker's legendary playwriting workshop at Harvard. Wolfe did turn out a few plays, and submitted *Mannerhouse* to the Theatre Guild. They were mildly interested, but asked Wolfe to cut down the script. The compulsive over-writer crafted a "cut" version that was longer than the original.[15]

Thomas Wolfe died in 1938, at age 37, without ever realizing his dream of writing a stage-worthy play. The task of forging a play from his massive novel was taken up by Ketti Frings 18 years after his death. The book's story spanned 20 years of Wolfe's life, and was 626 pages long. When Ketti undertook the project, friends asked her about it "with the same awe as if she were sweeping out the Augean Stables."[16] John Toohey referred to it as "the Herculean task of jamming this steamer trunk of a book into the tight confines of the stage."[17] But Frings claimed that she did not find the task too difficult. She said that, for one thing, during the year that the project took, "I didn't read anything else about Wolfe or by Wolfe that might have confused me."[18]

After getting the rights to Look Homeward, Angel from Wolfe's last editor, Edward Aswell, Ketti made a list of all the moments in the book that touched her the most. In distilling the time period down to a few pivotal weeks, Ketti searched for what she called the "point of not-blindedness. ... In a play," she insisted, "the protagonist should have a blind spot about something. When that blind spot is removed for him, the play is over."[19]

Ketti decided that for Wolfe's autobiographical protagonist, Eugene, the "blind spot is his feeling that he must accept the embraces of his family and be bound by the ties of family love." She felt that the moment of not-blindedness came in a talk that Gene had with his brother, Ben. Once she had hit on that moment, Ketti was able to reduce the play's action to the weeks surrounding Ben's death. She juggled sequences and speeches to increase the play's impact. Her innovations included having Ben say on his deathbed a speech he had made earlier in the book.[20]

Originally, Frings wrote a prologue and epilogue that featured Thomas Wolfe as a shadowy narrator, describing the main characters before important speeches. She abandoned this device as slightly pretentious (and perhaps too similar to The Glass Menagerie in form). "Still," she maintained, "I'm glad I did it.... It helps define the characters in my mind, and all of those speeches now appear in actual scenes."[21]

Ketti greatly enlarged the role of Eugene (Gene), as well as the romance between Gene and Laura, a vital ingredient in the build to the play's climax. She made no attempt to follow the novel's dialogue, and some of the favorite lines of her producer (Kermit Bloomgarden) were purely inventions of Frings.[22]

"I hate to say this about Wolfe," Ketti confided, "but I had to work my way around an awful lot of clichés in the dialogue." On the other hand, she doubted there could be a more inspirational and "beautiful line for the theatre" than Thomas Wolfe's painful observation:

> I understand that men are forever strangers to one another, that no one really comes to know anyone, that imprisoned in the dark womb of our mother we come to life without having seen her face, that we are given to her arms a stranger, and that caught in the insoluble prison of being, we escape it never, no matter what arms may clasp us, what mouth may kiss us, what heart may warm us. Never, never, never, never, never.[23]

This passage, part of which became Ben Gant's anguished enlightenment of his brother Gene, helped to convince Ketti that Wolfe's intent was best revealed in his novel's subtitle, A Story of the Buried Life. The stonecutter's angel was a symbol of the beauty that had been buried in the life of Gene's father, W.O. Gant. Beyond that, the angel stood for the pain of all misspent lives; but it was of special significance to artists, who agonize when their work falls short of their dreams. In this respect, the angel was evocative of Wolfe himself, whose work often depicted the torment of the artist in an insensitive world.[24]

"I didn't worry about the number of different scenes," Ketti confessed. "I hoped that somehow the scene designer would work it out."[25] Producer Kermit Bloomgarden took the script to Jo Mielziner who indeed worked it out, as he had worked out a similar challenge in designing *Death of a Salesman*. Mielziner's solution for letting scenes flow without stopping was to depart from literalness, and to use a revolving stage. A shift from the living room of the Gant Dixieland Boarding House to an upstairs bedroom was made by a turn of the revolve. The whole boarding house also moved back and forth, to allow for scenes to be played in front of it (against projections of locales).[26] A fluid, cinematic feel was brought to the production's staging by George Roy Hill, "a television man."[27]

On Thanksgiving eve, 1957, *Look Homeward, Angel* opened at the Ethel Barrymore Theatre, with Anthony Perkins in the role of young Eugene Gant, and Jo Van Fleet as his manipulative mother, Eliza. Hugh Griffith played the hard-drinking but soft-cored W.O. Gant. "How Tom would have rejoiced in this event," Wolfe's editor Edward Aswell declared. "It would have been for him the final consummation."[28] In his introduction to the published script, Aswell went on to applaud the "extraordinary insight and dramatic skill of Ketti Frings."[29] The New York critics seemed to be trying to outdo each other in praising Frings' work. Walter Kerr wrote:

> The world of the Gants, as the late Thomas Wolfe lived it and wrote it, was eternally two-faced.... It offered affection and solitary confinement in the same chilling breath.... What makes the Ketti Frings adaptation of Mr. Wolfe's autobiographical novel so fascinating in the theatre is the perfect, perfectly sustained tension with which it holds these violently opposed emotions in balance.[30]

In the *Daily News*, John Chapman cheered, "Ketti Frings has made a magnificent play which was given an almost miraculously beautiful performance last night. Hers is a drama which ranks with, perhaps above, Arthur Miller's *Death of a Salesman* in strength and compassion ... it is a work of splendid artistic creation on the part of Miss Frings."[31] Brooks Atkinson of the *New York Times* declared, "What Thomas Wolfe could never do, Ketti Frings has done admirably. She has mined a solid drama out of the craggy abundance of *Look Homeward, Angel*."[32]

An appropriate analogy was that Ketti Frings had played the stonecutter to the monumental rock which was Wolfe's novel. She had carved from it a perfectly featured and balanced Carrara angel of a play.

So universal was the admiration and acclaim for Ketti's achievement, that she was honored with both the Pulitzer Prize for drama and the Drama Critics' Circle Award (not to mention the *L.A. Times* "Woman of the Year" tribute). Her triumph was made more impressive by the fact that the Broadway season had been an exceptionally fine one. Also-rans included *The Dark at the Top of the Stairs*, *Sunrise at Campobello*, *Two for the Seesaw*, and the musicals *West Side Story* and *The Music Man*.

Of Ketti Frings' remaining three Broadway ventures, only one — her book for the 1966 musical *Walking Happy* — met with real approval from the public or press. Her stage adaptation of a book titled *The Long Dream* had a short-lived run produced by Cheryl Crawford. Ketti herself made an attempt at producing a new play (*The Umbrella*) in the 1962 season; but that venture fell short of success, despite a cast line-up that included Geraldine Page and Anthony Franciosa.

In 1972, Geraldine Page, E.G. Marshall and Timothy Bottoms starred in a television presentation of *Look Homeward, Angel*. Ketti Frings wrote the teleplay for the 90-minute special, which launched the *CBS Playhouse 90* series.

Ketti's career as an acclaimed writer was complemented by her husband's career as a top-flight Hollywood agent. The client list of Kurt Frings included such talents as Elizabeth Taylor, Audrey Hepburn, and Maria Schell. The Frings somehow found time to raise two children — a son, Peter, and a daughter, Katherine — and to have a magnificent Beverly Hills home built to their specifications. The ultra-modern house on Ladera Drive, with its spectacular Japanese gardens and pool, bested any home that Ketti would have described in her days as a fan magazine writer. Cleveland Amory called it "one of Hollywood's most showy showplaces."[33]

However, Ketti's favorite room was anything but showy. Unlike the rest of her picture-windowed house, this room had no window, only a skylight. Ketti explained, "You can't look out, you have to look in. It's a darn good thing, too, not only for writing but for everything else."[34]

After more than 20 years of marriage, Ketti and Kurt Frings were eventually divorced, but remained friends. During her last decade of life, Ketti spent less time writing than she did being a grandmother, three times over. She was in her seventies when she died of cancer in 1981.

Ketti Frings did acknowledge that playwriting requires more than knowing the "Real Meaning of Santa Claus." She decided that it takes complete devotion:

The greatest mistake anyone can make is to undertake a play as a casual excursion in creative work, to treat it as an alternate occupation. It's quite the other way. It demands the most complete dedication. And even with that kind of dedication you can't be sure of the result, but you have to possess it anyway.[35]

THE PLAY—*LOOK HOMEWARD*: A BOARDING HOUSE IS NOT A HOME

The time is World War I. The place is Eliza Gant's "Dixieland" Boarding House in Altamont, North Carolina, which also serves as a makeshift home for the Gant family: stonecutter W.O. Gant and his penny-pinching wife Eliza; their married daughter Helen and her husband, Hugh; and two of the Gants' sons—Ben and Eugene, both of whom are idealistic would-be writers. W.O. Gant is now a hard-drinking shadow of the romantic artist he once was. For years, he has tried in vain to copy the serene marble angel that once inspired him to become a stonecutter.

In Act One, some of the 15 shabby rooms of "Dixieland" are visible. In one of them, 17-year-old Eugene reads aloud a poem he has written about his older brother and mentor, Ben. Meanwhile, Ben is on the veranda steps with his "generous, somewhat boozy" companion, Fatty Pert, a long-term boarder. Today's headlines remind Ben that he would love to enlist, to be a pilot in the war. Fatty replies that he's too underweight, and asks how his family would feel. Ben counters, "What family? The batty boarders? ... Except for Gene, nobody'd know I was gone."[36]

The paying boarders are clearly the top priority with Eliza, who enters with her brother Will Pentland, a real estate broker. The two of them are conspiring about a potential sale of Gant's "precious old marble yard." After Will goes, Eliza nags Ben about spending time with Fatty Pert and for reading the boarders' newspapers. At the sound of the midday train, Eliza calls for Gene to run to the station and hand out business cards, a chore he despises. Ben retorts that "Gene should be *on* that train—going to college!" Ben goes off to his newspaper job, rejecting Eliza's dinner offer of the boarders' leftovers. The boarders swarm onto the porch for their coffee.

Eliza is welcoming a new boarder, young pretty Laura James (who is clearly a cut above the others), when Gene runs in with the news that his father has been drinking at Laughren's again: Dr. Maguire is steering him home now. Gene barely acknowledges Laura's presence before Gant is helped in, roaring that this is not his home. He passes out cold and is carried inside. Ben returns, having heard about his father; and Gene asks him a heartfelt question: Why has their father stayed here, if he hates it so much? Ben says, "It's like being caught in a photograph."

Ben corners Dr. Maguire for a medical okay for the flying corps; but as Maguire prods his chest, Ben collapses with coughing. "They'll have to save the world without you," Maguire counsels, and goes off. The disheartened Ben urges his brother to get away from here and from their mother, whatever it takes. "I let her hold on until it was too late. Don't let that happen to you." Before leaving for work, Ben assures Gene that he wouldn't enlist yet, anyway: "I have to bring you up first, don't I?" Laura James comes out to retrieve her hat from a bench, and smiles at the flustered Eugene.

Scene Two, that night, starts on the veranda. Ben reminisces to Fatty that his father once seemed to be an invincible Titan (who built the home that Eliza traded for this drafty barn). Laura draws Gene into talking about his hopes for college and travel, his love of trains. They both fib about their ages, Laura pretending to be younger (21), and Gene claiming to be older (19). A tender connection is formed between them. Inside the house, Eliza comes to Gant's bedroom "with pity in her heart," and tries to reminisce about their first meeting, long ago. Gant only groans his regret at coming to the "rag end" of his life, here. When Eliza brings the subject around to the sale of the marble yard, Gant is enraged. "Let me die in peace," he wails, "and *leave me my work!*"

Eliza descends to the porch and flings her anger at Ben and Fatty. Gene tries to make peace, and Eliza includes him in her rant, demanding their gratitude. Ben yells, "For what? Moving us into this drafty barn, where we share our roof, our food ... our privacy, so you can be Queen Bee?" He shrieks that she has made Gene into a huckster—"He isn't a son, he's an investment"—and Eliza slaps his face. Ben takes off, with Fatty Pert following. Again, Gene tries to soothe Eliza, who still mutters about all she's had to put up with. After she boasts to Gene about her latest property deal in Doak's Park, he persuades her to go inside. Alone, Gene calls to Laura, and apologizes for the family fight. They go for a walk, hand in hand. Eliza emerges with a property map, and calls into the darkness, "Ben? ... Eugene?"

Act Two, Scene One is in Gant's stone shop and yard, where his beloved angel stands. Eliza enters shouting for Gant, but finds only Gene at work by the emery wheel. Eliza talks about Gene's future, dangling the prospect of college. But she urges him to work in her brother Will's realty office, first. She finally goes and Gant returns, having seen Eliza leave. With Gene, Gant gazes at the smooth beauty of the marble angel, a contrast to the hardness of Eliza.

Laura arrives with a surprise picnic lunch for Gene. Gant teases them a bit, then retreats to his office. Laura confides to Gene that people are starting to "know about us." She confesses that she is 23, and knows that he is only 17. Gene insists that it does not matter; Laura is now his world. Their embrace is curtailed by Mme. Elizabeth, the town madam, who has come to her old friend Gant for a headstone. One of her girls has died, and she wants a special monument. In fact, she wants Gant's marble angel. Her insistence upsets Gant to the point that he escapes to his office, leaving Gene to deal with her. Gene says that he thinks "Papa is saving the angel for his own grave." The madam relents, and agrees to the stone lamb that Gene offers.

As she exits, Eliza returns with Will, and calling a family conference, Eliza rudely dismisses Laura. Ben arrives as ordered, and Gant urges Eliza to get to the point. She produces a check for the marble yard, and wants Gant to sign it, so she can deposit it. But Gant quickly pockets the check for his own plans: to take Gene off to college, then travel. Eliza frantically grabs the check away and tears it up, threatening to have Gant declared insane. To his wail of "Why don't you let me go?" Eliza snaps, "Because you're my husband, Mr. Gant."

After she and Will exit, Gant goes off to the bar, and Gene laments to Ben that their parents' love could turn to such hatred. "They're strangers," answers Ben, who collapses suddenly, his eyes closed. Realizing that Ben is ill, burning with fever, Gene phones for Dr. Maguire.

Scene Two is back at Dixieland that night. In Ben's room, Dr. Maguire hovers over Ben's still body. Laura and Eugene are in the yard. Gant is shouting into the phone, inquiring after his seaman son, Luke. Eliza huffs, "It's all nonsense ... Ben is far from dying," and tells Gene to go in to Ben and "make a big joke out of it." When Maguire has Eliza come to Ben's bedside, Ben turns away and asks for Fatty instead. Maguire allows Fatty in, and she sings Ben a lullaby.

To Eugene, the doctor whispers the truth: that Ben is dying. Maguire goes next door to phone for oxygen to "ease it a little" for Ben. While Gene is dumbstruck, the others chatter around the arriving Luke, who sardonically surveys "the same old happy household." A sudden cry from Fatty sends Gene to fetch Doc Maguire, who arrives in time to admit that nothing could be done. Ben's final words are to Fatty: "It's one way to step out of the photograph." Outside, Laura's heart goes out to Eugene, who kneels to pray: "Whoever you are, be good to Ben."

Act Three begins two weeks later, about dawn. Gene has spent the night in Laura's room; knowing that she is to leave today, he blurts out that they will get married. He will take the job with his Uncle Will. Later, downstairs, Eliza overhears Gene telephone Will and ask for the job because he is marrying Laura. Horrified, Eliza rails at Gene about this mistake, as she calls it, and about her plans for him. Unyielding, Gene goes to pack his things, and Eliza storms in to confront Laura James. Laura calmly explains that she is not marrying Gene. She is engaged to a man back home whom she will grow to love "after a while." Yes, she did feel for Gene a love she has never known, but she knows Gene must be free to pursue his dreams. She gives Eliza a note for Gene and says, "Someday you're going to have to let him go, too."

When Gene finds Laura gone, and Eliza waves the note as proof that Laura walked out on him, she scoffs that this was puppy love. He will "look back on this and laugh." She dangles the promise of college—next year—and Gene finally explodes: "Mama, what more do you want from me? ... Do you want me to collect more bottles? ... Do you want more property?" At her claims that she has provided a roof to call their own, he shouts that nothing has been their own. He never had a bed or even a quilt that wasn't taken "to warm the mob that rocks on that porch." Now immune to Eliza's weeping, Gene goes off to pack.

The oblivious Gant emerges, grumbling about the lack of heat and breakfast. Gathering firewood, he snarls that he would love to burn down Dixieland. He is stunned when Eliza answers, "I wish you would," and even threatens to shake down its pillars herself. Gant gladly joins in the manic attack on a pillar, scattering the screaming boarders. When Will arrives, just in time to grab away a hatchet and subdue them, Eliza is horror-struck at what they've done. She sends Helen after the boarders: "Tell them he's been drinking ... get them back."

The crestfallen Gant takes heart when he sees Gene with suitcase in hand, and tells him to "go for both of us." Eliza makes a last pathetic effort to keep Gene. "You know that lot of mine on Sunset Terrace? ... we could be in our own home by spring." She relents with a weak "try to be happy, child," and he goes.

In a brief epilogue, Gene starts his journey, as the voice of Ben reminds him that the world he seeks is inside: "*You* are your world."

The family spotlighted in Frings' *Look Homeward, Angel* is the most brutal example, so far, of a family of strangers. This horribly divided house is nothing like a family home: In Eliza Gant's Dixieland, the material needs of the boarders come first. The spiritual and emotional needs of the Gant family have been neglected or deeply buried. So much so, that the fight for survival of the three dreamers—W.O. Gant, Ben, and Eugene (Gene)—is well under way when the play begins.

Ben has already lost that fight before the opening curtain. Ben's story is the point to which Eugene's story is the counterpoint. The play's conflict and suspense derive from the question of whether or not Gene will manage to secure for himself what Ben could not, by pulling free of the forces of family. Gene does escape, with help from Ben and Laura. Both of these supportive people leave Gene; but not until they have helped to remove his blind spot—his belief that he must endure the embrace of family, the smothering grasp of Eliza.

As a matriarch, Eliza Gant is more aggressive and power-wielding than any patriarch found in these plays. She is the one, here, who has set up selfish and powerful myths to control her family. A match for Eliza is difficult to find in the whole body of prize-winning American drama. (Two other domineering wives are Harriet Craig of *Craig's Wife* by George Kelly, and Ann Downs in Joseph Kramm's *The Shrike*, which Frings adapted for the screen.)

What is so striking about Eliza is not that she shows the aggression and competitiveness usually associated with men; but that she is so devoid of the impulses toward nurturing and connection that are considered inherent in women. Eliza's children have lived and looked as if they were orphans, bereft of anything but the boarders' leftovers—in food, bedding, and above all, Eliza's attention. As Gene finally cries out near the end "... all these years—feeding us on *their* leftovers—do you know what it does to us? When it's ... *you* we needed for us. Why? Why?"

The answer is that the boarders are the family that Eliza has created, to suit her own very material needs. The paying boarders feed her skewed sense of self-worth. Ketti Frings' stage version of Eliza comes off as more ruthless than the mother of Wolfe's original novel. In the book, Eliza's greed is given some mitigating explanation: While her husband was raised amid the plenty of a Northern farm, and knows nothing of the privation that plagued the South after the Civil War, Eliza knows it full well. This is behind the "insatiate love of property" among Eliza and her brothers. In Frings' play, only a brief line by Mme. Elizabeth hints at this: "Mrs. Gant and I both understand that property is what makes a person hold one's head up!"

But Eliza has imposed the public sphere on her private family sphere with disastrous results. Her cold, consuming interest in the dollar value of Dixieland makes her the mortal foe of her idealistic sons and husband.

Ben has already relinquished his dream of writing, resigned to being a "hack on a hick newspaper." He divulges to Fatty Pert his fleeting, futile dream—to fly "up with the angels" and help "drive the Huns from the skies." Ben's dream is fueled by his desperate wish to escape from Dixieland and the family "photograph" in which he feels forever trapped.

Eliza is so oblivious to the needs of her son that Ben is dying before her eyes. He is being drowned by consumption, which Frings draws as an apt symbol for the consuming clutch of Eliza. As Ben tells Fatty, dying is "one way to step out of the photograph." Fatty Pert is Ben's created family: She sings to him, knits socks for him, and listens to his dreams. She fills for Ben the voids of mother, wife, friend, and confidant. A parallel relationship is formed between Gene and Laura.

Ironically, the women who become surrogate mothers and lovers to Eliza's sons both come from her hodgepodge of boarders. But they are not like the rest. These two are examples of the "outsider-strangers" who can be more kind than kin.

Laura has even been brought to Dixieland—and to Gene—by the business cards that his mother forces him to hand out at the depot. (Laura found a card that he'd rebelliously discarded.) The hawking of Dixieland is one of the degrading tasks that Eliza has foisted on Gene. "He hasn't anything else to do," she grumbles. "Spends his time up there dreaming, scribbling." In dismissing his dreams, Eliza negates the very essence of her son. She can't see in him what is so clear to a caring outsider. Laura genuinely loves Gene, but lets him go, knowing that he needs "the whole world to wander in," while she herself must go back and live by the "good rules for marriage."

Through Laura James, Ketti Frings questions the same biases about women and marriage that the previous playwrights have questioned. Laura does not relish the prospect of marrying her fiancé, Philip, back home. She says of herself "I never liked responsibilities.... I like music, I like to walk in the woods, I like—to dream." Yet, at age 23, she is getting married for practical reasons that are imposed, to a man she does not love but hopes she will grow to love. (Scores of young women in the era's audiences no doubt identified with this mind-set.)

Laura's part in saving Gene is not the usual role of a rescuer. Quite literally, by loving and then leaving him, she gives Gene the impetus to break away from family and Dixieland. Laura's warmth and caring let him know what love should be like. But his marriage to Laura would keep Gene trapped: To marry her, he is ready to take the menial office job with his Uncle. This choice would give a perverse victory to Eliza, and destroy Gene's dreams of college, and travel, and the writing that is his destiny.

Two sorrows, one on the heels of the other, bring about Gene's unblinding and escape. One is the death of Ben, the only family tie of affection for Gene. The other is Laura's departure. If it were not for these events, Gene might remain in Altamont, trapped in the family photograph by his anguished loyalty to family.

According to Ben, being stuck in this photograph is what has held their father here, long after his perfect marriage turned to perfect torture. All the passion and romance of Gant have dwindled down to "riot and confusion." His search for the intangible has been locked in demeaning combat with Eliza's avid pursuit of tangibles. All that remains of Gant's old dream is his precious angel statue, whose beauty he cannot replicate. (But Gant's work is still "clean and pure" to Gene.)

To Eliza, Gant's stonecutting is useless, either as art or business. She has already betrayed Gant by trading in their real family home—proudly built with Gant's hands—for what he calls the "bloody barn" of Dixieland. Now, she is determined to cash in Gant's marble yard for its cold dollar value, the only value Eliza sees.

Ultimately, Eliza is the most blind and wretched in the Gant family portrait: The more she counts her profits, the more she loses of all that matters. Even the death of Ben and the loss of Gene do not awaken her. For one chilling, uncharacteristic moment, she joins Gant in his violence upon the boarding house. Eliza seems to revel in their vengeance on the "miserable unholy house." "I'll kill you, kill you, house," she shrieks. And for that lightning moment, love and union exist between Gant and Eliza. But it is short-lived, a false hope. Snapping back to reality, Eliza surveys with horror what they have done, and sends Helen to placate the boarders.

Gant's final comfort comes with his son's departure. If Gene leaves, part of Gant will escape, too. Gene knows that his escape from Dixieland is the start of another fight. "I shall spend the rest of my life getting my heart back, healing and forgetting every scar." Still, a redeeming light has dawned for him: the realization that self-nurturing is far better than abuse at the hands of family. Gene can carry his dream within; this is Ben's final message to his brother. Look in, not out, counsels the spirit of Ben.

There is an appealing full-circle postscript attached to the story of the play's creation: Ketti Frings re-coined those closing thoughts of Thomas Wolfe in her favorite room at home, the room with a skylight and no windows—where she could "not look out, only *in*."

PART III

Whose Woman Is She? Henley, Norman, and Wasserstein

"What happened?" is a question that surrounds the next three plays: a trio of plays by women who took the Pulitzer Prize in the 1980s. The question has a few applications. First, it asks why there was a lapse of 23 years between the award of the 1958 Drama Pulitzer to Ketti Frings and the award to Beth Henley in 1981. Even the Pulitzer for Fiction—regularly awarded to women between 1920 and 1943—had no women recipients in the 20 years following World War II. And the Drama Critics Circle, which handed six awards to women between 1941 and 1960, let 21 years pass before they again honored a woman's work with their award to Henley's *Crimes of the Heart*.

Another, happier shade of the question "What happened?" arises from noting that, after this lengthy lapse, all three of the plays in this section— by Beth Henley, Marsha Norman, and Wendy Wasserstein—took the Drama Pulitzer in one decade. The plays by Henley and Wasserstein also took the Drama Critics' Circle Award, and Wasserstein's play won the Tony Award for best play. What happened to create such a reversal in the 1980's, even after the spirit of feminism had begun to break up and decline?

A look at the plays themselves prompts the question, "What happened?" as well as the question, "Whose woman is she, anyway?" The women characters in these plays are compelled by their unhappiness to take radical action as a means of taking charge of their lives. What happened to bring Babe MaGrath to the point of shooting her husband? To bring Jessie Cates to the point of shooting herself? To bring Dr. Heidi Holland to the point of desperate unhappiness—of feeling so betrayed, stranded, and worthless despite her achievements?

The answer, in each case, has to do with self-esteem and self-determination, two qualities that go hand in hand. Unless a woman holds a positive definition of herself above any negative judgments of others, she has slim chances of becoming her own free person. As Beth Henley put it, "Self esteem is the only thing that can save a woman from the traps of other people's definitions."[1] How do you define "self-esteem," without resorting to tricky psychological jargon? A good jargon-free definition is given by Dr. Nathaniel Branden, leading author and psychotherapist in the field of self-esteem. In a series of articles for *New Woman* magazine, Dr. Branden wrote (emphasis is his):

> *Self-esteem is the experience of being competent to cope with the basic challenges of life and of being worthy of happiness.* It consists of two components. *Self-Efficacy*—confidence in our ability to think, learn, choose, and make appropriate decisions. *Self-Respect*—confidence in our right to be happy; confidence that achievement, success, friendship, respect, love, and fulfillment are appropriate to us.
>
> "The basic challenges of life" include ... being able to earn a living and take independent care of ourselves in the world; being competent in human relationships ...
>
> Positive self-esteem operates as, in effect, *the immune system of the spirit*, providing resistance, strength, and a capacity for regeneration. When self-esteem is low ... we tend to be more influenced by the desire to avoid pain than to experience joy....
>
> Self-esteem empowers, energizes, motivates ... and allows us to take pleasure and pride in our achievements.

Dr. Branden underscores the reasons why women have had problems in building self-esteem:

> Throughout history, self-esteem has not been a trait that most cultures have prized in women.... "Femininity" has been identified with passivity, not assertiveness; with compliance, not independence ... with self-sacrifice, not self-celebration. To challenge this traditional view of womanhood, and to uphold a vision that honors a woman's strengths and potentials, is itself an act of self-esteem.[2]

(Upholding a "vision that honors a woman's strengths and potentials" would be at the core of the women's movement of the 1960s and '70s.) Women's battles for self-esteem and self-determination have been running currents in other plays of this series; but they're brought centerstage, to a glaring spotlight, in these three. To appreciate these plays and their contexts, and to tackle the questions raised here, it's vital to bridge the gap from 1950 to 1980 in terms of "What happened" to women—before and during the women's movement.

10

Being Female in the 1950s, '60s and '70s

Looking back, one could see a clear pattern: Only in times of national crisis had women in large numbers been allowed real participation in their world. The Depression and World War II had formed a stretch of some 15 years during which women held many of the privileges normally reserved for men. Women had played key roles in keeping the nation moving; they had achieved new status in both the public and private spheres; and they had proved to themselves and others that women could swiftly acquire new skills, even the most technical ones. This should have marked a turning point toward more self-determination and rights for women.

Yet, the 20 years following World War II became what writer Carol Andreas called an "age of the New Victorians." Women were plunged back into the same dependent homebound roles that their grandmothers had battled.[1] In retrospect, the 1950s would generate one of the most haunting questions of the century: Why did so many women give up the world so completely, and apparently so agreeably?

No one has attacked this question more avidly or offered more documented answers than Betty Friedan. A postwar mother herself, Friedan knew that, in their suburban dollhouses furnished to the envy of women everywhere, American women of the fifties were being crushed by the old social myth—that a woman's role as wife and mother is her sacred destiny. This recycled myth, which Friedan named "The Feminine Mystique," had a potent, hypnotic hold on young women, who were marrying and having children before they were adults themselves. By the late 1950s, the average marriage age for women was 20 and dropping into the teens:

Fourteen million girls were engaged by 17.... A century earlier, women had fought for higher education; now girls went to college to get a husband. By the mid-fifties, 60 per cent dropped out of college to marry....

Then American girls began getting married in high school. And the women's magazines ... urged that courses on marriage, and marriage counselors be installed in the high schools.

By the end of the fifties, the United States birth rate was overtaking India's.[2]

Writer Betty Friedan set out to topple the mega-myth that enjoined women "to seek fulfillment as wives and mothers," and to pity "the neurotic, unfeminine, unhappy women who wanted to be poets or physicists or presidents."[3] For years, Friedan interviewed—and confronted—experts in sociology, psychology, education, and in the media. "But the puzzle did not begin to fit together," she claimed, "until I interviewed at some depth, from two hours to two days each, eighty women at certain crucial points in their life cycle." Friedan's findings confirmed her suspicions that "I and every other woman I knew had been living a lie ... and our homes and schools and churches and politics and professions were built around that lie."[4]

When her findings were rejected by every magazine for which she wrote (all of which had an investment in the lie), Friedan realized, "I'll have to write a book to get this into print." It took her five years. "I wouldn't have even started it if the New York Public Library had not, at just the right time, opened the Frederick Lewis Allen Room, where writers working on a book could get a desk, six months at a time." She got a baby-sitter three days a week, took the bus from her Rockland home, and stretched the six months at her Allen Room desk to two years. Friedan never dreamed, then, that her book would become the bible of the new women's movement, and that she would become its ultimate spokeswoman.[5]

The Feminine Mystique was a strongly documented exposé of the myth that was destroying women's lives. Women revealed to Friedan the depression and despair they felt in what she called their "comfortable concentration camps." Of the 28 wives in one model suburb, Friedan found that 18 were on tranquilizers, 16 were in analysis, several had attempted suicide, and a number had been hospitalized for depression or "vaguely diagnosed psychotic states."[6]

(Friedan is not the only writer to compare the mental anguish of suburban wives to that of war prisoners. Others have included Mary P. Ryan and sociologist Stephanie Coontz. In her book *Womanhood in America*, Ryan wrote that in "the suburbs of the 1950s, wives and mothers were the most frequent visitors to psychotherapists and the household members most likely to be consigned to mental institutions."[7] Of course the treatment that was considered appropriate often enforced what was devastating women: In *The Way We Never Were*, Coontz described a study of supposedly schizophrenic women in the San Francisco area who were subjected to "institutionalization and sometimes electric shock treatments ... to force women to accept their domestic roles and their husbands' dictates." Shock treatments were also prescribed for women seeking abortion, since it was assumed that "failure to want a baby signified dangerous emotional disturbance."[8])

One of the 80 women Friedan interviewed was pregnant with her seventh child. The woman wept, "When I'm pregnant and the babies are little, I'm *somebody*, finally, a mother. But ... I can't keep on having babies."[9] When women became ill or despondent, they often blamed themselves for failing to adjust to their feminine roles. Friedan aimed her book at unraveling this puzzle: How had the mystique gained such a stranglehold on the minds and spirits of American women?

Friedan found a host of conspiring causes, from the producers of TV series to the precepts of Sigmund Freud. However, Freud was at the top of Friedan's culprit list, in carrying the weight of authority. Writer-editors Betty and Theodore Roszak also claimed that "Sigmund Freud made the most enduring and perhaps cruelest anti-feminist contribution."[10]

Gone were the days when Freud's theories helped to fuel a sexual revolution, or Susan Glaspell used the café chatter about Freud as fodder for a comedy. Freud was invoked with lethal seriousness in post-war America. (Freudian analysts had fled from Europe, causing a psychoanalytic movement here.) Freud's "Anatomy is Destiny" theory was touted in textbooks and all forms of popular culture. In the gospel according to Freud, a woman was innately inferior, doomed to lifelong penis envy: "Her self-love is mortified by the comparison with the boy's far superior equipment." The best a woman could do was to give birth to a "little boy, who brings the longed-for penis with him."[11]

Certainly women of the fifties had every reason to envy men—as did women of the Victorian era—not because of their "superior equipment," but because men held the privileges of a virtual ruling class. Freud's own family was a classic patriarchy: To Sigmund's docile mother, her husband (a man twice her age) was absolute ruler. When Sigmund's studies were disturbed by his sisters' piano playing, "the piano disappeared," Anna Freud recalled, "and with it, all opportunities for his sisters to become musicians."[12] To his own bride, Sigmund was supremely paternal: "You are my precious little woman," he wrote her, "even if you make a mistake ... my sweet child."[13] More telling was the letter Freud wrote attacking Stuart Mills' views on "female emancipation":

> [Mills] finds the suppression of women an analogy to that of Negroes. Any girl, even without a suffrage or legal competence, whose hand a man kisses ... could have set him right.... I believe that all reforming action in law and education would break down in front of the fact that ... Nature has determined woman's destiny through beauty, charm and sweetness.... The position of women will surely be what it is: in youth an adored darling and in mature years a loved wife.[14]

Freud's old-world Jewish culture compounded the bias about male "superiority": Jewish men recited the daily prayer, "I thank thee, Lord, that Thou has not created me a woman."[15] Freud's unbalanced view of women was firmly set in the cement of prejudice.

In the rapid, and rabid, spread of Freud's tenets, even misguided women joined the post-war frenzy. Dr. Helen Deutsch, whose hefty two-volume *Psychology of Women* held sway in the U.S., endorsed the idea that anatomy is destiny and declared that American women who achieved acclaim did so at the expense of their feminine fulfillment.[16] In their book, *Modern Woman: The Lost Sex*, Marynia Farnham and Ferdinand Lundberg condemned the "deep illness" of feminism. Women were lost, they wrote, because they had become too dominant for their own good. The happy woman was the one who could be docile, and totally submissive during sexual intercourse: "It is not as easy as rolling off a log for her. It is easier. It is as easy as being the log itself. She cannot fail to deliver a masterly performance by doing nothing whatsoever except being duly appreciative and allowing nature to take its course."[17]

Textbooks for social studies courses offered other absurd—and absolute—advice for women. Imagine the impact of this excerpt from the college text *Marriage for Moderns*, on the woman student hoping for a career:

> For the first time in history, American young women in great numbers are being faced with these questions: Shall I voluntarily prepare myself for a lifelong celibate career? Or shall I prepare for a temporary vocation, which I shall give up when I marry and assume the responsibilities of homemaking and motherhood? ... The problem of combining marriage and homemaking with another career is especially difficult.... The former, to be successful, requires self-negation; the latter, self-enhancement.[18]

Even Margaret Mead, "the symbol of the woman thinker in America," gave mixed signals to women in the fifties.[19] Mead was widely studied in colleges; quotes from her books and articles appeared everywhere. In her post-war writing, Mead showed the effects of "Anatomy is Destiny" theories. In *Male and Female*, she wrote,

> The recurrent problem of civilization is to define the male role satisfactorily enough. In the case of women, it is only necessary that they be permitted by the given social arrangement to fulfill their biological role.... If women are to be restless and questing, even in the face of childbearing, they must be made so through education.[20]

It was a sad irony that the impulses of women toward education and achievement should take more blows from Margaret Mead—world scholar, author, anthropologist, and wife. Only much later, in 1962, did Mead seem to awaken and wave a red flag about the cavewoman-like retreat of American women:

> Why have we returned, despite our advances in technology, to the Stone Age picture? ... Woman has gone back, each to her separate cave, waiting anxiously for her mate and children to return.... In this retreat into fecundity, it is not the individual woman who is to blame. It is the climate of opinion that has developed in this country.[21]

As Betty Friedan suggested, apparently Mead did not recognize her own role as a builder of that climate of opinion. Other builders included the educators who designed coursework along sex-role lines. Among the women students that Friedan interviewed across the country, most were resigned to being trained as homemakers. One college junior confided to Friedan:

> Ever since I was a little girl, science has had a fascination for me. I was going to major in bacteriology and go into cancer research. Now I've switched to home economics.... I'm not so intensely interested in home economics ... but I realize it was better for me to change.... I'll go home and work in a department store until I get married.[22]

America's education of its young women fell appallingly below average. Friedan quoted disturbing figures from studies on higher education for women, and warned that, "If the present situation continues, American women may soon rank among the most 'backward' women in the world."[23]

In exposing the builders of the feminine mystique, Friedan uncovered another powerful group headquartered on Madison Avenue: the "hidden persuaders" behind the marketing of household products. Housewives were, as Friedan discovered, "the chief customers of American business." Yet they held absolutely no power in the economy.[24] Friedan was not alone in stressing this paradox. As sociologist Marlene Dixon noted, "The housewife is the purchasing agent for the family.... This is not, of course, to say that she has any power in the economy. Although she spends the wealth ... it simply passes through her hands."[25]

Housewives were then making 75 percent of all purchases. *Fortune* magazine tied the big 1950s business boom to the fact that more "nubile females are marrying than ever before."[26] In the post-war push to make consumer sales take the place of profitable war contracts, marketers had turned their sites on "the psychology of housekeeping" and on young, suggestible wives. One of the men Friedan interviewed was "paid approximately a million dollars a year ... for services in manipulating the emotions of American women to serve the needs of business." Friedan was allowed to study reports and saw, in brazen terms, how wives were trained to seek the "identity, purpose ... even the sexual joy they lack—by the buying of things."[27] Excerpts from the hidden persuaders' memos spoke for themselves:

> Every effort must be made to sell X Mix, as a base upon which the woman's creative effort is used.... It might be possible to suggest through advertising that not to take advantage of all 12 uses of X Mix is to limit your efforts to give pleasure to your family. A transfer of guilt might be achieved.[28]

By making the housewife feel that her very identity and value depended on her skill as a consumer for her family, the manipulators gave her a skewed sense of "achievement" that even they saw as lacking in her "profession" of housewife: "Her time consuming task, housekeeping, is not only endless, it is a task for which society hires the lowliest, least-trained, most trod-upon individuals and groups.... Anyone with a strong enough back (and a small enough brain) can do these menial chores."[29]

Their solution was to make the housewife feel like a specialist who knew how to use "one product for washing clothes, a second for dishes, a third for walls, etc."[30] They persuaded her to identify their mundane products with "the physical and spiritual rewards she derives from the almost religious feeling of basic security provided by her home."[31]

Betty Friedan realized that these cunning marketers were not the prime creators of the feminine mystique, but they were the most ruthless force in perpetuating it. Friedan's bitter conclusion was that, "Like a primitive culture which sacrificed little girls to its tribal gods, we sacrifice our girls to the feminine mystique, grooming them ever more efficiently through the sexual sell to become consumers of the things to whose profitable sale our nation is dedicated."[32]

Friedan claimed that she "did not set out consciously to start a revolution." Her book, and her part in the women's movement, grew from her own experience in trying to conform to, then break away from, the feminine mystique:

> I didn't blame women for being scared. I was pretty scared myself. For fear of being alone, I almost lost my own self-respect trying to hold on to a marriage that was based no longer on love but on dependent hate. It was easier for me to start the women's movement which was needed to change society than to change my own personal life.[33]

In summarizing the 1950s, it is hardly a stretch to say that they became something of a dark age for women. Women lost precious hard-won footholds in all areas of life, private and public: in education, governments posts, professions spanning both the arts and sciences. It was not surprising, then, that part of the aftermath was women's absence from the major theatre awards.

In the following decades, as women moved into the light and furiously informed themselves about the world, they found the news of that world to be blazing with race riots, assassinations, and wars. Women would seize the methods of the day to create their own stages of protest and raise a new cry of feminism.

Betty Friedan's book did much to unleash the minds and voices of American women, and was a necessary prelude to the women's movement. But it was not altogether sufficient to launch and carry its momentum. A train of events through the 1960s forged a social and political climate that was ripe for the rebirth of feminism.

LEAVING HOME FOR THE REVOLUTION

Quite by accident, the American government helped lay the groundwork for a new women's movement—at about the time Betty Friedan's book appeared. A few Washington transactions backfired, and produced benefits for women not intended:

First, there was President Kennedy's Commission on the Status of Women (the last project ever headed by Eleanor Roosevelt). The Commission was formed, in part, to make up for the administration's lack of high appointments to women. But the Commission's biggest benefit was a tangential one: It spawned state commissions on women's status—almost 40 by mid-decade. Hence, growing like a mushroom was a network of women taking stock of women's place in family and society.

Another boon to the women's movement came with the Civil Rights Act of 1964. When that proposed act was hanging in the balance, a racist and sexist ploy by a Southern congressman backfired, and made women's rights a piece of that legislation. A part of the act, Title VII, banned employment discrimination on the basis of race. As a joke and a delaying tactic, Virginia representative Howard Smith urged an amendment that would ban discrimination on the basis of sex. Smith hoped it would slow or even stop the bill's passage.

However, the Civil Rights Act was eventually passed, with the amendment intact. Violations of its laws were to be handled by the EEOC—Equal Employment Opportunities Commission. When it became clear that women's grievances were being slighted, "a seething underground of women" in the government and press led a rallying cry for Betty Friedan to start "an NAACP for women." The result was NOW—the National Organization for Women—and the rise of the new women's movement, on its Phoenix-like wings.

Friedan later recalled "how pitifully few we were, how little money we had, how little experience."[34] It all started at an impromptu luncheon in Washington, with Friedan and a few of the "seething underground" of women:

> At the luncheon we each chipped in a dollar. I wrote the word "NOW" on a paper napkin; our group should be called the National Organization *for* Women, I said, because men should be part of it. Then I wrote down the first sentence of the NOW statement of purpose ... to "take *action* to bring women into full participation in the mainstream of American society now ... in truly equal partnership with men."[35]

Perhaps the biggest boon to the women's movement was the "consciousness raising group." This practice (which would appear in Wendy Wasserstein's Pulitzer play) was borrowed from the civil rights movement, where it was used to rally black solidarity and awareness. But, as Nancy Woloch explained, it also became a perfect tool for the women's movement: "Consciousness raising was at once a recruitment device, an initiation rite, and a resocializing process aimed at transforming group members' perceptions of themselves and society."[36]

All that is required for consciousness raising, said the editors of *Liberation Now!*, is at least two women, and a place to meet:

Other requisites are that those raw feelings just beneath the surface are bared, those feelings that come pouring out during 2:00-A.M. feedings ... beginning housework after a day's work outside the house; asking your husband's permission to buy something ... Feeling isolated, alienated. Or just feeling that there is a possibility that it doesn't have to be this way.[37]

Feminists were starting to realize that women needed a revolution within—a self-esteem revolution—as much an external one. More energy for both revolutions sprang from college campuses, as women marched for civil rights or protested Vietnam. Young women activists found that, even in the middle of a revolution for equal rights, they were being treated unfairly. Writer-editor Betty Roszak lamented:

Here they were, radical women involved in a struggle for human equality ... willing to dedicate years of effort to effecting political change, and what were they being allowed to do? Typing, mimeographing ... providing coffee and sexual diversion for the vigorous young men who were making all the decisions.[38]

Their frustration fostered the offshoot movement called "women's liberation." The tidal waves of women's lib and consciousness-raising may have been unleashed by women college students (who actually outnumbered men students by 1979); but they quickly washed across cities and suburbs, mobilizing housewives who both desperately desired and feared taking control of their lives. Secretly or openly, many a wife joined up, knowing that there was a risk of, as sociologist Alice Rossi noted, "tension in her marriage" if not a "threat to her marriage."[39]

Risk of losses on the home front did not prevent the swelling of the ranks of NOW, from its humble 28 in 1966 to more than 15,000 by the start of the 1970s. Betty Friedan later recalled some way stations of the movement:

Going to lunch at the for-men-only Oak Room at the Plaza Hotel with fifty NOW women and demanding to be served ... bundles of newspapers dumped onto the floor of the EEOC in protest ... against sex-segregated "Help Wanted: Male" ads (for the good jobs) and "Help Wanted: Female" ads (for the gal Friday–type jobs) ... testifying before a judge in Foley Square, because the airlines were outraged at our insistence that they were guilty of sex discrimination by forcing stewardesses to resign at age thirty or upon their marriage.[40]

Then there was the national strike of women on August 26, 1970, when thousands of women across the country linked arms and voices to bring "attention to the unfinished business of equality." In New York, Betty Friedan reported "starting that march with the hooves of policemen's horses trying to keep us confined to the sidewalk.... There were so many of us they couldn't stop us; they didn't even try."[41]

On one front, women were staging fierce battles for control of their lives through equal rights in education and employment. On another, they fought for control of their bodies—through reproductive rights. (Illegal abortions were still a desperate underground business in 1973. The Supreme Court case of *Roe vs. Wade* made headlines and history, when the outcome granted women the right to abortion in the first trimester.) After the Supreme Court sanction of contraceptives, the Pill helped to shape the sexual revolution that also rode the waves of protest.

Throughout the seventies, feminism colored politics, as laws and court decisions made bows to women's demands. Enforcing the new laws proved more difficult than enacting them. Still, Nancy Woloch noted, "the federal government in a few years made more efforts to end sex discrimination than in the entirety of the nation's history."[42]

Impacts of the women's movement were visible everywhere. For the 1972 Democratic Convention, 40 percent of the delegates were women. In education, changes in texts and curricula helped erase age-old sexual biases. Girls' sports programs finally received approval and funding. In higher education, doors to the male strongholds were cracked open and women elbowed their way in. By 1977, women were earning one out of five law degrees, and one out of six medical degrees. Women's-studies courses, introduced in the late 1960s, were expanded into full programs.[43]

From the mid-'60s until 1981, one galvanizing force of the women's movement was the ERA—Equal Rights Amendment—a simple 52-word clause intended to make sexual equality part of the law of the land. Although the national ERA was finally defeated, the fight for it spurred states and cities to enact equal-rights measures.

Not surprisingly, marriage and birth rates took sharp plunges during the women's movement, while divorce soared by 80 percent. This was a reflection of women's new independence, but also a meter of how false the '50s image of domestic bliss had been. In the 1970s, half of all marriages ended in divorce—but four out of five divorced women remarried. Women were not flatly rejecting marriage; rather, they were giving more thought to it, and refusing to remain in a compromised relationship. At last, women were making choices in shaping their own lives.[44]

"Choices" is the key word. Even the most radical feminists of the movement conceded that "a lifetime as a wife and mother may well be the choice of many women—what we are saying is that we are not given the choice."[45]

The main thrust of the movement was exactly that: to secure for women the right to choose, the gift of self-determination. The life-and-death importance of choice is vividly sketched in the Pulitzer plays of the next three playwrights—Henley, Norman, and Wasserstein.

Beth Henley finished *Crimes of the Heart* in 1978, when the spirit of the women's movement was waning but still palpable. Her three main characters, the Mississippi-raised MaGrath sisters, stage something of their own women's movement. They struggle toward self-determination and self-esteem in ways that are both deadly serious and wildly funny, which makes them perfect examples of how Beth Henley has viewed life and translated it for the stage.

11

Beth Henley's Funny-Terrible World View

In a black-walled studio theatre, much like other "black box" theatre spaces in Chicago, Beth Henley is perched on a chair (also black) in a lotus-like position. She still looks younger than 29 years, the age at which she garnered the Pulitzer Prize in 1981. She reads from the notebook balanced on her knee,

> My name is Anton Chekhov.... I am involved in this workshop because I believe that art increases our awareness of the beautifulness and the horribleness of life. I have written some short stories and a few plays. I'm from Florence; my parents were both painters.... I have fond memories of singing around the piano. Personal situation: I am very much in love with an artist named Georgia O'Keefe.... We have three beautiful children. My Fear: That a lifetime is not long enough to satisfy all my needs for love, art, and enlightenment.[1]

Obviously, this is not a thumbnail autobiography by the famed Russian playwright. Rather, it is Beth's version of her own assignment, given on the first day of her playwriting workshop at Center Theater. Beth has asked members to write briefly around the questions: What is your best fantasy? Your worst nightmare? What is your personal situation? What are your dreams? Your fears? And why are you in this class? Answers are a blend of fact and fantasy, assumed identity and real self. Beth switches identity gears, and shares her more real response with the class:

> My name is Beth Henley.... I've never done a workshop. I don't know what the fuck I'm doing. I'm afraid you'll find out that I'm

Beth Henley

a phony in sheepskin clothing.... My personal life is fine.... I have a dog, Chippee. We had a Christmas card made up together; Chippee wore this cute little hat. My dream is to be married to a wonderful man ... but I can write lots of plays that are big hits and he'll still love me anyway.

Despite her uncertainties, Beth's workshops are a hit and become repeated events in Chicago and elsewhere. In workshops, she tends to preach what she practices as a playwright:

> What I want to let you try ... is your sense of place, of character, of conflict, and stakes. Stakes are very important in drama: Even something kind of small, like a writer's workshop, can be a life and death thing. Everyone has this need, to show they're worthwhile. I think *stakes* are important; and *secrets*, too. What secrets characters keep from each other ...
>
> This is what I do sometimes when I'm working.... You have a place written down, like a setting ... and why it would be a good place for a play. And then you write: a page for conflicts; a page for characters; a page for stakes; a page for secrets; a page for senses.

Another part of this assignment is to write "*five tasks* you could do in this place ... If it's a garden, maybe pulling weeds. If it's a kitchen—cutting lemons."

In Beth's play *Crimes of the Heart*, the act of cutting lemons in a kitchen is indeed laden with high stakes. Her character Babe Botrelle, who's fond of lemonade with lots of sugar, has cut up ten lemons for a pitcher of lemonade. The trouble is, Babe has done this right after shooting her husband, Zackery, in the stomach. Hence, the split image: Zackery, oozing blood on the living room rug; Babe slurping lemonade in the kitchen. Henley paints this ironic picture through Babe's vivid recount of the event for her attorney, Barnette. What puts a cap on the image, and makes Henley's comedy inch toward the absurd, is that Babe actually offers a glass of lemonade to Zackery while he's oozing blood on the rug.

Henley's place for high stakes can be a common-enough family setting; but her stage families rally around an uncommon event: a shooting, a beauty pageant, a debutante ball. She uncovers the humor behind the shooting and the horror that haunts the ball. Beth's knack for split images—for jumbling the grotesque and gothic together with the simple and familiar—is largely derived from her Southern roots. (The South holds its own split images, of graceful belles against a backdrop of war, of cool mint juleps against heated racial tension, of tranquil gardens against the brute force of hurricanes.) The crosscurrents of the South have greatly influenced Beth's writing. So have the dynamics of family: About her major plays, she comments, "I seem to have been driven to explore different Southern families in different situations.... Maybe the plays are all variations on the same theme."[2]

At least, her characters and themes hold common traits: "I think practically everyone in my plays is searching for a family."[3] She tends to explore "how people need love so badly that the need cripples them in their struggles to attain it." A big hurdle in the struggle, as Beth puts it, is "overcoming ghosts of the past and letting go of what other people have said you are, what they have told you to be."[4] Typically, her characters most in need of overcoming ghosts are women.

Beth Henley has had to overcome some ghosts of her own past. Looking at her now, it's hard to believe her claim that she was a "shy and lonely fat kid" back in Jackson, Mississippi, a kid whose allergies often forced her to get shots and stay in bed. "At night, Mama'd come into my room and ask me why I was crying. I'd tell her I was pretending to be Heidi."[5]

"Mama" was Lydy Becker Caldwell, an important force in bringing Beth to a life in the theatre. Lydy was an actress at Jackson's New Stage and other regional theatres. Beth would linger over scripts and tag along to watch her mother rehearse. "I just loved going to the theatre and ... watching. I thought it was glamorous. She'd come out in this green dress and stand on stage and get kissed by a man. I thought it was the most wonderful thing for a mother to do."[6]

Her mother and her lawyer-congressman father were both from small Mississippi towns—Hazlehurst and Brookhaven—that would serve as settings for Beth's plays. Being one of four daughters also gave Beth a wealth of insights about the love-hate relationship of sisters, which she would weave into *Crimes of the Heart*.

Beth maintains that, in high school, "I was a mediocre student, I was terribly shy, I didn't go to homecoming."[7] Her parents' divorce in those years did not help Beth's shyness or isolation. (Still, she pulled a few adolescent stunts, like dying her hair orange and getting ejected from movie houses.) Her love of the stage pulled her into a theatre major at Southern Methodist University, where she pursued acting. She was studying playwrights, and said that "the veils of the mind lifted" on seeing stagings of Chekhov, Shaw, and Albee. "This was alive theatre, someone bringing you in touch with a world you hadn't understood before."[8]

But Beth's first play, *Am I Blue*, was the result of a playwriting course she took just to avoid a class in scene design. The one-act features two youths who've been bounced from a New Orleans bar for being underage. Quirky 16-year-old Ashbe—wearing red galoshes and cat-eye glasses—invites John Polk to the cluttered flat she shares with her absent alcoholic father. John is a serious business student with two hours to kill before his frightening appointment with a prostitute (an eighteenth-birthday gift from his frat brothers). The two lonely teens gradually move from exchanges of insults to a fragile connection. When the play was produced her senior year, Beth was still shy and uncertain of its merit; so she used a pseudonym— "Amy Peach." A decade later, after the play had been done at Hartford Stage and elsewhere, Beth reminisced,

> When I wrote *Am I Blue*, I was so emotionally covered up that I didn't even realize what I was saying about myself or about life or loneliness, family situations.... When I went back to it, I was so glad I'd written it down because I'll never be that innocent again.[9]

With her B.F.A. in hand, and still set on acting, Beth performed with a Dallas repertory group while doing odd jobs, like photographing kids for a large store. Then, dreams of breaking into films made her drop out of the University of Illinois' graduate school and head for Los Angeles. Reality set in when film studios would not hire her, but a dog food factory did. Beth found it impossible to land auditions. "I couldn't cope with the business side of acting much less the rejection."[10]

Her frustration compelled her to return to scriptwriting; but in Los Angeles, the logical form is the screenplay. So Beth wrote one, about a small-town girl who is lured to L.A. when a suave set designer passes through her town. "But no one at the studios would read [it] because I didn't have an agent," Beth lamented; "so I thought I would write a stage play that might at least get performed in a small theatre somewhere. That's when I wrote *Crimes of the Heart*."[11]

To help her chances of production, Beth kept to one set and six characters. For her three protagonists, the MaGrath sisters, she drew on her own experiences as a sibling:

> My little sister I've always just adored. My other two sisters were closer in age, so we always ganged up against each other. We had horrible, normal battles.... I don't know whether we loved each other more than most sisters, or whether we hated each other more than most.[12]

The play's three MaGrath sisters seem to love and resent each other with equal gusto. But each sister is ready to bolster the others through depression and trouble, which run rampant among MaGrath women. (Their mother hung herself along with her pet cat, after their father hit the road.) The big trouble in the play is that the youngest sister, Babe, has shot her lawyer husband "slap in the gut." This, plus the stroke that fells Old Granddaddy, reunites the three sisters: Lenny, the eldest, who has become Granddaddy's live-in caretaker; Meg, whose muddled pursuit of a singing career has ended badly in L.A.; and Babe, who has resorted to near-homicide to end the abusive "society" marriage that Old Granddaddy contrived for her.

Contrasted with these three protagonists is their antagonistic cousin, Chick. The play's cast ratio of four women to two men is the upshot of another influence on Beth's writing.

> I had women friends who were actresses and wanted parts and, you know, there seemed to be a lack of them.... I don't know why women always have to be supporting characters ... or just *one* woman in a play with five or ten men. So I'm proud of that. I'm happy that I've given women an opportunity to have leads.[13]

Crimes of the Heart was the first of four major plays set in Beth's home state. They hold bizarre images derived from Beth's vantage point on the violence that is peculiar to Mississippi:

> I think violence happens everywhere ... but there seems to be something scary about Mississippi; it just feels—different. [Violence] does seem to be prevalent. I mean, I went home and one of my mother's friends had just been hit in the head with a hatchet by

her son on Halloween—it *was* Halloween when I came—and he had lit all these green candles and played the organ around her.[14]

Whenever Beth steps off the plane in Mississippi, the incredible stories are "in the air":

> Oh, Lord, the stories I hear ... there are dope fiends living next door. Hermits live over here. The police are out after people breaking in windows. Somebody's drowned, and somebody's shot themselves. And that's just the houses on my block.[15]

This in part accounts for Beth's fascination with certain sordid images: of death, deformity, and violence with a twist. But her vision does not end there. Because, for example, alongside the array of dark images in *Crimes*— a bloody shooting, a dead horse, Mama's suicide, Old Granddaddy's coma— there is also a parade of happy images, like pecan pies, moonlight rides, shared memories, and birthday cakes. Henley may focus on horror, but not without hope. She takes the good with the bad, even when it's very bad: "The grotesque combined with the innocent, a child walking with a cane, a kitten with a swollen head, a hunchback drinking a cup of fruit punch. Somehow these images are a metaphor for my view of life. They're colorful."[16]

While much of the colorful plot of *Crimes* was pure invention, the memory of one family crisis did help to shape the play: While Beth was in college, her grandfather disappeared on his farm. "He fell off his horse, and it came back without him." The family converged to form search parties, until he turned up unharmed. Beth says the feeling of uniting in a family crisis "started me thinking."[17] But she adds that her views of crisis veer toward the comic, in spite of herself:

> All these things that I feel inside are desperate and dark and unhappy. Or not unhappy but searching. Then they come out funny. The way my family dealt with hardships was to see the humor or the ironic point of view in the midst of tragedy. And that's just how *my* mind works.[18]
>
> I like to read Chekhov and Shakespeare ... great tragedies; but in my own writing I can't see the situations I look at without laughing. I back into comedy. I can't help it.[19]

With *Crimes of the Heart*, Beth Henley "backed into" comedy and an amazing sweep of awards, an outcome she never imagined. After finishing *Crimes*, Beth had met with a round of rejections from theatres. Then, a friend secretly entered her script into the Great American Play Festival at Actors Theatre of Louisville. It was produced and named co-winner for

1979. What struck artistic director Jon Jory was that "most American playwrights want to expose human beings. Beth Henley embraces them." And Beth's comedy "didn't come from one character, but from between the characters."[20] Still, before the play's first preview in Louisville, Beth had the jitters: "I was waiting out in the parking lot ... and all these people showed up, dressed up. They were paying money to see my show, without having any idea what it was like. I just started crying."[21]

Those dressed-up people liked her play so much that it was picked up by other regional theatres. And Beth acquired what had eluded her as an actress; namely, an agent. But New York theatres still played hard to get: Rejections included one from Lynne Meadow at Manhattan Theatre Club. That's when fate stepped in again—or Beth backed into it—when director Melvin Bernhardt took a liking to her play. Bernhardt (a Tony winner for *Da*) told Meadow that he wanted to direct *Crimes of the Heart*, and Meadow did a turnabout. The off–Broadway production opened in December 1980, featuring Mary Beth Hurt and Mia Dillon. Houses were full, responses were hearty, and a chorus of critics sang Henley's praises. In *New York*, John Simon cheered: "From time to time a play comes along that restores one's faith in our theatre. This time it is *Crimes of the Heart* by Beth Henley, a new playwright of charm, warmth ... and authentically individual wisdom."[22]

Even before *Crimes* moved to the Golden Theatre on Broadway, it won the Pulitzer Prize. Editors of *Notable Women in the American Theatre* said this made it the only play to win the award "prior to a Broadway opening."[23] Actually, this was not the case; it shared that distinction with Glaspell's *Alison's House*. (Beth also shared with Zona Gale the distinction of winning the prize with her first full-length play, a feat later matched by Maggie Edson.)

For Beth, receiving the Pulitzer was "the moon"—"I was very excited and thrilled."[24] And, she adds, surprised: "One day, the phone rang, and a voice said, 'This is the Associated Press. Do you know you've won the Pulitzer Prize?' My sweetie was sitting there, and he said my face went through about five different emotions." They celebrated by getting drunk with friends, then getting more drunk at home. Television interviewers were on their way, Beth recalled: "So a friend of mine put me in this nice-looking outfit and pearls ... And told me not to have anything else to drink. By the time the television people came, I don't know if they thought it was liquor or just ecstasy."[25]

Beth was the first woman in 23 years to win the Drama Pulitzer. That acclaim was followed by the Drama Critics' Circle Award for best play, which made her the first woman in 21 years to take that honor. By then,

Beth also had a million-dollar contract for the rights and for writing her own screenplay of *Crimes*, to be directed by Jonathan Demme.

On the eve of her play's reopening at the Golden, Beth was struck by a new apprehension. "I hate the pressure of feeling that the play has to be seen as really great instead of just an enjoyable evening in the theatre."[26] But her play was hailed as both: the *New Yorker*'s Brendan Gill declared, "Though it is Miss Henley's first play, it has a daffy complexity ... that old pros like Kaufman and Hart would have envied."[27] The *Saturday Review* alleged that "the Pulitzer Prize for Drama is looking up a little, anyway."[28] (Quite a compliment, since the preceding Pulitzers had gone to Sam Shepard and Lanford Wilson.) The *Times* critic proclaimed that *Crimes* overflowed "with infectious high spirits."[29] It proved infectious enough to run for 535 performances, then take stages in Los Angeles, England, France, and Australia.[30]

A few reviews of *Crimes*, and subsequent Henley plays, have complained that too much action takes place offstage and is merely reported. However, this could be seen as a stylistic choice—and strength. Beth's comedy crystallizes in the reporting of events. Her recountings are so delightfully personalized by the recounters that it becomes a great device for revealing character. Vivid examples in *Crimes* include Babe's replay of shooting Zackery (rife with blood and lemonade), and Meg's recall of her own mental breakdown in L.A. Counted among Henley's strengths must be her exercise of audience imagination and her stubborn belief in the power of words to evoke images.

With the huge success of her first play, Beth had gained the freedom to write, and the assurance that her dog-food factory days were over: "Just being awarded the luxury of being able to make a living at something you love was a great gift."[31]

However, like others before her, Beth discovered a down side to winning: "I think it was hard getting a lot of notoriety when I was young and not really that sure of myself as a writer."[32] There were impacts on her family too: Beth's mother was accosted by people who recognized themselves in the play's characters, people whom Beth had never even met. To Beth's sister, C.C., one woman blurted, "You're just as smart as your sister; why don't you go out and get you one of those Pulitzer Prizes?"[33] Beth's father did not live to see her success or change his evaluation of her writing: "He thought the work was completely abysmal," she says. "He didn't see me as a writer."[34]

When Beth visited back home, and old lukewarm acquaintances turned suddenly friendly, she "felt false.... I thought, why do they like me now? They didn't like me then."[35] Still, having her play staged there, and such "a big hit," was a satisfying thrill. "It's like something you wish in high school, being so shy, not really making good grades."[36]

Crimes was still on Broadway when Beth's next play, *The Wake of Jamie Foster*, opened at the O'Neill in late 1982. This time, her stage family gathered for the title character's funeral: Foster, who dreamed of being a great historian, has met with a shameful death (he was kicked in the head by a cow), after a roll in a field with his mistress. Again, Henley's cast was replete with roles for women. They represented, by her design, "different images of women in their state of fertility: Marshael, who has had children; Katty who wants to but can't; Collard who'd had the abortion; and Pixrose, the virgin who dreams."[37]

Most critics, like Brendan Gill, judged *The Wake* to be a "clumsy reworking ... of Miss Henley's excellent earlier play."[38] The play's closing, after 12 performances, was perhaps another down side of winning. As Beth put it in our interview, "It's never the same.... They judge each play by your previous play; and it's like they've got a litany of testimony for and against you, which wasn't true your first time out."[39]

Elsewhere, Beth commented, "I think the fate of *The Wake* ... is part of the cost of winning. They just make sure you don't get overwhelmed by it. 'They' meaning the Fates, not necessarily the critics."[40]

One critic, Clive Barnes of the *New York Post*, defended Henley's efforts with *Wake*. He argued that other artists are allowed to have an individual style; yet if playwrights develop a trademark voice, they're attacked for being repetitious.[41] As Beth herself phrased it, "No one said, 'Degas, don't paint anymore ballerinas.'"[42]

The opinion of critics aside, for Beth herself, her themes are always "exquisitely different ... glittering colors that I've seen but haven't dealt with fully before."[43] This is a fitting image for Beth's play *The Miss Firecracker Contest*. Its action even culminates at a Fourth-of-July carnival. This time, the play's family rallies around a beauty contest in Brookhaven. The main character, Carnelle, is desperate to win it with her baton-twirling and tap-dancing act. Her cousin Elain is a former Miss Firecracker, on the run from a stifling marriage. Elain's high-strung brother, Delmount, has returned to sell his inherited house, in which Carnelle is living. At his offer to split the proceeds so she can get out of Brookhaven, Carnelle is hesitant: She might go, if she can just win the contest and leave in a "crimson blaze of glory."[44]

In his review of *Miss Firecracker*, the *Times* critic, Frank Rich, quipped that:

> This time, we hear about midgets, orphans and deformed kittens— and they're the fortunate ones. Other characters, whether on stage

or off, are afflicted by cancer, tuberculosis, venereal disease and, most of all, heartbreak, Even so, the the evening's torrential downpour of humor ... almost never subsides.[45]

Again, Beth's dip into despairing images was offset by things giddy and gaudy and oddly meaningful—like an outrageous red antebellum dress, and bullfrogs in tiny clothes. (Beth took the latter conceit from her family: An aunt actually sewed costumes for frogs.[46])

The Miss Firecracker Contest provided a tour-de-force showcase for high-powered actress Holly Hunter. So perfect was Hunter for the role of Carnelle and other off-center Henley heroines, that the association between playwright and actress has become a lasting dynamic duo. "Everybody thinks of us in tandem," says Hunter.[47] Their first encounter was an aptly comic crisis: The two women were trapped between floors in an elevator when Hunter was rushing to meet Henley at the behest of a casting director. The rest became stage and screen history.

The Miss Firecracker Contest had been guided to success by director Stephen Tobolowsky, Henley's significant other since college. Tobolowsky also staged her next play, *The Debutante Ball*, set in an opulent Southern parlor and a bathroom. Henley used the split image to reveal the animal within the socialite, the "many scars" and "many secrets" of the debutante's family, who gather for the event. While the besieged debutante Teddy almost self-destructs (she slashes herself with a cheese knife and has a miscarriage in her ball gown), her mother Jen tries to overcome a past scandal: Jen was once tried for killing her husband with a frying pan.

Henley's split-image humor has made an easy transition to film. Before she had translated *Miss Firecracker* into a four-star film with Holly Hunter and Mary Steenburgen, Beth had already scored film kudos. Her screenplay of *Crimes of the Heart* (starring Diane Keaton, Jessica Lange, and Sissy Spacek) was nominated for an Academy Award. Her 1986 film *Nobody's Fool* was Beth's revamp of her first screenplay, written in 1977. Rosanna Arquette played the small-town girl who is lured to L.A. by a charismatic set-designer (Eric Roberts).

Beth relishes the power of film in evoking location. "Films allow you to do that in a way theatre doesn't."[48] Still, she has never lost her awe of theatre's intimacy and immediacy:

> I think certain things are more effective on stage ... A character slashes her face with a razor blade. That's very effective on stage.... I think nudity on stage is more potent, because it's a live person right there.... There are certain things, like cutting lemons on stage—

that's more potent because it's right there. You can see the squirt of lemon, maybe smell the lemon.[49]

Luckily for her audiences, Henley has remained stagestruck: "I think I'm born for the theatre," she admits. "It's so alive. Audiences can pull it one way or another, and after the play you can go out and talk."[50] In recent years, talking has held Beth in good stead, in her workshops and pep talks with fellow artists. She is even considered a "den mother" to a group of theatre and film artists based in Los Angeles. Beth gives one-on-one support, too: When long-time friend, Colleen Dodson, did her one-woman show in Chicago, Beth gladly served as supervisor. "I felt honored I could help.... I love artists and try to be helpful if I'm able to."[51]

Of women who have mentored or inspired her, Beth's list includes "my mother, Carson McCullers, Eudora Welty, Lillian Hellman," with Hellman being a key writing inspiration. "I was really fascinated by her. It's sad to say that most playwrights we study have been men."[52] Beth realizes how fortunate she has been, since discrimination still looms for women playwrights:

> Yes, I think there is [discrimination] because there are still a lot more men than women in charge of our theatres, producing, directing.... Men generally can't help but be more moved by a man's play because they relate to it in a personal way. Women are more used to identifying with men, because they're raised on it, they've got to be.[53]

Beth's feminist impulses emerged early in life, from seeing her mother "trapped in with all that talent she had, by kids and husband and the world." Beth insured herself against a similar fate: "I didn't learn how to cook or sew ... things that would make me something I didn't want to be."[54] In my post-interview correspondence with Beth, she wrote, "I am a radical feminist." Still, she balks at labels because she feels "categorizing artists can dwarf their gifts."[55]

But no label could dwarf Henley's gift for what one writer called her "comically apocalyptic vision."[56] And the bulk of her work has been feminist. As Karen Jaehne noted in *Film Comment*: "Since Henley's first play, *Crimes of the Heart* ... she has analyzed the ways women conform to or rebel against standards of femininity, standards more rigid than the Honor Code at Notre Dame."[57]

Beth's characters may not be knowing emblems of feminism. In a *Modern Drama* article on Henley's women, "Aborted Rage," Alan Shepard wrote,

> Henley's heroines seem not to recognize as such the feminist awakenings that bubble to the surfaces of their consciousness, as

they seek to repair and preserve their lives within the system they have inherited.... Osmotically, the heroines have absorbed some of the energies of the feminist movement, and in their own ways, they grope toward liberty.[58]

From a less political viewpoint (since Beth claims she wants to "look at the world," not change it), her work explores the struggles of women as they search for family, for love and belonging. Quite often, the love they need most is self-love; the struggle they wage most valiantly is for self-esteem. A Beth Henley credo (noted earlier) is that: "Self-esteem is the only thing that can save a woman from the traps of other people's definitions."[59]

Beth's women don't always succeed in eluding those traps, especially in her plays of the last decade. Her comedy vision has grown darker, and wider. At times, she has abandoned her Southern setting and has even allowed a male protagonist or two: In *Abundance*, she takes a searing look back at the shocking plight of two mail-order brides of the frontier West—women warring against deprivation and their inhuman status as chattel. Their beauty and dreams are disfigured; they end up as little more than freaks in a sideshow. In *Control Freaks*, the protagonist "Sister" is trapped in a sadistic, incestuous bondage to her brother, Carl. The play's mood is surreal, the language startling in its poetry: Sister despairs to the audience, "I have scars on my tonsils from secret screaming."[60]

In Beth's even more abstract *Signature*, she satirizes a futuristic Hollywood, where people can line up at a Pharmaceutical Distribution Center to get their "emotional equalizers" and "pain executioners." Main characters are the two T-Thorp brothers; but the title refers to the character of the Reader, whose scam is reading lives from people's signatures.

Beth Henley ended the twentieth century with an off–Broadway comedy, *Impossible Marriage*, that was a more typical blend of humor and heartbreak. Its setting was again a Southern family, a triangle of a mother and two daughters. Holly Hunter played the "immensely pregnant" Floral, bent on halting the marriage of her sister to an older philandering man. (Since Floral's pregnancy is not the result of her own asexual marriage, complications abound.)

While Beth was busy suggesting what an impossible enterprise marriage can be, she was pregnant with her son Patrick. She tried to take her mother's advice—to write a happy play—but "it ended up being sadder" than intended. "I guess that's how life is," says Beth.[61]

Life for Beth's own family has taken some extremely sad turns in recent years. In 1996, Beth's teenaged nephew, Craig, was murdered in Jackson in an unsolved crime. And in fall 2002, Beth's mother—actress Lydy

Caldwell—was stabbed to death during a break-in at her Jackson home. It took the true grit of the Henley family to recall, in that dark hour, the brightness of Lydy's irrepressible humor and generous spirit. Close friends described her as being "funnier than any stand-up comedian." In an earlier news item, Beth had stressed how her mother "brought out the humorous side of things, instead of the tragic or banal ... even in the most ghastly situations."[62]

Things close to home and family have continued to inform Beth's plays; and still, she takes the good with the bad. Her play *Family Week* (2000) is set in a recovery center in a nameless desert, where dysfunctional patients gather with family for a therapeutic retreat. A main character, Claire, is trying to reclaim who she was before her teenaged son was killed in an unsolved murder. Claire's family members—mother, sister, daughter—bring their own emotional baggage. A few wounds get healed in the play, but it ranks as one of Beth's darkest comedies. (Critic Elyse Sommer called its billing as a comedy "misleading," but found some "quirky" Henley humor in it.[63])

Beth's newest play, *Exposed*, had staged readings and workshops at Arena Stage in Washington, the New York Theatre Workshop, and at Vassar's Powerhouse Theatre (all in 2003). In a phone conversation with Beth, she described *Exposed* as "very expressionistic":

> It takes place in Los Angeles at the winter solstice. So it's the darkest and longest night of the year. And it's about a kind of disparate group of people that, through coincidence and otherwise, intertwine: A married couple, and the man's mistress. Then the mistress's lover—a young man and his friends—they're from a foster home. So it's these desperate people ... trying to get through a very dark night.[64]

Beth has commented that writing "helps me feel not so angry." But she also has claimed, on a lighter note, that "all writing is creating or spinning dreams for other people so they won't have to bother doing it for themselves." When asked what dreams she has helped to spin for women through her plays, Beth answers, "Embrace life now—even though it's not perfect."[65] That slogan might serve as the motto for the MaGrath sisters at the end of *Crimes of the Heart*. Despite whatever disasters they face tomorrow, for a few sweet carefree moments, the sisters rejoice in life and each other, and in a perfectly decadent birthday cake.

Perhaps what makes Beth Henley's work so appealing is her relentless reminder that life is perched on a split between the hilarious and the horrific, and we need to keep our balance.

THE PLAY—CRIME IS IN THE EYE OF THE BEHOLDER

Act One lights come up on the large, cluttered MaGrath kitchen in Hazlehurst ("five years after Hurricane Camille"). Lenny comes in the back door and sets down a suitcase, saxophone case, and a small sack. She removes birthday candles from the sack, and is trying to stick a candle into a cookie, when Cousin Chick yells from the door, then barges in. Chick snarls that she won't be able to "hold her head up" after today's news reports. She collects the pantyhose that she had Lenny fetch in town, and while pulling them on, she tells Lenny that they've got to get over to pick up Babe. But Lenny is loathe to leave the phone: She has wired her sister Meg to come home (from L.A.) and hopes Meg will at least call. Outraged that Meg will add to the "mighty negative publicity" around town, Chick agrees that Lenny should stay, but to stop Meg from coming. Chick remembers that she has a birthday gift for Lenny—a box of chocolates.[66]

As Chick goes, Doc Porter arrives, with fresh pecans for Lenny, and more bad news. Lenny's horse Billy Boy, who was boarded with Doc, was struck dead yesterday by lightning. Doc is sympathetic to Lenny's tears; but when he hears Meg might be coming, he's interested in spite of himself. "I'd like to see her ... sad to say, but I would." After he goes, Lenny returns to her cookie project and sings "Happy Birthday" to herself till the phone rings. It's Babe's sister-in-law, reporting that Zackery's liver is spared, but his spinal cord is in question. Lenny hangs up with a sigh.

The "family whistle" is heard, and to Lenny's amazement, Meg walks in. After hugs and greetings, Lenny exclaims that they've taken Babe to jail; they're saying she shot Zackery. To Meg's question, "*Who's* saying it?" Lenny responds, "Everyone! ... even Babe is saying it." And the only reason Babe will give is that she "didn't like his looks." Meg insists that they must get Babe the best lawyer in town. Unfortunately, that would be Zackery. But Lenny assures her they already have a lawyer—the Lloyd boy suggested by Uncle Watson—who's getting Babe out on bail, now.

Meg is surprised to hear that Old Granddaddy is in the hospital, and admits she has not read Lenny's letters; they give her "slicing pains." Asked how her singing career is going, Meg replies that it's not; she's been clerking at a dog-food company. When Meg asks where the pecans came from, Lenny reluctantly tells her from Doc (Meg's old flame, now married, with two "half–Yankee" kids). After Chick returns, ranting at Babe whom she has collected, Chick and Meg exchange insults. Word comes that Chick's children have eaten their paint, and Chick and Lenny dash off.

Alone with Meg, Babe relays the awful things Chick has said: That their mother's suicide had been embarrassing to her; now Babe's crime is, too. They sadly recall how their mother incurred publicity, by hanging herself and her cat after their bastard daddy left. Meg prods Babe about why she shot Zackery, but Babe is "sort of protecting someone." Babe remarks that Lenny seems old already, sleeping on a cot to be near Granddaddy, getting fussy. Meg thinks that Lenny's "shrunken ovary" makes her shy with men; and Granddaddy has "made her self-conscious about it ... the old fool." But Babe reports that Lenny did meet one man via "lonely hearts": She even spent a weekend in Memphis with Charlie, before she broke it off. The cheap candy from Chick suddenly reminds them to order a cake for Lenny. But Barnette Lloyd arrives, and Babe flees upstairs, leaving Meg to talk to him. He may be a new lawyer, but he is very motivated; he has his own vendetta against Zackery. He also has evidence—Babe's medical reports—suggesting she shot him in self-defense. Outraged at the reports, Meg tells him to return later, and yells for Babe.

Babe reluctantly admits to Zackery's abuse, and discloses who she is protecting: the son of her cleaning woman—the black boy with whom Babe has had an affair. After she agreed to keep Willie Jay's dog for him, things just "started up" between them. Then, one day, she and Willie Jay were playing with Dog when Zackery came home and assaulted Willie. Babe went inside and, almost automatically, took out the gun they keep for burglars. She put it to her head, then realized that she didn't want to kill herself; she wanted to kill her husband. This made her think their Mama might have felt the same way. But Babe actually picked up a gun and shot Zackery. Meg says it's a "good thing," and starts to call Barnette. Babe slams the phone in the refrigerator, then relents, and hands the phone to Meg.

As Act Two opens, Babe is eating oatmeal while Barnette questions her. "You've just shot one Zackery Botrelle, as a result of his continual ... abuse—what happens now?" Bit by bit, Babe tells him how she was dying of thirst, went to the kitchen, and made lemonade. She gulped three glasses, then went to offer one to Zackery. He was writhing on the floor, gesturing for her to call the hospital, which she finally did. Babe fears that she's on the "brink of doom"; but Barnette is warmly reassuring. When Zackery calls, claiming he has "blackening evidence" on Babe, Barnette says he'll go right to the hospital. Before going, he tells Babe of his own vendetta against Zackery, who ruined his father.

Lenny enters, fuming that Meg lied to Granddaddy at the hospital, telling him she had made a movie and a record. On finding that Meg has sampled all her candy, Lenny unfurls old childhood anger about Meg, who always seemed to get what she wanted. Babe reminds her that Meg was the one who found their mother's body: She had cried for a week, then started a binge of strange behavior, staring at disgusting photos to stop "being a weak person." They also recall how Meg baited Doc into staying through Hurricane Camille, then left him for Los Angeles.

After Meg returns with bourbon and a newspaper (which Babe starts clipping), Meg erupts to Lenny, "All right—I lied." Granddaddy looked so pathetic, she says, that she couldn't help it, although she hates herself when she lies for that "old bossy man." Babe's work on her scrapbook evokes shared memories and a momentary truce. They decide to play cards, like old times. But a call from Doc sets Meg to primping for his arrival and renews Lenny's rage at Meg. Meg counters that it's not her fault if Lenny has had no men—or "maybe just that one from Memphis." At this, Lenny turns on Babe for revealing this secret. But it's out now, so Meg pushes further: Has Lenny asked this man if he cares that she can't have kids? Lenny storms upstairs, crying, and Babe follows.

Meg is drinking bourbon when Doc arrives. She pours him a drink, and Doc broaches the old question of why Meg left? She tells him that she didn't want to care, but did anyway. She recounts how she could not sing, then went crazy and wound up in a mental ward. Doc lifts the mood with, "There's a moon out," and persuades her to take a ride in his truck. When Babe comes down to find them gone, she blows notes on her saxophone until Barnette returns. He shows her Zackery's "blackening evidence"— photos of Babe in the garage with Willie, taken by a hired detective. Aghast, Babe "bangs herself hopelessly into the stove" while Barnette tries to soothe her. Lenny comes down, with more bad news: Granddaddy has had another stroke.

Act Three opens the next morning. As Babe and Lenny return from the hospital, Chick pops in with a list of people to call about Granddaddy, who's fallen into a coma. After she leaves, Babe and Lenny are listing their woes when Meg enters, singing and hobbling on a broken heel. At Lenny's glare, Meg blurts that "nothing happened"; no fantasy about Doc came true. Yet she is happy, just to feel that she could care for someone—and she sang, all night.

At the mention of Old Granddaddy, Meg vows that she'll do the right thing and tell him the truth, even if it puts him in a coma. At this, Babe and Lenny share a look and dissolve into helpless laughter—because it's "too late!" After they settle down, Lenny sighs that she'll be so alone in the house, now. Her sisters badger her to go out, to call this Charlie.... What does she have to lose? Lenny goes off to call; meanwhile, Meg gets word that Lenny's cake is ready. But before she leaves to get it, Babe shows her the incriminating photos. Barnette arrives; he admits that the photos had him worried, but he now has papers that could prove Zackery guilty of "graft, fraud and forgery." They might settle out of court, which is good for Babe, but bad for Barnette's planned vendetta. (He doesn't mind; he has come to care for Babe.)

After Meg and Barnette leave, Lenny comes down; she just couldn't make the call. Chick enters, oozing false sympathy for Lenny over Meg's behavior. She saw Meg stumble from Doc's truck. "I mean, to have a sister like that," she huffs. This time, Lenny gets riled up and builds to a quick boil. She grabs a broom, and shrieking, "Get out!" she paddles Chick out into the yard.

Babe is alone when Zackery calls, threatening to have her declared insane. Distraught, Babe pulls a rope from a drawer, and mutters "I'll do it ... I will." Lenny re-enters, smug and laughing over Chick. She feels daring enough to phone Charlie now. As it turns out, he is not fond of "snot-nosed" kids anyway, and they make a date. Elated, Lenny floats out to the yard. There's a terrible thud, then Babe comes downstairs, the torn rope dangling from her neck. Frustrated, she goes to the oven, turns on the gas and sticks her head in. Just as she mumbles something about why Mama "done it," Meg enters with the cake. She quickly pulls Babe from the oven and tends to her, while Babe describes Zackery's call. Meg assures Babe that she's as sane as anyone in Hazlehurst; Zackery is only bluffing. Babe calms down enough to share her revelation with Meg: She knows, now, why Mama hung her cat along with herself; she was afraid to die alone.

Meg exclaims that they've got to learn how to "get through these real bad days." She helps Babe realize how much she wants to stay alive—to surprise Lenny and all. Meg gets Babe to light the candles on the cake, while she fetches Lenny. The astonished Lenny can't think of any wish. When she finally does, it's not so much a wish as a vision of the three of them—smiling and laughing together—which is exactly what they're doing now, while scooping up mounds of birthday cake. They are suspended like this, in a "golden, sparkling glimmer," before the stage goes to black.

The real crime among the MaGrath sisters is their runaway lack of self-esteem, a lack they seem to have inherited from their mother, who was made to feel so worthless by their father that she erased herself altogether. But the same bossy patriarch who raised their self-effacing mother has also raised the sisters: Old Granddaddy is an offstage villain in their battles for self-esteem. (A relevant note is that he is the sisters' maternal grandfather; Henley has confirmed this. She also says that her characters—even off-stage—are "more than real" for her ... "more real than people you might get to know."[67])

Old Granddaddy contrived the marriage of Babe at 18 to Zackery Botrelle, in what was—as Meg recalls—Granddaddy's "finest hour." The shame is that it led to Babe's darkest. Lives led to please Old Granddaddy have brought Babe to the point of homicide, Meg to the brink of insanity, and Lenny to being a sad homebody by age 30. Meg's angry appraisal of Old Granddaddy sums up the hold that he's had over the sisters: "I hate myself when I lie for that old man ... I feel so weak. And then I have to go out and do at least three or four things that I know he'd despise just to get even with that miserable, old, bossy man!"

It may be a stretch to say that Babe has shot Zackery to get even with Old Granddaddy. But that is the upshot of her bullet: Little Babe MaGrath, an uneducated naïf cornered in a bad marriage, has shot her bigwig husband, "the most powerful man in all Hazlehurst."

The play's three unseen men—the girls' father, Old Granddaddy, and Zackery—hover above the action as palpable ghosts of the sisters' past. The sisters' task, in "overcoming ghosts of the past and letting go of what other people have said you are," is especially hard for these three.[68] The other people who have slapped harmful labels on them have been the very people (family) who should have comforted three girls down on their luck. Having their father take off, and their mother take her life, should have evoked compassion in their family and community. But thanks to a Chick Boyle mind-set pervading Hazlehurst, it made the sisters guilty of various social crimes. Chick has fostered the myth that the sisters are playing out some shameful trashy family destiny, living down to expectations about them.

Self-esteem gets eaten away (gobbled) by chronic shaming, as psychologists and even common sense will confirm. In the words of Dr. John Bradshaw, when shame becomes a constant, it becomes "toxic ... you don't feel you *have* a flaw, you feel you *are* a flaw ... unlovable and unworthy of love."[69] Of the sisters, Lenny has become most convinced that she is an unworthy flaw. She has been stuck in this house, trained to tend to Granddaddy and others, and to clean up their messes (like Chick's discarded pantyhose). For years, Lenny has absorbed Chick's diatribes on the shame of MaGrath women. However, the renewal of sisterly love and solidarity works its magic on Lenny's self-esteem and outlook.

For each of the MaGrath sisters, Henley has included a turning point that involves an awakening coupled with a catharsis. For each sister, this "awake and sing" experience marks a move toward self-awareness and esteem. For Lenny, that point comes with the laughing fit she shares with Babe, in their comic-relief response to Old Granddaddy's coma. There is a lightening of Lenny's outlook after this, and a swift move to her broom-wielding showdown with Chick. No more will Lenny tolerate her cousin's shaming, degrading slurs. The broom-beating pursuit of Chick out the door and up a tree is an appealing catharsis for Lenny—and the audience, too. One liberating action spawns another: "My courage is up ... the time is right!" she yelps, now ready to risk a phone call to Charlie of Memphis. Lenny's modest victory is not a wildly feminist stroke. Nonetheless, she makes a clear move toward embracing self-worth over the scorn of others.

Meg puts on a pretty good show of self-esteem; some might even call her behavior selfish. Lenny does, in fact. Meg's indulgences include her raid on Lenny's candy, and a certain audacity with men. Meg talks a great game of aggression, set off by "Chick the Stick" or Zackery's abuse of Babe. ("I'll kill him ... I'll fry his blood.") It even seems that Meg selfishly escaped family problems by fleeing to L.A. However, Meg has not escaped, and like her sisters, has been living a lie to this point. Since their mother's suicide, Meg has been on a rampage of emotional denial, to immunize herself against caring about others. When she started to care for Doc, she ran away from her emotional ghosts; but they caught up with her in L.A. As Meg recounts for Doc, one day she "ran screaming from the apartment," and tried to stuff all her valuables into a March of Dimes box. "That was when they nabbed me. Sad story. Meg goes mad."

Meg's turning point centers on her reunion with Doc, and their moonlight ride. Even though Doc didn't ask her to run away with him, Meg returns happy, glad to know that she could care about someone, and that she could sing, "right up into the trees! But not for Old Granddaddy. None of it was to please Old Granddaddy." With one exorcism, Meg ousts two ghosts that have hampered her need for caring and her joy of singing. With her zest for life and self-image repaired, Meg is able to help Babe decide that life is worthwhile, despite those "real bad days."

Babe's self-image is understandably fuzzy. She was Granddaddy's "Dancing Sugar Plum," preened by him to skyrocket to "the heights of Hazlehurst society," married off for that purpose. Then Babe's overbearing husband began abusing her. "He started hating me, 'cause I couldn't laugh at his jokes," she confides to Meg. "Then the sound of his voice got to where it tired me out ... I'd fall asleep just listening to him at the dinner table." In Henley style, the grim issue of abuse is couched in the comic image of Babe nodding off into the gravy. Babe tolerated Zackery's abuse to herself, but struck back when he turned on the gentle Willie Jay.

In a real sense, Babe forged a created family with her young lover and Dog: She found comfort and affection in those ties. Zackery's violence toward those is what brings her to violence. (Zackery does not know of their affair until his sister shows him the photos she hired a detective to get. He attacks Willie just because he is a black boy on his property, in the company of Babe, also his property.)

Babe's "awake and sing" turning point is the most complex. It springs from her realization that she is *not* as much like her Mama as she feared. Like her Mama, Babe has had a destructive marriage, and even considers suicide. (Babe's two suicide attempts are failures; and by Henley's design, they are even comedic failures.) But unlike her Mama, Babe opted for killing her husband, not herself. And as Babe realizes and shares with Meg, "I'm not like Mama. I'm not so all alone."

When she did feel alone, Babe sought created family in her link to Willie Jay; for Lenny, a kind of created family was found in her pet horse of 20 years. (Henley herself says, "Yes, I think Babe and Lenny felt love from Willie Jay and Billy Boy."[71]) But by the play's end, the sisters reunite as three stronger and feistier women, who are family created anew. Their jubilant, golden last scene becomes a group awakening and catharsis. The sharing of hunks of birthday cake (like a communion ritual, but happier) works well as a symbolic giving-in to self, of feeling worthy of joy.

On one hand, Henley's depiction of marriage and family presents the most scathing critique so far: The consequences of MaGrath marriages have been suicide and near-homicide. On the other hand, Henley sends up a renewed cheer for family potential with her portrait of the sisters. Their affirmation of self and each other becomes a family triumph.

Henley shies away from the image of being a political writer; she downplays the domestic abuse in her play. But she does strikes political chords, since domestic abuse remains the number one cause of death and injury to American women. And, as editors of *The Aching Hearth* note, "It can and does happen every day to poor, middle-class, and well-to-do women ... to any racial and economic group."[71] Babe is not alone in picking up a gun. More women do each year. (A television special of the mid-1990s aired the story of four women released from prison by a controversial ruling. They had killed their husbands after suffering repeated abuse.) Anti-feminists have pointed to increased gun-wielding by women as a symptom of too much liberation. More likely, as the evidence suggests, it's a sign of too much oppression and fear on the homefront—still.

Despite the sweet and salutary successes of the women's movement, ongoing losses have threatened to reverse the gains. In the 1980s, huge obstacles in the path of the movement caused its virtual halt. Feminism was confronted with what was called a backlash, or even an "undeclared war on women."

12

The 1980s: Backlash and Beyond

"Yes, I am a feminist," the majority of American women declared at the start of the 1980s. National polls confirmed it. Yet somehow, by 1989, a clear turnabout had taken place. More than sixty percent of women were responding in the negative.[1] What happened to the women's movement, to the spirit of feminism, in what Barbara Ehrenreich called "a decade of greed"—"the worst years of our lives"?[2]

Gloria Steinem, a strong voice and leader in the women's movement, offered one explanation: "Once you get a majority consciousness change, you also get a backlash. It's both an inevitable tribute to success and a danger."[3] Even before the outside danger of a backlash, an ironic inside threat to feminism's gains was found in an apathy among younger women. As Nancy Gibbs noted in *Time* magazine, "one measure of the success of the women's movement is the ease with which it is taken for granted."[4] Betty Friedan even used one of her *Cosmopolitan* articles to scold her daughter (a Radcliffe student) for her disregard for the movement's ideals:

> I hope there will come a day when you, daughter mine, or your daughter, can truly afford to say, "I'm not a feminist, I'm a person" ... when I can stop fighting for women and get into other matters that interest me now.... I think of the many women who have moved, whether from bitter necessity or new choice, and have ended up alone (but still would not go back) or have paid what seems too bitter a price. And I think how much better the endings are that may be possible for you, my daughter. But right now, you still have to pay your dues.[5]

Of course, there were obvious gains to point to, including the increase in women holding prominent positions: the first woman Treasurer and Director of the Mint (Azie Morton in the late 1970s); the first woman U.S. Supreme Court Justice (Sandra Day O'Connor in 1981); and the tripling of women state legislators between 1969 and 1981 (up from 300 to 900).[6]

Good news, yes; but not enough to balance out the ongoing bad news. In pay envelopes, women were still getting 66 cents for every dollar paid to a man. And women still comprised only 12 percent of total state legislators. The news was worse at the federal level, with women at less than five percent of the House, and a slight two percent of the Senate. Worse yet, the fragile gains in women's federal appointments were to be overturned by the Reagan regime and its clearly anti-feminist climate. Women swiftly vanished from federal office (their numbers plunging by 50 percent). Capitol Hill brought out and waved "traditional values" to rout women from public life and send them back home.

Barbara Ehrenreich decried the hypocrisy of the Reagan cohort's revised "family values." In her caustic book on the eighties subtitled *Irreverent Notes from a Decade of Greed*, she observed that

> Throughout the Eighties, the winning political faction has been progressively "pro-family." They have invoked the "family" when they trample on the rights of those who hold actual families together, that is, women. They have used it to justify racial segregation ... And they have brought it out, along with the flag and faith, to silence any voices they found obscene, offensive, disturbing, or merely different.[7]

In print and on podiums, front-line feminists denounced Reagan and his spokesmen for trampling on the rights of women and fueling the backlash. But the most detailed documentation of the backlash and the "no girls allowed sign on the White House lawn" was journalist Susan Faludi's book, *Backlash: The Undeclared War Against American Women*. Written 30 years after *The Feminine Mystique*, Faludi's book echoed Friedan's in that it, too, became a bestseller and was, essentially, an exposé of the myths intended to control women.

Faludi stressed that, by Reagan's second term, "not a single woman ranked high enough to report to the President or attend daily staff meetings."[8] Existing agencies that promoted women's appointments were dissolved. In speeches and conferences, President Reagan aired (quite clumsily) his own biases about women and their employment. *Time* magazine quoted Reagan's declaration of April 1982 that the cause of rising unemployment was "not as much recession as it is the great increase in the people going into the job market, and ladies, I'm not picking on anyone, but [it is] because of the increase in women who are working today and two-worker families."⁹

Faludi condemned the Reagan regime's cruel cut to women and, like Ehrenreich, saw the "family values" hype as an attempt to return women to homebound and subordinate roles. A major anti-feminist spokesman was Gary Bauer of the family policy office in the Department of Education. Bauer put out a 52-page policy statement, "The Family—Preserving America's Future," which, as Faludi noted, served to "excoriate all manner of independent women who aren't doing their duty: women who work, women who use day care, women who divorce, women who have babies out of wedlock."¹⁰ (Typical of Reagan henchmen who preached what they did not practice, Bauer and his congressional-assistant wife had used day care for their children for nine years.) In 1981, the anti-feminist founder of the right-wing Heritage Foundation, Paul Weyrich, boasted of his college tours:

> I see great hope because there is new receptivity out there.... Ten years ago, when I talked on campuses about the lie of women's liberation ... I got an absolutely hostile reaction. People hissed and booed. Now I get great interest ... Women are discovering they can't have it all.¹¹

Spokeswomen were also drafted into the war on feminism. Beverly LaHaye led her Concerned Women for America under the credo: "Feminism is more than an illness. It is a philosophy of death." The glaring hypocrisy among anti-feminist women like LaHaye was that they acted nothing like the models of homebound womanhood they claimed to salute. As Gloria Steinem wryly stated, "You don't get work selling out a movement until there is a movement."¹²

Susan Faludi's book denounced promoters of the backlash for distorting the goals of feminism to serve their greedy purposes. She accused "women's magazine publishers, television programmers, and marketers of fashion, beauty, and household goods ... all merchandisers who still believe they need 'feminine passivity' and full-time homemaking to sell their wares."¹³

(Faludi's protest echoed Betty Friedan's lament, three decades earlier, that "we sacrifice our girls to the feminine mystique, grooming them ever more efficiently through the sexual sell to become consumers of the things to whose profitable sale our nation is dedicated."¹⁴)

In the selling-out of the movement in the '80s, the mass media played its leading part. The main messages put out to women were: (1) that feminism and career pursuits had made women desperate; and (2) that delaying marriage and children had caused them severe marriage and infertility crises.

A prime example of media hype was the 1986 Yale study of women's marriage patterns. It supposedly showed that women who put education and careers before marriage had slim chances of making it to the altar: Their odds were 20 percent at age 30; a mere 1.3 percent by age 40. After the Associated Press had a field day with these figures, they found their way into places as diverse as *Newsweek* and the television sit-com *Designing Women*.[15]

However, the Yale study was severely flawed, with a census sampling of only 60,000 households. Susan Faludi countered it with the more valid study by Dr. Jeanne Moorman. In that study—involving 13.4 million households—women's chances of marrying at age 31 were 58 to 66 percent; at age 40, they were 17 to 23 percent. And college-educated women were *more likely to marry*, not less, than those with only high-school diplomas. When Moorman described her findings to reporters, none were interested.[16] Other findings passed over by the media included those of demographer Paul Glick, which showed that "being married is about twice as advantageous to men as to women" in terms of survival.[17] And sociologist Jessie Bernard reported that

> There are few findings more consistent [and] more convincing, than the sometimes spectacular and always impressive superiority on almost every index ... of married over never-married men. Despite all the jokes about marriage in which men indulge ... it is one of the greatest boons of their sex.[18]

In her derisive response to the marital "man shortage" hype, Barbara Ehrenreich wrote:

> Everywhere I look there seems to be a shocking man excess. Take the U.S. Senate, with ninety-eight men and two women—a man excess of ninety-six.... Once you start looking for it, you'll see [it] everywhere—for example, on the op-ed page of your daily newspaper.... Or there's the tenured faculty at Harvard ... a man excess of 808. It's even possible to be alone in a room with one's husband, lover, or boss, and discover that, as far as you're concerned, there's a local man excess of exactly one.[19]

But the Yale-study frenzy did have its effect. By the next year, women's ages at first marriage had dropped, and a 20-year trend had reversed: The number of family households had grown faster than non-family households. In a *New York Times* article, human scientist Jib Fowles predicted a "resurgence of the conventional family" (working father, at-home mother). He later commented, "There's not even going to have to be a veneer of ... subscribing to feminist thought. Men are just going to be more comfortable with the changed conditions." (Fowles' own wife had just given birth and gone right back to work in a Texas school district.[20])

A dire infertility crisis was as much a myth as the marriage crisis. The root of it was very skewed reportage of a French study of 2,100 apparently infertile women. The women were "all married to completely sterile men and trying to get pregnant through artificial insemination." The French researchers never meant their study to apply to all women. But their findings supported the backlash in America, so they were recycled and exploited. The *New England Journal of Medicine* reported that women between 30 and 35 faced a staggering 40 percent chance of being infertile. It advised women to reevaluate their goals and put childbearing before careers. Those warnings reappeared as headline articles in major magazines and newspapers.[21]

Using potent documentation, Susan Faludi countered that "the afflictions ascribed to feminism are all myths."

> From the "man shortage" to the "infertility epidemic" to "female burnout" ... to "toxic day care," these so-called female crises have had their origins not in the actual conditions of women's lives, but rather a closed system that starts and ends in the media ... and exaggerates its own false images of womanhood.[22]

The "toxic day care" frenzy was fostered by backlash engineers who found they could easily instill guilt in working mothers. Working women of the '80s were chastised by a rash of harrowing headlines: "Day Care Can Be Deadly"—"When Childcare Becomes Child Molestation." *Newsweek* did an eight-page cover story on "the dark side of day care." Yet, the largest study made on abuse in day care centers (by Family Research Labs of New Hampshire) suggested that if there was a child abuse crisis in progress, it was in the home. In the mid–1980s, reported cases of abuse by family members outnumbered day care cases by almost 100 to one.[23]

Hollywood joined the sensational rout of strong, independent women. While the rural wife and mother was heroine in such films as *Places in the Heart* or *Tender Mercies*, the single career woman was detestable in films like *Three Men and a Baby*, or *Fatal Attraction*. (In the latter, Glenn Close played a homicidal career woman who shrieked at her prey: "I'm 36 years old! It may be my last chance to have a child.") Mass culture was flooded with images of women made desperate by pursuing "too much equality."[24]

The backlash effectively halted the women's movement by the end of the 1980s. Since then, one encouraging sign of a heartbeat in the movement has been the steady stream of books by concerned feminists. Gloria Steinem was moved to write *Revolution from Within* because, after working so long on the external barriers to women's equality, she recognized the power of internal ones:

> I saw women who were smart, courageous, and valuable, who didn't *think* they were smart, courageous, or valuable.... It was as if the female spirit were a garden that had grown beneath the shadows of barriers for so long, that it kept growing in the same pattern, even after some of the barriers were gone.[25]

While only one of the three Pulitzer plays of the eighties (*The Heidi Chronicles*) carries the explicit message that the women's movement is far from complete, the plays by Henley and Norman give credence to the idea. They bear dramatic witness to the lack of self-esteem that continues to encumber women. As Gloria Steinem remarked, "Self-esteem isn't everything; it's just that there's nothing without it."[26]

Steinem's remark is an echo of Beth Henley's words, quoted earlier: "Self-esteem is the only thing that can save a woman from the traps of other people's definitions." Henley's play gave a piercing but playful look at how these traps can be built by family expectations. A more sobering picture of the danger of these traps—for a woman—is found in the art and the life of Marsha Norman.

13

Marsha Norman: Getting Out the Truth about Family and Self

"I was born into a family to which I did not belong," Marsha Norman explains, in a matter-of-fact voice. "If I was to survive, I knew that I had to find another group to support me ... and even see who I was." Not one to varnish truth in her plays, Marsha is just as disarmingly honest in person—about her work, herself, her family.

> My own family, my mother in particular, was so confused about who I was that, for years, I would get Christmas presents for another girl.... All those dolls that came year after year ... they were for the girl who did belong there, not me.[1]

The antipathy between Marsha and her immediate family has helped to produce her exquisite sympathy for a character whose break from family is a matter of life and death. Unlike her characters, however—Arlene in *Getting Out* or Jessie in her Pulitzer play *'Night, Mother*—Marsha managed to get out and create a whole new family. Growing up in Louisville, the first of four children for Bill and Bertha Williams, Marsha could never see the world in stark black and white as her Fundamentalist mother did. However, Marsha veered toward other women, in her home town and beyond, who were more kindred in mind and spirit. As she puts it, Marsha "adopted a matriarchy"; and of "these women—this family" she recalls:

> The first was my Great Aunt Bubbie, who never married, who worked for the phone company for a hundred years and was always

having her picture taken in bars in strapless red dresses.... Bubbie loved me and took me in; I was her little kid.... She was my savior early on.²

Next came Marsha's demanding piano teacher, Olga, who cured her of any impulse to "get by ... just by being clever." But Marsha's most enduring mentor was her English teacher at Durrett High, Martha Ellison, who awakened Marsha to her own writing talents and the work of Lillian Hellman (Marsha would later dedicate her volume of *Four Plays* to Ellison).

One male figure cropped up in Marsha's matriarchy: her grandfather, who, because he grew up in old New Mexico "had many stories about growing up in the West.... I had [his] stories and books, and the piano. I didn't have any friends, but I knew as long as I was reading or playing the piano, I was safe.³

Marsha's lack of friends stemmed from her mother's firm rules about what she considered suitable company. Marsha even quips that "maybe the people in my plays are all the folks Mother wouldn't let me play with as a kid."⁴

Her own childhood fostered an abiding impulse to help children who are somehow detached from others. While in college, she did volunteer work in the pediatric burn unit of an Atlanta hospital. After her return to Louisville, she married English teacher Michael Norman, whose name she retained despite their divorce a few years later.

The pull to help troubled children took Marsha to a job in the adolescents' unit of a mental hospital. The seed for her first play (which became *Getting Out*) took root when she encountered a 13-year-old who was so violent that she was "absolutely terrifying." The play, which centered on a young woman's release after eight years of prison, reflected Marsha's own feelings of isolation.

> I was an alien creature in my immediate world. So, why was I concerned about behaving well? Once I understood *that*—that isolation was absolutely as much as they (the world, my family, the people around me) could do to me—then suddenly I was free. The door was open and I might as well do what I wanted. And what I wanted was to write for the theatre.⁵

Luckily, Marsha had a world-class theatre in her home town. The Actors Theatre of Louisville, which launched the career of Beth Henley, would also introduce *Getting Out* and Marsha Norman to the theatre world. Marsha's first encounter with that theatre was, ironically, shared with her mother:

Marsha Norman

My mother ... got the idea that she and I would go to the theatre together. She had never been to the theatre before that and hasn't really been much since, but she did take me, when I was 12, up the stairs to the tiny loft-like theatre that was the beginning of Actors Theatre of Louisville.[6]

In *Getting Out*, "Arlie" is the violent adolescent buried within Arlene, out of prison on her first day of parole. Two actresses portray Arlie/Arlene, who struggles to break from her past of theft and prostitution—the tortured outgrowth of abuse she received from her parents. Arlene's first day out ends hopefully, with her neighbor Ruby giving help and the promise of a created family.

Getting Out garnered raves from critics, an off–Broadway run (1978–79), and an Oppenheimer-*Newsday* Award. In this same season of triumph for Marsha, she was made playwright-in-residence at Actors Theatre, and married Dann Byck, one of its founders. In the next few seasons, Marsha's scripts continued to explore family relationships both literal and surrogate. Typically, her characters are what she calls society's invisible people, but people who need "to find out what the truth is ... whatever it costs them."[7]

Her one-act *The Laundromat* was an encounter between two women in an all-night laundry. The talkative young DeeDee is doing wash to escape the humiliation of waiting for her unfaithful husband to return. The widowed Alberta is trying to let go of her late husband by washing his clothes. Gradually, the two women connect, and exchange painful truths.

Marsha's 1980 comedy, *The Holdup*, was set in a barren New Mexico of 1914 and was inspired by her grandfather's stories. It opened with a 17-year-old boy, Archie, fleeing a coyote by diving under a cookshack (as her grandfather had). But for Archie, a bigger threat is his 30-year-old brother Henry, a hot-headed rancher who bullies and degrades him. Archie's liberation is assisted by an unlikely pair of visitors: an over-the-hill Outlaw and his feisty ex-lover, Lily.

The harsh response to the comedy made Marsha feel the same old confining isolation: "What people thought was ... 'This is the queen of tragedy, what is *she* doing writing this? ... Does she think we're fools ... is she lost—what's going on?' ... If you try to get out of your category, again you get this *isolation* business."[8]

Marsha channeled her anger into writing *'Night, Mother*, an intense truth-baring encounter between a mother and daughter on the night of the daughter's planned suicide.

Having just moved to Manhattan (with producer-husband Dann), Marsha spent the summer of 1981 writing the play "unprotected," as she said, because "I didn't care if anybody ever saw it.... I just had to get this straight for me."[9] Marsha's anger at the theatre (and its critics) compelled the writing of *'Night, Mother*, but other forces informed the play's creation. Again, Marsha's fascination with parent-child dynamics underscored her script; and again it included elements of the antipathy between Marsha and her mother. Even Arlie's mama in *Getting Out* had borrowed from Marsha's experiences:

> Do you think I got [that] mother out of thin air? ... My mother once came to see *Getting Out*, saw the mother character walk in the door with the cleaning supplies and didn't recognize herself at all. My mother once broke into her sister's house to clean it. Broke a window![10]

The mismatch of mother and daughter that underscored Marsha's plays was a reflection of her mismatch with her own mother. Their disparate belief systems were manifest in Marsha's chosen work and her mother's response to it:

> She was highly suspicious of everything that I would take great pleasure in: writing and language and stories and contact with the big world.... She hated all my work—thought it was all vulgar, it was all filthy, it was all doomed—and my collective work was going to send me straight to hell. And she was going to have to answer for it when she got to the Pearly Gates. St. Peter was going to say, "What did you do that caused Marsha to write those ugly things?"[11]

In a sense, Marsha's mother did compel her to write. But what her mother saw as ugly or evil, Marsha has seen—and written about—as simply part of life: "I think white is very pale black and black is dirty white; and it's all so much more complex than they tried to tell me that I felt lied to."[12]

Her character Jessie in *'Night, Mother* also feels lied to. Jessie feels that too much of her life has been out of her control, everything from her epilepsy to her brief doomed marriage. So Jesse seizes dignity by taking control of her death. While suicide is usually interpreted as an act of ultimate despair, Marsha Norman views Jessie's suicide as an act of ultimate choice:

> I don't say suicide is "really wonderful, a great thing...." What I say is, when Jessie says, "My life is really all that I have that belongs to me, and I'm gonna say what happens to it," she's free.... Whatever she decides to do, whether it's kill herself or go to beauty school, is fine with me. But that's the part I wanted to watch and describe.[13]

'Night, Mother intensified the mother-daughter relationship, since the only characters are Jessie and her Mama, Thelma. As Marsha observes: "To put mother-daughter on stage all by themselves was new. We'd seen father-son on stage for centuries."[14]

Marsha did not even know if audiences could withstand her intense 90-minute drama. But when it was done as a reading at Circle Rep, "it was so funny and the audience was able to laugh. Not until that point did I know the audience would be able to take it."[15] Once production seemed possible, Marsha immediately thought of actresses Kathy Bates and Anne Pitoniak, associates from Actors Theatre of Louisville, for the roles of Jessie and Thelma.

Unlike other producers who balked at the play's subject matter, Robert Brustein said, "When can I do this?"[16] 'Night, Mother premiered at Brustein's American Repertory in Boston in January 1983 and opened two months later on Broadway. The play would run for almost a year at the Golden Theatre (which had housed Henley's Crimes of the Heart).

Even before its Broadway opening, 'Night, Mother took the Susan Smith Blackburn Prize, an annual award given to an outstanding play by a woman. In reviews of its opening, a few critics grumbled about what they felt was the play's contrivance: Jessie's suicide announcement in the opening moments. However, most critics praised what Frank Rich of the New York Times called "an intense eavesdropping on two people."[17]

To the strong roles for women that Marsha had already created with Getting Out, she had added two more: For her portrayal of Jessie, Kathy Bates won a Tony Award nomination and an Outer Critics Circle Award. Two other powerful actresses—Anne Bancroft and Sissy Spacek—would recreate Thelma and Jessie for the screen version of 'Night, Mother.

No one was more surprised than Marsha when her script went from a reading at Circle Rep, to an acclaimed Broadway opening, to her "lifelong dream" of a Pulitzer Prize. Yet, Marsha was to discover (as others had) that the coveted Pulitzer could bring mixed blessings.

Her next play, Traveler in the Dark, met with hostile critical response. The play was a departure for Norman: Her protagonist was male and very visible—a noted surgeon, Sam, who can't forgive himself for failing to save his nurse from cancer. Sam has also never stopped blaming the death of his mother (when he was 12) on his preoccupied preacher-father. Once again, Norman's parent and child were strangers. Sam's father concludes, "I guess you can be a big part of somebody else's life without even understanding the first thing about it."[18] In the end, Sam faces the truth that both science and faith can fail to work: They leave gaping holes in human experience. All that life can offer to fill those holes is love and forgiveness, which Sam's wife Glory freely gives to him.

The brutal reviews of Traveler in the Dark made Marsha feel that the Pulitzer had relegated her to another form of confinement: "Marsha Norman?—Oh, fine, if she'll stay over there ... we'll be happy to go by and say,

'Oh, there's Marsha Norman on *that* pedestal'—like a statue in the park. Well, who wants to be a statue in the park?"[19]

While trying to figure out how to get down from that pedestal, Marsha took a break from theatre. She wrote a suspense novel titled *The Fortune Teller*. In crafting the book, Marsha stuck to her creative pattern of arriving at character first. As she phrases it, she finds "someone I would really like to nominate for memory."[20] In her book, that person is Fay Morgan, a psychic who does fortune-telling to make a modest living for herself and her daughter. A third main character is Fay's old boyfriend, Arnie Campbell, a detective for the police station down the block. Although Marsha "knew from the beginning that the book was about how we inevitably lose our children," she was quite surprised when a serious social issue emerged in her story: Fay is called in by the police to help solve a crime, a terrorist act by an anti-abortion group.[21]

In that break from theatre, Marsha also gave birth to her son Angus (whom she proudly described as the "cutest child on the earth").[22] Being a mother would give Marsha a new perspective on the parent-child relationship, and new insights with which to inform her writing.

Nothing could keep Marsha away from the theatre for too long. When Actors Theatre of Louisville featured the next play by Marsha, its plot even centered on members of a prestigious theatre company in rehearsal for a Biblical drama. The main characters of *Sarah and Abraham* were the fictional company's most celebrated actress Kitty, her actor-husband Cliff, and their director Jack. The action sprang from this tense triangle, and the ultimate decision Kitty must make—between her husband, her director, and the baby she is carrying. Response to *Sarah and Abraham* was glowing; and when no other productions followed, Marsha felt she was still trapped on her limiting pedestal. The two things that came to her rescue were those that had saved her in the past: a matriarchy, and music: "If it weren't for my friend Heidi, I still wouldn't be down. If Heidi hadn't finally heard me and said, 'Yeah, okay—come on, let's do a musical,' I still would be up there ... like a statue."[23]

The Heidi in question is Heidi Landesman, a top-notch designer and producer (of *Into the Woods*) who had done the set for *'Night, Mother*. When she called Marsha with her idea for a musical based on Frances Burnett's classic, *The Secret Garden*, Marsha was ready and willing. The production team became an unprecedented matriarchy: Heidi Landesman as producer and designer; Marsha Norman as writer of book and lyrics; Susan Shulman as director; Grammy-winner Lucy Simon (Carly's sister) as composer; and the late Frances Burnett, author of the original 1911 children's book—whose presence was strongly felt by Marsha.

> I felt that it was my responsibility to recreate for her multitude of fans that same feeling they had when they read the book. I knew that to translate the book directly would not produce that feeling, so what I basically had to do was to say to Frances, "Look, I'm going to have to change some things in order to get the same effect, but it's going to be okay."[24]

The Secret Garden was perfect for Marsha to recreate, with its two troubled children—the bedridden Collin, who is crippled in spirit more than body; and the orphaned Mary, who struck a strong chord in Marsha: "I looked at that lost little girl ... who was looking for a place where she belonged. That was me." Despite pressures on the creative team, Marsha recalls the easy comradery among the women: "We would eat a bunch of chocolate, we would talk about our kids, and then we would get our work done."[25]

Their work resulted in three Tony Awards for *The Secret Garden*, including Marsha's award for best book. (Marsha remains one of only two women playwrights, to date, to win both a Tony and a Pulitzer Prize. Wendy Wasserstein would win both for *The Heidi Chronicles*.)

Her Broadway triumphs have not kept Marsha from returning to her roots at Actors Theatre of Louisville. Near the century's end, their Humana Festival featured Marsha's script *Trudy Blue* before it was restaged off-Broadway. Another script much informed by Marsha's own experiences, the play featured a woman character who receives a medical misdiagnosis (as Marsha had five years earlier) which quickly and radically changes her life. The character—also a writer—is forced to stop living in her mind and face terrifying realities about herself and her relationships to her mother, husband, daughter.[26]

Marsha's recent play, *The Last Dance*, also centers on a woman writer, and premiered at Manhattan Theatre Club in the summer of 2003. Jo Beth Williams played Charlotte, a novelist from the American South who tries to retreat to the French seaside; but even there, her lover, her goddaughter, and an old friend all vie for Charlotte's attention.

Marsha Norman claims that "If it's feminist to care about women's lives, yes, I'm a feminist writer."[27] She also maintains that "until the producing world is 50 percent women, we won't have 50 percent plays by women."[28] But Marsha believes that part of the problem in getting more women's plays to mainstream theatre lies in "what constitutes a discussable issue":

> Men are always discussing status; that's what they're always negotiating; that's what men's plays have to do with. Women's plays have to

> do with status not at all. Women's plays have to do with connection, have to do with rapport.... You never see plays about women arguing, "I want it. It's mine. It's a proof that I matter." No, for women the proof that "I matter" is in the relationship with the other person. And you establish that relationship perhaps around the object, but if you take the object away, the relationship is still there. For men, what's worth fighting over is the object, in that trophy world.
>
> I think among men there is the expectation that someone will be vanquished ... but women fight that. Women will insist there's some way to help you get by.[29]

Now that no one from her old adopted matriarchy is still living, Marsha feels that the tables have turned and it is her turn to be mentor: "I think, Well, all right. I wait, until someone comes along and says, 'I need you, Marsha. You be my matriarch now.'"[30] She has been thrilled to be a role model for aspiring women playwrights:

> I did three years of lectures on college campuses with the idea that I would simply go and give these women the thing I never had, which was simply the sight of someone like me ... Lillian Hellman— who was "it" for me—where was she? ... But I could go to the campuses and say, "Look. See, I'm alive and I'm working."[31]

The South has not been the strong force in Norman's plays that it has been in those of Hellman or Henley. But Marsha believes her legacy from the South is that of storyteller who gets to the bottom of a story—"that thing about, 'You're going to sit on this porch and rock until this is straightened out.'" She adds, "I think the quality that allows Southern writing to exist is the idea that you can't escape family."[32]

Marsha Norman has had, to quite a glorious degree, what her character Jessie Cates has lacked: supportive, created family. Jessie has been trapped in a remote house with a mother who, as Marsha states it, "does not know enough about her to save her life if she had to." 'Night, Mother is the story of a mother and daughter who have shared space but little of themselves—until one chilling night.

THE PLAY—MAMA AND JESSIE:
INTIMATE STRANGERS IN THE *NIGHT*

The setting is a house "way out a country road," shared by Thelma and her daughter, Jessie. Jessie is about 40 years old, "pale and vaguely unsteady.... It is only in the last year that Jessie has gained control of her body, and tonight, she is determined to hold onto that control."[33] The living room is cluttered with magazines, candy dishes, needlework; it opens onto the kitchen. Visible are a set of pull-down attic stairs, and a bedroom door that is the "focal point of the entire set." The time is evening, in the present.

Lights come up on Mama, searching a kitchen cabinet for one of her treats—a "snowball." She calls to Jessie that it's the last one: "Put it on the list, O.K.?" Jessie enters from her bedroom, asking about old towels that Mama no longer wants. Thelma tells her not to make a mess, and reminds her that it's Saturday night, almost time for Jessie to give her a manicure. Jessie has it on her list; but first she wants to find her father's old gun. Mama tells her that it's in the attic, in a shoebox, then regrets telling her: She's concerned about Jessie going up there, and the thought of a gun makes her uneasy. When Mama asks why she wants it, Jessie answers, "Protection." Mama scoffs, "This is way too far to come out for what's out here to steal." The subject of robbery turns to Jessie's son Ricky, who has become a thief and other unsavory things. Jessie speaks the cold truth about her son while Thelma shrugs it off with, "It's just something Ricky's going through."

When Jessie cleans and oils the gun, Mama tries to grab it away from her. But Jessie pulls it to her and says, with calm and quiet resolve, "I'm going to kill myself, Mama ... Shoot myself. In a couple of hours." Thelma is incredulous. Jessie must be feeling ill; it must be time for her medicine. No, Jessie responds; she feels fine. "Waited until I felt good enough, in fact."

Finally realizing that Jessie is serious, Mama begins grasping at tactics to stop her: The gun and ammunition are too old and might not work. But Jessie tries the gun's action and it is fine. Besides, the bullets are new, procured through her brother Dawson, who thought protection was a good idea. When Mama moves to call Dawson, to put a stop to this, Jessie snatches the phone: "This is private. Dawson is not invited." If Mama calls him, Jessie will just do it sooner.

Thelma tries to take charge, to forbid Jessie to kill herself, because the house—and gun—belong to her. Jessie patiently tells Mama there is no use in fighting her over this. Also to no avail is Mama's mention of Jessie's upcoming birthday, and the gifts awaiting her. Jessie can guess every one, including the usual pair of slippers from Dawson in the wrong size.

When Jessie takes the gun and towels into the bedroom, Thelma reaches for the phone, then thinks better of it. Jessie returns and goes down her list—refilling the candy jars, instructing Mama about ordering groceries. More talk of Dawson and Loretta reveals that Jessie resents her brother and his wife; they intrude on her privacy and make hurtful assumptions about her. Thelma promises that they'll "not set foot" here again, then adds that Jessie could even move away if Mama bothers her. But Jessie simply responds: "Mama, I'm just not having a very good time and I don't have any reason to think it'll get anything but worse."

Thelma desperately tries to suggest things that might make life better: If the state of the world makes Jessie sad, they can stop having newspapers or television. If she wants, Mama will happily assume the household chores. (They both know, and now admit, that Mama has been letting Jessie do them just to keep her occupied.) Maybe Jessie could get a driver's license, now that her epilepsy seems under control—maybe even a job. Jessie reminds Mama about the jobs she has already tried; she couldn't do them. "The kind of job I could get would make me feel worse." Jessie adds that she can't do anything about her life, either, to make it work. "But I can stop it. Shut it down ... It's all I really have that belongs to me and I'm going to say what happens to it ... And I'm going to stop it."

Mama is pained at this impasse. Jessie quickly urges, "We can't go on fussing all night.... I can ask you things I always wanted to know and you could make me some hot chocolate." In a momentary truce, Mama gladly fixes the cocoa, buying time by pulling out every pot and pan.

During the making and hesitant sipping of the cocoa (neither of them really likes milk), Jessie questions Mama about some things and receives honest answers at last. The reason Mama's friend Agnes won't come to the house is that she's afraid of Jessie's cold hands. She fears that Jessie has "shook the hand of death" and it might be "catching." Jessie is relieved and amused to hear that Agnes does not dislike her, but is scared of her.

Thelma confirms Jessie's suspicion that Thelma did not love Jessie's father; there was no real communication between them. But Jessie did love her father, who did "nothing but farm and sit." She would have long talks with him, which made Thelma feel excluded and jealous.

Their interval of calm erupts into storms again, with Thelma tossing pots and utensils, telling Jessie to throw it all out; she won't use it. Jessie refuses and suggests that Agnes might come over and cook now, or even move in. But Mama won't hear of this.

The topic veers to Jessie's ex-husband Cecil, and truths emerge about him and the marriage. Thelma did devise the match, hiring Cecil to build a porch she didn't need. But Jessie admits that she truly loved Cecil and tried, too hard, to be what he wanted. As for their son, she adds, "Ricky is the two of us together ... in too small a space ... tearing each other apart, like always."

Mama has lost all interest in her weekly manicure, so Jessie enlists her help in replacing the sofa cover she washed. As they work, Jessie has Mama describe what one of her seizures looks like. Thelma slowly tells her this, and another truth about her seizures: They began long before Jessie took a fall during a horseback ride with Cecil. Jessie has had fits since childhood and probably inherited them from her father, who had them, too. "Well, you took your time telling me," Jessie flares. Mama says she thought it best not to tell Jessie; she didn't want her to "feel like a freak." Stunned and angry at being denied this vital knowledge about herself, Jessie snaps at Mama to "get the manicure tray and sit down!" But Mama throws the tray on the floor; and breaking down, she wails, "It has to be me that's the matter.... I didn't tell you things ... or I took you in and let your life get away.... I don't know what I did but ... everything you do has to do with me!" Jessie answers, "What if it does! What if you are all I have and you're not enough?"

As Jessie moves toward the bedroom, Mama grabs her arm and pleads, "Don't leave me Jessie." Carefully releasing herself, Jessie explains that she's just getting "a box of things I want people to have." When she emerges, Mama begs her to try living a little longer; something might work to make it better. And she asks how she can let go: "You are my child!" Thelma cries. Jessie counters, "I am what became of your child."

However, Mama must go on fighting; she can't just say, "O.K., kill yourself if you want to." "Sure you can," corrects Jessie. "You just did. Say it again." Mama responds with a vehement outburst: "How dare you! You think you can just leave whenever you want like you're watching television here.... You are so wrong!" Thelma rails on, "I guess you think they'll all have to talk about you now! ... You know who they're going to feel sorry for? Me! How about that! Not you. Me!"

When Jessie responds that she should have just left a note, Thelma shouts, "Yes!" then quickly, quietly erases it with "No. No. I might not have thought of all the things you've said." Emotionally spent, Mama settles down as Jessie instructs her about the funeral, even paints a picture of the service and who will come. Mama momentarily imagines it herself, asking Connie Richards—if she comes—where she gets "that Irish yarn." Jessie helps Mama find the right words for telling people why Jessie did it: "It was something personal." She also tells Mama what to do, after the gun shot. Call Dawson, then the police, then keep washing the cocoa pan till they come.

There is now a unity and calm about them as Jessie tells Mama about the small gifts she is leaving for people. Some gifts are sarcastic, like the sack of slippers for Loretta—the ones from Dawson. Others are in earnest, like the odds and ends of presents for Mama. "For whenever you need one," Jessie says. Mama is surprised and pleased that her daughter has done all this. Somewhat recovered now, Mama tells Jessie that she is ready for her manicure. But Jessie stands up and evenly announces, "It's time for me to go, Mama."

Her fear and panic renewed, Mama leaps up to follow Jessie: "We're not through yet. We've got lots of things to take care of." Mama fights hard to hold Jessie back, while Jessie resists just as hard. The two physically struggle until Jessie reaches her bedroom door and pulls free. "Night, mother," she whispers, and vanishes inside.

The quick sound of the lock makes Thelma scream "Jessie!" She pounds on the door shrieking that she won't do any of the things Jessie has told her to unless she comes out and makes her. But to Mama's final plea, "Jessie! Please," the gun shot that rings out sounds like Jessie's answer. Thelma collapses, sobbing, against the door. Then, slowly, she collects herself and with automatic purpose, moves to the kitchen. She picks up the cocoa pan, and clutching it like a life-line, goes to the telephone and dials. "Loretta, let me talk to Dawson, honey."

A book that might serve as a companion piece to Norman's play is Nancy Friday's landmark book *My Mother, My Self*. In it, Friday paints the following mother-to-daughter exchange as "a scene that could never have taken place":

> I'm not really good at this mothering business. You're a lovely child, the fault is not with you. But motherhood doesn't come easily to me. So ... try to understand that it isn't because I don't love you. I do. But I'm confused myself.... We'll try to find other people, other women who can talk to you and fill the gaps. You can't expect me to be all the mother you need.[34]

Friday suggests that the myths of motherhood are so powerful, no reasonable mother could admit to her daughter that she is not all-loving, all-knowing of what is best. Rather than expose this painful truth, she will lie and say, "It's for your own good," to dismiss what her daughter questions. Eventually, her daughter learns to adjust, to respond with other lies. The result is a relationship of two false selves, closely tied yet forever distant. While no other relationship holds such potential for sharing and closeness as mother and daughter, biology does not guarantee compatibility.[35] So, as Friday suggests, no other relationship can be so limiting, even threatening:

> The unspoken fear is that if one partner leaves, if either questions the perfection of mother-daughter love by being "different," we are

both destroyed.... There is only one thing in this world that approaches letting go of our mother, more wrenching than giving up the illusion that she loves us unambivalently. It is separating from—letting go of—our daughters.[36]

'Night, Mother gives audiences a chance to eavesdrop on another mother-daughter scene that probably could never have taken place if it weren't for Marsha Norman. However, Norman makes it clear that this night of intense honesty and connection has only come after a lifetime of distortions, untruths that have kept Thelma and Jessie intimate strangers. In them, the denial and deceit that can haunt mother and daughter are exaggerated. Given their isolation, Thelma's limited understanding, and Jessie's bouts of epilepsy, Thelma could never be "all the mother" that was needed to nurture Jessie, to nourish or educate her. As Marsha Norman herself insists, "This woman's mother does not know enough about her to save her life if she had to."[37] Mama and Jessie have been in joint yet separate "solitary confinement," as Marsha puts it.

Marsha's belief that we are all in some form of solitary confinement informs all her work, but especially 'Night, Mother. The concept, for her, is both literal and metaphorical:

> Real solitary confinement is used to separate people ... because they are perceived to be dangerous; because they don't fit in. And, by nature, this person in solitary confinement wants to be able to get out of there ... so they can continue to search for the place where they belong. The metaphor is useful to me. I've been aware of it from the early moments of my life ... that we are in solitary, and they are not going to come in and get you. But the door ... is not locked. That's the realization of a grownup. What is required, I now know, is ... to open the door and go out to where the other people are who will help you.[38]

The fact that Mama and Jessie know each other so little, and could not get "out the door" to find help, has brought them to this night of Jessie's suicide. What makes this night riveting is that now, before she kills herself, Jessie wants to invoke Thelma's true self. We witness a desperately delayed mother-daughter bonding.

Mama has long been dishonest about vital areas of Jessie's life: Her illness (epilepsy), and the men in Jessie's life (her father, ex-husband, and son). Regarding Jessie's illness, the deceit has been practiced for years. Thelma's pretense of depending on Jessie around the house is a well-meaning lie. But Jessie knows that she has been acting in the charade of Mama's helplessness. And it's not a charade that promotes self-esteem. (Jessie even says, "I feel used.") A happier past scenario for her would have been the one that Mama paints: "You never should have moved back in here with me. If you'd kept your little house or found another place when Cecil left you, you'd have made some new friends at least. Had a life to lead ... You never should've come here."

The worst deceit surrounding Jessie's illness has been Mama's cover-up of her childhood seizures. And Mama's motives have been unwittingly cruel: "I didn't want anybody to know," she rants, "least of all you." Jessie's anguish at this unleashes her disgust with people usurping what belongs to her: "That was mine to know, Mama, not yours."

But Mama's whole mind-set about knowledge is vastly different. Mama asks, "Why do you have to know so much about things?" and declares, "I don't like things to think about." Her outlook borders on the idea that ignorance is bliss, while Jessie harbors a need to know. Survival skills appropriate for herself, she could never get from Mama. What sustains or appeals to Thelma—her crocheting or phone chats with her odd friend, Agnes—would never do for Jessie. Their senses of humor are even at odds, a big factor in their solitary status, as Marsha Norman stressed in our interview:

> I've often said that if Jessie had had a better audience, she would still be alive ... Whatever Mama thinks is funny, Jessie thinks is absurd; and whatever Jessie thinks is funny, Mama thinks is stupid. This is a real problem. This is really how you know you don't belong there. Because laughter is how you live, laughter is how you stay alive. If somebody is not laughing at your jokes, you've got to get out of there.[39]

Jessie has been psychologically stuck with Mama since the death of her father. Tonight, lies and buried resentments surface, about their respective ties to the man. The fact is that Jessie was closer than Thelma to the "old faded blue man" who sat quietly and made pipe-cleaner creatures. The man who had nothing to say to Thelma, right up to his dying moment, could sit whispering with Jessie each night. It didn't matter that the topics were his corn, or boots, or "why black socks are warmer."

Tonight, what matters to Jessie is having her lifelong impressions verified. About Mama not loving her father, she admits it just "feels good to be right about it." Mama can only add, "It didn't matter whether I loved him.... It wasn't important." But love was important to Jessie. And ironically, she did love Cecil, the husband Mama contrived for her by "flirting him out here" to build a porch. Thelma concedes, "All right! ... I married you off to the wrong man." The fact that Jessie loved him might have made him "right"; but she was a poor match for an outdoorsman like Cecil.

At one point, Thelma reveals that Cecil had cheated on Jessie with Agnes' girl—a tactic Mama uses to get Jessie riled up enough to stick around and take action. But minutes later, Mama takes the opposite tack, and pleads with her to find Cecil and urge him to come back. Jessie counters with another truth laid bare. She already begged Cecil to take her along; but when he left without a note, Jessie composed the one she showed Mama: "I wrote it. Not Cecil. I said, 'I'm sorry, Jessie, I can't fix it all for you.'"

About her contemptible son, Jessie is brutally honest: "I hope they put him away ... I'd turn him in myself, if I knew where he was." But not until the end of this raw night does Mama stop whitewashing Ricky's behavior. When Jessie leaves her watch for Ricky to "buy a good meal," Thelma realistically admits, "He'll buy dope with it." Jessie cannot lie to herself about Ricky because he is so like her: He, too, feels trapped in an unfair world that he distrusts. The difference is that Ricky wants to get even; Jessie just wants to get out. A big factor that sets apart Jessie's confinement from her son's, or her Mama's, is that Jessie has also been trapped in her unreliable body. About this, Marsha Norman comments, "Jessie was told that the door was locked ... 'You have this problem; people don't want to deal with you; you can't trust your body.' Jessie has lived for a long time imprisoned in a body that would fail her, that was unreliable."[40]

The anguish of this for Jessie is that whenever she lost control of her body through a seizure, others (mainly family) took control. Mama cleaned her up, then called Dawson to move her to the bed or ambulance. This invasion of her self is an outrage to Jessie: Brother or not, Dawson is an unwelcome intruder. "He just calls me Jess like he knows who he's talking to."

Mama and Dawson know little about the true self of Jessie, yet they are privy to knowledge that should be only "hers to know." This irony—that family can lack knowledge to help you, yet hold intimate information that can hurt you—is one that Marsha Norman knows well, and expresses fearlessly:

> I think what's really threatening about the idea of family—what the trap is ... is their power to define you, and the knowledge that they hold about your past. I remember one of the most threatening incidents of my life was at an opening night party ... and Mother started telling this producer about a Junior Miss contest that I was in when I was in high school.... I was horrified. I felt she was revealing something to him that wasn't hers to tell.[41]

In 'Night, Mother, Jessie makes Mama understand her anger about family knowing too much: "They were there when it happened and it don't belong to them, it belongs to you, only they got it."

A family that knows too much, yet so little; a mother who is right there, but worlds apart: These are the life issues which drive *'Night, Mother* to its forceful conclusion in Jessie's death. "I didn't know!" wails Thelma; "How can I get up every day knowing you had to kill yourself to make it stop hurting and I was here all the time and never even saw it." Mama asks another key question, one that will eventually allow her to forgive herself: "How was I supposed to learn anything living out here?" Mama could not make a gift to Jessie of life skills she never owned. Tonight, Jessie wants another gift impossible for her to give: "Just let me go easy, Mama."

The most shattering truth that Mama must accept is that Jessie does not belong to her. (After the gun shot, Thelma weeps, "Jessie ... forgive me. I thought you were mine.") However, before Thelma experiences this most painful letting-go, she gains something that she might not have had in another 20 years with Jessie. This night becomes something supremely private, almost sacred, between them. Again, the words of Marsha Norman are apt and eloquent: "After a lifetime of missing this daughter ... just living in the same space, they finally had a moment when they lived together, when the issues of their lives were standing there with them, in silent witness of their meeting."[42]

At first glance, *'Night, Mother* seems a far cry from Beth Henley's comedic *Crimes of the Heart*. However, they share serious family—and life—issues: In both plays, mothers are lost to daughters through suicide. In both settings, clearly the biological family has not been enough to sustain its members. Other plays in this series describe the power of family to smother with expectations rather than embrace with love. Norman joins Gale, Glaspell, and Akins in giving stage to women whose lives have been controlled by non-empathic family. But Norman's play goes farthest in spotlighting the most drastic route to self-control a family member could take.

When asked if Jessie could only have been helped by a woman, Norman firmly replied, "Oh, absolutely. But there just wasn't anybody there."[43] She makes a compelling case for an argument that underscores Nancy Friday's book and surfaces in the recent work of Gloria Steinem. To quote Steinem's *Revolution from Within*, "The biological family isn't the only important unit in society.... We have needs and longings that our families cannot meet."[44]

One of the ideals of the women's movement has always been a collective, helping spirit that speaks to this very issue. Women still need other women to foster the self-confidence and drive required to forge a satisfying place in the world. To borrow again from Norman's imagery, too many women still wait in solitary confinement, needing help to "get out that door."

The breakdown of the collective spirit of feminism was what compelled Wendy Wasserstein to write her Pulitzer play, *The Heidi Chronicles*. Wendy's own life, like that of her character, was clearly changed and shaped by the women's movement.

14

Wendy Wasserstein: Lola's Well-Rounded Daughter

"My mother wasn't like other mothers," Wendy Wasserstein insists. "They made Jell-O. They got their hair done on Kings Highway once a week ... sort of puffed up and teased." Of all the mothers of Yeshiva Flatbush, Wendy's mother Lola was a renegade. She kept her hair cropped so short, Wendy adds, that "basically, she looked like Bertolt Brecht."[1]

Other writers have used their family background as a source of stage material. But no one does it quite like Wendy Wasserstein. Then again, no one could have a family quite like hers.

Her mother Lola is a dance fanatic and has taken dance classes most of her life. A funny and eccentric woman, Lola Wasserstein once showed up at Wendy's college residence dressed like Patty Hearst—complete with beret and toy machine gun. Witness to this was Wendy's close friend, playwright Christopher Durang, who thought Wendy was exaggerating about Lola until that moment.[2] "In an era personified by Donna Reed," Wendy explains, "my mother preferred Carmen Miranda." Like Carmen, Lola even wore plastic fruit on her head, a practice that led Wendy and her brother to cut all the cherries off Lola's hat, to make her "like the other mothers."[3]

Despite four children, of whom Wendy was the youngest, Lola Wasserstein would never act like other mothers. A close friend of Wendy recalls, "Her mother didn't cook.... She didn't clean. I never saw any evidence of laundry.... Lola sort of operated in a different sphere."[4] The family dined in restaurants, or Lola had meals delivered, including the whole Thanksgiving feast. Since Lola could not be a Rockette, she settled for taking her brood to see the holiday shows at Radio City, where she avoided lines by lamenting to the ushers that they were only in from Kansas for the day. (Wendy laughingly recalls that her mother chose Kansas "the day after we watched *The Wizard of Oz* on television. I don't know why those ushers didn't tell us to click our heels together three times and get lost."[5])

While growing up, a Saturday ritual for Wendy included a dance class at June Taylor's studio, followed by a Broadway matinee. Lola felt that exposure to the arts would make Wendy a well-rounded person. Luckily, the fabric business of Wendy's father, Morris, could support the family's dining out, the Rockettes, and well-roundedness. Two of Morris Wasserstein's patents were for velveteen and bendable gift bows.

In school, the four Wasserstein offspring were already superachievers. Wendy skipped grades; so did her "very very smart" sister Sandra, and her financial-wizard brother, Bruce. Being the youngest left its mark on Wendy. As longtime friend Betsy Carter (an editor of *New York Woman*) explained, "Wendy grew up in a complicated, smart, verbal family. The way she dealt with it was by becoming a brilliant observer."[6] In school, Wendy became her class commentator:

> I was an elementary school Falstaff. Being perceived as funny served me well even when it got me into trouble. My comments about Mrs. Haskell, our seventh grade teacher ... were apparently so scathing that for an entire semester I was forced to stay after class for two hours every day. But I didn't mind.... I got a good early start on my homework.[7]

Betsy Carter found the Wassersteins a "funny family to see together. Sort of antic ... proud of and amused by each other." She credits the siblings' success to their parents' acceptance of "whatever they did ... no matter how wacky"; they grew up feeling they could "go as far as they wanted."[8] The oldest, Sandra, became one of the first women to break into senior corporate management. Bruce has become a legend in the investment banking world. (Wendy once received a terse message from his office: "Your brother can't come to the play tonight. Is buying Nabisco."[9]) Their sister Georgette opened a Vermont bed-and-breakfast.

But even after these three siblings married and produced a total of nine grandchildren for Lola Wasserstein, she impatiently waited for another one from her youngest child. Wendy would receive phone messages from her mother saying, "Your sister-in-law is pregnant and that means more to me than a million dollars or any play."[10]

The ironic fact is that Lola helped to create in Wendy a theatre monster who took a wildly different route than her siblings. As Wendy relates it,

Wendy Wasserstein

I knew my brother didn't have to become "well-rounded." It was me.... But the problem was that when a girl fell in love with what was making her well-rounded—that, all of a sudden—was a little drastic....

I assure you, my parents never said, "Wendy, please grow up to be an off–Broadway playwright. What we really want is for you to have a life as insecure as possible."[11]

Longing for a life in theatre but doubting that she could have one, Wendy made her script-writing debut from other motives: At her girls' school, she wrote the "mother-daughter fashion show" to get excused from gym. "I didn't know *anything* about fashion ... but I knew that they'd let me out of gym if I wrote these mother-daughter fashion shows.... I also *wanted* to write shows."[12] From her girls' high school, Wendy went on to the women's college Mount Holyoke, where she was "an intellectual history major—God knows why." She was also studying to be a political intern, but kept falling asleep over the Congressional Digest. When a friend said, "Wendy, why are you doing this, when we could take playwriting at Smith, then go shopping?" an important light dawned. Wendy realized that you can "get equal credit in life for what you really like to do. I could get four points for playwriting ... or for being a Congressional intern and falling asleep."[13]

Her first real encounter with male peers came in 1969 during an experimental exchange year with Amherst. The experience was a milestone for Wendy, and for the women's movement.

> There were twenty-three women and twelve hundred men.... I was scared to death! ... I remember going to the student-faculty meeting and saying, "You have to let us stay here." The speaker said ... "We have Kent State, we have Cambodia ... what's the big deal about a little girl wanting to stay at Amherst College?" I thought, "This is one of the most important things happening in terms of long-range changes for women."[14]

Wendy was so struck by "how much more confident the male students were," that she "started reading all this feminist stuff and going to consciousness raising groups."[15]

After her return to New York, Wendy took writing classes at City College—short story with Joseph Heller, and playwriting with Israel Horowitz. "That was wonderful for me ... because my mother had told me that all writers live in garbage cans in Greenwich Village, and I was happy to see that they both had apartments."[16] On the strength of this, Wendy wrote her first play, *Any Woman Can't*, about a college girl who comes to New York, fumbles a tap-dance audition, and ends up making an unfortunate marriage. The play and Wendy's career got an inadvertent boost from Lola Wasserstein:

> My mother Lola was walking down the street and she ran into a lady named Louise Roberts (who used to be the receptionist at June Taylor's). And Louise said to my mother, "How's Wendy?" and my mother started hyperventilating and saying, "She's not a lawyer,

she's not married to a lawyer, instead she's writing plays." And I think this woman, to stop my mother there on the street, said, "Well, give me Wendy's play, because I work in a new dancing school called the Clark Center and it's across the hall from a new theatre called Playwrights Horizons in the 'Y' [YMCA]."[17]

While the production was not outstanding, the link between Wendy and Playwrights Horizons would become an enduring, most successful one.

Her mother became upset again when Wendy decided to study playwriting at Yale, rather than business at Columbia. But her parents finally gave their blessing "because it was *Yale*, and I could meet a doctor or lawyer there."[18] Wendy recalls the pros and cons of those years:

> My classmates and the people at the school ... were Meryl Streep and Sigourney Weaver, Christopher Durang ... a whole world of people. So it was an interesting place, but very difficult; because when you're in a drama school ... you realize that your friends who are at other professional schools—when they get out, there will be some track for them to go on. When you get out of drama school, it's "whoopie!"[19]

Still, Wendy was driven by her belief that "it's worth it in life to risk trying to do what you really want to do."[20] She found a like spirit in Christopher Durang, who became a permanent member of Wendy's family of friends. ("Chris Durang is just my brother, you know.... I think he's just another brother of mine."[21]) At Yale, they swapped stories about their zany families and co-wrote a musical revue called *When Dinah Shore Ruled the Earth*. But Wendy was never fully comfortable at Yale, especially with the messages she was receiving about women, and theatre:

> It amazed me in terms of the perception of women ... we were reading a lot of Jacobean drama; and, excuse me, but it seemed that men were basically kissing the skulls of women and dropping dead from the poison. And I thought ... "I don't identify with this. This doesn't happen to any of my friends." So I decided as an almost political act ... that I would write a play for the Yale School of Drama in which there was an all-woman curtain call.[22]

Wendy drew on her undergraduate experiences at Mount Holyoke and its traditions for her thesis play, *Uncommon Women and Others*:

> There were characters I thought were stageworthy, and I thought there was humor that had not really been touched. Because I noticed that humor—in terms of women and women's lib—was often very "high" and "bitchy" ....

You know, I think the whole idea of women "vixens" and femme fatales would be a masculine idea ... because it "ain't so." And so the truth of the matter had not been written.[23]

In her nine-woman play, a cohort of friends help steer each other through graduation and into a world already changed by feminism. The teas and other rituals of gracious living promoted by their women's college do not prepare them for the options and obstacles they face. But they confidently predict that they will be "pretty fucking incredible" by the time they're thirty. The first and last scenes of the episodic play are set in a restaurant, at a reunion of five of the women. Reality has altered their expectations; and so their timetable must change, too: "When we're forty, we can be pretty amazing." The final scene mixes hope with skepticism. The question of one character hangs in the air: "I wonder what it's like when you stop thinking there's a lot of time left to make changes."[24]

In *Uncommon Women*, the character of Holly was a thinly disguised Wendy. Holly's father is "the inventor of velveteen" and donates to the school 2,000 slightly damaged bows. Holly's sister becomes a director at Proctor and Gamble, while Holly flounders for a career and gets probing phone calls from her mother: "Are you married to a root canal man, are *you* a root canal man?" Wendy felt the play explored "the fact that the Women's Movement has had answers for the Kates of the world [she becomes a lawyer]; or the Samanthas [she gets married]." But not for creative women like Holly. "There isn't a specific space for them to move into."[25]

Some of the issues in the play were paralleled in its production. Predictably, the first all-woman curtain call at Yale Drama School provoked some male resistance. Wendy relates one particular incident:

> What I'll never forget about *Uncommon Women* was, there was an after-play discussion ... and the dramaturg raised his hand and said, "I can't get into this—it's about girls." And this was ... 1976. And I said to him, "Well, you know, I've spent my life getting into *Hamlet* and *Lawrence of Arabia*, so why don't you just try it?"[26]

The play went from a reading at Playwrights Horizons to an off–Broadway production at the Phoenix Theatre. With a cast of such uncommon actresses as Swoosie Kurtz and Glenn Close, the play ran for all of two weeks ("with better reviews than *The Heidi Chronicles*," Wendy later recalled).[27] Its short life was partly due to a conflict about the theatre space, but also to the fact that producers still doubted the value of a play about women.

> Only one producer wanted to move the play ... and it was *only* if I made this girl (Holly) who meets a doctor in a museum and then

makes a phone call to him—if she married the doctor at the end.... And I said to this producer ... "Well, you know, she would have to have a nervous breakdown, and so would I. So, I guess we're not moving!"[28]

But the television producer of *Great Performances* saw the play and was so struck by "the unique voice of this young woman facing this era of liberation" that he optioned *Uncommon Women* for television. (When Glenn Close had a conflict, Meryl Streep stepped into her role.) Wendy laughs her enormous giggle and says, "I'm one of the few writers you'll meet who made a three-figure deal for their play! ... But I knew ... if I sold it to public television, I could maintain control of the play."[29] When it aired again a decade later, Wendy and the actresses gathered to watch it. And, as Wendy recalls, all of them were "fine, pursuing their lives":

> And I often thought that if they wrote a mini-series about what happened to actresses who'd been in a play ten years ago, you know that one would be a drug addict, one would be a maniac, one would have died.... But these were really all people who were fine and doing well.[30]

Wendy described her next play, *Isn't It Romantic*, as being "pretty much about me and my mother Lola, and my best friend and *her* mother.... Most of my plays come from something that happens in my life ... and I can't stop thinking about it.... Anyway, my best friend was getting married, and it made me very angry ... so angry that I thought, 'I'll write a play about this.'"[31]

In *Isn't It Romantic*, the best friends are Janie Blumberg, a "slightly unkempt" writer; and Harriet Cornwall, a "put together" corporate hopeful. They've come home to New York after college, to support each other in launching new lives and careers. Janie's meddlesome mother Tasha is a flamboyant dance-class fanatic who arrives at Janie's door with everything from a mink coat to a potential husband (a Russian cab-driver). Janie breaks off a relationship with a wealthy Jewish doctor because he is simply not right for her. But when Harriet becomes engaged to a man she's known for two weeks, Janie feels betrayed and furious. She wails to Harriet: "You've been waiting for some man to come along and change your life. And all the things you told me about learning to live alone and women and friendship, that was so much social nonsense."[32]

Janie finally convinces herself, and her mother, that it's all right to be alone—a realization that Janie celebrates, all by herself, in a tap-dance finale to the play.

When *Isn't It Romantic* was first staged at the Phoenix, response was cool. Wendy blamed a too-static production that featured a set with five couches. She went to artistic director Andre Bishop, and they remounted a livelier version ("in fact, there were four moving men in the set") and the play ran for two years.[33] The production became unusually personal for Wendy, since the role of Tasha was being played by Betty Comden, of musical-comedy's Comden and Green: "We had Betty Comden playing my mother, and I've always loved Betty and always been interested in musicals. And it's interesting ... for Marsha Norman, her mentor was Lillian Hellman. And for me ... I've always liked Betty!"[34]

By the mid 1980s, Wendy was busy writing for television (PBS's *Great Performances* and CBS's *Comedy Zone*) as well as articles and essays for magazines. However, a number of influences pointed her toward what would become her landmark play:

> I was seeing a lot of plays in which I found the image of women disturbing again. I was beginning to feel like I felt at Yale ... like seeing Madonna in *Speed the Plow*. It's not that they weren't good plays ... it's just that I felt, again, that the image of women was not being fully represented. So I thought, I can either go out to drinks with my friends and get angry about this, or I suppose I could write a play, which is always harder.
>
> The other thing was, I was beginning to think, Well, what's happened to feminism—to all that political commitment? ... Because I actually have always had an interest in history ... in how we got from the past to the present, when everything seems to be breaking down.[35]

So Wendy began writing *The Heidi Chronicles*, for "very personal" reasons: "*Heidi* was a play I wrote very much for myself.... Basically, I didn't think a play about a feminist art historian who becomes sad could be a commercial hit."[36] Coincidentally, to get funding to write the play, Wendy got a hand-up from Marsha Norman (who, by then, had won the Pulitzer Prize): "Marsha Norman recommended me for this grant [from the British American Arts Association], and it was for a 'mid-career stimulation' ... which I thought sounded lewd when I got it.... So I had a mid-career stimulation and loved it! And I wrote a lot of the play then."[37]

For her episodic play spanning 24 years, Wendy chose as her central character "a woman who has internalized all of the values of the women's movement."[38] While tracing the routes by which feminist art historian Heidi Holland has internalized these values, Wendy also depicts "a generation for whom friends are their family." Wendy includes herself in that generation:

> My friends really are my family.... My mother is Lola the dancer; and my sister, Sandra, she used to run the card division at American Express. So they were two very different kinds of role models, more interesting to me than nurturing. My nurturing has always come from my friends.[39]

In *Heidi Chronicles*, all Wendy reveals about Heidi's given family is that they live in Chicago. Heidi's created family is clearly paramount. And first in that family is Peter Patrone, who enters her life at a school dance, and is a kindred spirit—a caring, "serious, good person." Very unlike Heidi is her friend Scoop Rosenbaum, the brash journalist she meets at a McCarthy rally. Scoop's confident swagger holds an enduring fascination for Heidi.

Heidi's life unfolds around milestones good and bad: consciousness-raising groups; demonstrations for women's art; the publication of her book; and various personal crises. Peter discloses that he is gay; the philandering Scoop marries a woman he won't have to "compete with." Heidi feels remote from the hot-shot women around her, who have traded feminist spirit for status-grasping individualism. She feels stranded—marooned by the very values that have made her who she is. Not wanting to feel so stranded, or that she "made the wrong choice," she arrives at a choice that's right for her. With the help of Peter, who's now a noted pediatrician, Heidi brings into her created family an adopted baby daughter: A child she hopes will "*never* feel she's worthless," or be told her life must be "either/or."

Heidi began its stage life with a reading at Playwrights Horizons, the theatre home with which Wendy has had a "long and wonderful" relationship: "For a playwright, it makes a huge difference to have a home.... The most important thing is to see your plays done, to hear the plays read."[40] After *Heidi* was given a workshop at Seattle Repertory Theatre (Wendy's second home), it was staged back at Playwrights Horizons. When response warranted a move to Broadway (the Plymouth) Wendy had mixed feelings:

> I wanted to keep [it] off–Broadway because of ticket prices and things like that; and it was really the producer and director who said to me, "This is gonna work better as a Broadway play." And they were right. The play took on a weight because of the space given to it.[41]

At the news that her play had won a weighty Pulitzer Prize, Wendy was utterly surprised: "I was wearing a Lanz flannel nightgown," she explains, "and I got a call."[42] *The Heidi Chronicles* went on to win the Triple Crown of the commercial theatre realm: the Pulitzer Prize, the Tony, and the Critics' Circle Award. It also took a Drama Desk Award and the Susan Smith Blackburn Prize (a record sweep of awards for a single work).

When asked to describe her feelings at receiving the huge accolades of the Pulitzer and the Tony, Wendy attempts to express the inexpressible. Much of her response emerges between words, in her exuberant body language and unabashed giggle:

> I've always been someone who's had a hard time taking myself seriously ... and getting people to take me seriously. I think, one, because I write comedy; and two, because I seem like a passive gentle permissive—which is basically what I *am*—with an enormous giggle! So to me, something like a Pulitzer Prize is heavy; that's like weight.... I never thought that would happen to me.
>
> I went to the theatre that night, and I ran into Edward Albee, and he said, "Aren't you going to take a bow?" I said, "Edward ... I'm too shy, I can't." And Edward said, "Wendy, take off your coat and go backstage, because you don't know when this would happen to you again." And I felt it was like ... from one generation to another. So I went.... I had never been onstage for a bow or something, so I just kept kissing all the actors.
>
> The Tony Award is ... much more nervous-making because you know it has to do with the financial future of your play. So *there*, you're thinking about the stagehands, producers, the prop people. And you think, "I want to win this thing, goddammit, because I want us to *run*! ... and I want you guys to work." So it's different.... And I think Marsha [Norman] is right—it is like a wave of approval from your community; and that feels wonderful because it's them![43]

Part of the thrill for Wendy was the resounding proof that a play about a woman (and a bright, independent one) could become a mainstream commercial success. She proudly notes, "because *Heidi* was successful, that opens a door."[44] The play's triumph—despite the '80s backlash—was evidence that the women's movement had borne fruit. As Wendy adds, "that *that* rap scene (in *Heidi*) was on Broadway and commercial, that it won not only the Tony but the Pulitzer, says that the ideology—in the best possible way—influences society. So I feel very much a beneficiary of that."[45]

Inevitably, mixed in with the applause for Wendy's play were some sounds of dissent. A few feminists even objected to it, especially the ending: Heidi's decision to adopt. They felt it suggested that Heidi's generation had been sacrificed to the women's movement. Or, that women can only find fulfillment through motherhood. To this, Wendy flatly replies, "That's silly."

> The women's movement, the movement that said, "Your voice is worthwhile," is the only reason I feel like a person. But what still needs to change is that women shouldn't beat themselves up for

their choices—for being a mother or a single mother, or being a playwright.... It's important that there isn't one woman slot that puts you all into competition.[46]

Most feminists embraced Wendy's play. Gloria Steinem cheered, "To have a play on Broadway about the change that a woman goes through in her life ... this is a revolution in itself."[47] In her best-seller *Backlash*, Susan Faludi noted that Wendy's heroine, "Heidi Holland, delivers a speech that would become one of the most-quoted lines by women writers of the female experience in the '80s: 'I feel stranded, and I thought the point was that we wouldn't feel stranded. I thought we were all in this together.'"[48]

Wendy Wasserstein admits that her experience with the play helped her feel less stranded: "The acceptance of *Heidi*, the respect from my peers while we were staging it, made me feel that."[49] But the play's runaway success gave Wendy her own hard act to follow. She topped her play about the bright, well-educated Heidi Holland with a play featuring three bright, well-educated women, the Rosensweig sisters. On one level, *The Sisters Rosensweig* is a bow to Chekhov and his immortal *Three Sisters*. But Wasserstein's three are quite distinct from those of Chekhov, or even those of Beth Henley. Again, Wendy drew on her own family, making the oldest sister, Sara, a top corporate bank executive. The middle sister is nicknamed "Gorgeous" after Wendy's sister Georgette. Like Wendy herself, the youngest sister, Pfeni, is a writer and a holdout when it comes to marriage.

In the play, the sisters convene at the lush London apartment of Sara to celebrate her fifty-fourth birthday. An expatriate, the brittle, businesslike Sara has also detached from her Jewish heritage. She is the antithesis of her quirky sister, "Doctor Gorgeous," a Boston housewife who does a pop-psychology radio talk show and leads sightseeing tours for a Temple Beth El Sisterhood. The roving travel-writer, Pfeni, has kept an intermittent home base in London, where she has had an intermittent love affair with a bisexual stage director, Geoffrey.

Wendy saw the play as a big departure from her past work, and not simply because "in this, someone winds up with somebody else. A woman and a man come together."[50] She comments, "To my mind *The Sisters Rosensweig* was my most serious effort—a one-set, non-episodic play, complete with unities of time, place, and action, deliberately set on the eve of a momentous historical event."[51]

The momentous event is the fall of the Berlin wall. The world is at a turning point; so are the lives of these sisters. Twice divorced, firmly independent, and just recovered from a hysterectomy, Sara intends to keep romance at bay. But her daughter knows that Sara "is in desperate need of hope and rebirth." The optimist Gorgeous is at a crossroads with her

Harvard lawyer husband, now jobless and holed up in their basement writing a mystery. And Pfeni's love for Geoffrey is at an impasse; he admits that he has begun to "miss men." Each sister confronts the painful issues of her life and takes a hesitant step toward "hope and rebirth." The step Sara takes is toward an unlikely suitor—a wise-cracking Jewish fake furrier.

Wendy did not have to search for a producer. Her friend Andre Bishop (*Heidi*'s producer) had just become artistic director at Lincoln Center Theater; he made her play his first booking. Dan Sullivan, director of *Heidi*, again applied his magic to the *Sisters*. And into this recipe for success came actresses Jane Alexander as Sara, Madeline Kahn as Gorgeous, and Frances McDormand as Pfeni. Wendy proudly notes, "I deliberately set out to write smart and funny parts for women over forty."[52]

Again, the sellout run warranted a move to Broadway. And again, critics hailed Wendy's bright, spirited heroines. The *Times* applauded her "captivating look at three uncommon women and their quest for love, self-definition, and fulfillment."[53] *New York*'s John Simon hailed Wasserstein's *Sisters* as her "most accomplished play to date," and added, "She's surely one of our wittiest one-liner writers, but under the bubbles and eddies of her wit are real people in deep water, trying to keep from drowning."[54]

Wendy's characters in the deepest water were yet to come, in her most serious and most political play, *An American Daughter* (1997). Its protagonist, Lyssa Dent Hughes, is an acclaimed health professional, the daughter of a senator, wife of a noted professor, and the mother of twins. She is also the President's nominee for surgeon general—until the media gets wind of the fact that she once discarded a jury-duty notice. The script was inspired by the real-life Nannygate frenzy that robbed Zoe Baird of an appointment as attorney general. Wendy felt compelled "to write about the resentment aimed at professional women who seem to have it all."[55]

But events in Wendy's own life also informed this darker work: "I wrote this play when my sister Sandra was dying and I was trying to spend time with her. It was a very difficult period." While her sister spent years battling cancer, Wendy spent years undergoing fertility treatments, "attempting, in vain, to have a child."[56]

Wendy's sister succumbed to cancer. But in 1999, at the age of 48, Wendy finally gave birth to a premature two-pound baby. Mother and daughter Lucy are now doing fine. "I take her to plays already," says Wendy. "I kind of think it's your birthright as a New Yorker to see plays." (To this end, she has launched a theatre program for disadvantaged New York public school students.[57])

Asked how parenthood has affected her writing, Wendy responds, "I waste less time." To do her writing, she still likes to "go to libraries that aren't busy"—her favorite workspace since childhood—and to write by hand. But her days now begin and end with Lucy. As a middle-aged new mom, Wendy says she's "not the youngest thing in the playground"; but says, on the other hand, "I think there's a lot of history for me and Lucy to draw on."[58]

Wendy's fans can enjoy some of that history by reading her books of essays. Her earlier collection, *Bachelor Girls*, holds comedic essays on such topics as "The World's Worst Boyfriends," and "Aunt Florence's Bar Mitzvah."[59] In her recent collection, *Shiksa Goddess (Or, How I Spent My Forties)*, Wendy shares her experiences and thoughts on everything from the state of the arts to the art of aging, and from the death of her sister to the birth of her daughter.[60]

In an e-mail exchange with Wendy, she said she now spends life "with my [daughter] and my aging parents—caught between generations." She adds that she "finds solace in work," which currently includes a stage version of her children's book *Pamela's First Musical*.[61] (The title character is treated to a Broadway musical for her ninth birthday.)

Wendy has made excursions into film, including her screenplay of *The Object of My Affection*, starring Jennifer Aniston. But theatre is her first, abiding love—even if she likens playwriting to "making stained glass" in the high-tech information age. "I come back to the theatre because it's how I think ... and it's still, for the writer, the most individual platform and frankly one that respects the writer the most."[62]

When asked about the progress of women playwrights in past decades, Wendy comments that there's a "much larger number of women playwrights since I started writing; but we are still categorized, no matter how successful."[63]

While Wendy typically writes many drafts of a script, she rarely goes back to change a completed play. But she did tinker with *An American Daughter*. Her amended version (the 1998 TheatreWorks staging) highlights the evolving friendship between the main women characters: surgeon-general nominee Lyssa Hughes, and a Jewish–African American oncologist, Judith Kaufman. As products of the same period and its media images, the two women battle skewed definitions of "having it all." Wendy claims, "I wanted to end it with the two women because ultimately, this is a play about two women of that generation."[64]

In Wendy's more recent play *Old Money*, she leaps generations to explore the power and perversions that attend great wealth. The setting is an Upper Eastside mansion at both the start and end of the twentieth century, with actors playing characters in both periods. Most critics faulted the "unfocused," "frustrating" structure of the play, which Wendy herself describes as "like a dance." But the *San Francisco Chronicle* praised the "most poignant scene" in which present-day Vivian Pfeiffer confronts his robber-baron father as a young man. ("Viv" has reversed his father's bigotry and union-busting with his own philanthropy in the name of Pfeiffer.[65])

Wendy describes *Old Money* as "comedic with serious intention," a phrase that fits most of her work. Her characters use humor for the same reasons Wendy does: "Because one, it makes one entertaining; two, it deflects.... Also, it helps you deal with things which are overwhelmingly tragic."[66] Wendy tries to strike a balance between the lighter and darker issues of life. She suggests that comedy itself is a balancing act, a way to "hide the pain" but also "to reveal it.... To explore it. And to break it, too."[67] She seems to live and write by what is, in effect, her comedy creed: "I believe in comedy, in its spirit, in its ability to lift people off the ground."[68]

A passage that Wendy wrote for her preface to *The Sisters Rosensweig* could apply to virtually all of her plays. And certainly to *The Heidi Chronicles*: "This is neither a serious nor a comic play. It is hopefully both. The trick in writing it, playing it, or even reading it, is to find the balance between the bright colors of humor and the serious issues of identity."[69]

The Play—*Heidi*'s Brave New Family

Both acts of *The Heidi Chronicles* start with a prologue followed by flashbacks of Heidi Holland's life, scenes that span 24 years in all. A good approach to the play is to chart how Wasserstein has dovetailed the issues of Heidi's life with those of the women's movement.

In her Act One prologue, Wasserstein deftly sets up the analogy between feminist art-historian Heidi and her long-ignored women artists. The audience becomes Heidi's class at Columbia (1989), viewing slides that range from the art of the sixteenth-century Anguissola sisters through Lily Spencer of the late nineteenth century. The work and lives of these women have been sidelined. So, too, their canvases reflect images of women sitting apart, detached. The analogy between Heidi and her subjects is directly made with her closing line:

> Frankly, this painting has always reminded me of me at one of those horrible high school dances. And you sort of want to dance, and you sort of want to go home and you sort of don't know what you want. So you hang around, a fading rose in an exquisitely detailed dress, waiting to see what might happen.[70]

Quickly, the scene changes to such a school dance, in 1965, when feminism and Heidi are both about to blossom. Here, Heidi is an updated wallflower, prepared to sit in a corner reading *Death, Be Not Proud*. Her friend Susan reminds her why they're here: "Girl meets boy ... they hold hands walking in the sand ... Get it?" Only Heidi doesn't want to get it. While Susan hikes up her skirt and aims herself at a boy who can "twist and smoke," Heidi sits with her book. But not for long; a boy in a St. Marks blazer—Peter Patrone—draws her into a witty repartee ("I was drawn to you from the moment I saw you shielding that unfortunate wench rolling up her garments").

Peter transforms the horrible gym dance into a mock farewell cruise of the Queen Mary, and Heidi gladly plays along. Despite their make-believe, the ease and affection between them is genuine. There is earnestness in their playful vows of friendship: Peter says, "I want to know you all my life. If we can't marry, let's be great friends," to which Heidi replies, "I will keep your punch cup as a memento beside my pillow." Peter's line is particularly prophetic: The reasons they never marry are revealed later, but he remains a great friend who is indeed family to Heidi.

The scene shifts to 1968, to a dance and rally for Eugene McCarthy (the senator who was chief sponsor of the ERA). Heidi is alone by the food table when she's accosted by the "intense but charismatic" Scoop Rosenbaum. Intimidated, Heidi mumbles half-hearted replies that prompt his rude but incisive remark, "You know, you really have one hell of an inferiority complex." He goads her until Heidi snaps back, "You are really irritating." For this, Scoop cheers her: "That's the first honest thing you've said all night!" Like Peter, Scoop has his prophetic speech: "Why are you so afraid to speak up? ... You're the one this is all going to affect. You're the one whose life this will all change significantly."

Heidi finally speaks up, and asks why some well-educated woman should spend her life making tuna sandwiches for Scoop and his children. "She shouldn't," Scoop replies, "... I'm on your side." (Scoop talks a good game of women's lib—even if it's part of his pick-up line.) Heidi enjoys the sparring with Scoop, in spite of herself. To his invitation that she sleep with him, Scoop adds a vision of the future: Maybe when they're 35, they'll fondly look back on this encounter, when he was "editor of a crackpot liberal newspaper," who thought he could fall in love with Heidi Holland, "canvassing art historian," that first snowy night in New Hampshire.

The next scene is a women's rap session: a consciousness-raising group in a church basement, 1970. Wasserstein draws it with a blend of comic satire, nostalgia, and respect. In fact, the opening sound is Aretha Franklin belting out "Respect" (an anthem of the movement). Two wildly opposite characters begin the scene: Fran is a lesbian physicist and militant feminist in fatigues. The hostess, Jill, is an ever-polite and self-effacing housewife. Heidi is brought in by Susan and holds back while others give testimony about how they've neglected their own needs to serve others. Jill has been what Fran calls "a fuckin' Hostess cupcake," always tending to her husband, children, and friends. Fran wants approval from her "sisters" for her own sexual identity. And Susan reports that, instead of starting a women's law journal, she's joining the Law Review, so she can change the male establishment from within.

A newcomer to the group, Becky, is a forlorn teenager. Her filmmaking father has run off with the blond flower child from his last film. Her mother has fled to California, where she's been "talking to a tree or something." The overextended Jill invites Becky to move into her home, because "women like us have to learn to give to those who appreciate it instead of those who expect it." Fran adds that those "assholes [men] have been expecting it for centuries."

Wasserstein gives to Fran a poignant speech about the women's movement:

> Heidi, every woman in this room has been taught that the desires and dreams of her husband, her son or her boss are much more important than her own. And the only way to turn that around is for us, right here, to try to make what *we* want ... to be as vital to us as it would undoubtedly be to any man. And then we can go out and really make a difference!

The speech compels Heidi to share her testimony: She knows her attachment to Scoop is wrong. Both of them are now at Yale, where she is an art-history graduate student. Scoop sees other women, but Heidi will drop anything to be with him. "I keep allowing this guy to account for so much of what I think of myself.... I would tell any friend of mine that's wrong." Now into the spirit of the session, Heidi unfurls an emotional appeal that, again, echoes the thrust of the movement: "I hope our daughters never feel like us. I hope our daughters feel so fucking worthwhile. Do you promise me we can accomplish that much, Fran?"

Heidi is given a full-fledged welcome to the group, with hugs and assurances of "I love you, Heidi" all around. The ritual is funny in its effusiveness, but it marks the key moment of Heidi's initiation into the movement. The scene closes on an upbeat image of solidarity and high spirits among the women. Arms linked, courage up, they capture the energy and zeal of the whole movement as they belt out together, "R-E-S-P-E-C-T ... Find out what it means to me ..."

The next scene is outside the Chicago Art Institute, 1974. Here, Wasserstein explicitly merges the women's movement with Heidi's campaign for women's art. Heidi is in her home town for only four hours for a protest against the museum's exclusion of women artists. She is astonished to see Peter here, since she called him earlier to explain why she couldn't see him.

Peter's witty banter has turned bitter: He is caustic about Heidi's liaison with "Poopsie" (Scoop), and insulting to Heidi's fellow protestor, Debbie. Heidi chides Peter for becoming "cruel in my absence." He concedes that her absence has contributed to his mood; he has not seen her for the eight months she worked on her dissertation. "I'm afraid I'm feeling sort of distant from you," he snaps.

Heidi insists that Peter just needs a girlfriend. But after Heidi reports that Susan is now a "radical shepherdess" in Montana who prefers women, Peter drops his bomb: He has become "a liberal homosexual pediatrician." At first, Heidi is stunned and disbelieving; she accuses Peter of mocking Susan's ideals. But ultimately she must believe the intensity with which he blurts out,

> Heidi, I'm gay, okay? I sleep with Stanley Zinc, M.D. And *my* liberation, *my* pursuit of happiness and the pursuit of happiness of other men like me is just as politically and socially valid as hanging a couple of goddamned paintings ... by someone named Nancy, Gladys or Gilda. And that is why I came to see you.... I am demanding your equal time and consideration.

To break the tension, Peter prods Heidi into giving him a playful punch. She gives him a good one for "not being desperately and hopelessly in love with me." Peter may have a new love, the waiter who is meeting him here. Nonetheless, Heidi is a huge part of his life. (And now, they openly share an understanding of what it means to be in an out-group, fighting for respect.)

Despite Heidi's closeness to Peter and Scoop, the two men never meet until Scoop's wedding. The next scene—at the Pierre Hotel—puts Peter, Heidi and Susan outside the reception for Scoop and his "blandish" bride, Lisa. Peter does a sarcastic replay of the vows they've just witnessed: "'Do you, Scoop Rosenbaum, take Lisa Friedlander to be your bride?' "Well, I feel ambivalent about her. But I am blocked emotionally and she went to good schools, comes from a very good family and is not particularly threatening. So, yeah, I do."

Scoop emerges, to coax the others back into the reception. Left together, Scoop and Heidi come to terms with why he has just married Lisa.

He may be a scoundrel, but Scoop is honest with Heidi. He explains that he could not expect Heidi to devote the next decade "to making me a home ... and a life so secure that I could with some confidence go out into the world ... and attempt to get an 'A'." (He grades everything.) He admits that Heidi is right to go after the same things he wants: achievement and fulfillment. But he doesn't want a wife who wants that, too.

When Heidi tells Scoop why she came today, her words foreshadow the next act: "Peter said if I witnessed your ritual, it would put an end to an era." In a larger sense, an era does end with this scene, because Act Two chronicles the 1980s and the aftermath of the women's movement. Before leaving the old era, Wasserstein has her characters celebrate it once more. Inside, the musicians play "You Send Me," which Scoop was to have danced with his bride. Instead, he dances the request with Heidi. When Scoop tells her "I'll always love you," Heidi dismisses it, with "Oh, please." But she is fully caught up in the moment, as Scoop croons to her: "Darling, you send me, honest you do ..."

The prologue to Act Two—another slide-show of art—again recalls the link between Heidi, her reclaimed artists, and their legacy to all women. Heidi comments,

> There is something uniquely female about these paintings.... What strikes me is both ladies seem slightly removed from the occasions at hand. They appear to watch closely and ease the way for the others to join in. I suppose it's really not unlike being an art historian ... being neither the painter nor the casual observer, but a highly informed spectator.

Heidi is such a spectator for the next scene, a baby shower for Scoop's wife, the "blandish" but affable Lisa (1980). The guests include Heidi and Susan, and Lisa's younger sister, Denise. The scene begs comparison to the earlier rap session. Obvious now is that the women's movement has stalled in the new generation. They have no sense of collective spirit, but Denise blithely takes for granted the movement's gains: "Once my career's in place, I definitely want to have my children before I'm thirty.... Isn't that what you guys fought for? So we could have it all?"

Heidi's life is still not that neatly plotted. Her career got a boost with the publication of her book, written in England via a grant. But her potential marriage there fell through when she got a job at Columbia and the man would not leave London. The smug Denise, who is an assistant for a TV talk show, tells Heidi they might feature her and her book on an upcoming segment.

When a phone call from Scoop takes Lisa from the room, the others discuss Scoop's flagrant cheating: Even today, he was in Central Park with a graphics assistant in fishnets. Heidi and Peter saw them. Denise says that Lisa does know; she's just being cheerful to cover up. But when Lisa returns, she crumbles and openly weeps, circled by her "fantastic women" friends. Their huddle is a contrast to the earlier rap scene; its spirit is derived from consolation, not celebration.

The next setting is that of the TV talk-show *Hello New York*, for which Denise is an assistant. (It's 1982; the ERA has been defeated.) For this show segment on baby boomers, Heidi, Scoop, and Peter are all guests. Scoop's magazine *Boomer* is now the oracle of trends, and Peter is the "leading pediatrician in New York under forty." In this TV-shoot-within-a-scene, Wasserstein highlights an irony of women's status: Dr. Heidi Holland has become successful enough to appear on this high-powered talk show. Yet she remains essentially invisible, because the two men dominate the taping. They cut off Heidi's every attempt to speak.

The talk show itself is depicted as pretentious and foolish. An upcoming segment features "Divorced Senate wives modeling coats for spring." Still, Heidi came today believing she might say something meaningful about women and art. She is furious at being sidelined; for once, she vents her rage at these men in her life (suggesting that her consciousness has been measurably raised). After she storms off, Scoop expresses his envy that Peter has remained closer to Heidi. Peter has even picked up Heidi's pet comeback phrase, "Oh, please." He uses it now, in response to Scoop's claim to have been changed by fatherhood.

In the next scene, at a restaurant, in 1984, the gap that now exists between Heidi and Susan reflects the rift between the old ideals of the movement and the new era's preoccupations. Susan has not "worked within the male establishment" to change it. As a TV producer, she has fully embraced the establishment and absorbed its values. Susan and Denise (now her assistant) actually plan to exploit what they see as the mistakes made by Heidi and Susan's generation. They want Heidi to serve as consultant on a series about three women in an urban loft, who "don't want to make the same mistakes we did." Heidi, who had expected this lunch to be a private get-together with her old friend Susan, is outraged, and wants no part of this: "I don't think we made such big mistakes. And I don't want to see three gals on the town who do."

After Denise and Susan spot Diane Keaton and go off to corner her, Heidi looks after Susan and glumly murmurs, "Keep the faith."

The loss of "the faith" among women is what the following scene—Heidi's monologue—is all about. At a Plaza Hotel luncheon, 1986, Heidi addresses the alumni of her old girls' school. Her speech becomes a painful diatribe that expresses her disillusionment on the topic, "Women, Where Are We Going?"

She builds a picture of herself in her health club locker room, surrounded by women with whom she has nothing in common: women obsessed with status and consumption. Among them, Heidi feels alien and humiliated, afraid they will find out that she is both "worthless" and "superior." The point of her outpouring is that, somewhere along the way, the ideals of the women's movement have gotten lost, and Heidi feels lost and adrift, too. She doesn't blame other women, she says. "It's just that I feel stranded. And I thought the whole point was that we wouldn't feel stranded. I thought the point was we were all in this together." (This is the speech which Susan Faludi described in *Backlash* as "one of the most-quoted lines by women writers of the female experience in the '80s."[71])

The next scene is Peter's hospital ward for immune-deficient children. It's Christmastime, 1987, near midnight. A young doctor (Ray) tells Heidi the ward is closed, but she says she has brought boxes of books and records she wants to donate. (What she truly needs and wants is to see Peter; she has been trying to reach him all week.) Peter enters, very upset, and apologizes to Ray for Heidi's intrusion. Ray exits, and Heidi works up to telling Peter that she is moving to the Midwest tomorrow, to teach at a college there. She has come to say goodbye.

The news is a blow to Peter and makes him more caustic: "So. You're going to Northfield, Minnesota, to start again ... Make new friends. Give donations to the old." Heidi tries to give reasons: "I've been sad for a long time. I don't want to be sad anymore." Feeling his way through this, Peter glances at the books she's brought. Their odd out-of-place titles, like *The Secret Life of Salvador Dali*, evoke old familiar banter between them. But tension builds again, because Peter is inexplicably hostile. Finally, Heidi cries, "Where is all this coming from?" He painfully explains that about once a month he goes to hear testimonials about a friend who has died of AIDS. Now his old friend Stanley is ill. He continues, "You see, my world gets narrower and narrower. A person only has so many close friends. And in our lives, our friends are our families. I'm actually quite hurt you don't understand that."

Heidi does understand that, and assures him, "There is no one precious to me in the way you are." Peter counters, "But obviously I can't help you. And you can't help me." After a moment Heidi offers, "We could try.... I could become someone else next year.... I promise you won't lose this member of your family." Picking up two paper cups, she invokes the night they first met: "Tell me, how long have you been on this cruise?" They hold each other, and as Peter cries, Heidi echoes his line of long ago, "If we can't marry, let's be great friends."

For the final scene (1989), Heidi sits in a rocker in her new apartment. The freshly painted walls suggest a clean slate, a new start for Heidi. However, there still are constants in her life—the incorrigible Scoop, for one. He drops in "to touch base," but really to tell her that he just sold *Boomer* magazine. Scoop claims he got the courage to make the change when he heard Heidi had adopted a baby. "I wasn't alone against the wilderness," she reports. She had help from Peter, who "still runs that ward" and now lives with the nice young doctor, Ray.

To Scoop's probing question of whether Heidi is happy, she divulges that she is dating an editor she likes. And although she's never been "a happy girl," there is a chance that someday Scoop's son and her daughter will meet on a plane over Chicago. "And he'll never tell her it's either/or ... And she'll never think she's worthless.... Maybe things will be a little better. And yes, that makes me happy." Scoop finally discloses his real reason for selling *Boomer*: he's planning to run for Congress. He kisses Heidi and says to her baby, "What do you think, Judy? A mother for the nineties and a hero for the nineties." Scoop dashes off; Heidi lifts her baby into the air and exclaims, "A heroine for the twenty-first!"

Wasserstein ends both of her chronicles on a positive note: She invokes a future in which women are active, recognized leaders; and she closes on a vision of Heidi at her most optimistic.

Certainly, a main theme in the play is the idea that the work of the women's movement is far from complete. Wendy's concern about this was the springboard for the script. But another vital theme emerges and becomes, in essence, the playwright's "plea to establish your own kind of family," which is what Heidi does.

Dr. Heidi Holland is a new-age pioneer, vastly different from the women protagonists of the previous plays. She is the first female protagonist to be very active in her world, pressing for a voice and place on many fronts: social and cultural, political and professional. Heidi moves into the public sphere on a grand scale, with an impressive parcel of skills. And yet, she shares with her earlier counterparts an acute lack of self-esteem.

As in the case of all pioneers, Heidi's journey is an uncertain one. Living by the ideals she has internalized means revising the map of women's roles in society, starting with herself. But this also means re-charting relationships—to men, to other women, to community, and of course, to family.

In the play, the notion that created family may omit marriage is not presented without ambivalence. Here and elsewhere, Wasserstein suggests that the women's movement rescued Heidi's generation from marriage equated with being dependent and homebound. But it offered no real solutions for combining marriage with hard-won independence. Certainly, part of the problem lies in a mindset among the kind of men of whom Scoop is a specimen. He is a man who talks a great case for women's equality and appreciates a bright, ambitious woman as a coworker or friend, but would never marry one. The 1970s gave rise to legions of Scoops, who upheld women's rights in general but weren't willing to practice real equality at home.

If Wasserstein presents a positive image of marriage, it's the merger of Peter and Ray, the gay doctors. The play's images of conventional marriage—that of Becky's far-flung parents, or that of the scoundrel Scoop—come off as shallow and faithless. (Heidi seems much better off with Scoop as an honest friend, rather than a dishonest husband.)

Asked if she has scoundrels like Scoop in her own created family, Wendy answered, "It's interesting, this concept of family, because I know even in my personal life, people will say, 'How can you like that person, he's so terrible?' And I think, Well, I've known this person a long time, and they're sort of my family, so good or bad, they've got me, and I've got them."[72]

Wendy is emphatic in saying, "I'm a single woman and my friends really are my family. My parents and brother and sister talk about family all the time ... and for me, so much of my life has been about friends.... My nurturing has always come from my friends."[73]

In the play, Heidi's most enduring family members are obviously Peter and Scoop. At times, they foster Heidi's self-esteem; at others, they clearly test it. But they do function as family for her. In both senses of the word nurture—"nourish" and "educate"—they provide nurturing. Heidi clearly learns from both of them. Peter provides more nurture of the "nourishment" kind; but his sensibilities make him more the kindred spirit of Heidi. In fact, it is the scene between Peter and Heidi, at the hospital ward, that holds the heart of the play, as Wasserstein calls it:

> That's the heart of the play, really. And actually, I found it through the writing of the play; it wasn't what I set out to write. When I set out to write the play, I thought the heart of it was Heidi's speech to the girls' school. But, in fact, Peter saying "our friends are our family" is, in summary, the heart of it.[74]

In her plays and essays, Wendy Wasserstein challenges the assumption that there is only one right kind of family, or life. "I don't think there are any lives that are ... *the* life to live.... I think you have different things at different times in life."⁷⁵ By choosing to be a playwright, and by embracing life as a single mother at almost fifty, Wendy practices what she preaches through her writing. Her lament in one essay, about women conforming to dictates that keep them from feeling whole and worthwhile, is particularly eloquent:

> What saddens me deeply is that any of us should feel privately inadequate or deserving of judgment.... The self-recrimination for not being a certain kind of woman, a certain kind of mother ... is a quiet but constant undertow, a persistent dull ache. I wish all my friends could accept how fine and admirable they really are. I wish we could all offer ourselves such critical kindness.⁷⁶

Wendy is an avid feminist, but wants feminism to be "expanding the idea of humanism; otherwise humanism is about great European heroes."

> I know that, for myself, that whole [feminist] movement—it did change my life. I know that. I think I would have wanted to write plays, you know, have had the talent to. Whether I would have pursued it, I don't know. I think that Marsha and Beth and I are very fortunate to have come of age when we did, at this time—when the women's movement had made enough of a dent in society that the repercussions of it were able to open up the theatre to our voices.⁷⁷

Part IV

Lessons Driven Home: Vogel and Edson

The twentieth century ended with a Pulitzer "first": women took the Pulitzer Prize for drama two years in a row: Paula Vogel won for *How I Learned to Drive* in 1998; Margaret (Maggie) Edson for *Wit* in 1999. Both Paula and Maggie were teachers before their playwriting successes. So it is, perhaps, no coincidence that both of their prize plays impart lessons through their main characters. In both plays, the protagonist is a woman who narrates her story by directly addressing the audience, introducing flashback scenes, then stepping into them. (Vogel's play even starts with the central character telling the audience, "Sometimes, to tell a secret, you first have to teach a lesson.")

Both writers use humor to make a highly distressing topic bearable, even entertaining. Vogel's play centers on pedophilia; Edson's play depicts a woman struck down by ovarian cancer. Both plays are performed in quick episodic fashion with no intermission. And both plays are often followed by talk-backs that open dialogues between audience and performers about the play's content. These dialogues, and the plays themselves, have helped to bring some of the most painful, harrowing human issues into a much-needed spotlight.

After taking the Pulitzer with her first play, Maggie Edson returned to the elementary classroom, content that her play might be teaching elsewhere while she gives first-graders lessons in basic phonics. Veteran playwright Paula Vogel continues to push hot-buttons with her politically charged plays. Vogel's scripts vividly uphold the idea that the personal is, and must be, political—a notion that pervaded the whole decade of the nineties.

15

The 1990s: Gender Crisis at the Crossroads (Or, Wrong Turn at the Men's Movement)

The last decade of the twentieth century was punctuated with what became known as a gender crisis. Mass culture was awash with images of men and women squaring off, head to head, in a new "gender war." As the editors of *The Utne Reader* put it (in a 1993 issue):

> It seems that animosity between men and women has hit a boiling point once again. Less obvious than it was in the early '70s, when the emerging women's movement challenged ... relationships between the sexes, the gender war is now being played out more subtly against a series of public events that have inspired heated debates in the work place, on the park bench, and in the bedroom.[1]

Among the public events that fueled this war were: the Senate hearings on Clarence Thomas, a Supreme Court nominee charged with sexual harassment; the media-saturated trial of O.J. Simpson for the murder of his wife; and the media frenzy around President Clinton's liaison with aide Monica Lewinski. (His personal actions aside, one of Clinton's most prowomen public actions was his reversal of the Reagan-era "gag rule" that banned Federal funding to any agency that mentioned abortion while counseling women.)

The decade's paramount public event was the Gulf War, although little truth of the conflict was ever released to the American public. (Later documentary films, like *Hidden Wars of Desert Storm*, exposed the horrors

15. The 1990s: Gender Crisis at the Crossroads (Or, Wrong Turn...)

behind the U.S. invasion and post-war sanctions.) At the time, the Gulf War provided a stage for U.S. military machismo to flex its muscles in what was depicted as a just intervention. As feminist writer Rosemary Ruether lamented, "This triumphant machismo on the government level was both reflected in and supported by renewed racism, sexism, and open hostility to issues of social justice in American society."[2]

The renewed sexism of the '90s took an ironic twist with the rise of what became "the men's movement." In protest against the effects of the women's movement—but also in undeniable emulation of it—men rallied in sports arenas and campsites to reevaluate what it means to be a man. The movement's book titles even included *The Masculine Mystique* by Andrew Kimbrell, which alleged that pressures from the government, media, and marketplace have been forcing men into false image types that include "Machine Man" and "Competition Man." (Kimbrell glosses over the fact that the government, media, and marketplace were created by men and are still dominated by them.)

If the men's movement had a bible, it was Robert Bly's best-seller, *Iron John*. Bly's book argued that men have been made soft by feminine influences and lack of initiation by older males. Bly offered a parable for men seeking a return to their "wild man" nature with a drawn-out analysis of the Grimm fairy tale about Iron John. In the tale, a boy is led through initiation tests (in wilderness and combat) by an enchanted mentor: the hairy wild man, Iron John.

Gloria Steinem's response to *Iron John* reflected other feminist voices: "Though he seems to have started out with some idea that men should explore the full circle of human qualities ... Bly seems to have returned to the easier sell of old warlike language of kings and battles ... and measuring adulthood by men's distance from mothers."[3]

But some voices of the men's movement were aligned with the ideals of feminism. In the book *Women Respond to the Men's Movement*, Riane Eisler gave credit and thanks to "those men who are working for gender equity, to stop male violence against women, and to change their own thinking and behavior so they can work in equal partnership with women."[4]

A leader of that movement was John Stoltenberg, whose book *Refusing to Be a Man* challenged "what goes on in men's minds and bodies ... to maintain their belief that they are 'men.'" Calling male supremacy the "honest term for patriarchy," Stoltenberg declares that "people born with penises learn an ethic that leaves out ... others, specifically anyone who is 'less a man.'" The belief that masculinity depends on male supremacy has produced what he calls the "devastating consequences" of pornography, domestic violence, and homophobia. (Paula Vogel would write her angriest plays around these volatile issues, including her script *Hot 'n' Throbbing*.) The answer, says Stoltenberg, is for men to reject these beliefs about male supremacy and to embrace a "selfhood rooted in capacity for fairness."[5]

In the '90s, even feminist voices argued that men need liberation from male supremacy, almost as much as women do. Gloria Steinem avowed,

> Make no mistake. Women want a men's movement. We are literally dying for one. If you doubt that, just listen to women's desperate testimonies of hope that the men in our lives will become more nurturing toward children, more able to talk about emotions, less hooked on a spectrum of control that extends from not listening through to violence, and less repressive of their own human qualities that are called "feminine"—and thus suppressed by cultures in which men dominate.[6]

Susan Faludi wrote her book *Stiffed: The Betrayal of the American Man* to target the way men are "imprisoned in cultural stereotypes." Since those stereotypes have largely worked in men's favor, Faludi was asked why she wrote the book. Her response was that feminism is not "only about women.... For women to live freely, men have to live freely, too." Faludi's interviews with scores of men convinced her that men "have this feeling that women are rising just as men are falling." However, she is quick to add that

> The truth is, of course, that women are moving from the subbasement to the basement. By any objective measure—pay, representation in boardrooms, status—men are still ahead. But psychologically, it's much harder to fall than to climb, even if you land at a higher point than those who are just beginning to rise.[7]

"Just beginning to rise" was an apt phrase for the status of women at the century's close. By any gauge of progress, the ascent of women since the 1970s has been modest. For example:

In pay equity: In 1998, women were earning 76 cents for every dollar paid to men (up from 59 cents in the early '70s), and still made up two-thirds of all minimum-wage earners.[8]
In government: In the 106th Congress, women made up 9 percent of the Senate and 12.9 percent of the House (up from 2 percent and 5 percent in the '70s); and 26 states sent no women at all to the 106th Congress.[9]

In 1999, the National Foundation for Women Legislators posted this calculated prediction: "At the current rate of increase, the number of years until women hold public office in numbers equal to men will be—584 years. (And men may still hold most policy-making offices.)"[10]

On almost all fronts, as the millennium ended, true partnership was still the exception and male supremacy the rule. And what Stoltenberg called the "devastating consequences" of male supremacy still abounded in homophobia, pornography, and battery of women.

In her talk at Loyola University in the fall of 1999, Gloria Steinem reminded her audience that "the most dangerous place for an American woman is not in the street but in her home." (Domestic violence remains the number one cause of injury to women.[11])

In the 1990s, the homefront also became a storefront for pornography via "e-porn" on the Internet. In an article titled "Lust for Profits," *U.S. News* bared the facts that "web surfers spent $970 million on access to adult-content sites in 1998." And, in 1999, "cyberporn sales" hit a total that was "about the same as the amount spent on-line for books (1.3 billion) and a good deal more than plane tickets."[12]

John Stoltenberg was moved to co-found Men Against Pornography to awaken men to "the power pornography can have over our lives":

> [Pornography] can make men believe that our penises are like weapons ... that women's body parts belong to us—separately, part by part—instead of to a whole real other person ... that women want to be raped, enjoy being damaged by us, deserve to be punished.[13]

Pornography supports a male sexuality that keeps "the other" very much separate—objectified, unequal and unfree.

What Stoltenberg claims, and what feminists have long stressed, is that there can be no real social equality until there is sexual justice for everyone. The 1990s spotlighted the idea that this must include men and women, straight and gay, of every ethnic background.

During the 1990s, the borders between the personal and the political became less distinct but highly electrified zones. This was partly the result of the media blitz around the president's sexual indiscretion and the First Family's turmoil. But on the level of the simple, quiet citizen, pressing questions called for answers with political overtones: Why can't gay couples have the same legal rights as other couples? Why can't women count on having the right and access to safe abortion, if necessary? And when will the government—the "system"—recognize the diversity of the family as it actually exits, now, instead of touting the values of a nuclear family that no longer exists in the clear majority of American households?[14]

The realization that the personal and political must overlap was not new. But in the '90s, it was given new emphasis in American life, and its art. Paula Vogel's plays are a case in point. To Paula Vogel, "politically correct" is the ultimate oxymoron: "In my sense of political, you can never be politically correct. To be political means to open up a dialogue, not to be 'correct.'"[15]

To provoke her audiences into exploring both sides of an issue, Vogel tries to take them "for a ride they wouldn't normally take," and make them "see highly charged political issues in a new and unexpected way."[16] There was perhaps no better artist-spokeswoman for the 1990s.

16

Paula Vogel's Winding Road to Victory

Being at a loss for words has never been a problem for Paula Vogel. She laughingly describes herself as a "motor mouth." And the truth is, she gives the strong impression that she never thinks, talks, or writes in anything but high gear. Paula has also described herself, quite candidly, as "a lesbian who loves men." In matters of the heart, as well as in her art and politics (both national and gender politics), Paula has avidly chosen the road less traveled. And when she has encountered obstacles, Paula has managed to turn them into milestones by applying hefty amounts of resolve and humor.

When talking about her family background, Paula spins off a lively narration, describing family members who clashed and cavorted in the most theatrical ways:

> You know, I don't believe in Hallmark family love. My parents were characters, and everyone who met them knew that they were characters. I've even had people meet my mother and say, "I think I've met your mother before," and I go "Okay, is it Tennessee Williams or is it Paul Zindel?"—name your play.... My family is larger than life. My brother Carl was larger than life....
>
> My family has always felt like stage plays. And I love plays. So really, if you're going to get into a fight, it's going to be a fight you remember. And if you're going to do something—I mean, my mother made gestures that were highly theatrical, that were wonderful. The loose screw incident actually happened.[1]

What Paula refers to as the "loose screw incident" took place when she was thirteen and involved Paula, her older brother Carl, and her

Paula Vogel

mother, Phyllis. To set the scene for this particular family "stage play," a bit of background on Paula's life is in order. She was born in 1951 in Washington, D.C.; but she and her two older brothers, Carl and Mark, grew up around Baltimore "on the wrong side of the beltway," as Paula phrases it. The turbulent marriage of her Catholic mother from the South (New Orleans) and her Jewish father from the North (New York) left Paula with something of a split personality—but a useful one in terms of a gift for story-telling. "Some people say that this is very traditionally Southern, this kind of great story-telling," Paula explains. "Others say it's *so* New York."[2] From her childhood vantage point, Paula experienced it as both. Her family members not only told great outrageous stories, however. They lived them. And when her mother and father split up—in the year in which Paula turned eleven—they faced off with as much hostility as the American North and South during the Civil War.

As for the "loose screw" caper, picture this scene unfolding: Paula's newly divorced mother Phyllis is raising her adolescent kids in a humble apartment near the Baltimore beltway. Phyllis complains to the Board of Health about the trash buildup in their building. The Board checks it and slaps a violation on the landlord, who retaliates with an eviction notice to the Vogels. Rather than fight it, Phyllis moves her clan to a new dwelling; but not without driving them back to their old place, armed with screwdrivers. She directs them to unscrew everything in the apartment, and inscribes a circle on the living room floor. With quick, quiet efficiency, they unscrew every light bulb and dismantle every fixture. They unhinge doors to every room, cabinet and appliance. They carefully line up the parts against a wall, and place each screw or bolt in a neat pile in the center of the floor. To this, Phyllis adds a terse note to the landlord: "Screw you!"[3]

The bold strokes of this Vogel family drama—the theatricality, the wry humor, the deft dismantling of the familiar to make a point in a startling way—would later become hallmarks of a Paula Vogel play.

Looking back at her family dynamics, Paula comments, "I would describe love in my family as 'life force.'" Between her parents, that force became wildly negative. The ferocity with which her mother came to hate her father would, in later years, become amusing to Paula. But during her childhood, she concedes, "It was not funny. It was very painful."[4] And it brought Paula closer to her brother and mentor, Carl. He introduced her to a world both exciting and terrifying:

> My brother shook me up at an early age. He told me that he was gay.... I was scared to death of it. And he brought me to John Waters films when I was seventeen; and he brought me to drag shows when I was eighteen.... It was frightening; and it was wonderful.... And the notion of theatre and gender—I think that came directly from my brother Carl.[5]

Carl was the aspiring writer, until thugs broke in and destroyed his work in cruel response to his gay activism. (Carl ended up as a San Francisco librarian.) "When he stopped writing," says Paula, "I started."[6] The idea of writing for theatre took root in high school, although Paula recalls her first exposure as "some god-awful opera at the National Theatre. It was a school trip ... and what I remember most is that the boys were leaning over the balcony [so] they could see the soprano's cleavage.... I think I knew even then that theatre had to be seductive in order to work."[7]

As a class president and good speaker, Paula briefly considered a political life. But when she became aware of her own sexuality, such thoughts gave way to thoughts of theatre. She "stumbled into a drama class" and felt "this is home." She adds, "I think I chose theatre because it was a home that could include my sexuality."[8]

In drama class, a scarcity of men landed Paula in leading male roles. ("I thought I made a superb John Proctor.") But she knew she would not pursue acting. "Why would I want to stand on stage, be directed by a man, and told how a woman feels? It seemed too close to the gender scripting that society was prescribing in the first place."[9]

So she spent three years stage-managing and doing technical theatre.

She found this appealing "because techies *watch*. They don't participate ... they observe. And that is extremely comfortable."[10] But by her senior year, she started writing "revues and that sort of thing.... More and more I thought maybe I could write, but I didn't know of any women writers."[11]

Carl encouraged her to go on to college, and Paula did. She won scholarships to Bryn Mawr, then was kicked out two years later for what she terms "naughty behavior." After completing her B.A. in theatre at Catholic University, she weighed the choices of becoming a playwright or a director, roles that she feels reflect and "play off traditional gender roles. ... I think it's under the surface; that we think of the director as the one that will be, in essence, the father of the production." But the choice and challenge of playwriting won out with Paula:

> Playwriting, I thought—well, the reason there's a real resistance to women being playwrights is that playwriting was conceived as a feminine role for men to play. It's like men do not want to give over the one place where they actually give birth and are involved in the creative process. And it's guarded very jealously because it is seen as a feminine role to the masculine role of the director....
>
> At the point where I was trying to sort out whether to be a director or a playwright, I was also sorting out whether or not I was going to indeed marry my fiancé, or act on other desires. [She was, at the time, engaged to a young man—who actually taught Paula how to drive.] And when I decided to not go in the direction of the men that I'd been loving, but go in the direction of the women, I suddenly thought, well, you are already bucking the gender system. Why not be a playwright?[12]

Paula applied for the playwriting program at Yale School of Drama (the class of Wendy Wasserstein), but was turned down: "I put my head on the table and wept."[13] She rebounded by deciding to teach and got into the Ph.D. program at Cornell; but then "used Cornell as a backdrop to continue the playwriting and ... figure out how to do it my own way."[14] Of her three plays introduced at Cornell in the late 1970s, perhaps the best harbinger of what was to come from Paula was *Desdemona: A Play About a Handkerchief*. The play bore the stamp of her feminism and her keen political sense, and it established some hallmarks of her theatricality. To shock viewers into seeing the familiar in new ways, Paula uses devices that include voiceovers, black-outs, slides, scene titles, and multiple-role casting. (Some of her devices evoke the theatricality of Bertolt Brecht, who was an admitted influence on Paula.)

For *Desdemona*, Paula used blackouts and cinematic jump-cuts to dismantle and tweak the givens of Shakespeare's *Othello* into a startling feminist version, or inversion, of the play. She literally takes the audience behind the scenes—"a back room of the palace"—to retrace the tragedy's action from the perspective of Desdemona, Emilia, and Bianca. Paula draws these women full-blown and willfully resisting the roles that men have forced upon them. Her restless Desdemona rebels against her narrow world by daring trysts that would give due cause for Othello's jealous rage. To her servant Emilia, Desdemona laments that "women are clad in purdah ... from the cradle to the altar to the shroud ... bridled with linen, blinded with lace."[15] After Emilia admits to her theft of the handkerchief for the husband she detests, the two women reach a point of mutual trust and confidence. But their trust and desperate plan to escape together in the morning come too late. The last scene, of Emilia counting brush strokes to Desdemona's hair, becomes a chilling count-down of their remaining minutes of life.

Desdemona took second place in Actors Theatre's New Play Festival in 1979 (the year that Henley's *Crimes of the Heart* took first place). Even then, the play's journey to New York's Circle Theatre would take another 14 years.

Resistance from the producing world has disappointed Paula, but not surprised her:

> The difficulty is that all drama by definition from Aristotle is about finding a *male* protagonist. And I have struggled against it for years, with people who say, "You know, we kind of liked *Desdemona*; but ... can we bring in Iago in the second act?" ... You'd want to laugh ... if it weren't all so tragic.[16]

After two years at Cornell, teaching theatre and women's studies, Paula was dismissed for what she calls political reasons. She managed to keep writing without doing the odd jobs she once juggled (like Navy typist, or moving-company packer), thanks to timely subsidies from her brother. "Carl was always bailing me out ... when the rent was due or I had no money for food. His check would conveniently arrive."[17]

With each script she wrote, Paula would start with something personal, that would "directly impact on my life," as she puts it. Yet the plot and characters would unfold around charged political themes. Her play *The Oldest Profession* opened with five elderly females on a park bench in New York City. Their talk reveals that these are not grannies idly gossiping, but proud senior prostitutes scraping by during the Reagan years. In a series of blackouts, their numbers dwindle as the ladies die, one by one. In a final wordless blackout scene, Vera, the youngest at 72, sits alone and forlorn on the bench. Like Vera, the audience is left missing the comradery and quarrels and simple human worth of her lost companions.

Among other things, *The Oldest Profession* depicted the feminization of poverty due to "Reaganomics." But Vogel's vanishing ladies are symbols of all women whose everyday work does not entitle them to any benefits or recognized social value. In his introduction to a volume of Paula Vogel's plays, David Savran (long-time friend and associate of Paula) comments, "All of her work is devoted to exposing not just how women are entrapped and oppressed, but the possibilities that figures like Desdemona or the oldest professionals have to contest, subvert, and redefine the roles they have been assigned."[18]

Two women subvert and wildly redefine their roles in Paula's play *And Baby Makes Seven*, which explodes the conventional image of family and supplants it with a fantastically constructed one. Ruth and Anna make a couple, and their gay friend and roommate, Peter, makes three. But Ruth and Anna have adopted three imaginary, mischievous little boys who have become their alter egos and far too real for Peter's comfort. He has fathered the baby that Anna is carrying, the real child that the three adults are to "have equal say in bringing up." So the three imaginary boys undergo elaborate deaths to prepare for the arrival of the flesh-and-blood child. The play is an almost voyeuristic look at unconscious constructs of identity, maturity and family.

By the mid 1980s, Paula had enjoyed some success as a playwright and was teaching at Brown University. When her brother Carl asked her to join him on a trip to Europe, Paula declined, never dreaming that Carl was HIV positive. As he was dying of AIDS a few years later, she began a script "to the memory of Carl—because I cannot sew" (an allusion to the AIDS Memorial Quilt). "One time he smiled at me and said, 'You're writing about this, aren't you?' I denied it; but I could never hide anything from him."[19]

In *The Baltimore Waltz*, a pajama-clad Carl and his sister Anna make a dreamlike pilgrimage to Europe, to seek adventure and a cure for Anna's illness, "ATD," a disease that strikes unmarried elementary school teachers. (Carl is a head librarian who gets his pink slip because he wears a "pink triangle.") Until the final scene, it seems that Anna is the victim of a fatal disease. Then the reality of Carl's death in a Baltimore hospital quickly hits, capped with a final bit of fantasy: Anna waltzes off the stage with the spirit of Carl.

The Baltimore Waltz took a 1992 Obie award and marked a turning point in Paula's career. She felt that this was, in part, yet another gift from Carl. But a few women also played key roles in shifting Paula's career into high gear. One of these was her longtime associate and friend Molly Smith, who gave *Waltz* its debut at Alaska's Perseverance Theatre. The story of how the play received its pivotal New York staging is best left in Paula's own words:

> I do also think that I would not exist if it weren't for Tanya Berezin. If Circle Rep had not had a woman as artistic director, who happened to have a woman literary manager, who happened to be an ex-student of mine who happened to say "You know what, Paula's plays work better on the stage than they do on the page. If I give you *The Baltimore Waltz* to read, you're not gonna get it on the page." And Tanya asked, "What do we do?" And she said, "Just give it a workshop. Just let it be on its feet." The combination of those three women with *Baltimore Waltz* is really what created a career for me.[20]

Waltz had a cast of only three—Carl, Anna, and the "Third Man/ Doctor." But the latter also played some dozen roles including a French waiter and "the little Dutch Boy at age 50." Paula had originally placed the action in a hospital room, featuring the bed. However, director Anne Bogart had other ideas, which would also influence the art and career of Paula Vogel:

> When we were doing *Baltimore Waltz*, Anne Bogart called me from the hospital. I said, "Are you alright?" She said, "Yeah, I'm here with the set designer. We're looking at the hospital.... We've decided we're going to set it in the lounge." I said, "You can't set it in the lounge, because it all takes place on a bed.... My brother died in a bed. And in childhood we used the bed as a sailing ship. I intended the bed to be the wagon of Mother Courage trotted around the landscapes of Europe." She said, "Oh, that sounds wonderful. That's *your* play.... I don't see a bed." I said, "You're joking.... Annie, I really want this bed." She said, "I tell you what. I will make you see a bed in the lounge.... If you miss the bed, we'll re-talk this." Well, she did. Not only did she make the lounge the bed, but she made it the Eiffel Tower and everything else. And at that point, something in my head went, "Shut up Vogel, you're talking to Anne Bogart. She's got some pretty interesting things in her head."[21]

The experience taught Paula that the ideal model in theatre might not be a "marriage," or the unified production that directors have traditionally strived for. "Anne Bogart taught me something really, really good.... It's not a synthesis. It's not about us coming together on a common vision. It's about us responding to each other's vision. That's a different model.... You start thinking about how you write a play that always resists the director, and that resistance is good." Bogart's idea of theatre harkens back to Brecht. It's the idea, says Paula, that "there has to be multiple interpretations ... so that the set designer is not doing the same thing as the acting; the director is not doing the same thing as the text."[22]

This is not to say that Paula does not enjoy seeing the production she had envisioned. With *Waltz*, she says, "I finally got a production ... almost identical to what I had seen in my head ... at the Studio Theatre. They gave me the bed, they traveled." But she is quick to add, "It's great when it happens. But it's great when it doesn't happen," and a different vision takes shape.[23]

When Paula wrote *Hot 'n' Throbbing* (1994), the script was shaped by her anger over two main issues: First, she was outraged at the prevalence of domestic violence, even in her small city of Providence (she had witnessed an incident first-hand). Second, she wrote the script on an NEA fellowship, just after Congress had ruled that recipients must sign a pledge to keep obscenity out of their art. Partly to test this new censorship, Paula wrote *Hot 'n' Throbbing*—"because obscenity begins at home."

The play's protagonist is Charlene, who has a restraining order against her abusive ex-husband. Charlene supports herself and her two teenagers by writing erotica for a feminist film company. (The work has liberated her from bed-pan duty on a hospital night-shift.) When Charlene's ex-husband breaks in and refuses to leave, she pulls a gun and nicks him in the buttock. He, in return, manipulates her guilt until she agrees to sleep with him; he then beats her and strangles her to death.

Paula got angry again when the play was rejected as too disturbing. She complained that while "the Simpson trial became a media frenzy, my play ... has been kept 'off-stage'.... If we cannot confront domestic violence on our stage, we will not be able to eliminate it from our living rooms."[24]

The experience did not deter Paula from pushing hot-buttons with her plays. *How I Learned to Drive* was her personal exploration of pedophilia. The play depicts a young girl's coming of age at the hands of her Uncle Peck, hands both mentoring and molesting. The compelling protagonist, L'il Bit, tells her story through memory flashbacks connected by sessions in her uncle's car. The play was inspired by Paula's fascination with Nabokov's novel *Lolita*, but Paula made a quantum shift for her play: "The empathy changes because ... Uncle Peck is an object rather than the subject." Another influence (one that is highlighted in the following section on "The Play") was the O. Henry story, *The Gift of the Magi*. The story provided a key metaphor for the play, in that Paula's characters "give each other gifts that are the wrong gifts ... but with great love."[25]

The fact is, Paula's uncle character is a loving and lovable figure—a caring complex man who, ironically, helps L'il Bit to create "the ego formation that allows her to escape the family, to survive him, to excel."[26] Along with the gift of the driving lessons, he gives her "the gift of how to survive." Paula does not excuse the harm Uncle Peck does to his niece. But, again, she bids her viewers to take a different look: "Without denying or forgetting the original pain, I wanted to write about the great gifts that can also be inside that box of abuse. My play dramatizes the gifts we receive from people who hurt us."[27]

How I Learned to Drive ran off-Broadway for more than a year. The kudos it gathered included a Drama Critics' Award, an Obie, a Drama Desk Award and, of course, the Pulitzer Prize.

Besides the roles of L'il Bit and Uncle Peck, the play's cast includes a Greek chorus, three actors who play L'il Bit's family members and all other roles. Multi-character roles have become a hallmark of Paula's plays for practical and artistic reasons: "I will do transformational devices till the day I die. Not only do I think it's more economical, but ... I think transformational acting is something that actors love to do. And I'm trying to write plays now—that you say 'How the hell would you do that?'"[28]

Such a play is Paula's most blatant political satire, *The Mineola Twins*. The play takes a frantic romp across the Eisenhower, Nixon and Bush-Senior eras through the lives of wildly dissimilar twins. One actress plays both the flat-chested "bad" twin Myra and the bosomy "good" twin Myrna, whose politics and life-choices could not be more in conflict (right-wing Myrna bombs the Planned Parenthood clinic of far-left lesbian Myra). The twins represent the warring sides of our grossly divided nation. In the playbill, Vogel noted, "Democrats and Republicans alike, despite pretensions of civility, are not talking to each other.... We do not progress. We regress. So we might as well laugh about it." Even at her most farcical, however, Paula employs comedy to make critical points. For her, "combining sadness and comedy heightens both."[29]

Like several Vogel plays, *Mineola Twins* was given its premier by Molly Smith. When asked why Smith is such an ideal producer and director for Paula's plays (Smith has done both), Paula answers,

> She's fearless. She never backs down from anything I do. I have spent decades in rooms with people going "Uuuucchh! Should we really be saying this?" ... Or I've actually had directors go, "Oooh, you're really sick." Which is devastating. Molly goes, "Yeah, can you do it a little bit more?" Molly gets thrilled.... She pushes me past my own limit of what I think is taboo.... I think she's the bravest director I've ever worked with.[30]

After years of collaboration at Alaska's Perseverance Theatre (which is where *Twins* began its stage life), the theatre arts of Vogel and Smith joined again at Arena Stage in Washington. The century ended with Molly as Arena's artistic director, and Paula as playwright-in-residence.

For the New York run of Vogel's *Twins* at Roundabout (1999), Swoosie Kurtz tackled the roles of Myra/Myrna, which include—counting dream sequences—ten roles in all. (Other actors double as the sisters' sons, lovers, etc.; hence the subtitle, *A Comedy in Six Scenes, Four Dreams and Six Wigs*.) In her review, Susan Thomsen claimed that Kurtz' performance was "exquisitely absurd" and the "reason you should make tracks to the Roundabout as soon as possible."[31]

Asked if she has consciously written plays to give women more dynamic and more leading roles, Paula responds, "Absolutely." And she purposely gives actors—male or female—much room to create specifics for characters. "I leave a lot of stuff offstage, deliberately. I don't talk about what people do for a living.... I don't care what they do for a living. Let the actors choose that." Overall, Paula believes in keeping the given circumstances sparse, since she wants a play to be "not the world itself, but a distillation of the world."[32]

Paula's personal distillations of the world present a challenge for actors, directors, designers, even audiences. (The dialogues that fly in talk-backs after a Vogel play can be as intense and provocative as the play itself.) In her playwriting classes, she also challenges her students to write scenes like "the end of the world in five pages," or other extreme scenarios. Even the circumstances in which Paula has taught playwriting have been, at times, extreme. Take her class in the women's maximum security prison in Providence. Paula's frustrations with the early rejections of *Baltimore Waltz* led her to that particular scenario:

> Carl had died.... I wanted to give back through drama; and the play that I wrote, I could not get on. And I was so frustrated that I thought, I will either kill myself wanting to give back with a thing that I love; or I will find another way. And I was driving home; and you can see the barbed-wire fences of the jail from Route 95. And I went, "Okay, so you're not supposed to be a playwright; you're supposed to be a teacher.... Go and teach these women how to write a play." I happened to have the year off because ... I got granted a leave of absence, which was supposed to go into nursing Carl. It went into the jails instead.[33]

Of course, Paula has also taught playwriting in more likely, mainstream settings. She has brought the New Play Festival at Brown University to much-acclaimed levels of excellence and experimentation. And on the Cape (where she has been trying to establish a permanent home), Paula has taught her "Playwriting for Teachers" workshop at the Provincetown Fine Arts Center. As for her teaching philosophy, Paula says, "This is my feeling about teaching. I'm training people to be my colleague. Anyone who writes in my class and puts their heart into it, I will support, encourage and love. Period."[34]

Paula's long-time partner, geneticist Anne Fausto-Sterling, has also taught at Brown University, and has been the first to read many drafts of Paula's plays. Paula's own given family has dwindled down to only one brother, Mark. But vital members of Paula's sizable created family include director-producer Molly Smith: "Molly is a main part of my family. She's a big part of my family."[35]

Did Paula ever actually have an "Uncle Peck"? No, she insists. And when asked how she did learn to drive, she smiles and answers:

> There was an older man for me. He was six months older; he was my fiancé. He's the man who taught me how to drive; and he's the man I went to the Beltsville Agricultural Farms with. He was, and is, a wonderful man.
>
> ... There's a lot of different men that I've had crushes on, or I've loved, including some teachers. But you know what ... and this is the only way I know how to say it—there's a lot of me in Peck. There's a lot of me, wanting not to hurt the people I teach ... And wanting to give gifts. I think *that*'s a part of me.[36]

THE PLAY—HOW I LEARNED ... THE REAL LESSONS OF THE ROAD

L'il Bit, the play's protagonist, tells her story in 20 scenes that take her back from age fortyish to age eleven. Aside from L'il Bit and Uncle Peck, the cast includes two women and one man who form the Greek chorus, playing family members and all other parts. Scenes are set up or shifted via titles that are spoken, and sometimes also displayed. (Slides were not used in the New York production but have been used elsewhere, including Chicago. Vogel gives much leeway with the visuals and sound.) Settings are evoked with chairs, a table, a drink glass or two—and titles:

Safety First—You and Drivers' Education. At the sound of a car ignition, the mature L'il Bit steps into a spotlight and tells the audience, "Sometimes, to tell a secret, you first have to teach a lesson." She evokes the scene of this lesson, a "warm summer evening ... in a parking lot overlooking the

Beltsville Agricultural Farms in suburban Maryland." It is 1969 and she is a "very cynical" 17 year old. She joins Uncle Peck in his Buick Riviera (two chairs); Peck inhales the scent of her hair and says, "A man could die happy like this." L'il Bit admonishes him to be good, and Peck insists that he has been good all week—not a single drink—and pleads for a small reward. With her reluctant consent, he unhooks her bra through her blouse, then tenderly feels and kisses her breasts (mimed with great reverence). When L'il Bit curtails this with "We've got to go," Peck says he lives "all week long for these few minutes" with her. L'il Bit replies, "I'll drive."[37]

Idling in Neutral Gear. The adult L'il Bit comes to the audience and introduces some of her family and their practice of giving nicknames after genitalia. When she was born, they were so excited to have a baby girl that they whipped down her diaper to admire her "l'il bit." So small was she that Uncle Peck could lovingly hold her "right in this hand." L'il Bit interjects that she was 16 before she realized "pedophilia" did not mean people who love to bicycle.

Driving in First Gear. The scene is "a typical family dinner," 1969. To L'il Bit's dismay and humiliation, the table talk centers on her blossoming bustline, with the cruelest taunts coming from her grandfather (Big Papa). Uncle Peck tries to make peace; he brings up L'il Bit's upcoming departure for college. But Big Papa mocks her hopes to study Shakespeare: "How is Shakespeare going to help her lie on her back in the dark." L'il Bit explodes and storms off, and Peck is sent by his wife Mary (sister of L'il Bit's mother, Lucy) to go talk to her. He tries, but L'il Bit just wants to borrow his car for a drive—alone. Peck asks when he can see her again; she answers, "Tonight."

Shifting Forward ... to Second Gear. L'il Bit confides to the audience why she was kicked out of college: She had company in her room—a fifth of V.O. With herself and her Mustang tanked, she would cruise the back roads, thinking all it would take would be a notch of the steering wheel. But a reflex kept her hands at nine and three o'clock; she never even got a ticket. "He taught me well."

You and the Reverse Gear. L'il Bit backs up to 1968: a dinner with Peck near the shore, to celebrate her first long legal drive. They're at an inn rich in history, some of which Peck shares with her. He keeps his promise not to drink, but persuades her to have a cocktail. (Interspersed with the scene is L'il Bit's mother Lucy giving "A Mother's Guide to Social Drinking." Its advice includes avoiding any ladies' drinks, made with "sugar ... or umbrellas.") L'il Bit opts for a martini; while sipping the three Peck orders, she asks him about the war and his past in Carolina. He alludes to his mother's disappointment in him, for not amounting to something. L'il

Bit slurs, "I think ... you've amounted a lot." She's obviously in the "soppy stage" as Peck pays the check.

Vehicle Failure. Leaving the inn, L'il Bit is so woozy, Peck has to carry her to the car. She is surprised he didn't take her upstairs. But Peck avows, "I've told you, nothing is going to happen between us until you want it to.... I'm a very patient man." Even drunk, L'il Bit knows "this is wrong ... someone is going to get hurt." But she's too sleepy not to cuddle against Peck for the ride home.

Idling in Neutral Gear. Peck takes the spotlight as a Voice announces "Uncle Peck Teaches Cousin Bobby to Fish." Peck's side of a talk with an imagined Bobby recreates the scene of their fishing jaunt, and Peck mentors Bobby in catching a pompano. But the sensitive boy cries at the plight of the fish, so Peck cuts the line and tries to soothe Bobby. His comforting of the boy moves into another realm as he tells him, "There's a really neat tree house where I used to stay for days.... But it's a secret place—you can't tell anybody we've gone there."

L'il Bit joins her mama and grandma at a table and introduces "On Men, Sex and Women: Part One." Both women complain that men only want one thing. Grandma, who was grabbed up and married at 14 by that "bull" Big Papa, has never had an orgasm and thinks they're a myth. She and Lucy decry the base urges of men, who've got to have it "on the spot ... nasty ... primitive!" Grandma boasts of wielding a broom; Lucy prefers an iron frying pan—"They're great on a man's head."

While Making a Left Turn, You Must Downshift... L'il Bit sets up a "bus trip to upstate New York," 1979. The boy seated beside her claims to be a senior at Whitman high, but is betrayed by a voice breaking into the "miserable equivalent of vocal acne." L'il Bit paints the scene of their night together: Dinner, then her place, for a "faltering and slightly comical 'first act'" but a "capable ... and *sustained* second act." Then, in the denouement, in the dark, "I thought about you, Uncle Peck. Oh, this is the allure. Being older ... Being the first ... the teacher.... This is how the giver gets taken."

L'il Bit reverses to her 15-year-old self for "On Men, Sex, and Women, Part Two." She haltingly asks her mama and grandma if it hurts, the first time you "do it." After her mother replies "just a little bit. Like a pinch," her grandma retorts, "Tell her it hurts! It's agony! ... especially if you do it before marriage!" This leads to a fierce verbal battle between the two women: L'il Bit's mother blames her mother for not equipping her with the facts of life. "If you and Daddy had helped me—I wouldn't have had to marry that no-good-son-of-a—" L'il Bit wails to the audience, "I still can't bear to listen to it," and flees to where the radio is playing in the car, where Peck waits for her.

You and the Reverse Gear. (Here, "it would be nice to have slides of erotic photographs of women and cars"—women draped over hoods, etc.) L'il Bit titles the scene "Initiation into a Boy's First Love." While Peck rhapsodizes about cars, L'il Bit editorializes that "long after a mother's tits, but before a woman's breasts ... after the milk but before the beer ... the boy falls in love with the thing that bears his weight with speed." When the scene shifts to Li'l Bit's actual driving lesson, Peck becomes serious, no-nonsense. He tells her that he wants to give her something that really matters to him: "There's something about driving"—a power that no one can take from you. Peck wants to teach her how to drive "like a man ... with aggression." How to "think what the other guy is going to do before he does it." How to survive an accident, and be the "one to walk away."

Defensive driving involves defending yourself from hazardous and sudden changes... L'il Bit subtitles this scene "Anthropology of the Female Body in the Ninth Grade—or a Walk Down Mammary Lane." (There is a beeping sound, like a transmitter.) In the school hall, a student named Jerome fakes a violent asthma attack brought on by an "allergy trigger." When L'il Bit is pulled in to help and asks what he's allergic to, Jerome grabs her breasts and yelps, "Foam rubber." He and his abettors laugh and retreat, as L'il Bit rages and kicks at him.

Good defensive driving involves mental and physical preparation. In the gym showers, two girls and L'il Bit are in towels. The two prod L'il Bit to go first. And when she drops the towel, they laugh and high-five each other. "Told you! It's not foam rubber! Jerome owes me fifty cents!"

Were you prepared? At the sock hop, L'il Bit stands with other girls. She declines an offer from a boy—Greg—to dance, and explains to the others that he's short and just wants to watch her jiggle. The other girls don't see the problem. (A beeping sound, again. L'il Bit becomes aware of Peck elsewhere on the stage, where he has set up a camera and waits for her.) L'il Bit laments that sometimes she feels like "someone's implanted radio transmitters in my chest at a frequency that ... girls can't detect, but they're sending out these signals to men who get mesmerized." At this, Greg is pulled to her in a trancelike state and again requests a dance. But L'il Bit must get away from the dance: the beeping changes to an electromagnetic force, pulling her to Uncle Peck's side.

You and the Reverse Gear. L'il Bit announces, "1965. The Photo Shoot." (Here, there could be slides of the actor playing L'il Bit, "interspersed with other models à la *Playboy*.") L'il Bit is now a "nervous but curious" 13 year old. Peck assures her that Aunt Mary is at the theatre, and that he'll shoot her with "Nothing showing. Just a peek." He unbuttons her blouse, halfway. Then, to the music he plays, he has her "pretend you're in your room all alone ... and the music feels good." He snaps the shutter; coaches her; snaps again. When he says, "You're a very beautiful young woman," he snaps her blush (and it becomes a slide). L'il Bit relaxes until Peck says, "If we keep this up, in five years we'll have a really professional portfolio." At his idea that she could then model for Playboy, L'il Bit is furious and hurt: "I'm never doing ... that! This is something—that you said was just between us.... I don't want anyone seeing this." Contrite, Peck swears to her that "No one will. I'll treasure this," but L'il Bit withdraws, her eyes closed so he can't "see through" her. He gently coaxes her to listen, at least. "L'il Bit," he intones. "I love you." He snaps her open-eyed startle (yet another slide). "Do you know that? I have loved you every day since the day you were born." L'il Bit nods "yes." Still looking at her uncle, she begins to unbutton her blouse. A voice proclaims, "As an individual operating a motor vehicle ... you must abide by 'Implied Consent.'"

Idling in Neutral Gear. Aunt Mary extols her husband Peck as "such a good man." He does the dishes. He does the yard work for her, for others. "Everyone in the neighborhood borrows Peck." She adds, "I know I'm lucky." At Christmas she gets a "new stole or diamonds," while her poor sister sits. But Mary also knows that Peck is troubled. (She wonders at times what happened in the war.) And she knows what's going on with her niece. "I'm not a fool.... She's twisted Peck around her little finger.... Yet another one borrowing my husband." Mary is counting the days until her niece leaves for school. "I'm a very patient woman. But I'd like my husband back."

You and the Reverse Gear. A chorus member announces L'il Bit's thirteenth Christmas, 1964: "Uncle Peck Does the Dishes." Peck is at the sink in dress clothes and apron, "quiet, brooding." L'il Bit seeks him out. "You're the only man I know who does dishes. I think it's really nice." Peck responds, "I think men should be nice to women. Women are always working for us." L'il Bit works up to asking "Uncle Peck ... Why do you drink so much?" He slowly explains: Some people have a "fire in the belly" ... others (like L'il Bit) have a "fire in the head." Peck has a "fire in my heart. And sometimes the drinking helps." Li'l Bit quietly asks, "Does it help—to talk to me?" Peck confirms, "Yes. It does." So Li'l Bit proposes a deal: "We could meet and talk—once a week ... as long as you stop drinking" and "let me draw the line." Much moved, Peck wishes her a merry Christmas.

Shifting Forward from Second to Third Gear. The chorus announces "Days and Gifts: A Countdown." They recite notes from Peck to L'il Bit at school. September 3, 1969: "You've been away only two days and it feels like months ... ninety days to go." September 25: "Got a post office box—write to me there. Sixty days—Love, your candy man." November 16: "Sixteen days to go. Hope you like the perfume." With each note there is a gift (chocolates, roses, a tape player). Then, L'il Bit recites her note to Peck: "Dear Uncle Peck ... Don't come up next weekend for my birthday..."

Shifting Forward ... to Fourth Gear. December, 1969: A hotel room with champagne chilling. Peck sits on the bed; L'il Bit paces. "I am so pissed off at you, Uncle Peck.... You were counting down to my 18th birthday." To Peck's reply, "You misunderstand," she insists, "I understand all too well. I know what you want to do five steps ahead." They attempt small talk, and both gulp champagne. Peck broaches how much he has missed her. But L'il Bit has only come to tell him, "I'm not doing very well. I'm getting confused.... I don't want us to 'see' each other any more." Peck rationalizes that she's just scared ... everyone has made her "frightened to death about something that is just like breathing." He entreats her to "just lie on the bed with me—our clothes on ... Because sometimes the body knows things the mind isn't listening to." L'il Bit complies ("half wanting to run ... half wanting to be held by him"). But she rises in the bed to join Aunt Mary in "Recipe for a Southern Boy": A drawl of molasses ... splash of Bay Rum ... His heart beating Dixie ... His mouth—"

L'il Bit bends to kiss Peck, then suddenly wrenches free. Desperately, trembling, Peck says, "I haven't been able to do anything but think of you." He pulls out a ring box and blurts, "I want you to be my wife." L'il Bit recoils. "What have you been thinking! ... Family is family. I am leaving. Now!" When she pauses in flight to ask if he's all right, Peck pulls himself up to reply, "I just ... need a real drink." While he drains shots lined up by a bartender, L'il Bit addresses the audience: "I never saw him again.... It took my uncle seven years to drink himself to death. First he lost his job, then his wife, and finally his driver's license." Now that she is older, L'il Bit wonders, "Who did it to you, Uncle Peck? How old were you? Were you eleven?"

You and the Reverse Gear. L'il Bit, at age eleven, is convincing her mother to let her drive to Carolina with Uncle Peck. Her mother is against her spending seven hours in the car with a man: "I don't like the way your uncle looks at you." But L'il Bit counters, "Just because you lost your husband—I still deserve a chance at having a father ... a man who will look out for me." Her mother relents, but adds, "I'm warning you—if anything happens, I hold you responsible."

L'il Bit joins Uncle Peck "On the Back Roads of Carolina," for the

"First Driving Lesson." She sits beside him, but her voice comes from a chorus member. Peck pulls the car over and offers to let her drive. At her objection that she's too young, and can't reach the pedals, he puts her on his lap. After guiding her hands into position on the steering wheel, he moves his hands to her breasts. "Please," says L'il Bit. "Don't do this." He takes "just a moment longer" to tense against her, then buries his face in her neck, and moans softly.

Driving in Today's World. Mature L'il Bit tells the audience, "That was the last day I lived in my body.... I've lived inside the 'fire in my head' ever since." But she finds herself "believing in things that a younger self vowed never to believe in ... like family and forgiveness." She still doesn't know how it feels to jog or dance, "anything that 'jiggles.'" But the nearest she feels to "flight in the body" is when she is driving. "Today ... I've got five hundred miles of highway ahead of me—and some back roads too." After doing the drill of checking her car, she slides in and adjusts the radio, changing the sound of old voices from her past to road music. "Finally, I adjust the rearview mirror." (As she does so, a light reveals the spirit of Uncle Peck in the back seat. She smiles at him in the mirror; he nods to her.) "And then," says L'il Bit, "I floor it."

The compelling, controlling concept of Vogel's play is the idea that Uncle Peck wants to give L'il Bit the skill of driving well, because it is "something that really matters" to him. However, along with the driving lessons, Peck begins his long, patient seduction: Seven years of delicate, near-reverent fondling of his niece that, in his fantasy, will end with her full acquiescence when she comes of age. The shattering of that fantasy is what ultimately destroys Peck and leaves him a casualty, while L'il Bit steers her life back onto a livable course.

Paula Vogel does not belittle or excuse the damage done to L'il Bit by their liaisons, but she compels her audience to consider that a child abuser might be hurting as much as his victim. Vogel draws L'il Bit and Peck with equal skill and sympathy. She leaves no doubt that, whatever other emotions flash between them, at the core of their connection is love.

In the flashbacks of L'il Bit's family life, she is closer to Uncle Peck than to anyone else. What makes him such a potent presence in her coming-of-age is that he is, essentially, both given family and created family for L'il Bit. She and Peck are drawn together as misfits in their squabbling "cracker" family circle.

L'il Bit's no-good father took off long ago. Her bickering mother and grandmother offer misguided, muddled advice. And her grandfather's degrading taunts—about L'il Bit's developing body, or her college plans—are a form of emotional abuse. L'il Bit and Peck provide an oasis for each other. He rescues her from the ego-eroding taunts and shores up her self-esteem. She saves him from his need to drink in order to quell the "fire in his heart." (Vogel only hints at the causes of Peck's "fire"—old traumas sustained in the war? older traumas from his own childhood?)

Peck's abstinence is one of the gifts he gives to L'il Bit: "As long as you're with me, I'll never drink," he vows. And in return, L'il Bit allows his intimate gaze and caress, his "reward" in measured doses. As audience, we see the pattern of their liaison in jumbled sequence (because memories are jumbled). So, also jumbled is the sequence of gifts that are exchanged between them. As Paula Vogel points out, "There are a lot of gifts throughout the play," and these are a vital key to understanding the play as Vogel designed it: "I'll tell you what one of the pivotal metaphors for me was—I was thinking of *The Gift of the Magi*. (O. Henry's classic Christmas tale is about an impoverished couple's exchange of gifts: She sells her long, lovely hair to buy him a watch fob. He sells his cherished heirloom watch to buy her a set of hair combs.)" Paula explains,

> I wanted the play to be that they give each other ... the wrong gifts, with great love ... That you give exactly the wrong thing, but you give it with great love and sacrifice.... So I was thinking *The Gift of the Magi*, when L'il Bit says, "Would talking to me help?" and Peck says, "Yes, very much."[38]

Paula even has this crucial gift exchange take place at Christmas time, in the flashback of L'il Bit's thirteenth Christmas. L'il Bit is worried about Peck, because he's withdrawn and has been drinking again. To rescue him, she urges, "I could make a deal with you, Uncle Peck.... We could meet and talk—once a week. You could just save up whatever's bothering you during the week—and then we could talk ... as long as you don't drink."

This gift from L'il Bit has a profound and ironic impact on both their lives. As Paula Vogel expresses it, the gift she gives in trying to save him "could be, in many ways, what ultimately destroys him."

The most evident gift from Peck to L'il Bit—and the most enduring—is the driving lessons. Uncle Peck, as teacher, is fixed on conveying to his student the importance of that power that comes with driving. But L'il Bit absorbs more than a sense of power and strength behind the wheel of a car. The survival skills she learns from Peck eventually allow her to surpass her teacher in the ability to withstand the shocks of living and keep going.

After L'il Bit rejects the desperate marriage proposal from Peck on her eighteenth birthday, his loss of control becomes complete: He drinks himself to death, losing his job, then his wife, and ultimately, his driver's license. Paula Vogel gives this insight about Peck's demise:

> The gift of the driving lessons, to me, is a gift that is actually teaching L'il Bit how to destroy him. It's telling her how to be a survivor: "You've gotta watch out for what the other guy's gonna do; stay five steps ahead." He's basically—not knowing it—but preparing her and giving her the ego formation to survive and destroy him. But in that strange way, that "Gift of the Magi" way.[39]

Other "Magi" gifts are exchanged in the play: In tolerating Peck's ardor for L'il Bit, Aunt Mary tries to "give him enough of what he needs" to serve as what Paula calls "a kind of homeopathic remedy." Paula even suggested (in our interview) that Mary has given Peck the camera and said, "You know what would be great—is if we could give Lucy a really beautiful portrait of L'il Bit..." Mary's attempts clearly backfire. But in leading to Peck's demise, his own gift of the driving lessons to L'il Bit becomes the most potent agent.

The stark irony of Peck's gift comes full circle at the play's end. L'il Bit gets into her car; and after making all the checks and adjustments drilled into her by Uncle Peck, she focuses the mirror on her passenger, the spirit of Peck in the back seat. L'il Bit the survivor can now smile at him, and with him. And as she confidently prepares to floor it, she gives the sense that L'il Bit the adult is now solidly in control of her car, her life—and her memories.

A striking feature about Vogel's character is how much she is in charge of the play's unfolding and the audience's connection to the action. Keeping L'il Bit the clear subject—and Peck and other men the objects—was part and parcel of Paula's design: "We're always looking for males to take over and then, Ahhh, we're fine.... I thought, Okay, we're going to switch it now. I will have men in the production, yes. Men are important to the play world. But they are going to start being objects ... and not the subjects.[40]

In Maggie Edson's play *Wit*, her protagonist Vivian Bearing also narrates and controls the play's unfolding. But the play centers on that character's journey from subject to object—from one who smugly teaches lessons to one who must, in the most dire circumstances, learn a lesson.

17

Margaret Edson's Advanced Course in *Wit*

The day after Maggie Edson won the Pulitzer Prize for Drama, she was back in her classroom in Atlanta, leading her two dozen kindergarten charges in their customary "Wiggle Down." Miss Edson's Pulitzer achievement was duly noted, however. The class had a round of celebratory donuts.

She was the most celebrated American playwright of the 1998–99 season. In addition to the Pulitzer Prize, Maggie and her play *Wit* reaped awards from the Drama Desk, Drama League, New York Drama Critics, Outer Critics Circle, and Dramatists Guild. Yet Maggie insists that she is first and foremost an elementary school teacher and that nothing could induce her to give that up. Her play may be loaded with revelations about the perplexing wit of John Donne's seventeenth-century sonnets, but in daily life, Maggie thrills to her students' revelations about alphabet sounds: "One guy today—I said something about a marker—and he said, 'A marker starts with mmm, mmm,' which means he's so close, he's going to get it tomorrow."[1]

Maggie loves such moments. "Learning to read—that's the biggest thing in your whole life," she exclaims. "It's the thing that opens your mind the most, that gives you the most power."[2]

Before she became a kindergarten teacher, Maggie was a teacher of English as a second language. And before that, she was a student of life in wildly diverse settings. One year, she went from being a waitress in an Iowa hog-farmers' bar to being a worker in a Dominican convent in Rome. To say that Maggie has many diverse interests is a huge understatement.

She grew up in Washington, D.C., across the street from American

University. With her next-door neighbor Julia Louis-Dreyfus (of later *Seinfeld* fame), she made up impromptu scenes and characters.

Maggie's mother was, and still is, a social worker. Her father, who died in the mid–1970s, was a newspaper journalist: "My father was a columnist.... He wrote a column about Washington that was syndicated around the country. But he was a lot older, so it was before we kids were a part of his life."[3]

("We kids" refers to Maggie and her two siblings—an older sister and a younger brother.) In high school at Sidwell Friends, Maggie began a close pivotal friendship with Derek Anson Jones who, years later, would figure largely in the success of Maggie's play. Like Derek, Maggie enjoyed taking part in theatre at Sidwell: "I was very interested in theatre in high school. And a group of friends and I were just very committed to it and very involved in it.... It was a great way to go through high school. And then in college, I just got more interested in academics."[4]

Maggie went on to major in Renaissance history at Smith; nothing about her life at the time pointed toward theatrical distinction. After graduation, she rambled to Iowa, where she took a day job selling hotdogs and a night job waitressing in a farmers' bar. She followed a summer there with her year of working in a Roman convent.

> I went right from one [the bar] to the other [the convent] ... And the guy who ran the bar was talking to me about it one night; and he said, "So, you're just gonna go live there, and sort of adjust to their customs and way of life?" And I said, "Yeah, just like here." And his face fell—I got him on that.[5]

Maggie was not at all seeking a convent vocation; she "just felt like doing it," which is the chief reason behind most of Maggie's endeavors.

After Rome, she returned to Washington and took a job as a clerk in the AIDS-Oncology unit of a research hospital, where the germ of her play *Wit* took root. Maggie felt that being a lowly clerk (something like the role of "Radar" on the TV series M.A.S.H., she says) was an ironic "key to any kind of insight" into exchanges between health-care staff and their patients. "Because I had no skills, I could see the whole exchange." She began to write about it, she says, because "I thought someone has to write it." She made her protagonist a terminal cancer patient in a research hospital, the job of which is "not to comfort the afflicted. It's to develop a cure.... So the intricacies of one person's little life are necessarily not the main concern of a cancer researcher. At the same time, they're the paramount concern of that person."[6]

In the summer of 1991, before she began pursuit of a master's degree

Margaret Edson (Photo credit: Dave Smiley)

in English at Georgetown, Maggie wrote the first draft of her play. She was living in an apartment above Georgetown Hairstyling and working at a Tenley Circle bicycle shop. "I was at the bike shop afternoons and evenings, and was working on the play in the mornings. So it balanced out well."[7]

When asked why a play, and not some other form of writing, Maggie responds, "I'm very interested in talk. In speaking and listening. So I would never want to write a novel, or a short story." Talking and listening took on special significance in Maggie's writing process: "I felt like voices were talking to me in my head, and I just wrote down what they said. I could see everything happening as I was working on it."[8]

The main voice and narrator of her play is Dr. Vivian Bearing, a supremely scholarly and aloof professor of seventeenth-century English poetry. Diagnosed with advanced ovarian cancer, Vivian is subjected to experimental chemotherapy at her university's hospital. The junior doctor on her case is a former student of hers, who is now Vivian's match in the smug pursuit of knowledge. Like Vivian, he has "preferred research to humanity." Only through Vivian's lonely and harrowing journey toward death does she learn what's essential in life: human connection and compassion.

Maggie made her character a specialist in the "Holy Sonnets" of John Donne because she was told at Smith that "Donne is the hardest." So Maggie spent long library hours educating herself about Donne. "To me, that's a wonderful day—a day spent in the library, rooting around, with all the footnotes and everything."[9] By evening, however, Maggie was working at the bike shop, toying with "a great idea that didn't really come to fruition, which was the bike-shop wedding registry." She laughingly adds that this could be the next frontier in "mellow merchandising."[10]

Maggie submitted her play to virtually every regional theatre, and went about her life as rejections poured in (citing "cast size, subject, too much talk, too academic.") As planned, Maggie started the English master's program at Georgetown. "The idea was, I would fall in love with it, and do a Ph.D.," she says. "That didn't happen." Instead, Maggie began to teach children English as a second language through a church program, and lost her heart to that. "So at the end of the year, it was clear to me that I wanted to be in the elementary classroom." What made it possible for her was the alternative certification program started by the D.C. school system at that time. Maggie was one of the first in the program, which allows people from other professions to start teaching while taking classes toward certification. Maggie credits that program with being "really the big break of my life."[11]

Meanwhile, an unusual first reading of Maggie's script had taken place in her mother's home. The central role of Vivian Bearing had been read by Maggie's old friend Derek Anson Jones, and the cast was rounded out by her family.

> It was at my Mom's dining room table. And Derek was working in theatre at the time in Washington.... So of course I asked him. And then my mother played E. M. Ashford [Vivian's old professor and

advisor], and my sister-in-law played Susie [the nurse].... And so they read it all the way through, and then they had a discussion afterwards. My partner, Linda, moderated the discussion. I left for the discussion.... I had planned it that way.[12]

(Maggie's life partner, Linda Merrill, has been an art teacher and curator in both Washington and Atlanta, where she and Maggie now share a home and two sons.) The upshot of the discussion was reported to Maggie ("this part was too long, this wasn't clear"), and she made revisions. She confirms that her family was "very helpful ... Really, they outdid themselves."[13]

Her script was given a professional reading by the Players Club in New York, in 1993, with Marian Seldes reading Vivian. Then, in 1995, South Coast Repertory in California took a chance on producing Maggie's play. "[They] read it as one of their thousand manuscripts they receive each year. And they just picked it out of the pile."[14] With their help, Maggie cut an hour off the play's running time. But even after the revised 90-minute *Wit* won six Los Angeles Drama Critics Awards, including Best World Premiere, Maggie could not land another production, or an agent.

Maggie's old friend Derek got her play noticed and produced on the East Coast. Derek had been carrying around a copy of *Wit* in his backpack. While assisting Doug Hughes on a production of *Henry V* in Central Park, Derek showed the play to Hughes and to Kathleen Chalfant, a veteran actress featured in *Henry V*. They were so intrigued that Doug Hughes allowed Derek to direct *Wit* at the Long Wharf Theatre in Connecticut, with Chalfant in the lead. In the fall of 1998, *Wit* opened in New York at the tiny 99-seat Manhattan Class (MCC) Theatre. Response was such that, by January, it was moved to the 499-seat Union Square Theatre.

Because teaching is her top priority, Maggie missed the opening performance of her play at MCC in New York. She got there just as it ended, then mingled with women wiping their eyes in the ladies' room. "But I made it for the party," Maggie adds.[15]

Maggie had moved to Atlanta with her partner Linda by the time her Pulitzer Prize award was announced. Even then, her celebration was far from flamboyant: They went out for pizza, then to Atlanta's popular Zesto ice cream shop, where Maggie indulged in a vanilla-chocolate swirl cone. "It was the best ice cream cone I've ever had," she reports.[16]

Maggie gives much credit for the success of *Wit* to the faith and direction of her friend Derek Anson Jones. He brought her play to light in New York, and in his hands, *Wit* became what Maggie calls "a fast-swerving drive. You're brought very quickly over to laughing, and then ripped right back into something harrowing." A sad and ironic postscript to the journey of *Wit* is that, after guiding the New York and touring productions to triumph, Derek Anson Jones died of AIDS complications in January 2000, at the age of 38. Four days later, Maggie returned to their alma mater, Sidwell Friends High School, where she was to have shared stage with Derek. Instead, she gave an affectionate tribute to her cherished friend who once stole the show as Touchstone (to her Rosalind) in their student staging of *As You Like It*." Maggie continues to honor Derek in program notations and dedications of *Wit*.[17]

When *Wit* came to television as an HBO movie in 2001, Emma Thompson starred as Vivian Bearing, and Mike Nichols directed. (Nichols and Thompson collaborated on adapting it for the screen, but dialogue changes were minimal.) Nichols commented, "One of the wonders of *Wit* is that it grows and grows and is about far more than the loneliness of death for one person."[18]

As Maggie Edson sees it, *Wit* is "about redemption," about a journey toward grace:

> To show the action of grace in someone's life, there needs to be some kind of "undoing." A play about somebody who starts out fine and ends up fine isn't going to reveal very much. And a play about somebody who starts out flawed and ends up repaired will reveal a lot more. But a person who starts out thinking she's fine, and is in fact flawed, and ends up thinking she's doomed, and is, in fact, redeemed—to me is the most interesting of those three possibilities.[19]

Despite her protagonist's painful undoing, *Wit* contains abundant humor. As its title implies, the script abounds with sharp ironies and clever word plays. The character Vivian uses her wit and her own sense of irony to fend off her rising panic and vulnerability. For example, as a scholar of distinction who has made elevated language her life's work, she is still struck dumb by the waves of nausea induced by chemotherapy. "God, I'm going to barf my brains out," she blurts—then quips to the audience, "You may remark that my vocabulary has taken a turn for the Anglo-Saxon."

In ways that evoke both laughter and anguish, this once smug and self-satisfied force in English literature drops her dignified defenses and skills. As Maggie Edson explains, Vivian "finds herself in a new situation where those skills ... don't serve her very well. So she has to disarm ... to become someone who learns new things."[20] And learn, she finally does, in the eleventh hour of her dire but necessary "undoing." According to actress

Kathleen Chalfant, who played Vivian for two years, "the end of the play is entirely triumphant."[21]

The phrase "entirely triumphant" also applies to the outcome of Maggie Edson's excursion into playwriting. But Maggie will tell you, it was just an excursion: "I just wrote this one little play." If *Wit* happened to work, she feels it's "because it's the one thing I had in my heart, and I'm not going to try to crank that up again."[22] She adds that "the things I want to say, I'm saying in my classroom."[23] (At the behest of South Coast Repertory, Maggie did write a second script; but it has not been produced and she insists it will remain so.)

Her good friend Derek might have encouraged Maggie to write more plays. As it is, Maggie never stops giving him credit: "The life of *Wit*, from 1997, belongs to Derek. He created the standard live performance of the text." Maggie even adds, "The life of me, of Maggie, from 1973 on, belongs to Derek, too." (They met at age twelve.) She downplays her own battles for the life of *Wit*, and continues to value the trials as much as the triumphs: "My experience of *Wit* came in three parts: The writing ... the rejection ... and the rising. At each stage, I learned a lot about myself. The last stage was the most fun; the first was the most important; the middle was necessary."[24]

Life for Maggie Edson is now very grounded in her Atlanta home and her classroom. The year 2003 marked her eleventh year in public schools, teaching the early grades of Title One "free lunch" children. "I feel very clear about what I'm doing," says Maggie. "I'm perfectly sure of the positive impact of what I'm doing."[25]

None of that has been changed by her playwriting celebrity. Among the post–Pulitzer interviews Maggie did was the one by newsman Jim Lehrer (whose daughter was once a schoolmate of Maggie's). Maggie's enthusiasm about her classroom topped her enthusiasm about the Pulitzer win. She was grateful for the bouquets from well-wishers, she said, because they much enhanced their lessons about bees. "We're studying about insects ... doing a big project on insects called Six Legs Over Georgia." They were also singing (as they do daily), having a "great time counting by twos to the tune of 'I Feel Good,'" the James Brown hit.[26]

When an ABC *World News* camera crew came to her classroom, the producer kept prodding Maggie about why she was a kindergarten teacher; she finally retorted, "Because these children are going to change the world."[27]

Now Maggie has two children of her own, who have much changed her world. In a recent follow-up exchange with Maggie, she proudly reported that her partner Linda "has given birth to two *big changes*. Our son Timothy was born in July 2000. Our son Peter was born in June 2002. All are healthy and thriving."[28]

Maggie still spends most days in a classroom world of primary colors, alphabet letters, and exercises set to happy tunes. ("Singin' in the Rain" is a favorite.) By all reports, including that of her Atlanta school principal, Maggie is "a wonderful teacher."[29] And is very unlike her play's character, Vivian, who has valued abstract knowledge far above human connection and kindness.

How did someone as warm and gregarious as Maggie create a character as arrogant and aloof as Vivian Bearing? Maggie was asked this question at some of the post-play talks she attended. Her favorite exchange on the matter featured her old friend Derek, in New York:

> I was there, and Derek, and Kathleen—we were all up on the stage ... and we had established that Derek and I had been in school since seventh grade. And a lady in the audience said, "Well, the play is about arrogance, as you said, and I don't see how such a simple person as yourself, such a plain, honest person as yourself—well, where did you get this understanding of arrogance?" And Derek just said right away, "She's had it since seventh grade."[30]

Everyone dissolved into laughter, and "that was the end of that question." But Maggie's play has also evoked sobering questions and comments from people who have experienced cancer personally. These are often directed at the actress playing Vivian. About Kathleen Chalfant, Maggie said, "People feel very strongly that they have things they need to tell her, about themselves or about people they know. And to me, that's a very interesting phenomenon."[31] The actress-audience bonding that takes place during Wit is often palpable. Maggie says,

> What I feel, and what other people have told me they feel, is that the audience starts out very alienated from her and by the end they're just aching for her and just pushing her over the edge with their wishes for her last move to happen ... there are 500 people that really want to see it.... As her character grows, it's only because she's had the audience with her.[32]

Maggie very much appreciates the audiences who have watched and supported her play. "I feel very grateful to them, 'cause they could have been doing something else."[33]

Maggie is also grateful that, while she is doing something else—say, lesson plans for her kindergarten kids—her play's message about human connection and compassion is reaching people in far-flung places. Asked how she feels knowing that her play will be taught in classrooms, that she may serve as a model for aspiring playwrights, Maggie modestly replies, "If my experience encourages people to try something that they wouldn't try otherwise, then I'll be very pleased to be part of that."[34]

At least one of Maggie's own young students is already thinking of a playwriting future. "He's going to give it a try," she reports. "Yep. As soon as he learns to write."[35]

THE PLAY: WIT—THOSE WHO CAN, LEARN

The main setting is a university research hospital, suggested by white curtains on a ceiling track. A few others are indicated by desks or chairs rolled on and off; scene changes are fluid. Lights come up as Vivian Bearing walks onstage, pulling her IV pole with her. She is about 50 years old, very thin, wearing two hospital gowns, and a baseball cap on her bald head. She says to the audience (with false familiarity), "Hi, how are you feeling today?" She changes tone to admit that this is not her standard greeting. But it is the standard around here—a question to which Vivian has generally answered "fine," despite the obvious:

> I have been asked "How are you feeling today?" while I was throwing up into a plastic washbasin. I have been asked as I was emerging from a four-hour operation with a tube in every orifice, "How are you feeling today?" I am waiting for the moment when someone asks me this question and I am dead. I'm a little sorry I'll miss that.[36]

It would be an ironic moment, and Dr. Vivian Bearing appreciates irony. She is a professor of seventeenth-century poetry, specializing in the "Holy Sonnets" of John Donne. She tells us that irony is a literary device that will be "deployed to great effect in this play.... It is not my intention to give away the plot; but I think I die at the end.... I've got less than two hours." The scene shifts as Vivian detaches the IV pole and says, "I'll never forget the time I found out I had cancer."

She moves to the desk of Dr. Kelekian, senior doctor on her case, who abruptly proclaims, "You have cancer." To the audience, Vivian remarks, "It was something of a shock. I had to sit down." While Kelekian explains stage-four ovarian cancer in medical jargon, Vivian mulls over the few words she catches: "Insidious ... Hmmm. Curious word choice ... must read something about cancer." The gist of Kelekian's spiel is that they will treat her with a course of experimental chemotherapy. It's the strongest thing they've got, "and it will make a significant contribution to our knowledge." When he asks if there is any family he should speak to, Vivian says "that won't be necessary." He counsels, "You must be very tough"; she replies, "You needn't worry."

To herself, and the audience, Vivian reviews her situation. She has insidious cancer, with pernicious side effects. "No, the *treatment* has pernicious side effects," she corrects. But she must stay the course. "It appears to be a matter ... of life and death"—her area of expertise. "I am, after all, a scholar of Donne's Holy Sonnets, which explore mortality in greater depth than any other body of work in the English language." She confirms that she is tough, which is why she chose to study John Donne as a student of the great E.M. Ashford. She steps back to the desk, where a middle-aged woman, Dr. Ashford, is in mid-critique of Vivian's essay on "Death be not proud." "Do it again," Ashford intones; and Vivian repeats to the audience, "It was something of a shock. I had to sit down." Ashford rejects her essay because Vivian used a text with "hysterical punctuation"—with semi-colon and exclamation-point flourishes. When Ashford uses the original punctuation ("And death shall be no more, *comma*, Death thou shalt die"), death becomes merely "a pause ... not insuperable barriers, not semi-colons, just a comma."

While Vivian struggles to comprehend, Ashford urges her not to return to the library right away: "Go out. Enjoy yourself with your friends." But Vivian is lost among the students gathered on the lawn, talking, laughing. "I went back to the library."

Snapping back to the hospital, Vivian is put in a wheelchair by her primary nurse, Susie, and whisked to various stations. As technicians process and prod her, Vivian gives the audience the highlights of her career. She boasts of her articles and her authoritative book on John Donne, whose sonnets require scrupulous study: They're known for their "itchy outbreaks of far-fetched wit." Vivian smugly concludes that, "Donne's wit is ... a way to see how good you really are. After twenty years, I can say with confidence, no one is quite as good as I."

Susie delivers Vivian for a pelvic exam with her junior doctor, Jason Posner, who once took Vivian's class for the challenge (and received, he reports, an "A minus"). Even the verbal part of Jason's exam is awkward for both of them: His questions, checked off on his clipboard, include "are you having sexual relations," to which Vivian quips, "not at the moment." In Jason's abrupt and inept bedside manner, he almost forgets that he must retrieve Susie before starting the pelvic exam. He leaves Vivian stranded and stirruped on the table, muttering to herself, "I wish I had given him an 'A.'" For comfort, she recites "Death be not proud" until Jason reappears with Susie and starts the pelvic. Jason attempts small talk about Vivian's classes, then suddenly halts and blurts, "Jesus!" as he feels the mass of her tumor. He lamely covers up his shock and dashes off.

Vivian rises, and utters to the audience, "That ... was ... hard." But it was just a small part of how she is "learning to suffer," learning that levels of pain and humiliation are relative. The mild discomfort of an electrocardiogram is swept from memory by the agony of a proctosigmoidoscopy. And, "yes, having a former student give me a pelvic exam was thoroughly degrading ... but I could not have imagined the depths of humiliation that—" Unable to complete the thought, she dashes to her hospital room and retches into a plastic basin. She slumps on the bed, retches again, and moans, "Oh, God. What's left? I haven't eaten in two days. What's left to puke?" At the thought that she might barf her brains out, she muses that it would be a loss to her discipline, but "not a few of my colleagues would be relieved. To say nothing of my students."

Susie comes in to collect and measure the "emises" (output) from Vivian's basin. Susie is cordial and concerned, asking "You're not having a lot of visitors, are you?" Vivian corrects, "None, to be precise." At Susie's offer to call someone for her, Vivian replies, "That won't be necessary." Alone with the audience, Vivian shares what it is like to be a cancer inpatient between the "dramatic climaxes." She lies back and intones, "You cannot imagine how time ... can be ... so still.... Yet there is so little of it." If *she* were writing this scene, she says, she would lie there "a full fifteen minutes." But after a long silence to convey her point, she introduces the spectacle of "Grand Rounds."

For this scene, she is the scrutinized subject of Jason and four medical fellows who are coached and questioned by Dr. Kelekian. It reminds Vivian of a graduate seminar "with one important difference ... *they* read *me* like a book." After Jason barks his "How are you feeling," he initiates the probing of Vivian's abdomen, then vies with the others to answer Kelekian's questions. When they leave Vivian, stomach still exposed, she chirps, "Wasn't that ... Grand?" She rises and does a recap on her bouts of chemo and their side effects: "hepatoxicity (liver poison)," and "neuropathy (nerve death)." She claims it has always been "my custom to treat words with respect. I can recall the time ... when I knew words would be my life's work.... It was my fifth birthday."

Vivian, now child-like, flops onto the floor near a stack of books. Her father sits reading a newspaper. Vivian stumbles on the word "soporific" in a Beatrix Potter tale about bunnies. Never distracted from his paper, her father has her sound out the word and gives her its meaning: "makes you sleepy." Ah yes, she sees that the book's picture of drowsing bunnies bears this out! The mature Vivian explains to us, "At the time, it seemed like magic." And so, she adds, imagine the effect of John Donne's words upon her. "Medical terms are less evocative," she admits. Still, she seeks their meaning, since "my only defense is the acquisition of vocabulary."

Key words for the next scene are "fever" and "neutropenia." Susie helps a shaking, feverish Vivian to a wheelchair and summons Jason, who orders "reverse isolation." Vivian's immune system has shut down from the chemo: "My treatment imperils my health," she notes. "Herein lies the paradox ... Donne would revel in it. I would revel in it, if he wrote a poem about it. My students would flounder in it.... If they were here ... how I would *perplex* them. I could be so powerful."

And suddenly, Vivian is the invincible professor, armed with a pointer and a screen that blazes Donne's sonnet, "If Poysonous minerals..." The poem asks why, if poisons and serpents are not damned, he is damned for his intellect? It entreats God to show the questioner mercy, by choosing to forget him. Thwacking the screen with her pointer, Vivian sternly dissects and explicates the lines. "The speaker does not need to *hide* from God's judgment; only to *accept* God's *forgiveness*. It is ... suspiciously simple. We want to correct the speaker, remind him of the assurance of salvation. But it is too late—" She's interrupted by Susie: Jason wants a new test. "No. Not now," snaps Vivian, "I am in the middle of—this"; but Susie gently insists and Vivian yields.

As soon as Vivian arrives at the technician's station, he goes off on his break. From her wheelchair, Vivian recites Donne's "This is my playes last scene...." She is now "very, very sick." But she has distinguished herself even in illness: She has "broken the record" for surviving full doses of their chemotherapy agents. Jason and Kelekian are thrilled. They foresee celebrity status from the "article they will no doubt write about me," she says, amending this to "about my peritoneal cavity.... What we have come to think of as *me* is, in fact, just the specimen jar."

Vivian changes her next line of the play to reflect her true sentiments: "It is such a relief to get back to my goddamn room after those goddamn tests." Jason sweeps in with, "How are you feeling," and checks her Input and Output chart. Vivian detains him, desperate for some human contact. When she asks him, "Why cancer ... why not open-heart surgery," he answers, "No way. Cancer's the only thing I ever wanted.... Cancer is..." and Vivian supplies the word "awesome." Jason rhapsodizes about cancer cells and their mind-boggling ability to replicate. He can't wait to get his own lab, he says. If he can "survive *this*...." Vivian adds, "the part with the human beings."

Jason leaves and Vivian says, "The young doctor, like the senior scholar, prefers research to humanity." She grudgingly continues, "Now I suppose we shall see ... how the senior scholar ruthlessly denied her simpering students the touch of human kindness she now seeks." Quick flashbacks show Vivian as the cold daunting professor, giving her students no allowance for being young, or unprepared, or needing an extension on a paper. She looks back at these scenes, and she feels "so much—what is the word?" But she finds no word.

Back in the hospital, Vivian slumps, chastened and so lonely that she summons Susie by creating a "little emergency" (she pinches her IV tubing). When Susie arrives, a tearful Vivian tolerates being called "sweetheart," and sharing a Popsicle. Susie works up to asking Vivian what she wants her "code status" to be. Susie explains that Jason and Kelekian will want her to be Code Blue—to resuscitate her—because "they always ... want to know more things." Vivian responds, "I always want to know more things. I'm a scholar. Or I was when I had shoes, when I had eyebrows." But Vivian opts for DNR: "Don't complicate the matter." As Susie heads out to tell Kelekian this, Vivian asks if Susie will still take care of her. Susie answers, "Of course, sweetheart."

Vivian sits up after this maudlin display, annoyed that her life has become so "corny." Yet, she admits, "now is not the time for verbal swordplays ... for wit." Now is the time for simplicity, for, "dare I say, kindness." Now is also the time for extreme measures: She can no longer tolerate the pain. Susie returns and summons both doctors. Kelekian ignores Susie's suggestion of a patient-controlled pump and orders a morphine drip. After they leave, Vivian struggles to give the audience her last coherent lines: "It came so quickly, after taking so long."

When Vivian has drifted off, Susie and Jason discuss her while they insert a catheter. Jason recalls how Vivian could give one "hell of a lecture" with no notes, yet a lot of students hated her. Her class felt like "boot camp," he says, partly because of the subject: John Donne couldn't accept the idea of salvation, so he wrote "screwed-up sonnets" that are "brilliantly convoluted ... like a game." After a while, "The puzzle takes over. You're not even trying to solve it anymore.... Great training for lab research." Susie asks, "Don't you get to solve the puzzle?" Jason says no; it boils down to "trying to quantify the complications of the puzzle." Jason leaves, and Susie thoughtfully rubs oil on Vivian's hands, then goes.

Into Vivian's room comes E.M. Ashford, now eighty, carrying parcels. She gently rouses Vivian, who cries with surprise and anguish at seeing her. Ashford explains that she's in town for her grandson's birthday. Removing her shoes, she climbs on the bed to comfort Vivian. "Shall I recite to you," she asks, "something by Donne?" Vivian moans "Noooo," so Ashford removes from her bag the book *The Runaway Bunny*. She reads about the bunny who would run away, but whose mother would follow and find him—anywhere. "Look at that," says Ashford. "A little allegory of the soul. No matter where it hides, God will find it. See, Vivian?" She rises, kisses Vivian and wishes for her that "flights of angels sing thee to thy rest."

After she goes, Jason strides in with a brisk "How are you feeling today" and checks the I&O charts. "Uh-oh, kidneys gone," he mutters. He quickly realizes that Vivian is, in fact, gone, and rushes to call a code. We hear it announced, and Susie sweeps in, yelling "WHAT ARE YOU DOING? ... She's DNR!" Jason counters, "She's research!" Susie shoves him away and dives for the chart, to show him. Despite her attempt to cancel, the Code Team swarms in and begins frantic CPR on Vivian, until Jason finally howls, "I made a mistake!" While the frenzy around the bed unravels, and Susie pulls the sheet over Vivian, Vivian slips from the bed and serenely walks away, toward a glowing light. She removes her cap, her hospital gowns, and her ID bracelet. She stands, finally, "naked and beautiful, reaching for the light."

Maggie Edson's play is, essentially, a lesson; a lesson in grace that her central character learns belatedly and most painfully, and shares with the audience. Vivian Bearing stands apart—far apart—from other women protagonists in this series. Vivian does not lack self-esteem. In fact, she possesses it "to a fault," as Maggie puts it. She is self-satisfied to the point of being arrogant.

Vivian's arrogance stems from her supreme confidence in herself as a scholar, which is all that she has aimed at being. Vivian's published writings are acclaimed; her teaching methods are notoriously rigorous. She has lived a very cerebral and independent life. In short, she has lived by her wits quite well—or thinks that she has.

Among the glimpses of Vivian's past is the moment, on her fifth birthday, when she realizes that words will be her "life's work." In that short scene, her father instructs her without relating to her, or leaving his newspaper. Meanwhile, Vivian becomes enthralled with the magic of words. This quick scene, by Edson's design, reveals to the audience what Vivian herself does not see:

> Vivian is narrating the scene. And she's an unreliable narrator.... So what she thinks the scene shows ... is the glamour of words. And what it does in fact show is the division between them.... Her dad is reading the newspaper; she's reading those books. They're

> not doing anything together. So that scene, which is very small, is very revealing. ... You see Vivian's *whole life* in that scene.[37]

The scene suggests that Vivian learned, early on, to put intellect before the human touch. And certainly, other flashbacks of Vivian as a college student and as the formidable professor reveal a woman who has "preferred research to humanity." But as the play and Vivian's illness progress, the aloof and powerful teacher becomes the ironic and impotent subject—the frightened lab rat being prodded and quantified with humiliating indifference. The irony is magnified by virtue of her junior doctor and former student, Jason, who is a cold impersonal researcher from the same mold as Vivian. Like an Ebenezer Scrooge flinching at scenes of his past unkindness, Vivian narrates and reenacts scenes of her past insensitivity to others.

Vivian's confident reliance on her mind is shattered by the breakdown of her body and her change into hapless specimen. But this process is what brings about her much-needed repair. Her cancer becomes a blessing in the most painful disguise. As Maggie Edson puts it,

> If she lived another 20 years, she would have had a heart attack in the stacks, probably, and she would have slipped through. She would have made it without being found out.... But cancer made her stop, and everything that she had built up to protect herself, she had to let go of. And the repair that she needed as a person came through this.... So her cancer is her "cross"; but it's her salvation as well.[38]

Vivian receives a kind of assurance of salvation in what many describe as the play's most poignant scene: Vivian's near-death visitation by her mentor, E.M. Ashford, who comforts her with the sweet children's story, *The Runaway Bunny*. (Some viewers interpret the scene as a morphine-induced vision. Others insist Ashford's visit is real. Maggie prefers not to specify.) Taken at face value, the scene suggests that Ashford, unlike Vivian, balanced her love of Donne's complexities with a love of life and family (she boasts of her grandson). And Ashford can, and does, find great meaning in simplicity: In the simple words of *Runaway Bunny*, she finds a message about God's love for soul, and it becomes part of Vivian's lesson.

In a way, Ashford is as close as Vivian comes to having friends or family. About this, Maggie says, "You don't see family, with mom and dad and the kids. But there is a definite generational structure ... that has many of the characteristics of family."[39] In an odd way, Kelekian and Jason and Susie do become a kind of family for Vivian at the end of her life. They "nurture" her in the sense of "educate": From them, Vivian learns the biggest lesson of her life.

In the last two Pulitzer plays of the twentieth century (Edson's and Vogel's), the central female character controls the play and the audience's connection to its action. That these two women protagonists are assertive and dynamic and blatantly theatrical is perhaps a welcome sign of changing times. These characters take center stage in no uncertain terms. Both roles have been called tour-de-force roles for women. And the bold strokes with which they've been written reflect a growing, gutsy kind of confidence among women playwrights, built on the awareness that stories of women's lives are compelling and stageworthy, and that no one writes them better than women themselves.

A new wave of women playwrights are providing bold and diverse role models for the next generation. Among them is Suzan-Lori Parks, the first woman to win the Drama Pulitzer in the new century, and the first African American woman to take the prize. In Park's Pulitzer play, there are no women, only two blood brothers. This marks a different kind of breakthrough by women playwrights: After millenniums of men telling women's lives for the stage, women are turning the tables—or the mirrors—on men. Of course, as more reflections of men's lives stream from the pens of women playwrights, so do more images of aggression, competition, and violence. The plays of Suzan-Lori Parks are replete with such images. They offer disturbing reflections of, and parables for, a violent twenty-first-century America.

PART V

History in the Staging? Suzan-Lori Parks and the Sisterhood of Black Playwrights

"I love to sit and watch people watch violent things," says Suzan-Lori Parks, the first black woman playwright to take the Drama Pulitzer. History repeats itself—and so does violence—in the stage art of Parks. "If I model my plays after anything," she explains, "it's Greek plays, where he's stabbing his eyes out, she's put on the poisoned dress, and the horses jump off the cliff."[1] Parks is also undeniably swayed by such diverse sources as Bertolt Brecht, James Joyce, and rap music; but the comparison to Greek tragedy is an apt one. Two of Parks' plays conclude with a mother bloodily murdering her own son; another ends with a bride receiving her would-be-husband's head on a platter; and, in Parks' most acclaimed play—her Pulitzer play—a brother shoots his only sibling in the head, after killing his girlfriend offstage.

Parks' 2002 Pulitzer play, *Topdog/Underdog*, is so laden with violence and testosterone, expletives and sexual swagger, that viewers have assumed its author was a man. After seeing the play off-Broadway, rap artist Mos Def ran backstage and said to one of the actors, "Ah man, what a great play. The guy who wrote this ..." and the actor laughed, since the script had been penned by Parks.[2]

Later, *Topdog* moved to Broadway, and Mos Def moved into the underdog role in Parks' play about two blood brothers who contend with each other and their dismal family history. Named Lincoln and Booth as a perverse joke by their father, the brothers taunt and provoke one another like pit bulls, in a seedy rented room where they compete at three-card monte and wind up (as their names project) assassin and victim. Yet the implicit verdict seems to be that both brothers are victims of a machismo myth that divides humanity into hustlers and their marks, the slayers and the slain, in a dire con game for power. Intended or not, the play seems to distill the state of the world into one room, with two men who are playing war for keeps.

18

The Early 2000s: "Bang, Bang—You're American"

Suzan-Lori Parks insists that her plays contain no metaphors. However, her spotlight on a violent game of vying for power makes her play an apt allegory for the cultural and political timbre of the times, allusions to Greek culture aside. Popular culture has been overrun with "survivor" and "reality" shows that pit people against each other in brutal competitions, and reward behavior that is cutthroat, risky and altogether senseless (*Fear Factor*, *Dog Eat Dog*, and *The Real Cancun*, to name a few). Overall, these new-century years have been awash in images that flaunt America's acknowledged culture of violence. To much of the world, America itself has become a gun-toting, swaggering outlaw, and the arts that most consciously mirror life are reflecting this image. As Michael Moore vividly depicts in his 2003 Oscar-winning documentary *Bowling for Columbine*, the U.S. has a uniquely pervasive gun culture. The reasons for this go beyond the handy access to weapons. (Moore rolled film in a bank that offers guns as premiums for new accounts.) Canada has as many guns per capita, but America's death count from firearms is 200 percent that of Canada.[1]

One reason suggested by Moore and others is that there is a trickle-down effect of the violent stance of our government, one that gives a tacit cheer for using weapons to dominate others. Moore notes that the day of the Colorado school slaughter was the day of heaviest U.S. shelling on Kosovo. Moore's point, that the school killers were products of our "institutionalized violence," was echoed by journalist Leila Matsui: "As home to the Lockheed Corporation where missiles and other weaponry are manufactured ... it's hardly a coincidence that Littleton has been turning out killers over several generations."² A few weeks after Moore won the Oscar, the Cannes Film Festival gave its top prize to another film inspired by American school violence. Writer-director Gus Van Sant set his massacre in an Oregon school and had it erupt from an almost lulling day of high-school routine. When the sudden horror explodes onscreen, the shock is staggering. The film and its title, *Elephant*, suggest that violence is as an enormous, unknowable beast that lurks in the American landscape. Violence is the elephant in the room—our room, our lives, our psyches—that we as Americans selectively ignore, revile, and revere.

The early 2000s became a test case for Americans' reactions to violence in varied and unprecedented forms. Red-letter events polarized people around questions of violence and appropriate responses to violent crime. The Internet provided a cyber-stage for debates on everything from sexual abuse by the clergy—which seemed ubiquitous—to corporate and political scams—which seemed interchangeable and more ubiquitous. But the Internet also became the handiest high-tech venue for vice. As author Kurt Vonnegut quipped, it did "what the Mob would have loved to do—put a pawn shop and a loan shark in every home"³ (and a porn ring to boot). Beyond that, computers have put into homes an interactive playing field of violence, where killing and brutality are rewarded. They've opened a cyber-world of grisly potential: a Pandora's "X-Box" of uses and abuses that may relentlessly feed the American addiction to violence.

In 2001, players of Sony Playstation's game "Grand Theft Auto" scored points by stealing cars, beating up cops, dealing drugs, and abusing and killing women. The taste for violence (and profits) led to the enhanced "Grand Theft Vice City," which escalated the violence, especially against women, and featured a "whopping 40 weapons with which to spread mass destruction."⁴ Microsoft's X-Box and other rivals offered competing virtual violence: With titles like "Brute Force," "Desert Combat," "Counter Strike," "Soldier of Fortune," "Command and Conquer," they offered a banquet of blood-sport games, many of which became web accessible. Descriptions were lurid: "Brute Force lives up to its name with tactics such as flanking, baiting, ambushing ... throwing grenades. Plus, characters use a 'rag doll' skeletal system, allowing them to do sick stuff like keel over in a flesh heap when you snipe 'em in the head."⁵ In "Command and Conquer," you "search and destroy [by using] the awesome firepower of the Comanche's machine gun, Hydra rockets, and Hellfire missiles."⁶ "Soldier of Fortune offers 27 separate gore zones on a victim's body, customized to explode according to rules of anatomy and the caliber of the incoming bullet."⁷ As one game reviewer put it, "the more you can kill, the more you'll want to play."⁸

Critics of such games argue that they are, in fact, "killing simulators." And because they're so interactive, they hold addictive powers much stronger than film and television, which are already culturally competing with video games. By 2002, game software sales had hit 221 million units: roughly two video games for every U.S. household.[9]

In recent years, on-screen violence in all media has sharply escalated, as monitored by groups like the National Institute on Media and the Family. Its research director, Douglas Gentile, remarked, "Why do we need more media violence and more graphic media violence? Because we've gotten bored by the old stuff."[10] This explains why a film like the original *Texas Chainsaw Massacre* just doesn't cut it anymore (so to speak): That version opened with a deranged hitchhiker pulling out a knife and slashing his hand. The remake opens with a crazed female hitchhiker pulling out a gun and blowing off the back of her head. On TV, the crime scenes must get ever more steeped in gore; the extreme stunts on *Fear Factor* ever more extreme: Somehow, this week's stunts—of being shackled in a tank with 100 snakes, shooting explosive pellets at flaming goblets, and plunging one's head into a vat of cow eyes to retrieve ten pig hearts with one's teeth—must be topped next week.[11] (What perverse think tank concocts these?) *Denver Post* critic Michael Booth asks, "What horrors must come with the next remake of *Texas Chainsaw* before anyone will buy a ticket?" And what's next, now that "once-unspeakable violence has moved from the unbalanced fringe into our surround-sound home theatre systems?"[12]

The early 2000s gave proof that, along with a culture of violence, Americans harbor a culture of addiction and attendant culture of excess. All three are kept well supplied by a huge controlling overlord: corporate America. Paddy Chayevsky said it 30 years ago (in *Network*):

> We are now a corporate society, a corporate world, a corporate universe ... a cosmology of small corporations orbiting around larger corporations who, in turn, revolve around giant corporations, and the whole endless, eternal, ultimate cosmology is expressly designed for the production and consumption of useless things.[13]

Except now, this cosmology promotes things much worse than useless. They are dangerous and addictive, and a waste of human potential and precious world resources. To add grim insult to injury, our corporate cosmology seems newly designed to swindle investors. In recent years, white-collar crimes—another kind of violence—have taken headlines like "World-Com Scam Could Total $9 Billion"; and "Big Banks Helped Enron (by disguising $8 billion in loans)"[14] It turned out that what *Fortune* magazine had for five years hailed as "the Most Innovative Company in America" had been most innovative in fabricating profits: It had played a mega-game that bilked thousands of average Americans out of their savings. Meanwhile, Enron's executives cashed out at more than $1 billion in company stock at its peak, and 600 of its favored employees received $100 million in bonuses weeks before it declared bankruptcy.[15]

Enron and its employees had been the single largest body of contributors to George Bush's campaigns.[16] No stranger to corporate fraud, Bush was on the board of Harken Energy when it played offshore shell games to evade taxes. Dick Cheney had been CEO of Halliburton when that Texas oil giant fabricated tax havens and cut its federal taxes from $302 million to *minus* $85 million (a rebate in 1999).[17] So perhaps it was business-as-usual when the White House installation of Bush and Cheney was cloaked in fraud and flagrant nepotism; standard procedure, when Jeb Bush skewed the Florida electorate by creating a list of 57,000 felons to be scrubbed from state rolls (and Bush Sr. court appointees did the rest). But much of the world saw it as a "Bush-Cheney Junta" that gave our government to corporate hawks and far-right fundamentalists. These were, Noam Chomsky warned, "almost the same people who ran the country in the Reagan-Bush years"—but now, even wealthier. (The "'poorest' among them" was multi-millionaire Condoleezza Rice, a former Chevron director with an oil tanker named after her.)[18]

Responses from outraged Democrats and progressives ran the spectrum. At one end was Congresswoman Cynthia McKinney's restrained lament, "We know now that the [Jeb Bush] list was a phony; and worse, the majority of those rightful voters were people of color."[19] At the other end was Michael Moore's unrestrained slam at the Bush-corporate oligarchy: *Stupid White Men and Other Sorry Excuses for the State of the Nation.* Beneath the book's glib title was a well-documented treatise that became a big bestseller, and spurred a sequel: *Dude, Where's My Country?* (Moore's later documentary-film censure of Bush, *Fahrenheit 9/11*, took the Cannes Festival's top prize for 2004.[20]) Droves of Americans obviously welcomed a political wake-up call from the baseball-capped Moore. Others preferred theirs from scholar-in-tweed Noam Chomsky, or from columnist Arianna Huffington—whose book *How to Overthrow the Government* had already cried for an uprising against a corporate-fat government of "politicians living on graft and sinecure [while] 35 million Americans live in poverty and more children are homeless than at any time since the Great Depression."[21] A spate of wake-up calls came from a chorus of writer-activists, including Gore Vidal, Ramsey Clark, Alice Walker, Arundhati Roy, and Howard Zinn. They warned of the reinstalled regime's agenda, one set on more favors for the rich, attacks on the rights of women and minorities, and more invasions of poor besieged nations to tighten the U.S. hold over world resources.

September 11, 2001, became a pretext for that agenda. Terrorists used our own technology to attack the Pentagon and World Trade Center, supreme icons of U.S. military and corporate might. That same chorus of activists saw the attacks as a global wake-up call: A call to address the real "gulf war"—the gulf between the world's "haves" and "have-nots"—and to amend a world in which almost one-fourth of its people get only one percent of its resources. While Washington rallied hawks in a war-cry for revenge, pacifists pointed to 50 years of brutal U.S. military attacks on a score of nations, from Laos to El Salvador. But as Noam Chomsky bitterly remarked, "the atrocities you commit somewhere else don't exist."[22]

So Washington pursued what Gore Vidal dubbed its "enemy of the month club." In books and in *Nation*, Vidal scoffed, "Was Afghanistan turned to rubble ... to avenge the 3,000 Americans slaughtered by Osama [on September 11]? Hardly." It was "made safe for Union Oil of California, whose proposed pipeline ... had been abandoned under the Taliban's chaotic regime."[23] Next, as journalist Christian Dewar put it, "the Bush administration managed a remarkable trick in morphing Osama into Hussein" and spinning a tale of WMDs in Iraq (which holds the world's second-largest oil reserves).[24] In the prelude to war on Iraq, even the families of the terrorist victims—"September 11th Families for Peace"—condemned the Bush cohort's "illegal, immoral, and unjustified military action" and its use of "the anniversary of our loved ones ... to call for a war on a country unrelated to Sept. 11th."[25] In what Cultural Freedom Prize–winner Arundhati Roy called "the most spectacular display of morality the world has ever seen," ten million people marched against the war.[26] Their petitions to the UN Security Council filled 12 ream-sized boxes.[27] Yet, once again, the U.S. sidestepped the UN to invade a nation already battered by U.S. attacks and sanctions, as starkly revealed in Audrey Brohy's bold documentary, *Hidden Wars of Desert Storm*. (The film supports reports from the AP and ex–Attorney General Ramsey Clark that Iraqi deaths resulting from the *first* Gulf invasion exceed 700,000, most of them children.)[28]

The U. S. is now "the Arrogant Empire." So *Newsweek* said in a 2003 cover story reporting that our military spending "will soon equal that of all other countries combined."[29] David Krieger, head of the Nuclear Age Peace Foundation, denounces our government "by the rich, for the rich" and its "militarization of America":

> We are now spending some $400 billion a year on our military.... It works out to $45.5 million per hour.... Imagine all of the important

social programs that will go unfunded to pay for a military that cannot defend us. For a small portion of what the U.S. government spends on its military, it could be saving lives and building friendships by humanitarian assistance in food, healthcare, education, and sanitation.[30]

Both Krieger and Arundhati Roy decry our military's ironic dependence on poverty: "a poverty draft of Whites, Blacks, Latinos ... looking for a way to earn a living and get an education."

In her speech for the Center for Economic and Social Rights, Roy also observed that as "American show business gets more and more violent and war-like ... America's wars get more and more like show business." She cited the $250,000 designer set from which General Franks "stage-managed news coverage of Operation Shock and Awe" and the right-wing Clear Channel stations that staged "pro-war Rallies for America," then made them "breaking news."[31] Objective coverage was not offered by networks like NBC (which is owned by GE, one of Washington's top military contractors).[32] In fact, the *Village Voice* gave credit to corporate media for producing a "new hyper-reality genre"—"the Shock and Awe Show."[33]

An ironic, full-circle footnote is that the military launched its own computer combat game: "America's Army," which features "missions from dangerous hot spots around the world."[34] *Crisis* magazine noted that the game "doubles, not surprisingly, as a marketing tool. It targets avid male game players at exactly the right age to consider a military career."[35]

The military had already teamed up with General Motors to bring avid SUV fans the most gas-guzzling vehicle of all: the Hummer, the 6,500-pound "star of Desert Storm" that costs $60,000. At a time when concerns about our dependence on oil should be uppermost, GM can't keep up with demands for the behemoth that gets eight to ten miles per gallon.[36] Sports and music stars favor them. Arnold Schwarzenegger owns six of them. As one Hummer critic ranted, "If we make cars in our own image, this is the ultimate American car: over consumptive, over pollutive, and unsafe."[37]

The question for the 2000s is: Will this image ever change? Will we "over-consumptive, over-pollutive" Americans ever shake our addictions to power and speed and convenience and endless devices and Having It Our Way? Will we admit that most of us daily wallow in and waste oil products (from pop bottles and spray cleaners and sport shoes to cosmetics and cell phones and a plethora of plastics)? Will we testify that we've let our political-corporate cosmology convince us that these things are essential; that they are worth the price of any and all violence on humanity and the environment?

What's a Woman to Do?

Now that once-unspeakable violence has moved into the most mainstream media, once-unconscionable debasing of women has gone mainstream, too. And it has provoked a flurry of "Action Alerts" from the National Organization for Women. NOW led the biggest outcry against video games that "encourage violence and the degradation of women."[38] (The latest degradation comes with the X-Box game "N.U.D.E," in which players create and control their "very own beautiful brainless robot women."[39])

NOW has also condemned the misogyny of "rage rap" which, thanks to "the Merchants of Cool"—as PBS's *Frontline* calls them—rules the music business. Rapper Eminem has racked up CD sales records and a slew of Grammy Awards for extremely violent lyrics like those in "My Name Is" and in "The Eminem Show."[40] Eminem's rapper persona blatantly refers to women as sluts and bitches, boasts of heaping physical harm upon them, and even threatens physical violence to a pregnant woman.

On the political front, NOW also stormed the capitol to protest the most misogynist legislation since the Reagan regime. Bush's first presidential act was to reinstate the global "gag rule," which bans U.S. funds to any agency that mentions abortion. He also blocked $34 million for the UN Population Fund which, among other things, provides birthing kits to Afghan women, whose maternal mortality rates are extreme. Activists note that these were "the very women Bush claimed to be 'liberating' last year"[41] and that "thousands of women and infant children will die needless deaths in the coming year because of Bush's edicts."[42]

How many more will die from war is incalculable. On that front, NOW's policies continue to reflect the behest of its president, Kim Gandy: "We must keep raising our voices for peace—and the harder that becomes, the more necessary it is."[43] But among the women who have most fervently opposed war, two have become a symbol for the hundreds of protestors across the nation who were arrested for peaceful anti-war demonstrations. They are Dominican nuns Ardeth Platte and Carol Gibson, who were imprisoned for their protest at the Colorado site of a Minute Man Missile—a nuclear bomb of 300 kilotons (20 times Hiroshima).[44] Michael Moore dedicated his new book to these women, who face sentences of up to 20 years for using their own blood to inscribe a cross on one of *our* weapons of mass destruction.[45]

Another nun was moved to write an article titled "Is There Anything Left that Matters?" published by CommonDreams. In it, Joan Chittister avowed that indeed, it matters that "a nation was destroyed by us under a new doctrine of pre-emptive war":

> If a president's sex life matters, surely a president's use of global force against some of the weakest people in the world matters ... and surely [his] word to the community of nations matters. And if not, why not? ... What is the depth of the American soul if we can allow destruction to be done in our name ... and never even demand an accounting of its costs.[46]

Pulitzer novelist and activist Alice Walker makes a kindred appeal in her book *Sent by Earth*. Violence committed in our name made Walker realize that "it is the very soul of the people of North America that is being lost, and ... if this happens, for the rest of our time on the planet we are doomed to run with the dogs of war.... This is the vision that I have of this period. Ravenous, rapacious dogs, mad with greed and lust, red tongues out and salivating, running loose across the planet."[47]

Walker adds that "the psyche recognizes this image ... because some part of it is internal ... which means, we must all look inside and get to know our own dogs of war.... Some of our war dogs, we have to own, are paying taxes that will be used to destroy people almost identical to us. Many of our war dogs are connected to heating our homes and driving cars."[48]

Walker's image of war dogs conjures up the illustration on the cover of Suzan-Lori Parks' play *Topdog/Underdog*. It bears the image of two dogs' heads: black pit bulls with red-rimmed eyes and mouths, on a blood-red background. The heads are one up, one down, like the Jacks on a playing card. They make a perversely ideal emblem for this heyday of dog-eat-dog contentions and dire politically powered deceptions.

19

Suzan-Lori Parks: Putting Dirt and Deadly Games Onstage

"If I said that I write for the audience," explains Suzan-Lori Parks, "I would be lying. I write for the figures in the plays." She calls them "the figures that take up residence inside me" in what she claims is a case of double possession: Parks possesses them, and they possess her.[1]

She was born in Ft. Knox, Kentucky, in 1964 to army colonel Donald Parks and his educator wife Francis. By age five, Suzan-Lori was already trying to write novels, and the penchant for writing would stick: Along with her brother Donald (now a social worker) and sister Stephanie (a marketing manager), she churned out a family newspaper called *The Daily Daily*. "We'd type it every day in our attic," she recalls.[2]

Raised as an "army brat," Suzan-Lori grew up across six states, from Texas to Vermont, until the family was transferred to Germany, where she spent her adolescence. "I've heard horrible stories about 12-step groups for army people," says Parks. "But I had a great childhood. My parents were really into experiencing the places we lived."[3] As she stressed to interviewer David Savran, however, hers was a decidedly "military family: we all packed guns and did drills," which may help to explain why Parks has always been ready for a fight.[4]

Back in the States, her first fight in theatre was about putting dirt—literal dirt—on stage. Parks was a student at Mt. Holyoke (also the alma mater of Wasserstein). Until then, Parks had avoided theatre, disdaining the "students who wore funny clothes and had lots of attitude."[5] But in

Suzan-Lori Parks (Photo credit: Stephanie Diani)

writing classes with James Baldwin, Parks kept reading her stories aloud and having the sense that the characters were "standing behind me ... acting it out." Baldwin told Parks, "Why don't you try writing plays?" and Suzan-Lori heeded him: This was James Baldwin. "Someone I respected was telling me what to do ... it wasn't some Whosey-Whatsit who runs La Fuddy Duddy Playhouse in Whosey-Whatsitville."6 But after she submitted her first play, *The Sinner's Place*, the set for which was lots of dirt, the battle lines were drawn at Mt. Holyoke. The English department hailed it while the theatre department railed, "You can't put dirt on stage. That's not a play!"7

Parks would go on to put hefty amounts of dirt—both literal and figurative—on stages in New York and beyond. The dirt, and digging, are key to Park's process of excavating history, especially African American history, and "re-membering" it:

> Because much of African American history has been unrecorded, dismembered, washed out ... one of my tasks as playwright is to ... locate the ancestral burial grounds, dig for bones, find bones, hear the bones sing, write it down.... I'm working theatre like an incubator to create "new" historical events.[8]

Parks didn't think studying theatre would help her that much. Instead, she studied acting at Drama Studio in London, although she "never wanted to be an actor. Never. Ever. Ever." Then, in Yale School of Drama's playwriting program, she forged ties with top-string theatre innovators who would help shape and launch her career. One of them was the major new force in stage direction, Liz Diamond, who would direct a string of Parks' plays.[9]

The first was *Imperceptible Mutabilities in the Third Kingdom*, in which Parks set up a quasi-phonetic language that would become a hallmark of her work. ("Mm gonna go on ... ssif nuthin ssapin yuh know?") She used stylized characters, and a flip-flopping dynamic of subject versus object. In Part One, three black women are observed by a white male naturalist through a camera disguised as a giant cockroach in their home. The three women, speaking in both first and third person, summon the "ssterminator, Doctor wipe-um-out-Lutsky," who is the naturalist in exterminator guise. As he trains his squirt gun on them, the women recoil at TV mages of Wild Kingdom host Marlin Perkins brandishing a gun and "SHOOTIN THUH WILD BEASTS!"[10]

Part Two of *Mutabilities* is a parable told by five "Seers" (Kin-Seer, Over-Seer, etc.) about the diaspora of African people across time and oceans: "Black folks with no clothes. Then all thuh black folks clothed in smilin. In between is ... uh wet space. 2 worlds: Third Kingdom." Part Three is the tale of a Saxon family: a father, Charles; two children; and their mother Aretha, who also plays a slave and servant across three locales, from a slave ship to a modern apartment. Throughout this, cameras click away; and Aretha undergoes the extraction of all her teeth, which Charles decries as giving up the last "verifying evidence." In Part Four, a Sergeant Smith returns home to his wife and his children who hardly know him. Smith has lost his legs saving a boy that was "fallin out the sky"; but the deed has earned him a longed-for "distinction.... Got my bars! See?"

Parks referred to *Imperceptible Mutabilities* as "African American history in the shadow of the photographic image."¹¹ The script holds another device that has become a Parks signature: "Repetition and Revision," or "Rep and Rev," as she terms it—a form taken from jazz and poetry, in which a phrase is used again and again but "slightly revised."¹² In a reprise in *Mutabilities*, the Seers of Part Two repeat variations of their lines, climaxing in an overlapping staccato sound-off (which is itself repeated four times):

KIN-SEER	SOUL-SEER	SHARK-SEER	US-SEER
Wavin wavin	Rock. Thuh boat	Shouldijump	Thuh sky
Wavin	Rock.	Shouldijump	was just
Wavin	Thuh boat.	Or whut?	as blue! THUP.¹³

(The effect is something of a military drill, suggesting that Parks also absorbed part of her concept of "Rep and Rev" from her army-base roots.)

Liz Diamond guided *Mutabilities* to a 1990 Obie Award. The Parks-Diamond duo reinforced Parks' protest against what she calls "Theatre of Schmaltz" (traditional plays with linear structures and realistic characters)—theatre that's "mired in ... stating some point, or tugging some heartstring ... or wagging a finger."¹⁴ Diamond shared Parks "hatred of smarmy psychological realism" and "love of high theatricality." About theatre and Parks' work, Diamond remarked:

> The theatre has one foot firmly in the mud of popular entertainment, you know—snake swallowers and flame throwers and jugglers and things like this. I think people want to be astonished, people want to be blown away.... I think that [Suzan-Lori's] plays do make that possible, but I think that they also offer up ideas that frighten people because they portray the world as a complex place ... they don't offer the comforts of plays that are structured along more linear lines.¹⁵

Another high-powered figure who would champion Parks' works was the artistic director of Yale Repertory, Stan Wojewodski. Parks was the first person he called when he took that post with the intent to give a home to "idiosyncratic writers who create a very special language for the stage."¹⁶ For Yale Repertory, Liz Diamond directed Parks' play *The Death of the Last Black Man in the Whole Entire World*. The script explodes racial clichés about African Americans, using characters like "Black Man with Watermelon," "Black Woman with Fried Drumstick." They move through a historical dreamscape woven around reports of the Black Man's demise. His deaths and lives have been many—ending in a brutal lynching, death by an electric chair, his plunge from "uh passin ship from space tuh splat on thuh pavement." The language hints at the rappers' riffs that Parks would blatantly evoke in later work. Black Man riffs on the Then and Now: "That me that was-be is uh me-has-been. Thuh Then that was-be is uh has-been-Then too." He resurrects repeatedly, and cants in reprise: "Missmemiss-mewhats-myname ... Re-member me."

In a lengthy study of Parks' work for *American Theatre* (October 2000), Shawn-Marie Garrett wrote that Parks' first two plays "did appeal strongly to a small yet unpredictable assortment of theatre artists, audiences, and critics who could see how Parks was inventing new ways of shaping dramatic characters and structure."[17]

For an Actors Theatre Humana Festival, Parks agreed to write a companion piece to a David Hwang play on interracial relations. When Hwang asked "What have you got?" Parks replied, "Three black women in white wedding dresses. And that's interracial, right?"[18] *Devotees in the Garden of Love* was set on a hill where a bride-to-be and her mother, both in white, look down on a war that rages between the daughter's two suitors and their troops. The women fuss over the bride's hope chest while tracking the war on TV and through spy-glass "bonocks." First-hand news from the front is brought by Mme. Pandahr, the bride's panderer who insists that no suitors could be better matched "than ThisOne and ThatOne." The steadfast bride declares,

> ThisOne may sever thuh arms and legs off uh all uh ThatOnes Troops ... puss green-slimed bile and contagion may grow from the wounds of thuh wounded seep intuh thuh ground and kill and kill and kill and kill and kill and kill ... thuh sky may shake and spit fire and crack open and swallow um all but itll all end nicely. Our word is "devotion".... We will hold fast ... we won't flinch. How come? Cuz thuh cause of Love.[19]

At the end of the gory "even–Steven" battle, Mme. Pandahr proudly presents the bride with her victor—a severed head on a platter—which Pandahr recognizes to be ThatOne "because I am after all his mother." When Parks was asked by interviewer David Savran if *Devotees* held any "feminist content" or "critique of masculine aggression," Parks replied, "I don't think that way. In my plays ... everybody's bad. And everybody's good."[20]

The America Play was the last of four Parks plays directed by Liz Diamond, and the first play by Parks to move from Yale Rep to New York's Public Theater. By that time, Parks had the support of George C. Wolfe, the forceful successor of Joe Papp at the Public. Wolfe had come to directing and producing by way of his own experimental playwriting and view of black history. His 1986 play *The Colored Museum* gave a guided history of black culture through "exhibits"—ranging from a "Celebrity slave ship" to a spoof of black musicals to a satire of *A Raisin in the Sun* (titled "the Last Mama-on-the-couch Play"). Wolfe said the play "liberated" his imagination, but "I got trashed by a lot of black people for it because they didn't see the flip side."[21] Yet, the play and playwright compelled Joe Papp to bring Wolfe to the Public, where he eventually became producer. Wolfe also became Suzan-Lori Parks' agent, producer, and avid champion: "I wanted to say, 'World, you should know this playwright. [She] is saying amazing things about the human condition ... about America.'"[22] Just what Parks is saying continues to puzzle and provoke critics into heated controversies about her methods and merits as a playwright.

In *The America Play*, Parks put dirt onstage in the form of "a great hole ... an exact replica of the Great Hole of History." Wandering this hole is a bizarre family: A black grave-digger obsessed with Lincoln, and his abandoned wife Lucy and son Brazil who search for him. Act One is mostly a monologue, the digger giving a much-repeated narration of how he became "Lincoln the Lesser Known"—a "Faux Father" who goes off to replay Lincoln's assassination in a sideshow. In Act Two, the Lesser Known's wife and son dig for him, led on by the echoes of gunshots and the artifacts they find while digging. Of these, they construct a "Hall of Wonders" for their own public sideshow. When the Lesser finally joins them and Lucy bids him to do his Lincoln for the boy, the Lesser takes yet another bullet in his head; and Brazil adds him to their Hall of Wonders: "Note thuh death wound: Thuh great black hole ... in thuh great head."[23]

Audiences and critics were, for the most part, frustrated or put off by *The America Play*. Shawn-Marie Garrett reported "disastrous box-office receipts, walkouts and mixed (but mostly negative) critical reactions.... Some of the same publications that favorably reviewed Parks' first two history plays skewered *The America Play*."[24] Even Parks had objections, this time, to Diamond's staging. Parks later said that the play "was much simpler than the production made it out to be." And much dirtier: The glossy set and performances were too sanitized. For example, the boy Brazil should be "the kind of guy who scratches his crotch when he knows you're looking. This is not the shiny, happy ... family that the production presented."[25] Of the play's better-received (dirtier?) West Coast premiere, critic Steven Winn wrote that it "provokes and frustrates in more or less equal measure.... It starts an itch you don't quite know how to scratch."[26]

Parks' next play, *Venus*, was co-produced by the Public and Yale Rep, and staged by Richard Foreman. It was based on the true story of Saartjie Baartman, a nineteenth-century African woman with huge buttocks who was exploited as a sideshow freak—"the Venus Hottentot." In Park's play, Venus is sold by The Man and his Brother to a cruel Mother-Showman.

19. Suzan-Lori Parks: Putting Dirt and Deadly Games Onstage

She is sold again to a Baron Docteur who takes Venus as his mistress and subjects her to the lewd scrutiny of a team of anatomists. Parks insists that she wrote *Venus* not as a critique of colonialism or objectification of the female body. "It was none of those things. I wrote it because I wanted to give this great character two hours [and] give a black actress a chance to play a really cool part."[27]

Interviewers who question Parks about the meaning or message behind her plays get her retort that none is intended: "If you want to send a message," she quips, "go to Western Union."[28] Parks avows that she has little interest in "meaning—whatever that word means.... I keep meaning to look up meaning." And she openly admits, "I know my plays aren't for everybody." [29] Even some within the black theatre community have taken exception to her politics: *Theater* magazine once planned a printed symposium on her work, but scrapped it when editors could find no African American critics willing to go on record with their opinions. Late in the year 2000, Shawn-Marie Garrett still noted that "Parks' plays are rarely produced at theatres exclusively devoted to the production of African American drama.... Her tendency to attract predominantly white audiences and directors sparks further questions in some minds about whether she is speaking to or for the African American experience."[30] (But Parks does have fans among current women playwrights: Paula Vogel calls her a "most original voice in theatre today."[31])

In Parks' three plays since *Venus*—*In the Blood, Topdog/Underdog*, and *Fucking A*—the violence of history shares the spotlight with interpersonal violence in the here-and-now and in a grisly projected future. Parks borrows less from a historical past and more from past writers and theatre innovators. For instance, *In the Blood*'s main character, Hester, is an updated and obvious hybrid of two classic mothers: the adulterous Hester of Hawthorne's *Scarlet Letter*, and Brecht's wartime Mother Courage. But Parks' black Hester is battling a social system that reviles her for being the homeless mother of five bastards by five fathers. The actors playing Hester's children, who live under a viaduct, also play a chorus of hypocritical authority figures—from a smug black female social worker to a scurrilous preacher—each of whom has had casual, lurid sex with Hester. (They admit to it in "Confession" monologues.) The illiterate Hester can write only the letter "A," which she practices on her viaduct wall, where some prankster has also scrawled "slut." Yet Hester declares, like a mantra, "All I need is a leg up. I get my leg up, I'll be ok." But failing to get one, she sinks into madness. In the end, while her other children look on, she bludgeons her son Jabber to death for using the word "slut" to taunt her.

Responses to *In the Blood* have ranged from one polar extreme to the other, after productions in New York and elsewhere. Nelson Pressley of the *Washington Post* hailed the play as "an electrifying drama" and Parks as "a relentlessly inventive phrasemaker."[32] *Chicago Tribune* critic Michael Phillips praised Parks for a "sleekly structured and unexpectedly lively piece ... reworking a few key signifiers from Hawthorne's 'The Scarlet Letter.'"[33] Regarding the same Chicago production, Justin Hayford (critic and former social worker) complained about Parks being "touted as an innovator for her semi-poetic, semi-epic work—apparently everyone's forgotten Brecht," and claimed that Parks tends to "keep things TV simple while creating a patina of complexity with a flurry of attention-grabbing theatrical devices." Hayford added—having himself "worked with numerous homeless clients in ten years at a legal-aid agency"—that Parks has a "laughably superficial understanding of the problems she addresses."[34]

It is true that the dark desperate worlds that Parks typically depicts are a far cry from her own personal experiences; she has enjoyed a privileged if not charmed life, and certainly a charmed career. Besides the invaluable "leg-ups" she gained through the theatre milieus of Yale and the Public and Wolfe, Parks has been showered with money awards, including a $50,000 Alpert "mid-career" award (which brought Parks to Cal Arts and led to her heading up their Writing-for-Performance Program); National Endowment and Guggenheim fellowships; Ford and Rockefeller Foundation grants; and the MacArthur Foundation's whopping $500,000 "genius" grant. Added to these mega–leg-ups have been two Obie awards, a Tony nomination, two Pulitzer-Prize nominations (*In the Blood* was nominated in 2000), and her win of a Pulitzer for *Topdog/Underdog*.

Parks' personal life holds no trace of the psychic and socio-economic traumas she depicts. For several years, she has shared homes in New York and Los Angeles with Paul Oscher, who was once the only white musician to play with the Muddy Waters band. (The two met when Parks wanted lessons on the harmonica—Oscher's forté.) Two days before *Topdog/Underdog* opened at the Public, Parks and Oscher were married and took off for an Amsterdam honeymoon. They missed the off–Broadway opening of her two-man play that would take the 2002 Pulitzer for Drama. This time, George Wolfe personally directed Parks' script, using the powerful talents of Jeffrey Wright (Tony-winner for *Angels in America*) and Don Cheadle (stage and screen actor of *Bulworth* and *Traffic*).

Parks claims that she wrote *Topdog/Underdog* in three days. "So far, it's the easiest thing I've written." Her notion for the play was itself a "rep and rev" of her earlier *America Play*. "I thought it'd be fun to write a completely different take on the idea of Lincoln and Booth."[35] But another huge inspiration came while she and Oscher were watching a three-card monte game on a New York street. "To my surprise," says Parks, "I started getting this running commentary from the man standing beside me. It turned out to be Paul.... I didn't know he used to do it for a living between music gigs." Parks made the con game the main action and catalyst for violence between her stage brothers, Lincoln and Booth. "I knew I had an expert in my life to tell me how to do it."[36]

Oscher taught her well. Most of the riveting moments of the play spring from the tension behind the three-card monte patter, and the fire with which actors like Wright and Cheadle perform it. They've brought to the play what *Variety* critic Charles Isherwood called "electric charisma": "These are actors with inventive theatrical instincts and heaps of natural talents; and their fertile performances are so captivating that it may take a while before audiences notice there's not a lot going on in this disappointing new play by Parks."[37]

What does go on in *Topdog* is a lethal rivalry between two street-smart but relationship-impaired siblings, who were long ago (as teenagers) abandoned by their parents. Now, Lincoln pays the rent on their dismal room by playing a white-faced Abe Lincoln in an arcade where patrons shoot him. Booth prefers to shoplift or "boost"—everything from designer suits to gourmet meals. But Booth envies and deeply resents the three-card monte skills that Lincoln, now retired from the hustle, still possesses. And therein lies the conflict that erupts into Booth's murderous revenge on Lincoln. The gun-toting Booth also takes revenge on his girlfriend Grace, who has stood him up for a date. "I popped her," he boasts. "Twice. 3 times." He "popped her good" until she was dead.

When *Topdog* moved to Broadway, to the Ambassador, it was neatly apropos that rapper Mos Def stepped into the role of Booth, who dubs himself "3-card" for his street scam. The con-game patter in Parks' script is closely akin to a rapper's riff. But even the men's more straightforward dialogue evokes the tough strut and gunfire volley of rap.

The new pairing, of Mos Def with Jeffrey Wright, created what *Nation* magazine called "the most thrilling duo on Broadway."[38] But, predictably, reviews of the play itself were wildly mixed. "When the play works at all, it's on the strength of the performances," wrote Matthew Murray. "Parks' script ... remains as unbelievable and dramatically lackluster here as it was there (at the Public)."[39] On one hand, Ben Brantley of the *Times* said the play showed that Parks "can shape a captivating narrative without sacrificing her thematic ambitions. She even incorporates one of her more far-fetched metaphoric devices from her 'America Play' in 'TopDog' (a black man playing Lincoln in a sideshow) and gets you to accept it without blinking."[40] On the other hand, *Variety* critic Isherwood complained that Lincoln's "unbelievable line of work strains belief in the realistic context of this play.... What's next door at this peculiar arcade, anyway: Let's Lynch Santa Claus? A Kill Kennedy videogame?"[41]

Just as far-fetched was the character Booth managing to shoplift two designer suits, with shoes and all accessories to match. But director George Wolfe had Booth do a provocative strip-tease of his stolen layers to a James Brown tune, and audiences ate it up.

Most reviews of *Topdog* focused on themes and metaphors, meanings that, again, Parks would negate. As she told her director "a hundred times, 'George there are no metaphors. I don't know what a metaphor is.... There are two men in a room.'"[42] *Topdog* was different from Parks' prior work, more realistic in its linear construction. It also drew a somewhat broader audience. *Nation* claimed that "the numbers of young people and black people in the audience ... could be considered a healthy sign."[43]

Parks herself has said that her earlier (history) plays were "the foundation" for her newer work: "Now the plays are different. Mothers killing children in *In the Blood*. The brother against brother in *Topdog/Underdog*. The servant decapitating the master in *Fucking A*." However, Parks adds with a grin, "One thing that hasn't changed is my love of vulgarity. In *Topdog*, one of the characters jerks off to 'fuck books'—dirty magazines—he keeps under his bed."[44]

Suzan-Lori Parks did make it to the Broadway opening of *Topdog/Underdog*. And her outfit for the event included a silver-studded dog collar borrowed from her pit bull: "Everybody thought it was some chi-chi thing I bought at Barney's."[45] On opening night, some of Parks' cohorts already knew about the Pulitzer Prize, but kept the news from her.

The Pulitzer committee that awarded the Drama Prize to Parks included Robert Brustein of American Repertory (and founder of Yale Repertory). Brustein admitted, "This play was not my first choice ... but as an admirer of her previous work, I was content to endorse the decision."[46] On receiving the award, Parks used the word she had disdained so often in interviews: she said her Pulitzer "has a lot of meaning. It's great for African Americans."[47]

Hopefully, Parks' win will open for other black women playwrights some of the doors that have been pushed and pulled open for her. Meanwhile, those doors are propped wide open for Parks and her new work; and where they go, controversy still follows.

Parks' "new" play for 2003, *Fucking A*, was actually written before *Topdog*, and is an outgrowth of her Hawthorne-Brecht hybrid, *In the Blood*. This time, Hester is a backroom abortionist for a grisly police-state of the future. Her friend, Canary, the "Mayor's whore," shares Hester's hate for the mayor's wife, who got Hester's son arrested for his first crime, stealing meat. Canary and Hester conspire to drug the First Lady and abort the fetus she's carrying. But the First Lady was impregnated not by the Mayor (who sings a song about his sperm—"My Little Army") but by Hester's escaped-convict son "Monster," who is the target of sadistic state bounty hunters and their dogs. The hunters plan to catch Monster and do a "run-through"—run a hot iron rod "up his bottom and out his throat" and then "let him wiggle on it." Hester begins the play steeped in the blood of aborted fetuses and ends it awash in the blood of her son, whose throat she cuts before the hunters can "have their fun" with him.

The play is punctuated by nine songs written by Parks, and by spurts of a language called "Talk," used to discuss things that are gynecological or scatological. (Examples: *Abah-nazip* means "abortion"; *Kaltie Bleehc* is "chilly twat.") The Talk is translated on above-stage screens.

When Bertolt Brecht used projections and character songs, he did so to create a distance or alienation that would curb audience empathy and spur social action instead. Parks gives no such reasons for copying the techniques, and critics have had a field day mocking her use of them. Reviewer David Hinkle quipped that "Parks has written a by-the-numbers tragedy. It's as if she had hied herself over to CompUSA, purchased some Bertolt Brecht software ... then followed the formula assiduously."[48] Ben Brantley of the *New York Times* (who had praised *Topdog*) wrote of *Fucking A* that the letter "A" is arguably "the liveliest character" in what amounts to "an animated diagram of a play.... [It] awkwardly mixes Brechtian distance and the kind of intense social melodrama associated with Clifford Odets."[49] Frank Scheck of *Hollywood Reporter* wrote that "the action, such as it is, is punctuated from time to time by dramatic musical numbers and by interludes in which characters ... lapse into Parks' made-up language, which resembles Klingon by way of New Orleans.... It's all extremely pretentious and off-putting."[50] Conversely, Gerald Rabkin of the Web's "Culture Vulture" alleged that *Fucking A* "may well be [Parks'] best work yet" and praised her Hawthorne-based "riff on themes of freedom and entrapment."[51]

Even when critics slam a script by Parks, they typically praise the actors, who tend to be high-profile and high-powered talents: Mos Def took his second Parks role as Monster in *Fucking A*, and S. Epatha Merkersen (of television's *Law and Order*) played the hapless Hester.

Parks—who admits she is "really not a theatre person but I love what I can do in it"[52]—writes for other venues. She authored the screenplay for Spike Lee's *Girl Six*, about a would-be actress's stint as a phone-sex operator. For Oprah Winfrey's Harpo Productions, she's been hired to adapt a Toni Morrison work. Disney has her on contract to write a new musical,

Hoopz, about the Harlem Globetrotters. And Parks' first novel, *Getting Mother's Body*, was released by Random House in 2003. Parks' off-stage storytelling features many of her signature images, with dirt, digging, and death high among them. There is humor, too; but as Steven Boone of *Show Business* remarked, "Parks has Richard Pryor's taste for crude, cruel humor."[53]

In her book *Getting Mother's Body*, Parks borrows from Faulkner's *As I Lay Dying*; however, Parks' story-family is on a quest to dig up the remains of a mother (Willa Mae), not bury them. The family hopes to cash in the jewels that Willa Mae was allegedly buried with: Aunt June needs a better false leg; Willa Mae's pregnant teenaged daughter, Billy, needs an abortion. (Willa Mae herself died from a bloody coat-hanger abortion.) The novel's ending is more upbeat than any of Parks' plays to date. The same goes for her outline of the Disney script, although violence is her entree to the plot of *Hoopz*. As Parks plans it, a basketball hotshot "with attitude … gets into it on the court with somebody … and he gets shot and killed…. But then! The guy gets a second chance at life … he time travels and has to hang out with the Globetrotters."[54] Perhaps these hints of a brighter outlook will work their way into Parks' plays. Critic Elyse Sommer of *Curtain Up* suggests that things like Parks' "Pulitzer Prize, numerous pending projects, and a happy marriage" might lead to "a little more sunshine being allowed into her future work."[55]

Maybe. But Parks appears to have little interest in uplift. Her art seems more fixed on mirroring what is cruel and vile in human nature—and American society—than on attempting to change it. Perhaps Parks has only taken Stokely Carmichael's observation that "violence is as American as apple pie" and brought it into the twenty-first century, center stage.

One thing about Parks seems certain: Her plays will continue to evoke both cheers and jeers from divided critics. What Frank Scheck of *Hollywood Reporter* said about *Fucking A* could apply to all of Parks' work: "This new effort from prolific Pulitzer Prize–winning Suzan-Lori Parks is certain to further provoke division between those who consider her a brilliant new dramatic voice and others who consider her the latest example of the emperor's new clothes."[56]

Depending on where you stand, Suzan-Lori Parks either turns out brilliantly-conceived cautionary tales, or derivative and pretentious paeans to nihilism.

Wherever you stand, Parks undeniably stands on the shoulders of a line of other determined and defiant black women writers who came before her. The place where Parks stands as a highly visible, highly rewarded black woman playwright was forged by the earth-moving talents and toils of women like Beah Richards and Alice Childress and Ntozake Shange. They and other women of color warranted Pulitzer Prizes before any Pulitzer jury could or would warrant their achievements. So, the next chapter (after the synopsis of Parks' play) will be a humble but sincere bow to a few of the women who gave Suzan-Lori Parks a "leg up" of incalculable value.

THE PLAY—*TOPDOG/UNDERDOG*: NO MATTER WHAT CARD YOU CHOOSE, YOU LOSE

The play is set in the "seedily furnished" room of Booth and Lincoln, two blood brothers in their thirties. As Scene One opens, Booth is awkwardly practicing his three-card monte scam atop two milk crates. (Other makeshift furnishings include a single bed and a reclining chair.) "Watch me close watch me close now: Who-see-thuh-red-card ... thuh-red-card-is-thuh-winner ..." In his patter, Booth pulls in and defeats an imaginary mark: "This card you say? Wrong! Sucker! ... Asshole ... I bet yr daddy heard how stupid you was and drank himself to death just cause he didn't wanna have nothing to do witchu!"[57] After Booth dodges imaginary cops and starts over, Lincoln quietly enters, in a top hat and beard (his Abe Lincoln garb) and stands behind Booth. Suddenly sensing his presence, Booth reels and pulls a gun from his pants. He berates Lincoln for coming in like that and for wearing that "bullshit ... that getup that motherdisfuckinguise" home from his arcade job. If Booth's woman, Grace, sees that getup, it's "gonna reflect bad" on Booth. He brags to Link that today he boosted (shoplifted) a "diamondesque" ring for Grace, one that's a half-size too small so she can't "take it off on a whim, like she did the last one."

Lincoln removes his costume and whiteface, explaining that he only had a minute to catch his bus. He adds that there was a kid on the bus who wanted old Abe's autograph. Lincoln gave it to him—for 20 bucks. When Booth announces that he has decided to change his name, Lincoln suggests an African name, but one easy to spell, 'cause "some of them fellas who got African names, no one can say they names."

They sit at the milk crate table to eat the take-out food that Link has brought; it's part of their deal. The room was Booth's until Link's wife Cookie threw him out; now Link sleeps in the recliner and brings food. He also brings home his weekly pay on Fridays. But this is Thursday, so Booth even orders Link to serve up the food. Booth eats ravenously; Lincoln eats slowly then cleans up, rejecting Booth's request to play cards. Lincoln "don't touch the cards no more." Yet, when Booth resumes his clumsy monte routine, Link advises him to "work on it in smaller bits."

Booth declares that his new name is "3-card": "Anybody not calling me 3-card gets a bullet." While Lincoln strums his guitar, Booth entreats his brother to get back into the street scam with him, to be partners. "No one throws the cards like you, Link. And with your moves and my magic ... we'd be golden, bro!" But Link is finished with all that.

Booth suddenly brings up their family history—something their mama told him the day she left. "She told me to look out for you. I told her I was the little brother and the big brother should look out after the little brother.... Not like you care. Here I am interested in an economic opportunity ... and all you can say you shiteating motherfucking pathetic limpdick uncle tom ... is how you don't do no more what I be wanting to do.... YOU STANDING IN MY WAY, LINK!" To Link's reply that he "cant be hustling no more," Booth counters that what Link does, "dressing up like some crackerass white man, some dead president and letting people shoot at you sounds like a hustle to me." Link says that it's not, because "people know the real deal."

Link strums and sings a woeful ditty that he's written: "My dear mother left me, my father's gone away...." It ends with "My luck was bad but now it turned worse / Dont call me up a doctor, just call me up a hearse." The brothers settle in for the night, and Lincoln confides to Booth, "Daddy told me once why we got the names we do.... It was his idea of a joke."

Scene Two is Friday night. Booth enters, toting a room-divider screen and looking bundled-up to the extreme. From his coat sleeves he pulls two shoes, then another pair. From beneath his coat, he sheds a new suit with price tags, revealing another new suit. From it, he pulls two folded shirts, belts, neckties—all of it shoplifted. When Lincoln arrives with his weekly pay, Booth jokes "Lordamighty, Pa, I smells money," and Link joins in the melodrama spoof, capped with a swig of whiskey. Booth gives Link his half of the clothing loot, and they admire themselves in the suits. After Booth "does the budget" with Link's pay, including $50 to get the phone turned back on (vital if "you gonna get a woman"), Link says "theyre talking about cutbacks at the arcade." He wants to keep this sit-down job. "Folks come in, kill phony Honest Abe with the phony pistol. I can sit there and let my mind travel." At Booth's retort, "But you aint living," Link says "Im alive aint I?" Not dead, like Link's street-scam partner Lonny. "Somebody shot him. I knew I was next, so I quit." Booth's advice, if Link wants to keep his arcade job, is "you gotta jazz up yr act." So Link asks Booth to help him with it, but Booth dashes off to meet Grace. Alone, Link puts on his Abe getup, pretends to get shot, and contorts in pretended death. He considers another attempt, but pours a tall whiskey instead.

Scene Three begins with Lincoln dead drunk in the chair. It takes the returning Booth two door slams to rouse him. Booth swaggers and boasts about how much Grace wanted him back. To Link's query, "She let you do it without a rubber?" Booth says "Yeah ... I put my foot down—and she *melted*." But when Booth retreats to his side of the room, he is furtively handling condoms and himself. Lincoln scoffs, "You didn't get shit tonight," and Booth rails, "I'm a hot man.... Not like you, Link.... You a limp dick jealous whiteface motherfucker whose wife dumped him cause he couldn't get it up and she told me so. Came crawling to me cause she needed a man."

After a long pause Lincoln says, "You can hustle 3-card monte without me"; but he tells Booth that he would need a better gun than the pop gun he carries. Their talk of guns comes around to whether Lincoln ever looks at the arcade customers who shoot at him. Link describes the "assassins"—the "little good for nothings in they school uniforms," businessmen smelling like martinis, tourists in theme-park shirts. Link does his best for them. "And now they talking bout replacing me with uh wax dummy." Booth offers to play assassin while Link practices dying: "I am Booth!! ... this is life and death! Go all out!" But when Lincoln does so, it's almost too real for Booth. Link says that people are funny about "they historical shit ... they like it to unfold the way they folded it up." In case Link does get fired, Booth urges him to show how the hook part of the card hustle goes. But Link says good-night and dozes off in his chair. Booth goes to bed with a girlie magazine.

In Scene Four, Lincoln wakes up first, stumbles around for a cup to use as a urinal, then tears off his Lincoln garb, ripping the beard. He curses about this, since his job's already on the line. To himself, Link reminisces about hustling, when he was the "be all end all." He recalls the days when he and Lonny took a man and his wife "for everything they had.... We took a father for the money he was gonna get his kids new bike with.... We took a mothers welfare check, she pulled a knife on us and we ran." He swore off the cards; but he was very good. Tempted by Booth's deck of cards, Link pulls out three cards and sets up a game. He starts slowly but is drawn into it. Unlike Booth, his moves and patter are smooth, "dangerous, electric." Unseen by him, Booth wakes up and listens closely, as Lincoln deftly finishes the routine.

Scene Five is very late Wednesday night. Booth is in his shoplifted suit, surveying the romantic dinner for two that he has boosted, including food, candles, table settings. To himself, he mutters "food's getting cold, Grace.... Don't worry, she'll get here." While he's pushing his dirty magazines further under the bed, Link enters; and Booth tries to hurry him out before Grace comes. Link groans that he needs to sit for a bit—he lost his job today. He promises to go when Grace arrives. But she was due at 8:00 P.M.; and it's now 2:00 A.M.

While Booth looks for Grace at the window, Link drinks whiskey and pulls out their ragged family album. He starts to get sentimental about their old house, which Booth reminds him had a "cement backyard and a frontyard full of trash." Thinking about when their Mom and Pops left them, Lincoln says, "I think there was something out there that they liked more than they liked us ... something they was struggling against." At least they didn't leave together; and they gave the brothers $500 each (their "inheritance") before they split. Booth says, "It was you and me against thuh world, Link. It could be like that again." Link says throwing cards "aint as easy as it looks." But he finally offers to show a few moves to Booth, who instantly clears the table for the monte setup. Booth wants to pretend to be the lookout and has his gun ready, but Link puts the gun aside: "We dont need nobody watching for cops cause there aint none."

Starting the game, Lincoln pretends to size up the crowd, including Booth. He tells Booth that "theres 2 parts to throwing thuh cards ... thuh moves and thuh grooves." He snaps, "Dont look at my hands, look at my eyes." After a round of moves, he has Booth pick out the deuce of spades. Picking the right card makes Booth cocky. Link adds his hypnotic patter for another go-round; Booth picks the right card again and gloats even more, until Link tells him to switch places. "Take thuh cards and show me whatcha got." Booth's attempts are so inept that Link collapses in laughter. Booth pockets his gun, angry and agitated. Lincoln suggests that he try to throw the cards with a light touch, "like Grace's skin." The reminder that Grace has stood him up fuels Booth's rage. He slams out the door in a vengeful mood, while Link stays fixed on the cards.

Scene Six is the next night. Link walks in drunk, pulls a big wad of cash from his pocket, and congratulates himself. "You got yr shit back in the saddle man ... Walking in Luckys and you seen how they was looking at you? Lucky starts pouring for you ... And thuh women be hanging on me and purring ... 3 of them sweethearts in thuh restroom on my dick all at once ... Cause they knew I'd been throwing the cards." Booth emerges, having been in the room all this time. He slips to the door and pretends to arrive with good news: "Grace got down on her knees ... asked *me* to marry *her*." He adds that he just had the night for their date wrong, that's all. The bad news is, Grace is moving in here, so Link has to go. Link says, "No sweat," and digs out a suitcase.

When Booth presses to know how it can be "no sweat" when Link has no job, no cash, Link claims he has a new job, as security guard. The suitcase reminds Booth that when their Pops left, he took no clothes.

Lincoln replies that "the man was a drunk"; he did everything "half fucked up." Their Pops was a womanizer, too. Sometimes he took Link along, even let him watch. Link says, "One of his ladies liked me, so I would do her after he'd done her. On thuh sly though." As Link is packing his tattered Abe getup, Booth remarks that he doesn't even have a photo of Link in it, for the album. So Link puts on the garb; Booth grabs his camera and snaps a photo. Angry and wanting to bait Link, Booth brings up the night he slept with Link's wife, Cookie. "I had her. Yr damn wife." Link responds, "I dont think about her no more," and prods Booth about how he intends to "bring home thuh bacon" for Grace. Booth plans to throw the cards. Link says, "You a double left-handed motherfucker who don't stand a chance," and tries to leave. But Booth stops him. "You scared I got yr shit.... Ima go out there and be thuh man and you aint gonna be nothin."

Lincoln takes the dare and barks at Booth to set up the cards, which he quickly does. Lincoln methodically throws the cards; when Booth again makes the right pick, he's pleased but less than before. "It didn't feel real," Booth says. It needs the thing that makes it real—"thuh cash." He knows that Link got a wad of bills on the street today. "You scared of losing it to thuh man, chump? Put it down." Link puts the $500 cash on the table and starts his moves. But Booth says that he's not doing "thuh real shit." And it won't be real, Booth claims, unless he puts money down, too. He goes to his hiding place and removes a knotted nylon containing cash—his $500 from their mama. It reminds him of when he caught her with her dress up with her "Thursday man." He caught her again later, asking the guy for money to get rid of a "mistake." Then two months later, she shoved all her stuff into plastic bags while the man waited in a car. "She musta known I was gonna walk in on her this time cause she had my payoff—my *inheritance*—all ready for me."

Link says, "Don't put that down," but Booth puts the stocking on the table and makes Link throw the cards. Booth picks the right card to "get him in," then has to pick the right card to win. The brothers lock eyes; Link turns over the card that Booth chooses. It's the wrong card. Link scoops in all the money and says, "Aint yr fault if yr eyes aint fast.... Throwing cards aint thuh whole world. You got other shit going ... you got Grace." Laughing, Link works at the knot in the stocking, to check if their mama was "for real about it.... I aint laughing at you," he says. "Im just laughing.... Theres so much about those cards ... And the first move to know is that there aint no winning.... The only time you pick right is when thuh man lets you." Booth snarls, "Fuck you Fuck you FUCK YOU!" As Link is about to take a knife to the knot, Booth blurts, "I popped her ... Grace ...

Who thuh fuck she thinks she is doing me like she done? ... Popped her good." Grace is dead.

Lincoln tries to give the stocking of cash back to Booth. But Booth refuses it and rants, "Think you can fuck with me, motherfucker think again! Think you can take me like Im just some chump some two left-handed pussy dickbreath chump...." He makes Lincoln open the stocking; but as Link brings the knife down to do so, Booth grabs him from behind, pulls out his gun and pushes it into Link's neck. "Don't," says Lincoln. Booth shoots; Lincoln's body lurches from the chair. Booth rails, "Think you can take my shit? ... You stole my inheritance, man.... You had yr own. And you blew it.... You aint gonna be needing yr fucking money-roll no more, dead motherfucker.... Watch me close now: Ima go out there and make a name for myself that don't have nothing to do with you." Booth starts to gather up the money, then crumbles. He sits down by Lincoln's body, takes it in his arms and sobs, "AAAAAAAAAH!"

Suzan-Lori Parks has insisted that her play holds no metaphors—no intended meaning. But her characters' names and their sibling status obviously evoke metaphors and speculation about Parks' symbolism. Critics tend to align the play with the stories of Cain and Abel as well as the history of Lincoln's murder by Booth. Critic Ed Blank of the *Tribune-Review* describes the brothers as prisoners of "a legacy foreshadowed by their identity as African American males, underscored by their father's labeling.... The metaphor passes for a plot."[58] Indeed, it seems that the whole play is driven not by plot, but by metaphors for destiny and domination. The only action is derived from the brothers' see-saw game of get-the-upper-hand. And through it all, Parks' form and content battle with each other as much as the brothers do.

This play is by far the most realistic of Park's canon to date. It has linear construction and observes the unities of time and place, which is why some features of the play are jarring and questionable in both the reading and the viewing of it. The degrading banality of the brothers' existence in their room is drawn as extremely real, very palpable. Lincoln's arcade job in this context comes off as an absurd contrivance. (As *Variety*'s critic Isherwood scoffed, "What's nextdoor in this peculiar arcade anyway ... a Kill Kennedy videogame?"[59]) Booth's shoplifting career rankles, too, for double-edged reasons. If Booth is really so cunning and agile at thieving as to steal full sets of men's attire, whole gourmet meals with swanky tableware to boot, and three-fold room dividers, why on earth can't he handle the cards with more skill? But more relevant to the play's over-determined outcome is this question: How could the supremely street-smart Booth, brother of a big-time hustler who was himself once part of the act, not know that "the only time you pick the right card is when thuh man lets you"?

Perhaps to distract viewers from such questions, Parks inserts interludes that are pure show biz. For Booth, there is his burlesque-like striptease out of his purloined clothing. Lincoln has at least two take-stage solos: One comes in his rehearsal of his namesake's last moments—sitting down in the theatre box, taking the bullet, convulsing to his death. Another comes in Link's hypnotic reenactment of his heyday card hustle. The brothers also share a limelight interlude in their melodrama spoof prompted by Link's payday. In performance, the tawdry glamour of these moments is heightened by director or designer touches. In the Chicago premier (at Steppenwolf), a row of footlights flared to give the feel of vaudeville, with huge shadows of the performers cast on a red backdrop. In New York, Booth did a provocative peel to a James Brown beat.

Amidst these undeniably entertaining bits, somber revelations about the brothers' past come out of nowhere and beg more questions: The brothers were teens when their parents bailed out—half their lifetimes ago. Is there any reason why their family agendas have not been addressed before now, besides dramatic convenience and contrivance? The build to the final violence seems equally forced. Parks uses a heavy hand on the trigger of Booth's rage, especially in the last two scenes. After Link reacts with laughter to Booth's inept monte attempt, Parks has to refocus Booth's anger on his no-show girlfriend, Grace. Parks has Lincoln remind Booth to "throw the cards with a light touch ... like Grace's skin." And presto, Booth revives his rage enough to storm out (with gun) and blow Grace away. Since killing Grace makes Booth top dog over her, it's a short hop to his dominating Lincoln with a bullet.

Despite the play's leaden contrivances and overly controlled outcome, it holds some compelling moments. In performance, the three-card street scam is mesmerizing (as it was when I witnessed it in my years of living in Manhattan, and still is when I see it as a furtive traveling scam on the Chicago "el-trains." But even I know that the dealer only gives the mark a token win to pull him in for the kill). Perhaps above all, Parks deserves credit for devising a vehicle that allows two dynamic black actors to strut their stuff. The energies of Mos Def and Jeffrey Wright in New York, and K. Todd Freeman and David Rainey in Chicago, attracted like electro-magnets. (*Chicago-Tribune* critic Michael Phillips called *Topdog* "worth seeing for the performances of K. Todd Freeman and David Rainey," but described the play as "hindered by an over-insistent, reiterative quality. Parks foreshadows like mad."[60])

For me, the play only works as metaphor; a metaphor for a deadly war game between brothers that has the entertainment veneer of vaudeville. Seeing it that way, I find Parks' play to be a perfect, perverse symbol for the cultural and political timbre of the times.

Regardless of what Parks intended in writing the play, or what the Pulitzer jury saw in considering it, I can and do cheer the fact that the Drama Pulitzer has, at last, gone to a woman of color. But I will save some of my cheering for later: for a day when the prize goes to a black woman for a play that depicts not the weaknesses and indulgent violence of black men, but the admirable strengths and solidarity of black women.

20

"Also in the Winner's Circle" (The Legacy of Black Women Playwrights)

Until *Topdog/Underdog* moved to the Ambassador Theatre in 2002, there had not been a play by a black woman on Broadway in 33 years, not counting one-woman shows. Arguably, one-woman shows should count; they have ranged from Whoopi Goldberg's 1984 run to the 1994 Tony-nominated *Twilight, Los Angeles* by Anna Deavere Smith. Smith played all the people she interviewed after the L.A. riots of 1992 (race riots that followed the acquittals of policemen whose beating of Rodney King was caught on tape). *Twilight* is part of Smith's body of work called *On the Road*, which merges drama with journalism. Another part inspired by racial tension, *Fires in the Mirror*, made Smith runner-up for the 1993 Pulitzer Prize.

Even counting one-woman shows—which have been, as editor Margaret Wilkerson suggests, a "primary vehicle for women playwrights" for centuries—black women playwrights have been sadly underrepresented in our nation's theatres. Near the end of the twentieth century, in a season that offered more than 1,100 plays nationwide, a mere 15 plays were by African American women. That's roughly one and one-half percent. Those are not odds that would encourage any reasonable woman to write plays. But luckily, increasing numbers of wonderfully unreasonable black women have persisted in writing plays anyway.[1]

A century ago, persistence required more courage, partly because there were far fewer role models, but largely because of the deplorable hostilities that black Americans confronted daily. The Jim Crow laws that mandated segregation in schools, public transportation, and accommodations also fostered the brutal violence of lynching. A uniquely American hate crime that often went unpunished, the lynching of black men (and sometimes women) continued well into the 1950s.

The arts of black women of the period were often outcries against these abuses. In fact, the first drama on record to be written and performed by a black in the twentieth century was by a woman: Angelina Weld Grimké. Produced in 1916 by the NAACP's Drama Committee in Washington, D.C., Grimké's play *Rachel* was, as its program declared, an important first: "This is the first attempt to use the stage for race propaganda to enlighten the American people relative to the lamentable conditions of ten million of Colored citizens in this free republic."[2]

In the play, Rachel is a caring and cheerful girl who adores children and longs for the day she'll have her own. Her outlook begins to erode when she learns that the deaths of her father and older brother, years ago, were caused by a lynching. Over time, Rachel also witnesses the severe damage that black children suffer at the hands of cruel white schoolmates. One of those black children is Jimmy, a sweet neighbor child whom Rachel adopts when smallpox claims his parents. Rachel swears to God that she will never bear children and see them hurt, so she rejects the marriage proposal of a young man who loves her. In the last act, she tells the child Jimmy a story about two "dear little boys" who lived amid such cruelty that they forgot how to laugh. When a kind woman tells them about "the Land of Laughter," the boys set off to find it—passing up entry into "the Land of Riches" (to gain castles and servants) or "the Land of Power" (to become emperors or kings)—because all they want is "to laugh again." At the play's end, a nearly-mad Rachel sobs for her children who might have been, but whom she will keep safe by never bearing.

Grimké's sentimental script was aimed, she said, at white women: "If anything can make all women sisters under their skin, it's motherhood."[3] Tisch Jones wrote in *Black Theatre, USA* that "with its 1920 publication, *Rachel* reached a larger female audience and became the subject of an ongoing debate among critics."[4] The debate was this: Should drama be propaganda for social change, or should it simply be art? And it spawned two main types of black native drama: race-propaganda plays on one hand; folk plays on the other. Women writers of both types were given support—and even prizes—by a few privileged, visionary black men. Harvard graduate W.E.B. DuBois, a founder of the NAACP and its magazine *Crisis*, promoted propaganda plays and fostered the Harlem Renaissance. DuBois formed the "Krigwa" Players (an acronym for "Crisis Guild of Writers and Artists") and launched a playwriting contest that attracted some 1,400 scripts by black writers—mostly women—in 1925. The contest was repeated for two more years, and most of the winners were also women. Among the many who became role models and forces in theatre were: Eulalie Spence, May Miller, Zora Neale Hurston, and Georgia Douglas Johnson.[5]

These and other black women writers were also encouraged through Howard University, where two more Harvard graduates—Montgomery Gregory and Alain Locke—promoted folk plays by way of the Howard Players and their top-notch theatre department. The Howard roster included Eulalie Spence, who wrote domestic suspense plays (such as *Undertow* and *Her*) and advised against propaganda: "We go to the theatre for entertainment, not to have old fires and hates rekindled.... A little more laughter if you please."[6] Zora Neale Hurston was a Howard student, then the first black graduate of Barnard, and a Guggenheim-fellowship anthropologist. Hurston embraced both art and propaganda in her work and became, as editor Kathy Perkins noted, the most "widely published black female writer of her era." Zora helped to write the 1931 revue *Fast and Furious*, then sold her car to put her own revue *The Great Day* on Broadway for just one day. Dire money problems forced her back to writing books and essays; yet, she was something of a theatre legend. While John Houseman was head of the Federal Theatre's Negro Unit, he found Zora to be its "most talented writer." He wanted to stage her black update of *Lysistrata*, in which the wives of a Florida fishing town withhold sex until their men win a fight with the cannery for fair wages. But the script "scandalized both the Left and Right."[7] Zora drew on her home town of Eatonville, Florida, for her best-known novel, *Their Eyes Were Watching God*. (Plans for an ABC teleplay of the book were launched by Oprah Winfrey in 2004.[8])

Playwright-poet Georgia Douglas Johnson also straddled the propaganda-or-art fence. In her most-anthologized play, *Plumes*, a black mother must choose between spending her last $50 for her dying daughter's surgery or for what may be the child's inevitable funeral. Johnson made a huge impact on black theatre with her four decades of "Salons on S Street" in her Washington home, which nurtured such talents as Langston Hughes, May Miller, and Marita Bonner. (Bonner won a *Crisis* contest with *The Purple Flower*, the first known surrealistic play by a black woman. Her protagonists, the Us's," struggle to reach the crest of Somewhere and the Purple Flower of Life, but they're beaten down by Sundry White Devils. Thirty years later, the plays of Adrienne Kennedy would be hailed as revolutionary for their surrealistic style.)

Having been born at Howard University to a dean's wife, May Miller was perhaps destined to write plays. She boldly merged history with propaganda, and put white characters in key roles to make a point or raise a question. In her play set at the Tomb of the Unknown Soldier, *Stragglers in the Dust*, a black woman and a dazed white soldier both insist that the tomb holds the woman's son. The drama asks if the Unknown Soldier could really have been a black boy. Several of Miller's plays (like *Sojourner Truth*) were written to teach her students about black history. Her *Nails and Thorns* is an unusual indictment of lynching: It centers on a white sheriff's wife who tries to stop the lynching of a retarded black man by going with her baby into the mob. Mother and child are knocked down, the baby killed in the crush.

Nails and Thorns is one of 15 poignant plays by women in the anthology *Strange Fruit*, which takes its title from the song performed by Billie Holiday. Like the song—in which "strange fruit" refers to the bodies of black lynching victims hanging from Southern trees—all of the plays are reactions to lynching. (Ten are by black women, five by white women.) They range from Grimké's *Rachel* to the 1994 play *Iola's Letter* by Michon Boston. Boston's play features Ida B. Wells, the activist who used her news column "Iola's Letter" to expose lynching crimes. *Strange Fruit*'s co-editor, Judith Stephens, duly notes Ida Wells' thoughts on lynching—that "white men used the ownership of the body of the white female as a terrain on which to lynch the black male." Stephens adds that not until the 1940s did women start to recognize that "male chivalry was largely a means of control ... and lynching was an extension of that control," as much over white women as over blacks.[9] The behest that white women wake up to their own bondage became a theme in the work of the era's black women playwrights. Their emergence, from the 1940s through the '60s, was tied to the explosive rise of civil rights protests.

A stunning example of a black woman's art merged with social activism, and framed in the one-woman show, was *A Black Woman Speaks* by actress-playwright Beah Richards. Long before her Oscar-nominated role as Sydney Poitier's mother in *Guess Who's Coming to Dinner* (and much later roles on television's *The Practice* and *ER*), Richards was startling audiences with her powerful, poetic solo play. She took the title from her own larger work, *A Black Woman Speaks*, which Beah performed in Chicago in 1950 for a white organization, Women for Peace. Her challenge to white women was daringly candid: "It is right that I ... should speak of white womanhood. My husbands, my fathers, my brothers, my sons, die for it."

> White womanhood stands in bloodied skirt
> and in slavery ...
> White womanhood too is enslaved; the difference is degree.

> They brought me here in chains.
> They brought you here willing slaves to man ...
> My sisters, there is no room for mockery.
> If they counted my teeth, they did appraise your thigh.
> Sold you to the highest bidder the same as I ...
>
> You bore him sons. I bore him sons. No, not willingly.
> He purchased you. He raped me.
> I fought. But you fought neither for yourselves nor me.
> Sat trapped in your superiority and spoke no reproach
> consoled your outrage with an added brooch ....
>
> You were afraid to nurse your young, lest fallen breast offend
>   your master's sight ...
> So you passed them, your children, on to me ...
> and as I gave suck, I knew I nursed my own child's enemy ...
>
> White supremacy is your enemy and mine.
> So ... remind me not of my slavery; I know it well.
> But rather of your own ...
> If you will fight with me, then take my hand, that our land
>   may come at last
> to be a place of peace and human equality.[10]

Richards took her one-woman show on tour. And in 1975, after the civil rights and women's movements had made enough inroads in the national conscience, *A Black Woman Speaks* was televised, and Beah Richards won a special Los Angeles Emmy Award. Her canon of writing would also include the play *One Is a Crowd*, which traces a black singer's quest for identity and healing after a white man's lust destroys her family.

Among the artists whom Richards inspired and mentored is actress-director LisaGay Hamilton, who says of Richards: "Not many people know what a prolific writer Beah was, in fact. But it's only through Beah's own words and writings that we really get a clear picture of who this woman *was*, in total." (Before Richard's death in 2000, Hamilton spent a year interviewing the veteran actress and gathering historical footage of Richards performing her hallmark work. The result was LisaGay's superb documentary tribute to Richards, *Beah: A Black Woman Speaks*, which was aired by HBO and garnered a Grand Jury Award in the American Film Institute Festival.[11])

From the 1950s through the '70s, black women playwrights reaped several crucial firsts: In 1955, Alice Childress became the first to have a play produced off–Broadway and to win an Obie Award. Her *Trouble in Mind* centered on a black actress resisting white supremacy in the theatre (a fitting microcosm of the world). In *Wedding Band*, Childress broke taboos about showing interracial love onstage. She depicted the demise of a ten-year affair between a black woman and her idealistic white lover, a simple baker who is cowed by his racist family.

Childress was a member of Harlem Writers Workshop, along with Lorraine Hansberry from Chicago. Hansberry made the earth-moving breakthrough into mainstream theatre in 1959 with *A Raisin in the Sun*, which made her the first black woman produced on Broadway and the first black writer to win a Drama Critics' Award. Hansberry's stage family, the Youngers, brought to white audiences an awareness and empathy for the black families among them who were fighting for their rightful share of the American dream. The play became a major film in 1961.

Hansberry died of cancer at age 34, leaving behind unfinished plays and the question of how much more she might have influenced theatre and society in another 30 years. Still, she became a potent role model for new generations of black women. Her former husband, Robert Nemiroff, collected fragments of her plays, poems, and other writings in a production called *To Be Young, Gifted, and Black*, which ran off-Broadway in the late 1960s, toured the country in the early '70s, and became a film in 1972. In a sense, Lorraine Hansberry won a Tony Award posthumously: Nemiroff's musical version of *Raisin* took that prize in 1974.

Vinette Carroll became the first black woman to direct a Broadway production when she staged her 1972 collaboration with songwriter Mikki Grant: *Don't Bother Me, I Can't Cope*. (Carroll reaped awards for this as well as for *Your Arms Too Short to Box with God*.)

September of 1976 marked the Broadway opening of an astonishing landmark play, Ntozake Shange's fearless work written for and about black women: *For Colored Girls Who Have Considered Suicide When the Rainbow Is Enuf*. Seven black actresses performed 20 poems revealing the grim realities of black women's lives. The first poem, "dark phases," expressed the rage and anguish of black women rendered silent and taken for granted by their men. Several poems detailed the shame and pain of living with sexual abuse, the squalor of ghettos, the violence of men against their own children. The chilling nineteenth poem, "a nite wid beau willie brown," told the graphic story of a volatile black man who dropped his own children out a fifth-story window to punish their mother for trying to leave him. In the twentieth poem, "a laying on of hands," the seven women joined to celebrate their strength, worth, and survival, in a ritual of sisterhood and self-realization. (I was lucky enough to see that production of *For Colored Girls*. Even living in Manhattan for 12 more years and seeing scores of Broadway plays since then, I have found nothing that surpassed the drama and impact of that exquisite event.)

For Colored Girls had been brought to the New York stage—from neighborhood bars on both coasts—by another visionary black man, Woodie King. King produced it at his New Federal Theatre, and later coproduced it on Broadway with Joe Papp. As a supremely feminist work, Shange's stage piece intensely engaged the national conscience, even as it polarized black men and women and reconfirmed theatre's power as a tool for social change.

Ntozake Shange went on to write other provocative pieces on race and sexism, like "Spell #7," and *Boogie Woogie Landscapes*. Meanwhile, her milestone *For Colored Girls* has been staged across the globe in languages ranging from French to Zulu. For its twentieth anniversary, Woodie King revived Shange's "choreopoem" at New Federal Theatre, with Ntozake directing and adding timely subjects like AIDS to her text.

No one has been more innovative or eloquent than Shange in fusing poetry, music, and street vernacular into powerful stage works. Her fearlessness in style and subject have inspired and empowered black women writers who have taken the limelight in the 1980s, '90s, and beyond. Shange credits them—"the new crop of women writers"—with being "even more daring than we are because they are willing to tackle the world in terms of women's needs and desires."[12]

One of the most prolific, multifaceted writers in this group is playwright-novelist-essayist Pearl Cleage. Much of the female reading public discovered Cleage when Oprah Winfrey selected her 1997 novel *What Looks Like Crazy On An Ordinary Day* for her Book Club, but Pearl had been around for decades. And, although she's been writing compelling plays for nearly as many years as Ntozake Shange, Pearl reports (in our interview and elsewhere) that Shange ranks high on her list of role models. Pearl says, "as an artist, I always try to give myself permission to just tell what I know ... just focus on figuring out what the truth is, and then, like Ntozake, be brave enough to tell it."[13] But Pearl also honors the much earlier, enduring influence of Lorraine Hansberry:

> I saw *A Raisin in the Sun* when I was young, in Detroit.... It was a great production, and the audience was just ecstatic. I mean, we all wept and hollered and screamed. It was just great. And it was a tremendous influence on me because it was a black woman writing about things I knew to be real ... And that was like my dream. That was all I wanted: A black theatre, in a black community, full of black people listening to what I had to say. So I said, "Okay, this is possible. If she can do this, I can do this." ... She was really the one who made it very real to me.[14]

Pearl Cleage is now a stellar role model for black women who hope to merge art with social activism. Main characters in her plays and books are often stubborn activists who show-and-tell it like it is, but also like it could be if sexism and racism were vanquished. Pearl takes aim at sexual abuse even above racial abuse because "you can't be a warrior in the fight against racism if you're not safe in your own house ... if you're afraid the man you love is going to come home and throw you across the room."[15] (She tackles abuse issues head on, in essays that mix scathing criticism with wit and feminist wisdom, in her book *Deals with the Devil and Other Reasons to Riot*.)

Much of Cleage's body of work is aimed at empowering black women to avoid abuse, to forge fulfilling lives, and to help sisters do the same. She weaves fact with fiction, history with advocacy, to spin scenes of black women making leaps to safer, satisfying lives. Her first major play, *Flyin' West*, honored the dauntless black women who trekked from the South after the Civil War to become homesteaders. The play's matriarch, Miss Leah, who lost ten babies to slavery, now heads a created family of three women on her land in Nicodemus, Kansas. "This was a woman who used to be property," says Pearl. "Then she became a woman who owned property."

> I loved working with this character.... If you have the kind of feeling I have about ancestors—black women who I know that I owe, who did such wonderful things—when you're writing historically, you get to talk about them in a way that honors them.[16]

Pearl imparts her feminist views with humor: Her character Miss Leah complains, "Colored men always tryin' to tell you how to do somethin', even if you been doin' it longer than they been peein' standin' up." But she also presents the dark side: She has Miss Leah conspire to murder the smug, abusive husband of the pregnant and battered young Minnie.

Pearl sets her play *Blues for an Alabama Sky* in a Depression-blighted Harlem, weaving the story of four friends (two Cotton Club artists, a social worker, and a physician) into the fabric of Harlem's history. Hovering just offstage are real figures like Adam Clayton Powell and birth-control crusader Margaret Sanger. Cleage merges their insights with her own to make dramatic points about racial violence, reproductive rights, and the "most deadly" of diseases, poverty. Her play *Bourbon at the Border* gives a lesson, lest we forget, about the racist cruelties inflicted on activists of the 1960s Freedom Drives. (The play received standing ovations during its 2003 run at Chicago's venerable Victory Gardens Theatre—proof of Cleage's power to galvanize audiences around volatile issues.)

Cleage's novels are shaped by her playwright's voice and activism. She tells the stories of the Johnson sisters of Idlewilde, Michigan, through lively first-person narrative in *What Looks Like Crazy* and *I Wish I Had a Red Dress*. Ava Johnson is a beautician whose Atlanta lifestyle has left her HIV positive. Yet Cleage makes Ava's homecoming a triumphant story of love between Ava and her old friend Eddie, a self-redeemed ex-addict and Vietnam vet. Ava's sister, Joyce, is a widowed social worker who's bent on giving teenaged mothers the tools to chisel out happy, worthwhile lives for themselves and their kids. Obstacles abound in abusive boyfriends, corrupt authorities, and a culture vested in violence. But Cleage's characters seem to echo her own upbeat words: "Tell me one good thing. Just one. So we can begin the repair work."

> I make it my business to look at the hard, bad things around me, because I'm an activist. So I want to know what I should be working on. But I'm really a very optimistic person.... I think I have a wonderfully blessed life: I get to make a living doing the work I love. I have a great child.... I am in love with a man who is very connected to me.... So I know that it's possible for human beings—and in my case, in terms of my writing, for black women—to have really exciting, productive and engaged lives....
>
> Everything that I write, I look at—politically—as a black conscious person ... and as a conscious woman activist. Because I always want my work to make black women stronger. And if it makes black men and women of other color stronger, then that's great too.[17]

Aishah Rahman, another playwright-activist, and a Howard alumna, made her theatre mark in the '80s and '90s. Growing up as a foster child in Harlem helped to shape Aishah's art and activism (with CORE and other agencies). Her first play, *Lady Day*, was a tribute to Billie Holiday. But Aishah's best-known anthologized work is *The Mojo and the Sayso*, staged in New York in 1993. The play sprang from a strong personal experience: "I was pregnant ... at the time of the infamous killing of Clifford Glover" (a ten-year-old black boy mistakenly shot by a Queens policeman). Thoughts of "what kind of world awaits this child within me" made her follow the case; "and it was the same old thing: they let the officer off." Ultimately she "had to write something about the story" to give a voice to the family and to address the question, "How does a family survive this ... because so many black families do."[18]

Aishah uses an imaginative mix of jazz, myth, and ritual to depict the emotional states of her characters. She gives them each a "mojo," a mechanism for magic that unleashes the "sayso," the power to survive a crisis. Mrs. Benjamin has her candles, her "spiritual things." Mr. Benjamin is building a literal Mojo—a car—in their living room, and trying to teach their surviving son Walter that a knife "is not a mojo." At the end, the family rallies together to shed the trappings of grief and anger, and climb into the revved up "Mojo 9" which, says Mr. Benjamin, "can take us anyplace."

The fact that Aishah was brought to Brown University by Paula Vogel—to do a guest professorship that became permanent—bears out Vogel's belief that women playwrights "write in a community. We have to create our own community. This goes back to the notion of family."[19]

The family tree of black women playwrights that was seeded in the early twentieth century has produced too many offspring to name or honor them here. Of the generation born since 1960, most still continue to merge stage art with social propaganda. Kia Corthron, Lynn Nottage, and Cheryl West are key examples. Chicago-born West was a social worker before her playwriting success, and this informs her intense family plays. Her *Before It Hits Home* depicts the impact of AIDS on a bisexual black man and his family. In her better-known *Jar the Floor*, four generations of women gather to mark the ninetieth birthday of their matriarch, MaDear. Their dreams and disappointments collide, while MaDear glides in and out of senility.

In her plays, Kia Corthron works at "balancing the political with the specific." Her *Cage Rhythm* explores the lives of women in prison and the injustice of the penal system (white women arrested for drug abuse go to rehab; black women go to jail). With their families outside broken apart, the women forge vital but explosive family ties with inmates. Corthron explains, "I hope that in my work ... despite the fact that these ugly things exist, that there is some sense that it doesn't have to be this way. Something in the work suggests hope, possibility."[20]

Paula Vogel was a shaping force in the career of Lynn Nottage, who was her student at Brown. Nottage's work with Amnesty International made her turn to comedy as a way to voice—yet detach from—the human suffering she witnessed at work. In her *Brooklyn After the Glow*, a wondrous glowing orb found in a junkyard by two homeless people turns out to be radioactive waste. In *Poof*, Nottage comically confronts domestic abuse: A battered wife blurts a curse at her husband, and he spontaneously combusts into a residue of smoking ash and eyeglasses.

Among other new-wave black women who have applied comedy and satire to social issues are Danitra Vance and Judith Jackson. Vance was the first black female regular on *Saturday Night Live*. Her solo play *Live and in Color* is peopled with Vance's alter-egos, like "Flotilda, the classical actress" (which Vance had planned to be); and "Aquanette, the avant-garde rap artist" who chants, "I am the Pulitzer Prize, I am the Nobel Prize, I am the prize in Captain Crunch.... We are all cousins ... we are all foreigners. We are all raisins, and raisinettes, and Ju-Ju-Bees."[21] The play has become a sadly ironic legacy from Vance, who died of breast cancer in her thirties, in 1994.

Judith Jackson puts herself in a generation of women who are "overt feminists because we were raised by the sacrifices of the subliminal feminists.... Our mothers were planting seeds in our heads." Jackson writes and performs social satires with characters that include archetypes, celebrities, ordinary folks, and spirits, like the "Anima-animas" figure in her *WOMBmanWARs*. The play was her response to the "primetime woman-bashing" that followed the Thomas-Hill and Tyson-Washington sexual abuse cases. Jackson says that "WOMBmanWARs are wars that women have with themselves in just trying to be whole in this world." Her oldest character Hilda, who was already an activist in the womb (her mother was a suffragette while pregnant), explains the acronym WOMB: "Women to Overcome Men's Beliefs."[22]

Jackson feels she has a responsibility to her mother's sacrifices and to "all the women of her generation who were my teachers; and other people who went before and wrote plays, books ... created music; and to those mothers who helped them to say you can do this thing."[23]

Jackson's comment about women's battles to be "whole in this world" brings to mind a remark by Alice Walker. In her book *Anything We Love Can Be Saved*, Walker subtitles a chapter with her belief that "If Women Were Comfortable in the World, the World Would Be a Comfortable Place." Certainly, a key reason among black women for writing plays is their desire to make themselves and other black women feel more comfortable in the world. But the idea seems to inform the work of a myriad of women playwrights, spanning generations and racial boundaries. The strongest motive for playwriting by women may well be the impulse to help themselves and other women feel more at home in the world.

Epilogue: Parting Thoughts on Family Flux and Cultural Flummery

The stories of the playwrights honored here suggest that crafting plays is one way in which these women have made themselves feel "more comfortable in the world." Forging families is another way. Among these women, both the plays and the families reflect a colorful spectrum—a diversity that I find remarkable and salutary.

Of course, the American family is now a kaleidoscope of configurations, defying definition. I know of one seven year old, Lisa, who says "a family is a bunch of people, or not too many, who love each other." Lisa's family includes no dad, but two moms, and is grateful for Today's Families Help Center, an independent agency that serves "Adoptive Families, Single-Parent Families ... Alternative Lifestyle Families, and Special Needs Families."[1] More and more non-traditional family units are finally getting noticed and even nurtured. In Stephanie Coontz's myth-busting book about American family, *The Way We Never Were*, she notes a *Newsweek* poll in which only 22 percent of respondents defined family "solely in terms of blood, marriage, or adoption.... Seventy-four percent declared, instead, that family is any group whose members love and care for one another."[2]

The idea that "untraditional" does not mean "uncommitted" is one that feminists have stressed for generations. The women's movement was, after all, one huge effort to change our value map of relationships in the family and across society.

In actuality, our value map of family *has* changed, and it now charts what our policy makers still tend to deny and obscure: the news that the nuclear family has, in essence, exploded into diverse and creatively constructed units. In an August 2003 article titled "Not Just Mom and Pop," a *Chicago Sun-Times* special edition reported that "politicians can debate it, and presidents and popes pander to protect it, but the American family is changing right before our eyes." The old mold has "bent to include such modern realities as divorce and same-sex unions." And now, "about one-third of all U.S. adoptions are by single parents, mostly women but also men." (While the Bush cohort has pursued a nationwide Defense of Marriage Act—to restrict it to "a union between a man and woman"—the reality is that single parents and gay and unmarried couples are changing the face and future of American family.[3])

Seven of the Pulitzer plays in this book imply that our long-held standards of family have needed revamping. The history linking the plays suggests that our touted model of nuclear family has worked to socialize individuals into being half a person. As activist Charlotte Gilman once argued, we have "bred one kind of qualities into half the species and another kind into the other half."[4] This does not foster a whole person, or, as Gloria Steinem puts it (in *Revolution from Within*) a "full self"—which only comes with "full equality. ... The full self necessary for self-esteem has been denied more to women," says Steinem, "but also to men."[5] Since the newer forms of customized family are themselves a testimony to more creative self-expression, they may prove (in the long run) to be more supportive of full-self potential.

Among these women playwrights, real-life family units tend to be models of customized families. Consider Zona Gale, who adopted a baby before her marriage at age 54; who did not wear a ring or take her husband's name (but loved him dearly). Susan Glaspell and Jig Cook were as much married to their theatre as they were to each other. They forged an extended family of artist-friends, much like Marsha Norman. Of the contemporary playwrights, Beth Henley and Wendy Wasserstein have both opted for motherhood outside of marriage. Paula Vogel and Maggie Edson happen to be lesbians whose life-partners are also role models of successful, creative women.

The social revolution to mark this century may be the family revolution: a movement to allow family to arise from individual need rather than social or legal mandates. This is not to say that new forms of constructed family will escape conflict. Stephanie Coontz reminds us that "families have always been in flux and often in crisis."[6] Playwrights since the classical Greeks have reflected this. Paula Vogel even remarks that "'domestic' is precisely the definition of tragedy."[7]

However, if family and tragedy go hand in hand, current front-line women playwrights suggest that comedy walks close behind. A striking, common feature in their work is the great degree to which they merge comedy with pathos, the personal with the political. Many of them manage to locate the state of the nation, or the world, within one family. A standout example is Connie Congdon. In her dreamlike *Tales of the Lost Formicans*, Congdon's characters are a three-generation family blighted by a failed marriage, senility, and our vacuous shopping-mall culture. But they are also aliens *observing* the customs and chaos of family on this planet. Congdon's play is an imaginative paean to the aspect of theatre that lets us see double: What we see onstage is both real and unreal, spontaneous and rehearsed. And in the same paradoxical way, it is often both art and propaganda for social change.

Because women playwrights have had to be social rebels even to become playwrights, perhaps they naturally bring propaganda to the writing table. Writer-activist Karen Malpede says "the woman playwright listens [and] takes the measure of her time ... speaks the hidden truths, exposes nightmare doubts of the culture in which she lives." As a playwright herself, Malpede goes on to note:

> Women dramatists inhabit the realm of the unfinished. We don't know what our lives would be if we had lived them fully, without terror, without disrespect. We struggle to imagine wholeness—an earth undefiled; a striking new balance between nature and culture ... a spiritual renewal untouched by fundamentalist violence and cant; and personal relationships based upon mutual respect.[8]

At times, when current women playwrights have talked to me about their "responsibility as artists," I've been reminded of the beliefs of the earliest playwrights represented here—Zona Gale and Susan Glaspell. Like those forebears, these new writers seem to view the artist as a spiritual singer for society: someone who is attuned to the "something more" Gale talked about, open to insights that uplift the race, that sustain the creative life force. Many of these women even talk about a force or energy that came to them as visions of characters, or as audible voices. (Two women described having to pull their cars over in order to attend to such voices and take notes!) Some of them try to tune into this energy and to evoke it with their work.

Pearl Cleage is one who strongly senses and describes a struggle between this creative energy and what she calls a "death energy" behind the violence that pervades our culture. In our interview, Pearl lamented,

> The violence just takes your breath away. Because it's so awful. And it's made to look so exciting and so beautiful, in all these beautiful color films ... And in these "thrillers," where the center of the movie is some terrified woman caught in the woods, or caught in the house alone. I think all of those are horrible violent messages.... And it's in the video games ... where the prize comes when you kill the policeman ... or you rape the woman and throw her out of the car—and these are real examples. I think that we are dehumanizing generation after generation of young people. And I don't know if those of us who are crying out against that energy have enough power—in fact, I don't think we do have enough—to overcome what the popular culture is putting out there.[9]

I would count most of the women playwrights I have talked with as being artists who are crying out against this energy of violence. The question is whether enough of them and their work will be heard and heeded to effect a change. Near the end of the twentieth century, Karen Malpede asked, "If women's plays were produced with the frequency, financial backing, and critical understanding accorded to the plays of men, would this change the culture, or would it herald a culture already changed?"[10] Perhaps both; the change would surely herald a big shift in the world of theatre production. In my interviews, most women have echoed Marsha Norman's sentiment that "until the producing world is 50 percent women, we won't have 50 percent plays by women."[11]

I think that Karen Malpede's question provokes a parallel one: If our culture of violence is ever to change to a culture that upholds and glorifies images of human compassion and creativity, will it happen only through the determined efforts and arts of *women*? (And through their equal participation not only in the culture, but in our government?)

Most of the women I know are aching for a salutary change in our culture, in our whole identity as a country. Like me, these women are artists, teachers, and mothers whose feelings of discomfort and disenfranchisement as American women have never run higher. To paraphrase the earlier quote from Alice Walker, I believe that if women were comfortable within the culture, our culture would be a more comfortable—and comforting—place to be.

Meanwhile, I get the strong sense that women playwrights take heart from their own subculture, or what is their own extended and ever-extending family. Here again, I think that Pearl Cleage gives an apt and eloquent description:

> For me, there has always been that sense of community among any women writers—black, white, Chinese-American, whoever I meet:

We're so glad to meet other women who are writing. We just start talking about our work ... and about who's doing what.... We're all so far flung, we don't get to see each other much. But we have that very real sense of community across all sorts of lines. It's very empowering. It's great.[12]

Chapter Notes

Introduction

[Note: I have included only solo women winners in my list and in this text: I exclude the 1956 Pulitzer win that Frances Goodrich shared with Albert Hackett for *The Diary of Anne Frank*.]

1. Hohenberg, *Pulitzer Prizes*, p. 4.
2. Angeli Rasbury, in "Pulitzer Winner Talks About Being a First," says that "in 1999, 8 percent of plays and 1 percent of musicals on Broadway were written by women." http://www.womensenews.org/article.cfm/dyn/aid/874 [cited August 24, 2002]. This is even a bit higher than noted by Julia Miles in the September 1998 issue of *American Theatre* (p. 17). Miles put the plays by women (then) at 6 percent of Broadway productions, and indicated that this figure creeps up about 2 percent every 5 to 7 years. Figures on federally funded theatres quoted by Frank, Introduction to *Facing Forward*.
3. Coughlin, "Changing Roles," pp. 110, 114–16; Skinner, "Women Are Misguided," pp. 73–75.
4. Jacobson, "Heidi Mystique," p. 26.
5. Moore, *New Women's Theatre*, p. xviii.
6. Lady Gregory, *Our Irish Theatre* (New York: Capricorn Books, 1965), p. 92.
7. Barlow, *Plays by American Women*, p. ix. Actually, Anna C. Mowatt's *Fashion* was later recognized as the best American comedy of the 19th century. See Barlow, p. xi; also Walter J. Meserve, *American Drama: An Outline History* (Totowa, NJ: Littlefield, Adams and Co., 1965), p. 85. Too bad she was not encouraged to write more.
8. Barlow, p. xiii, citing Virginia Frame, "Women Who Have Written Successful Plays," *Theatre Magazine*, October 1906, pp. 264–67.
9. Hohenberg, p. 19.
10. Ibid., p. 45; Toohey, *Pulitzer Prize Plays*, p. 13.
11. Hohenberg, pp. 47–49, 269. The phrase about "raising the standard of good morals" was deleted in 1929; in 1964, the citation was shortened to read: "For a distinguished play by an American author, preferably original in its source, and dealing with American life."
12. Flexner, *American Playwrights*, p. 174.
13. Bonin, *Major Themes*, p. 6.
14. Ibid., p. xv.
15. Scanlon, *Family, Drama and American Dreams*, p. 4.
16. Adler, *Mirror on the Stage*, p. x.
17. Bonin, pp. xiii–iv.
18. Adler, p. 5.
19. Scanlon, p. 4.
20. Norman, interview.

21. Wasserstein, interview, letters, and e-mail.
22. Edson interview.
23. Betsko and Koenig, *Interviews*, p. 9.
24. Norman, interview.
25. Vogel, interview.
26. *Ibid.*

Prologue

1. Norman, *'Night, Mother*, p. 19.
2. Napier, *Recreating Your Self*, p. 19.
3. *Ibid.*, pp. 51, 177–79.
4. Swerdlow et al., *Families in Flux*, p. 18.
5. Scanlon, *Family*, p. 4.
6. Norman, interview.
7. Carol Gilligan, *In a Different Voice* (Cambridge, MA: Harvard University Press, 1982), pp. 6–8, 16–17.
8. Personal interview with Marsha Norman, August 16, 1991.

Part I: Family Lies and the Unwed Woman

1. Catton, "The Restless Decade," pp. 5–6.

1. The 1920s: Those Not-So-Good Old Days

1. Allen, *Only Yesterday*, pp. 50–51.
2. *Harper's Magazine* quoted in Allen, p. 51.
3. Bruce Bliven, "Tempest Over Teapot," in *The 1920s: American Heritage*, vol. 16, no. 5 (August 1965), p. 21.
4. *Ibid.*; Charles L. Mee, *The Ohio Gang* (New York: M. Evans and Co., 1981), especially pp. 134–35, 158–164.
5. Allen, pp. 70–71.
6. *Ibid.*, pp. 55–56.
7. Malcolm and Robert Cowley, eds., "Memoranda of a Decade," in *The 1920s: American Heritage*, vol. 16, no. 5 (August 1965) p. 38.

8. Allen, pp. 73–74.
9. Skolnik, *Fads*, p. 45. Also, regarding Fitzgerald and the Flapper, see Matthew Brucolli, Scottie Fitzgerald Smith, and Joan P. Kerr, eds., *The Romantic Egoists* (New York: Charles Scribner's Sons, 1974), pp. 62–63, 148–49.
10. Allen, p. 77.
11. Skolnik, p. 45; Allen, p. 77.
12. Catton, p. 14.
13. Woloch, *Women*, p. 397.
14. Prost and Vincent, *History of Private Life*, p. 539.
15. *Ibid.*, pp. 555–57.
16. Woloch, *Women*, pp. 332–33.
17. Schneir, *Feminism*, p. 72.
18. Woloch, p. 216.
19. Sanger, *Woman*; Woloch, p. 379.
20. Woloch, p. 388.
21. *Ibid.*, p. 392.
22. Elaine Showalter, ed., *These Modern Women: Biographical Essays from the '20s* (Old Westbury, NY: The Feminist Press, 1978), pp. 3–4. This volume reprints the series of feminist essays and articles which appeared in *Nation* magazine, 1926–27.
23. *Ibid.*, pp. 52, 141.
24. Woloch, p. 393. Unfortunately, Margaret Mead's writing lost its feminist stance by the 1950s, after she came under the influence of Freud's tenets. In fact, Mead was partly responsible for the return to domestic confinement of droves of young women in the '50s. This is discussed in this text in Chapter 10.
25. Woloch, pp. 406–408; Prost and Vincent, p. 557.
26. Woloch, p. 408.
27. Prost and Vincent, p. 547.
28. *Ibid.*, p. 553.
29. *Ibid.*, pp. 554–55.
30. Pruette quoted in Woloch, p. 411.
31. Emily Blair excerpt in Woloch, p. 386.
32. Toohey, *Pulitzer Prize Plays*, p. 92.
33. Zona Gale, letter to her friend Edith Rogers, August 25, 1933; Archives, State Historical Society of Wisconsin at University of Wisconsin, Madison, Gale Letter Files; and: Zona Gale, letter to

"Dear Miss Madden," January 24, 1929; Gale Files, Wisconsin Archives.

34. While most of Glaspell's plays treat this theme, *The Verge* and *The Outside* do so most directly, and are replete with such phrases as "otherness," "meeting the Outside," and "the edge of life."

35. August Derleth, *Still Small Voice*, p. 112.

36. Barlow, *Plays by American Women*, p. xx.

37. Zona Gale, letter to friend Edith Rogers [undated] Gale Files, Wisconsin Archives.

2. Zona Gale and the Real Village Tale

1. Sumner, "Everlasting Persistence," p. 137.
2. Derleth, *Still Small Voice*, pp. 286–87.
3. *Ibid.*, pp. 97–98.
4. *Ibid.*, p. 98.
5. Sumner, pp. 137–41.
6. *Ibid.*; Zona Gale, *The Loves of Pelleas and Etarre* (New York: MacMillan, 1907), p. 115.
7. Sumner, p. 137.
8. *Ibid.*
9. Derleth, p. 93.
10. Sumner, pp. 137–41; Derleth, p. 66.
11. Derleth, p. 85.
12. *Ibid.*, p. 87.
13. Derleth, p. 88.
14. *Ibid.*, p. 84; Simonson, *Zona Gale*, p. 31.
15. Derleth, pp. 81–82.
16. *Ibid.*, pp. 81–82; and Simonson, pp. 29–31.
17. Derleth, p. 100.
18. *Ibid.*, p. 62.
19. *Ibid.*, p. 154.
20. *Ibid.*, p. 108.
21. *Ibid.*, p. 110.
22. *Ibid.*, pp. 118, 212–13.
23. *Ibid.*, p. 111.
24. *Ibid.*, p. 112.
25. Simonson, p. 77.
26. Derleth, pp. 120–21.
27. Simonson, pp. 80, 83; Derleth, p. 142.
28. Zona Gale, *Miss Lulu Bett* (New York: Grosset & Dunlap, 1920), p. 1.
29. *Ibid.*, p. 3.
30. Simonson, p. 79.
31. *Ibid.*, p. 82.
32. Fannie Hurst, letter to Zona Gale, 1920 [no exact date affixed], Gale Files, Wisconsin Archives.
33. Derleth, p. 143.
34. Brock Pemberton, letter to Zona Gale, postmarked October 24, 1920, Gale Files, Wisconsin Archives.
35. Sumner, p. 140.
36. Brock Pemberton, letter to Zona Gale, postmarked November 13, 1920, Gale Files, Wisconsin Archives.
37. Derleth, p. 144; Toohey, *Pulitzer Prize Plays*, pp. 18–19.
38. Toohey, p. 19.
39. *Ibid.*, p. 21.
40. *Ibid.*
41. Gale, *Miss Lulu Bett*, in *Plays by American Women*, p. 161.
42. *Ibid.* Barlow includes both play endings in this volume.
43. Toohey, p. 21.
44. Derleth, pp. 145–46.
45. Brock Pemberton, telegram to Zona Gale, January 15, 1921, Gale Files, Wisconsin Archives.
46. Derleth, p. 146.
47. *Ibid.*, p. 149.
48. Hohenberg, *Pulitzer Prizes*, pp. 50–51.
49. Derleth, p. 157.
50. *Ibid.*, p. 153.
51. *Ibid.*, p. 164.
52. Simonson, pp. 64–65.
53. Derleth, pp. 161–62.
54. Zona Gale, letter to "My Dear Mr. Gerling," n.d., Gale Files, Wisconsin Archives.
55. Gale, *Preface to a Life*, excerpted in Derleth, p. 194.
56. *Ibid.*, p. 195.
57. Simonson, p. 101.
58. Derleth, pp. 205–08. Simonson also alludes to Leslyn (p. 125), and papers in the Wisconsin Archives document

Gale's devoted mothering of Leslyn and journaling of the child's progress.
59. Simonson, p. 117.
60. Derleth, p. 207; Simonson, p. 125.
61. Derleth, p. 207.
62. Zona also insisted on compensating anyone who inspired a story. Once, when a hobo died before she could reward him, she had a gravestone made and spent weeks locating his burial site.
63. Simonson, p. 125; Derleth, p. 212.
64. Derleth, p. 109.
65. Ibid., p. 211.
66. Ibid., p. 213; Simonson, p. 126.
67. Simonson, p. 133.
68. Derleth, p. 263.
69. Simonson, p. 132; Riley, "Zona Gale: Her Life and Writing."
70. Derleth, p. 258.
71. Brock Pemberton, letter to Zona Gale, August 29, 1935, Gale Files, Wisconsin Archives.
72. Zona Gale, letter to Brock Pemberton (no date, but the letter closes "Happy New Year"; placing it in December 1935 or January 1936). Gale Files, Wisconsin Archives.
73. Derleth, p. 259.
74. Simonson, p. 16.
75. Ibid., pp. 137–38.
76. All dialogue quotes taken from Gale, Miss Lulu Bett, in Plays by American Women, start page 98.
77. Simonson, p. 80.
78. Barlow, Plays by American Women, p. xxiii.
79. Ehrenreich, Worst Years, p. 154. Ehrenreich discusses the influence of this idea—the "right to be supported by a man"—in the matter of the ERA's defeat.
80. Napier, Recreating Your Self, p. 179.
81. Quote found in Zona Gale's manuscript dated April 1, 1932, for her preface to One-Act Plays for Stage and Study, 7th Series, p. 7. The manuscript galleys, in various forms, are located in the Wisconsin Archives and in the New York Public Library at Lincoln Center Performing Arts Archives.

3. Susan Glaspell: From Iowa Village to Greenwich Village

1. Most sources give Glaspell's birth year as 1882; Drake University records suggest it was 1876 (putting it two to seven years after Gale's birth year of 1874).
2. Gould, Modern American Playwrights, p. 27.
3. Ibid., p. 28.
4. Waterman, Susan Glaspell, p. 18.
5. Ibid., p. 17.
6. Ibid., Preface, n.p.
7. Waterman, p. 34.
8. Gould, p. 29.
9. Ibid., p. 30.
10. Ibid., p. 35.
11. Waterman, p. 35.
12. Ibid., p. 20.
13. Ibid., pp. 35–36.
14. Ibid.
15. Gould, p. 30.
16. Bigsby, Plays by Susan Glaspell, p. 6.
17. "The Road to The Temple," review with excerpts in The Advocate (Provincetown, Mass., April 14, 1927). Glaspell files, New York Library at Lincoln Center Performing Arts Archives.
18. Ibid.
19. Malpede, Women in Theatre, p. 148; Gould, p. 32.
20. Glaspell, The Road to the Temple, quoted in Malpede, p 150.
21. Ibid.
22. Ibid.
23. Ibid., p. 151; Gould, p. 33.
24. Malpede, p. 152.
25. Ibid.; Gould, pp. 34–35.
26. Gould, p. 35.
27. Malpede, p. 152. See also Sarlos, Jig Cook, pp. 22–24.
28. Malpede, p. 153.
29. Ibid.
30. Ibid., p. 154.
31. Barlow, Plays by American Women, p. xx.
32. Malpede, p. 154.

33. Gould, pp. 39–40.
34. Sarlos, p. 73.
35. *Ibid.*, p. 82.
36. *Ibid.*, p. 73.
37. *Ibid.*, p. 85.
38. Bigsby, p. 14.
39. Sarlos, pp. 68–70.
40. Press release/Article dated May 31, 1919, composite of *Bernice* reviews, Glaspell files, Lincoln Center Archives.
41. *Ibid.*
42. Bigsby, p. 15.
43. James Agate quoted in Bigsby, p. 16.
44. Eugene Solow, "America's Great Woman Dramatist: Susan Glaspell," in *New York World-Sunday*, February 9, 1930, n.p., Glaspell files, Lincoln Center Archives.
45. Glaspell, *The Verge*, in *Plays by Susan Glaspell*, ed. Bigsby, p. 58.
46. *Ibid.*, pp. 71, 98.
47. Waterman, p. 80.
48. Kenneth MacGowan, "Curtain Calls," *The Globe and Commercial Adviser*, December 12, 1921, n.p., Glaspell Files, Lincoln Center Archives.
49. Sarlos, p. 93.
50. *Ibid.*, p. 130.
51. Ben-Zvi, "Susan Glaspell's Contributions" p. 164.
52. Sarlos, p. 139.
53. Gould, p. 45.
54. Gould, p. 46; Rapp, "A Self-Made Greek Hero," p. 3.
55. Kenneth MacGowan, letter to Zona Gale, dated only "September 18," Gale files, Wisconsin Historical Archives. MacGowan also wrote that "Roland Young, Clare Eames, Frank Conroy ... have already promised conditional on Broadway Engagements"—testimony to the MacGowan-O'Neill regime's commercial, star-oriented stance.
56. Bigsby, p. 30.
57. All dialogue quotes from Glaspell, *Alison's House*.
58. Waterman, pp. 88–89.
59. Chamberlain quoted in Waterman, p. 103.
60. *Ibid.*, p. 89.

4. The Depression Years: Gaining Despite the Losses

1. Woloch, *Women*, p. 458.
2. Toohey, *Pulitzer Prize Plays*, p. 127; Burns Mantle, *Best Plays of 1934-35* (New York: Dodd, Mead, 1935), pp. 144–45.
3. Woloch, p. 458.
4. Marshall, *Great Events*, p. 222.
5. *Ibid.*, pp. 256–58.
6. Woloch, p. 44.
7. Prost and Vincent, *History of Private Life*, p. 558.
8. Woloch, pp. 419–20.
9. *Ibid.*, pp. 420–21.
10. *Ibid.*, p. 421; Christine Lunardini, *What Every Woman Should Know About Women's History* (Holbrook, Mass: Adams Media Corp., 1997), pp. 246–48.
11. Lois Decker O'Neill, ed., *The Women's Book of World Records and Achievements* (Garden City, N.Y.: Anchor Press, 1979), pp. 331–32.
12. Woloch, p. 455. Woloch notes that Perkins was in the New Deal's "hot seat" as the first female: "When cabinet members were seated by ranks (for formal occasions), Perkins was usually placed with their wives."
13. *Ibid.*, pp. 430–31.
14. *Ibid.*, p. 439.
15. Woloch quotes (p. 447) a *Harper's* magazine article from 1935, n.d.
16. Woloch, p. 458.
17. Peter Skolnik, *Fads*, p. 71.
18. *Ibid.*
19. "The Movies," in *The Swing Era, 1936-37* (Time-Life Books, 1975), pp. 14–15.
20. Skolnik, p. 75.
21. *Ibid.*, p. 89.
22. Woloch, p. 458.
23. *Ibid.*, p. 459.
24. *Ibid.*, p. 435.
25. *Ibid.*, p. 459.
26. *Ibid.*, p. 453.

5. Zoe Akins, Escape Artist

1. "Miss Zoe Akins to Make Debut in Romeo and Juliet," press release and photo (1904), Zoe Akins files, Lincoln Center Archives.
2. *Ibid*. Akins' comment—"Ever since I can remember I have been wild about the stage"—was echoed 36 years later in a column by Benson Inge (*New York Herald Tribune*, May 11, 1941, p. 1). Inge said that Akins still exuded "a buoyancy that one associates with stage-struck novices."
3. Morehouse, "Broadway After Dark," n.p.
4. See note 1 above.
5. *Ibid*.
6. *Ibid*.
7. Inge, "Author of Twenty Plays," p. 1.
8. See note 1 above.
9. *Ibid*.
10. Alice M. Robinson, Vera N. Roberts and Milly S. Barranger, eds., *Notable Women in American Theatre: A Biographical Dictionary* (New York: Greenwood Press, 1989), p. 11.
11. Chapman, "Zoe Akins," p. 2; see also "The Girl Who Wrote *Declasse*," *Kansas City Star*, November 2, 1919, n.p., Akins files, Lincoln Center Archives.
12. Inge, p. 1.
13. Robinson, et al., p. 11.
14. "Zoe Akins, Amoralist," *Town and Country*, December 1, 1916, n.p., Akins files, Lincoln Center Archives.
15. Nathan, *The Theatre*, p. 87.
16. Chapman, p. 2.
17. *Ibid*.
18. "Brief Sketches of Winners of Pulitzer Prizes," *New York Herald Tribune*, May 7, 1935, n.p., Akins files, Lincoln Center Archives.
19. A report on "Prohibition and The Drama" in *New York Sun*, May 15, 1920 (n.p., Lincoln Center Archives), said that, in those prohibition days, an onstage mention of alcohol could "change a serious drama into a farce." So it was a "tribute to both vehicle and star" that audiences "never lost sight of the tragedy of Lady Helen Hadden's death when she gasped for wine."
20. Mantle, "Declasse," p. 54.
21. Inge, p. 1.
22. "Daddy's Gone A-Hunting," p. 315.
23. Yongue, "Zoe Akins," in *American Women Writers*, ed. Faust, pp. 14–15.
24. Akins, "Philosophy of an Adaptation," pp. 1, 3.
25. Chapman, p. 2.
26. Reston, "New York by Day and Night," n.p.
27. *Ibid*.; Chapman, p. 2.
28. Chapman, p. 2.
29. Alexander Woollcott, "The Stage," *New York World*, March 9, 1928, n.p., Akins file, Lincoln Center Archives; see also Atkinson, "The Play."
30. "Zoe Akins to Wed Hugo Rumbold," *New York Times*, March 2, 1932, n.p., Akins files, Lincoln Center Archives.
31. "Artist and Playwright at Their Wedding Luncheon" (photo with 5-line caption), *New York Herald Tribune*, March 15, 1932, n.p. Akins file, Lincoln Center Archives.
32. Morehouse, n.p.
33. Akins, "Philosophy of an Adaptation," p. 1.
34. *Ibid*. Akins' *The Greeks* ran 250 performances, despite pans from critics, because of producer William Harris' belief in it.
35. Akins, "Philosophy of an Adaptation," p. 1.
36. *Ibid*.
37. "Brief Sketches of the Winners," n.p.
38. Burns Mantle, ed., preface to *The Old Maid* summary, *Best Plays of 1934-35*, pp. 144–45.
39. Quoted in Toohey, *Pulitzer Prize Plays*, p. 127.
40. Slide, *Selected Theatre Criticism*, p. 178.
41. Toohey, p. 127.
42. Mantle, p. 145.
43. Toohey, p. 128.
44. Hohenberg, Pulitzer Prizes, pp. 149–50; Toohey, pp. 125–27.

45. Reston; see also Blum and Kobal, *Talkies*, p. 118.
46. Reston.
47. Akins, "The Playwriting Passion," p. 106.
48. Reston; see also Inge, pp. 1–3.
49. Inge, p. 3. Although Akins admitted she was "not thoroughly at home" in these languages, she was praised for her "grasp of the emotional impulses" held in these scripts.
50. McClintic directed *The Old Maid*; Cukor staged *The Furies* on Broadway and directed Akins' screenplay of *Camille* with Garbo.
51. Woollcott's spoof ran in the July 1922 *Vanity Fair*, pp. 67, 108. An included photo caption notes that "Zowie: or The Curse of an Akins Heart" was also performed as part of a staged vaudeville devised and performed mainly by New York critics. Woollcott's quote about Akins' "ever restless imagination" in review fragment from *N.Y. Times*, September 1, 1921, Lincoln Center Archives.
52. Oliver P. Sayler, *Our American Theatre* (New York: Brentano's Publishers, 1923), p. 21.
53. Inge, p. 1.
54. Morehouse.
55. All dialogue quotes taken from Akins, *The Old Maid*.
56. Ferguson, *Images of Women*, p. 14.

Part II.
Domestic Wars

6. The 1940s: Women in a World at War

1. Woloch, *Women*, p. 462.
2. *Ibid.*, pp. 461–65, and Marshall, *Great Events*, p. 328.
3. Skolnik, *Fads*, p. 76.
4. Capt. Barbara A. Wilson, "Women in World War II," in "Female Veterans" [cited December 7, 1992], http//userpages.aug.com/captbarb/femvets5.html.
5. Woloch, pp. 462–63, 467; see also Skolnik, p. 77.
6. Corbett, *Daddy Danced the Charleston*, p. 118.
7. Woloch, p. 463.
8. Marshall, p. 326; Woloch, pp. 466–67.
9. Woloch, p. 467.
10. *Ibid.*, p. 464.
11. Skolnik, p. 77.
12. *Ibid.*
13. Corbett, pp. 115, 119.
14. Skolnik, p. 77.
15. Corbett, p. 120.
16. Marshall, p. 324; Woloch, p. 469.
17. Prost and Vincent, *History of Private Life*, pp. 565–67, 569; see also Woloch, p. 464.
18. Woloch, pp. 464, 469.
19. Prost and Vincent, pp. 566–67.
20. Prost and Vincent, p. 567; see also Woloch, p. 473.
21. Woloch, p. 473. A slew of the era's journalists reminded us that "Women Aren't Men."
22. Woloch, pp. 473–74.
23. Woloch, p. 462.
24. *Ibid.*, p. 469.
25. *Ibid.*, pp. 468, 473.
26. Prost and Vincent, pp. 570–71.
27. Death toll statistics from Marshall, p. 327.

7. Mary Chase and Her Wartime Rabbit

1. Willingham, "Introduce Them to Harvey," p. 6. Two of the most thorough treatments of Chase are this Master's thesis by Willingham and a 1970 Ph.D. dissertation by Maurice Berger from University of Denver, cited below in note 11.
2. *Ibid.*, p. 7; Rothe, *Current Biography*, p. 98.
3. Willingham, p. 8.
4. *Ibid.*, p. 7.
5. Rothe, p. 99; see also Willingham, p. 7.
6. Reef, "She Didn't Write," p. 109.
7. Rothe, p. 98.
8. Willingham, p. 8.

9. *Ibid.*, pp. 9–10.
10. *Ibid.*, p. 10.
11. Berger, "Mary Coyle Chase," p. 12.
12. Reef, p. 109.
13. Perkin, *The First Hundred Years*, p. 500.
14. Willingham, p. 27.
15. Perkin, p. 499.
16. Willingham, pp. 28–29.
17. *Ibid.*, pp. 41–42. Mary happily discovered that her aunt had played the Baker in 1900.
18. Rothe, p. 99; see also Willingham pp. 39–42. By marriage, Mary was even related to politicians: her husband was cousin to Sen. Margaret Chase Smith.
19. Willingham, pp. 41–42.
20. *Ibid.*, p. 42.
21. *Ibid.*, pp. 47–49.
22. *Ibid.*, pp. 51–53, 55; see also Reef, pp. 109–10.
23. Willingham, p. 55.
24. *Ibid.*
25. Berger, p. 21.
26. Melrose, "Mrs. Chase Pleased," p. 8.
27. Rothe, p. 100; see also Willingham, p. 67.
28. Willingham, p. 68.
29. *Ibid.*, pp. 73–74. One of Chase's fanciful children's books is *The Wicked Pigeon Ladies in the Garden* (Alfred Knopf, 1968).
30. Seymour P. [Last name illegible], in "PM Visits: The White Rabbit Lady," p. 16; Willingham, pp. 79–80.
31. Mary Chase, "My Life with Harvey," p. 54.
32. Chase, pp. 56–57; see also Willingham, p. 81.
33. Willingham, p. 81.
34. Chase, p. 54; Willingham, p. 13.
35. "Wednesday Editorials: Mary Chase," p. 50.
36. Willingham, p. 82.
37. "PM Visits: The White Rabbit Lady," p. 16.
38. Willingham, p. 84.
39. *Ibid.*; Rothe, pp. 99–100.
40. Chase, p. 54.
41. *Ibid.*

42. Willingham, p. 85.
43. *Ibid.*
44. *Ibid.*, p. 96.
45. *Ibid.*, pp 101–3, 131.
46. *Ibid.*, pp. 109–11.
47. Chase, p. 54; Reef, p. 110.
48. Boston reviews of *Harvey* quoted in Willingham, p. 112.
49. *Ibid.*, pp. 112–13.
50. Chase, p. 54
51. Chapman excerpt in Toohey, *Pulitzer Prize Plays*, pp. 199–200.
52. *Ibid.*, p. 200.
53. Willingham, p. 114.
54. Slide, *Selected Theatre Criticism*, p. 98.
55. Chase, p. 57.
56. *Ibid.*, p. 54.
57. *Ibid.*, p. 57. Mary Chase added a heartfelt postscript to this article—a note which read: "Dear Editor, I am grateful that you asked me to do this, because in the doing of it I have received much benefit in the way of therapy. I feel better than I have for a long time. I got rid of a lot of things."
58. Betty Caldwell, "Winning Pulitzer Prize Makes Mary Chase's Dream Reality," *Rocky Mountain News*, May 8, 1945, p. 5.
59. Chase, p. 58.
60. Willingham, p. 132.
61. Hohenberg, *Pulitzer Prizes*, p. 207.
62. Brady, "Hollywood Digest," p. 5.
63. Reef, p. 109.
64. Chase, p. 58.
65. Willingham, pp. 144–45.
66. *Ibid.*, p. 175; see also "Wednesday Editorials: Mary Chase," p. 50.
67. Melrose, p. 9.
68. All dialogue quotes from Chase, *Harvey*.
69. Rothe, p. 99; see also Willingham, p. 7.

8. The 1950s: An Uncomfortable Homecoming

1. Pres. Roosevelt's opening of the RCA Exhibit Hall was televised. See Campbell, *Golden Years*, pp. 55–58.

2. Campbell, pp. 58–60; and Marshall, *Great Events*, p. 280.
3. Marshall McLuhan, *The Medium Is the Massage* [sic] (New York: Bantam Books, 1967), p. 63.
4. Marshall, pp. 404–7; Skolnik, *Fads*, pp. 99–100. In the St. Louis elementary schools in the '50s, we practiced these air-raid drills regularly; the proper "crouch" is indelibly etched in my mind.
5. Marshall, p. 406. See also Howard L. Hurwitz, *An Encyclopedic Dictionary of American History* (New York: Washington Square Press, 1970), pp. 415–16.
6. Jezer, *The Dark Ages*, pp. 98–99.
7. Marshall, pp. 375, 407.
8. Skolnik, p. 103.
9. Prost and Vincent, *History of Private Life*, p. 573.
10. As Stephanie Coontz noted in *The Way We Never Were*, '50s television sidestepped any real family problems and ignored cultural diversity, adopting "the motto 'least objectionable programming' which gave rise to the least objectionable families, the Cleavers, the Nelsons, and the Andersons" Coontz, p. 30.
11. Prost and Vincent, p. 579.
12. *Ibid.*, p. 577.
13. *Ibid.*, p. 578.
14. Shearer, *Woman: Her Changing Image*, p. 67.
15. Coughlin, "Changing Roles in Modern Marriage," p. 110. See also Skinner, "Women Are Misguided," pp. 73–75.
16. *Look* magazine excerpt in Shearer, p. 56.
17. Shearer, p. 60.
18. *Ibid.*, p. 64.
19. *Ibid.*, p. 61.
20. Jezer, pp. 299–302. Parks' action prompted a mass bus boycott by blacks, which eventually led to integrated transportation.
21. Friedan quoted in Shearer, p. 67.
22. Oscar G. Brockett, *History of the Theatre*, fourth edition (Boston: Allyn & Bacon, 1982), p. 652.
23. Campbell, p. 60.
24. Sona Holman and Lillian Friedman, *How to Lie About Your Age* (New York: Collier, 1979), p. 142.

9. Ketti Frings and Her Stageworthy Angel

1. Battelle, "A Write Nice Salary," p. 7.
2. Charles Moritz, ed., *Current Biography—1960* (New York: The H.W. Wilson Co., 1960), p. 151; Robinson, Roberts and Barranger, eds., *Notable Women in American Theatre*, p. 316.
3. *Ibid.* Frings' early background information is drawn from both sources above.
4. *Ibid.*
5. Battelle, p. 7.
6. "Fan Mag Author Wrote Own Life—And Sold It," *Brooklyn Daily Eagle*, October 5, 1947, n.p., Frings file, Lincoln Center Archives.
7. Ketti Frings, "Her Trick Got Quick Reading for Script," *New York World-Telegram*, December 13, 1941, n.p., Frings File, Lincoln Center Archives.
8. Battelle, p. 7.
9. Atkinson quoted by Lina Mainiero, ed., *American Women Writers* (New York: Frederick Ungar, 1980), p. 93.
10. Cook, "Ketti Frings," p. A-16.
11. Moritz, *Biography—1960*, p. 152.
12. Press Release, "Ketti Frings," from Seymour Krawitz and Merle Debuskey, August 1961; Frings File, Lincoln Center Archives. See also Toohey, *Pulitzer Prize Plays*, pp. 243–45.
13. John Chapman, *Broadway's Best—1958* (Garden City, NY: Doubleday, 1958), p. 21.
14. "Sketches of Pulitzer Prize Winners," *New York Times*, May 6, 1958, p. L-38.
15. Toohey, *Pulitzer Prize Plays*, p. 295.
16. Hewes, "Broadway Postscript," p. 27.
17. Toohey, p. 296.
18. Hewes, p. 27. Also Chapman, p. 21.
19. Hewes, p. 27.
20. *Ibid.*
21. *Ibid.*, p. 28.
22. *Ibid.*

23. *Ibid.* See also Frings, *Look Homeward, Angel*, p. 65.
24. *Ibid.*; Chapman, p. 21.
25. Hewes, p. 27.
26. *Ibid.*, pp. 27–28.
27. Chapman, p. 21; Toohey, pp. 293, 297.
28. Moritz, *Biography–1960*, p. 152.
29. Aswell's introduction to the Scribner script (1957) quoted in Moritz, p. 152.
30. Walter Kerr review excerpt in Toohey, pp. 296–97.
31. John Chapman quoted in Toohey, p. 297.
32. Atkinson, "Look Homeward, Angel," p. 33.
33. Moritz, *Biography–1960*, p. 152–53. See also note 14 above.
34. Moritz, *Biography–1960*, p. 153.
35. *Ibid.*, p. 153.
36. All dialogue quotes taken from Frings, *Look Homeward, Angel*.

Part III. Whose Woman Is She?

1. Jaehne, "Beth's Beauties," p. 11.
2. Branden, "A Woman's Self-Esteem," pp. 56–58.

10. Being Female in the 1950s, '60s and '70s

1. Carol Andreas, *Sex and Caste*, pp. 134–35.
2. Friedan, *Feminine Mystique* (1963), p. 16.
3. *Ibid.*, pp. 15–16.
4. Friedan, *Feminine Mystique*, tenth anniversary edition, p. 9. This will be the Friedan edition cited hereafter unless otherwise noted.
5. *Ibid.*, p. 7.
6. *Ibid.*, pp. 234–37.
7. Ryan, *Womanhood in America*, p. 287.
8. Coontz, *Way We Never Were*, p. 32.
9. Friedan, p. 236.
10. Roszak and Roszak, *Masculine/Feminine* (New York: Harper & Row, 1969), pp. 19–20.
11. Friedan, p. 116. Another feminist vantage point on Freud is found in Steinem's *Moving Beyond Words*, pp. 21–98. Her annotated footnotes on Freud give a documented account of Freud's prejudices regarding women; while her amusing text gives a hypothetical look at what psychology might be like if Freud had been "Phyllis."
12. Friedan, pp. 106–110; also Steinem, in *Moving* (p. 37 fn), quotes Freud's biographer Ernest Jones, who states that "Freud's aversion to music was one of his well-known characteristics."
13. Friedan, p. 110.
14. *Ibid.*, pp. 110–11. Freud's letter also reprinted in Steinem, *Moving*, p. 47.
15. Friedan, p. 108.
16. *Ibid.*, pp. 120–21.
17. Lundberg and Farmham, *The Lost Sex* quoted in Ryan, p. 283.
18. Henry A. Bowman, *Marriage for Moderns* (New York, 1942), p. 21.
19. *Ibid.*, p. 135.
20. Margaret Mead, *Male and Female* (New York: William Morrow, 1949), p. 160.
21. Mead's excerpt from *Saturday Evening Post*, March 3, 1964, quoted in Friedan, p. 148.
22. Friedan, pp. 155–56.
23. *Ibid.*, p. 403.
24. *Ibid.*, pp. 206–07.
25. Marlene Dixon's "The Rise of Women's Liberation" reprinted in Roszak and Roszak, pp. 186–201. Quote cited is found on pp. 194–95.
26. Ryan, p. 301; Friedan, p. 208.
27. Friedan, p. 208.
28. *Ibid.*, pp. 212–13.
29. *Ibid.*, p. 215.
30. *Ibid.*
31. *Ibid.*, p. 218.
32. *Ibid.*, p. 231.
33. Friedan quoted in Woloch, *Women*, p. 488; Friedan, p. 381.
34. Friedan, p. 386.
35. *Ibid.*, p. 384.
36. Woloch, p. 516.

37. Babcox and Belken, *Liberation Now!* p. 2.
38. Betty Roszak, "The Human Continuum," in Roszak and Roszak, p. 297.
39. Alice Rossi, "Sex Equality: The Beginning of Ideology," in Roszak and Roszak, p. 178.
40. Friedan, p. 388.
41. *Ibid.*, pp. 390–91.
42. Woloch, p. 523.
43. *Ibid.*, pp. 525–26.
44. Prost and Vincent, *History of Private Life*, pp. 583–84.
45. Babcox and Belken, p. 3.

11. Beth Henley's Funny-Terrible World View

1. Henley, Playwrights' Workshop.
2. Betsko and Koenig, *Interviews*, p. 217.
3. Henley, interview by author, 1992; Henley, letters, 1992.
4. Betsko and Koenig, p. 218.
5. Charles Moritz, ed., *Current Biography—1983* (New York: H.W. Wilson, 1983), p. 186.
6. Betsko and Koenig, p. 215. See also Moritz, p. 186.
7. Jaehne, "Beth's Beauties," p. 11.
8. Moritz, *Biography—1983*, p. 186.
9. Betsko and Koenig, p. 213.
10. Walker, "Beth Henley," pp. 30–31.
11. *Ibid.*
12. Betsko and Koenig, pp. 213–14.
13. Henley, interview by author, 1992.
14. *Ibid.*
15. Haller, "Her First Play," p. 44.
16. Betsko and Koenig, pp. 215–16.
17. Haller, p. 42; Moritz, *Biography—1983*, p. 187.
18. Betsko and Koenig, p. 216.
19. Jaehne, p. 12.
20. Haller, p. 42; Moritz, *Biography—1983*, p. 187.
21. Haller, p. 42.
22. Simon quoted in Moritz, *Biography—1983*, p. 187. Also excerpted on bookjacket of Henley, *Crimes of the Heart*.
23. See Robinson, et al., *Notable Women*, pp. 418–20. These editors have published some other misinformation here: They write (p. 420) that Beth Henley "ranks with Lorraine Hansberry as a Pulitzer Prize winner for drama." Hansberry did not win a Pulitzer, but did garner a 1959 Drama Critics' Circle Award. Also, Beth was only the 6th, not the 7th woman to receive the Pulitzer, excluding Frances Goodrich's shared win with Albert Hackett for *The Diary of Anne Frank*, 1956.
24. Henley, interview by author, 1992.
25. Haller, p. 42.
26. Moritz, *Biography—1983*, p. 188.
27. Brendan Gill quoted in press release for (and bookjacket of) Henley, *Crimes of the Heart*.
28. Kauffmann, "Two Cheers," p. 54.
29. Frank Rich review quoted in press release for (and bookjacket of) Henley, *Crimes of the Heart*.
30. Moritz, *Biography—1983*, p. 188.
31. Henley, interview by author, 1992.
32. *Ibid.*
33. *Ibid.*; Betsko and Koenig, p. 214.
34. Betsko and Koenig, p. 214.
35. Jaehne, pp. 11–12.
36. Betsko and Koenig, p. 214.
37. *Ibid.*, p. 220.
38. Gill, "Wake of Jamie Foster," p. 161.
39. Henley, interview by author, 1992.
40. Betsko and Koenig, p. 215.
41. Clive Barnes quoted in Moritz, *Biography—1983*, p. 188.
42. Betsko and Koenig, p. 217.
43. *Ibid.*
44. Henley, *Miss Firecracker*.
45. Frank Rich, "Firecracker," p. 11.
46. Jaehne, p. 12.
47. *Ibid.*, p. 14.
48. *Ibid.*, p. 12.
49. Henley, Playwrights' Workshop.
50. Walker, p. 31.
51. Henley, interview by author.
52. *Ibid.*; Henley, letters to author.
53. Betsko and Koenig, p. 221.
54. *Ibid.*, p. 220.
55. Henley, letters to author.
56. Walker, p. 31.
57. Jaehne, p. 11.
58. Shepard, "Aborted Rage," pp. 106–07.

59. Jaehne, p. 11; Henley, interview by author.
60. Premier of *Control Freaks* at Center Theater, Chicago, September 17, 1992. Holly Hunter was in the audience; she later played the role of "Sister" in the Hollywood production. See review: Jacobs, "Control Freaks," p. 35.
61. Sydney, "Mission Impossible."
62. Jack Bertram, "I Can't Imagine a World Without Her," *The Clarion Ledger*, October 25, 2002 [cited January 12, 2003], http://www.clarionledger.com/news/021 0/25/m01a.html.
63. Sommer, "Family Week."
64. Henley, telephone interview, 2003.
65. Henley, letters to author, 1992; Betsko and Koenig, p. 215, 221.
66. All dialogue quotes taken from Beth Henley, *Crimes of the Heart* (New York: Dramatists Play Service, 1982).
67. Jaehne, p. 14.
68. Betsko and Koenig, p. 218.
69. Bradshaw quoted by Caryl S. Avery, "Shame," *New Woman*, May 1991, p. 49.
70. Henley, letters to author.
71. Deats and Lenker, *Aching Hearth*, pp. 1–4.

12. The 1980s: Backlash and Beyond

1. Conniff, "Interview: Susan Faludi," p. 38. See also Gibbs, "War Against Feminism," p. 54. The article includes results of a survey demonstrating that 63 percent of American women still did not consider themselves feminists in 1992—even though more than 80 percent felt that they enjoyed more freedoms than their mothers did (an indirect but clear tribute to the women's movement).
2. The subtitle of Ehrenreich's book *The Worst Years of Our Lives* is "Irreverent Notes from a Decade of Greed." When I met Ehrenreich before her address at Loyola in 2003, she said, "I wish I'd saved that title [for now]."
3. Gibbs and McDowell, "How to Revive a Revolution," p. 57.
4. Gibbs, "Dreams of Youth," p. 12, from a *Time* magazine Special Issue of fall 1990, with the cover title "Women: The Road Ahead."
5. Friedan quoted in Bassnett, *Feminist Experiences*, pp. 17–18.
6. Jackal and Manning, "Long March to Equality," p. 13.
7. Ehrenreich, p. 4.
8. Susan Faludi, *Backlash: The Undeclared War Against American Women* (New York: Doubleday, 1992), p. 257.
9. Jack Cocks, "How Long," p. 23.
10. Faludi, p. 263.
11. Ibid., pp. 229–30.
12. Ibid., p. 239; Gibbs and McDowell, p. 56.
13. Faludi, p. 56
14. Friedan, p. 222.
15. Faludi, p. 9.
16. Ibid., pp. 11–14. "The Man Shortage Myth" by Susan Faludi was also reprinted in *Cosmopolitan*, July 1992, pp. 66–70, 100.
17. Faludi, pp. 16–17.
18. Ibid., p. 17.
19. Ehrenreich, pp. 110, 114.
20. Faludi, pp. 18–19.
21. Ibid. Nancy Gibbs plays devil's advocate to some of Faludi's points about infertility and marriage odds for women over 40 (see Gibbs, "The War Against Feminism"), but on the whole she notes that Faludi's "big picture is accurate."
22. Faludi, p. xv.
23. Ibid., pp. 41–43. Another account of how unsafe children are at home is given in Deats and Lenker, *Aching Hearth*. They report that "each year abusing parents kill more children than do leukemia, cystic fibrosis, or muscular dystrophy," and "more children are injured by violence in the home than in any other place" (p. 4). See also Coontz, *Way We Never Were*, Chapter 9, "Toxic Parents."
24. Faludi quotes (p. 121) the anti-feminist sentiments of Adrian Lynne, director of *Fatal Attraction*: "My wife has never worked. She's the least ambitious person

I've ever met. She's a terrific wife ... I come home and she's there." And Gibbs in "War Against Feminism" (pp. 50–53) quotes a movie theatre worker's report that men in the audience regularly screamed "Beat that bitch. Kill her off now."
25. Gloria Steinem, *Revolution from Within*, p. 3.
26. Ibid., p. 26.

13. Marsha Norman: Getting Out the Truth about Family and Self

1. Norman, interview by author.
2. Ibid.
3. Ibid.
4. Ibid.
5. Stout, "Marsha Norman," p. 31.
6. Harriott, *American Voices*, p. 148.
7. Ibid., p. 152.
8. Norman, interview by author.
9. Ibid.
10. Betsko and Koenig, *Interviews*, p. 338.
11. Norman, interview by author.
12. Gross, "Marsha Norman," pp. 257–58.
13. Norman, interview by author.
14. Harriott, p. 155.
15. Ibid., p. 161; Norman, interview by author.
16. Norman, interview by author.
17. Charles Moritz, ed., *Current Biography—1984* (H.W. Wilson, 1984), p. 305.
18. Norman, *Traveler in the Dark*, in *Four Plays*.
19. Norman, interview by author.
20. Harriott, p. 151; Norman, interview by author.
21. Marsha Norman, *The Fortune Teller* (New York: Random House, 1987); Norman, interview by author.
22. Norman, interview by author.
23. Ibid.
24. Ibid.
25. Ibid.
26. April Gornik interviewed Norman regarding *Trudy Blue* for *Bomb* magazine, spring, 2000 [cited February 4, 2003], http://bombsite.com/norman/norman2.html.
27. Harriott, p. 156.
28. Dace, "Sexism in the Theatre," pp. 20–25.
29. Norman, interview by author.
30. Ibid.
31. Ibid.
32. Ibid.
33. All dialogue quotes and set notations from Norman, *'Night, Mother*.
34. Friday, *My Mother/My Self*, p. 19.
35. Ibid., Chapter One, especially pp. 19–32.
36. Ibid., p. 33.
37. Norman, interview by author.
38. Ibid.
39. Ibid.
40. Ibid.
41. Ibid.
42. Betsko and Koenig, p. 329.
43. Norman, interview by author.
44. Gloria Steinem, *Revolution from Within*, p. 179.

14. Wendy Wasserstein: Lola's Well-Rounded Daughter

1. Hoban, "The Family Wasserstein," p. 35.
2. Ibid., p. 37; see also Wendy Wasserstein, *Bachelor Girls*, p. 19.
3. Wasserstein, *Bachelor Girls*, p. 16.
4. Hoban, p. 36.
5. Wasserstein, *Bachelor Girls*, p. 17; also Wasserstein speech, "He and She."
6. Hoban, "Family Wasserstein," p. 36.
7. Wasserstein, *Bachelor Girls*, p. 184.
8. Hoban, p. 37.
9. Cawley, "A playwright's birth pangs," pp. 22–23; Wasserstein, interview by author.
10. Wasserstein, *Bachelor Girls*, p. 20; interview by author.
11. Wasserstein, address at Pace University.
12. Ibid.; Cohen, "An Interview with Wendy Wasserstein."
13. Cohen, p. 258; Wasserstein, interview by author.

14. Betsko and Koenig, *Interviews*, p. 427.
15. Hubbard, "Bio: Wendy Wasserstein," p. 104.
16. Wasserstein, address at Pace University.
17. *Ibid.*
18. Hubbard, "Bio: Wendy Wasserstein," p. 101.
19. Wasserstein, address at Pace University.
20. *Ibid.*
21. Wasserstein, interview by author.
22. *Ibid.*
23. *Ibid.*; Wasserstein, address at Pace University.
24. Wendy Wasserstein, *Uncommon Women and Others* (New York: Dramatists Play Service, 1978).
25. Wasserstein, interview by author; Betsko and Koenig, p. 324.
26. Wasserstein, interview by author.
27. Wasserstein, address at Pace University.
28. *Ibid.*
29. Hoban, p. 37; Wasserstein, interview by author.
30. Wasserstein, address at Pace University.
31. *Ibid.*
32. Wendy Wasserstein, *Isn't It Romantic* (New York: Doubleday, 1984), p. 76.
33. Wasserstein, address at Pace University.
34. Wasserstein, interview by author.
35. *Ibid.*; Wasserstein, address at Pace University.
36. Wasserstein, address at Pace University.
37. *Ibid.*
38. Horwitz, "The Playwright as Woman," p. 23.
39. Wasserstein, interview by author; Burleigh, "The Wendy Chronicles," p. 8.
40. Wasserstein, address at Pace University.
41. *Ibid.*
42. Abby Cohn, "Wendy Wasserstein Brings Wit, Midlife Wisdom to MJCC," *Jewish Bulletin*, June 7, 2002 [cited October 11, 2002], http://www.jewishsf.com/bk02067/bn26.shtml.
43. Wasserstein, interview by author.
44. Burleigh, "The Wendy Chronicles," p. 8.
45. Wasserstein, interview by author.
46. Hubbard, p. 106.
47. Steinem quoted in Jacobson, "Heidi Mystique," p. 26.
48. Faludi, *Backlash*, p. 58.
49. Hubbard, p. 106.
50. Wasserstein, interview by author.
51. Wasserstein, preface to *Sisters Rosensweig*, p. ix.
52. *Ibid.*, p. x.
53. *New York Times* review excerpt in press release of November 1992; also on fly-leaf of Wasserstein, *Sisters Rosensweig*.
54. Simon, "The Best So Far," p. 100.
55. Hedy Weiss, "Wasserstein's Political Chronicle," *Chicago Sun-Times*, August 30, 1998 [cited October 13, 1998], http://suntimes.come/output/weiss/30stag.
56. Wasserstein, preface to *Sisters Rosensweig*, p. x.
57. Cohn, "Wendy Wasserstein Brings Wit."
58. *Ibid.*
59. Wasserstein, *Bachelor Girls*.
60. Wasserstein, *Shiksa Goddess*.
61. Wasserstein, e-mail to author.
62. A. H. Home, "Wendy Wasserstein," an interview for *Bomb* [cited February 18, 2003], http://www.bombsite.com/wasserstein/html.
63. Wasserstein, e-mail to author.
64. Norma Faingold, "Wendy Wasserstein Confronts Strong Women, Tough Choices," *Jewish Bulletin*, September 4, 1998 [cited August 10, 2000], http://www.jewishsf.com/bk980904/etwendy.htm.
65. Steven Winn, "'Money' Lacks Payoff," *San Francisco Chronicle*, January 21, 2002, p. D-3.
66. Cohen, "Interview with Wendy Wasserstein," p. 265.
67. Wasserstein, interview by author.
68. Betsko and Koenig, p. 431.
69. Wasserstein, preface to *Sisters Rosensweig*, p. x.

70. All dialogue quotes taken from Wasserstein, *Heidi Chronicles*.
71. Faludi, p. 58.
72. Wasserstein, interview by author.
73. Ibid.
74. Ibid.
75. Cawley, "A Playwright's Birth Pangs," p. 23.
76. Wasserstein, *Bachelor Girls*, p. 148.
77. Wasserstein, interview by author.

Part IV. Lessons Driven Home

15. The 1990s: Gender Crisis at the Crossroads

1. Introduction to "Women and Men, Can We Get Along?" p. 52.
2. Ruether, "Patriarchy," p. 15.
3. Gloria Steinem, foreword to *Women Respond to the Men's Movement*, p. viii.
4. Eisler, "What Do Men Really Want," p. 47.
5. John Stoltenberg, *Refusing to Be a Man* (New York: Meridian, 1990), pp. 4–5, 50.
6. Steinem, foreword to *Women Respond*, p. v.
7. Halpern, "Susan Faludi."
8. Statistics from Women's Bureau at: http://www.gov/dol/wb/public/wb_pubs/7996htm [cited May 4, 2000].
9. "Gender Gap in Government," at: http://www.gendergap.com/governme.htm [cited April 30, 2000].
10. Ibid. See also statistics posted at: http://www.womenlegislators.org/didyoukn.html [cited April 30, 2000].
11. Steinem, address at Loyola University.
12. Koerner, "A Lust for Profits," pp. 36–37.
13. Stoltenberg, p. 134.
14. One source among many on this is Judith Stacey, *Brave New Families* (New York: Harper Collins Basic Books, 1990), especially p. 5.
15. Drukman, "A Playwright on the Edge Turns Toward the Middle," *New York Times*, March 16, 1997, sec. C, p 6.
16. Ibid.

16. Paula Vogel's Winding Road to Victory

1. Vogel, interview by author.
2. Ibid.
3. Ibid. See also David Savran, "Loose Screws," introduction to Vogel, *Baltimore Waltz*, pp. ix–x.
4. Vogel, interview by author.
5. Ibid.
6. Ibid.
7. Savran, "Driving Ms. Vogel," p. 17.
8. Ibid., p. 18; Vogel, interview by author.
9. Vogel, interview by author.
10. Ibid.
11. Savran, "Driving Ms. Vogel," p. 18.
12. Vogel, interview by author.
13. Savran, "Driving Ms. Vogel," p. 18.
14. Ibid.
15. Vogel, *Desdemona*, in *Baltimore Waltz*, p. 193. "Purdah" refers to the veils covering women's faces in certain Asian and Middle Eastern cultures.
16. Vogel, interview by author.
17. Ibid.; Sid Smith, "Brother-Sister Act," *Chicago Tribune*, April 18, 1993, sec. 13, p. 16.
18. Savran, "Loose Screws," p. xi.
19. Hughes, "In the Driver's Seat," p. 99.
20. Vogel, interview by author.
21. Ibid.
22. Ibid.
23. Ibid.
24. Vogel, *Baltimore Waltz*, p. 231.
25. Vogel, interview by author.
26. Ibid.
27. Arthur Holmberg, "An Interview with Playwright Paula Vogel," for "Hippodrome: Perspectives" [cited May 2, 2000], http://hipp.gator.net/drive_perspectives_vogel.html.
28. Vogel, interview by author.
29. Arthur Holmberg, "An interview with Playwright Paula Vogel."
30. Vogel, interview by author.
31. Susan Thomsen, "The Mineola

Twins," for "Sidewalk New York" [cited March 15, 1999], http://newyork.sidewalk.com/detail/95986.
32. Vogel, interview by author.
33. Ibid.
34. Coen, "No Need for Gravity," p. 26.
35. Vogel, interview by author.
36. Ibid.
37. All dialogue quotes and set notations taken from Vogel, How I Learned to Drive in The Mammary Plays.
38. Vogel, interview by author.
39. Ibid.
40. Ibid.

17. Margaret Edson's Advanced Course in Wit

1. Sack, "Margaret Edson," p. 1.
2. Edson, interview by author.
3. Ibid.
4. Ibid.
5. Ibid.
6. Ibid.; Sack, "Margaret Edson."
7. Edson, interview by author.
8. Ibid.
9. Ibid.
10. Clay, "Donne Deal."
11. Edson, interview by author.
12. Ibid.
13. Ibid.
14. Ibid.
15. Ibid.
16. Kelly, "Wit and Wisdom."
17. Edson, interview by author; Pressley, "A Teacher's 'Wit' and Wisdom."
18. Rosenthal, "Matters of Life and Death."
19. Edson, interview by author.
20. Ibid.
21. Brief personal interview with actress Kathleen Chalfant, New York City, May 23, 1999.
22. Pressley, "A Teacher's 'Wit.'"
23. Edson, letters to author, July/August 2000.
24. Edson, letters to author, November/December 2002.
25. Ibid.; Pressley, "A Teacher's 'Wit.'"
26. Jim Lehrer, "Love and Knowledge."
27. Kelly, "Wit and Wisdom."
28. Edson, letters to author, November/December 2002.
29. Linda Jacobson, "Kindergarten Teacher Takes Home a Pulitzer Prize," Education Week, April 21, 1999 [cited May 13, 1999], http://edweek.org/ew/vol-18/32prize.h18.
30. Edson, interview by author.
31. Ibid.
32. Albis, "In the Spotlight."
33. Edson, interview by author.
34. Ibid.
35. Ibid.
36. All dialogue quotes and set notations from Edson, Wit.
37. Edson, interview by author.
38. Ibid.
39. Ibid.

Part V. History in the Staging?

1. Savran, Playwright's Voice, p. 252.
2. Fanger, "Pulitzer Prize Winner," p. 19.

18. The Early 2000s: "Bang, Bang— You're American"

1. Michael Moore, Bowling for Columbine (Salter Street/DogEatDog Films for Iconolatry, 2002). Also, one of scores of articles I found on our gun culture is Michael G. McFadden's "A much needed and overdue study (on gun violence)," Baltimore Afro-American, October 18, 1999, p. A-5.
2. Matsui, "Regime Change Begins at Home."
3. David Hoppe, "Still Vonnegut ... After All These Years," Utne Reader, May–June, 2003, p. 88.
4. Cindy Yingst, "'Grand Theft Auto' Video Game Is Target of Protest," The Olympian, December 14, 2003 [cited October 27, 2003], http://www.theolympian.com/home/news/20021214/southsound/27761.shtml.

5. "Brute Force (Xbox)," *Gamenow*, April 1, 2003, p. 22.

6. "Command & Conquer: Attack Copter," at *Gamezone* [cited October 26, 2003], http://www.gamezone.com/gamesell/p22080.htm.

7. "Soldier of Fortune" description in Booth, "The Media Death Watch Machine."

8. James Bottorff, "'Half-Life' a Whole Experience," *The Cincinnati Enquirer* [cited October 29, 2003], http://www.cincinnati.com/freetime/games/reviews/halflife.html.

9. Francis X. Maier, "Why Video Games are Great," pp. 35–36.

10. Gentile quoted in Booth, "The Media Death Watch Machine."

11. These were precisely the stunts on the October 27, 2003, episode. (Over time, I've taped and watched *Fear Factor* episodes as research.) All I omitted from the October 27 show was the devouring of 8 to 24 stink beetles, determined by numbers under flaming goblets at which contestants shot explosive pellets.

12. Booth, "The Media Death Watch Machine."

13. Excerpt from Chayevsky's *Network* (speech of character Howard Beale) in "Corporate Television: Who Owns the Networks?" [cited November 5, 2003], http://www.netreach.net/~kaufman/network.ownership.html.

14. "Associated Press Report: WorldCom Scam Could Total $9B," *Milwaukee Journal-Sentinal*, Sept. 20, 2002 [cited October 26, 2003], http://www.jsonline.com/bym/news/ap/sep02/ap-worldcome 092002.asp.

15. "Background on Enron, Government Probe," *The Indychannel.Com* [cited October 28, 2003], http://www.theindychannel.com/news/1188641/detail.htm.

16. Ibid., and Pratap Chatterjee, "Enron: Pulling the Plug on the Global Power Broker," *CorpWatch*, December 13, 2001 [cited October 26, 2003], http://www.corpwatch.org/issues/PID.jsp?articleid=1016.

17. Arianna Huffington, *Pigs at the Trough: How Corporate Greed and Political Corruption Are Undermining America* (New York: Crown Publishers, 2003), pp. 58–65. Excerpts from this chapter, "Our MBA President and His CEO Sidekick," appear in *Utne*, May–June, 2003, p.52. See also Robert Scheer, "Cheney's Grimy Trail in Business," *The Nation*, July 16, 2002 [cited November 5, 2003], http://www.thenation.com/doc.mhtml?i=20020716. In *Dude, Where's My Country*, Michael Moore also has a well-documented Enron section, pp. 148–155.

18. Noam Chomsky, "Iraq: A Test Case of Imperial Violence," Speech at Metro State College, Denver, published by Alternative Radio, Boulder Colorado, April 2003. One of several reports on the Condi Rice oil tanker is "The Condi Rice Renamed," in *Multinational Monitor*, June 2001, issue 6.

19. Rep. Cynthia McKinney, "Thoughts on Our War Against Terrorism," *Counterpunch*, April 13, 2002 [cited May 12, 2003], http://www.counterpunch.org/mckinney0413.html.

20. When introducing Michael Moore for his appearance at Borders Bookstore, State St., Chicago (October 14, 2003), the Borders official announced that *Stupid White Men* was in its 59th printing and had sold more copies in the last year than any book except "the Harry Potter books." (Moore arrived to cheers from a crowd packed throughout two levels of the store.) Moore spoke briefly and signed copies of *Dude, Where's My Country*, research for which also informs *Fahrenheit 9/11*, his documentary denouncement of the Bush cohort. *Entertainment Weekly* hailed the film as "the highest-grossing non-concert, non–IMAX documentary of all time" (July 9, 2004, issue, p. 32).

21. Huffington, *How to Overthrow*, p. xviii.

22. Chomsky, *Power and Terror*, p. 17. A thorough treatment of U.S. military atrocities elsewhere is that by ex-statesman William Blum: *Killing Hope: U.S. Military and CIA Interventions Since World War II* (Common Courage Press, 1995; updated edition due 2003).

23. Gore Vidal, "We Are the Patriots," *The Nation*, June 2, 2003, p. 11; Gore Vidal, *Dreaming War: Blood for Oil and the Cheney-Bush Junta* (New York: Thunder's Mouth Press/Nation Books, 2002), pp. 16–20. Michael Moore also makes a good case for the pipeline motive for Afghanistan in *Dude, Where's My Country*, pp. 30–35.

24. Christian Dewar, "Speaking Truth to Ignorance: An Open Letter to Charlie Daniels and the Warmongers," *Democratic Underground*, April 5, 2003 [cited November 2, 2003], http://www.democraticunderground.com/articles/03/04/p/05_letter.html. Also: Iraq's "2002 proved oil reserves" were 115 billion gallons, second to Saudi Arabia with 261 billion. One of several web sites giving such statistics is www.factmonster.com.

25. Letters to Bush posted on their web site, "September Eleventh Families for Peaceful Tomorrows" [cited May 20, 2003], http://www.peacefultomorrows.org/letters/whitehouseletter.html.

26. Arundhati Roy, "Instant-Mix Imperial Democracy." Also: "Ten Million Join World Protest," press release from the *Guardian/ UK*, February 13, 2003.

27. I'm a member of MoveOn.org, one of the peace agencies that gathered and delivered the petitions. Two e-mails I received in early March 2003 reported the delivery of the boxes of protest petitions to the U.N. Security Council.

28. Audrey Brohy and Gerard Ungerman, *Hidden Wars of Desert Storm* (Free-Will Productions, 2000). See also Ramsey Clark, *The Children Are Dying: The Impact of Sanctions in Iraq* (New York: WorldView Forum, 1996), especially pp. 9–10. Also Jackson, "Burying the Number," p. 15. Jackson quotes an Associated Press report on Iraqi war-related deaths. See also www.iraqibodycount.com.

29. Zakaria, "The Arrogant Empire," pp. 26–27.

30. David Krieger, "Bush's War on the Poor." The $400 billion per year figure does not include Iraq.

31. Arundhati Roy, "Instant-Mix Imperial Democracy."

32. "Corporate Television: Who Owns the Networks?" [cited November 5, 2003], http://www.netreach.net/~kaufman/network.ownership.html. Also, *Columbia Journalism Review* has a great site, "Who Owns What," at http://www.cjr.org/tools/owners/asp. Another such site, "MakeThem Accountable.Com," states that there is "no corporation in the world more powerful than General Electric," and details how GE Chairman Jack Welch set an agenda to "make George W. Bush president" via corporate media (see http://makethemaccountable.com/coverup/part_04.htm). NBC's fictionalized coverage of the Iraq war was topped only by its fictionalization of the staged "Rescue of Private Lynch." We now know from reports by the BBC, the AP, and Middle East Bureau that Lynch was actually injured in a vehicle accident and treated very well by Iraqi doctors, who tried to return her in an ambulance that was fired on by U.S. troops. The damage done by the unnecessarily violent U.S. "rescue" (there were no Iraqi soldiers in the hospital at the time) included the destruction of 12 hospital doors and a special-traction bed, and the contamination of a sterilized operating room. See Mitch Potter, "The Real 'Saving Pvt. Lynch,'" *Toronto Star*, May 5, 2003 (www.thestar.com) and Robert Scheer, "Saving Private Lynch: Take 2," *The Nation*, May 20, 2003 [cited June 9, 2003], http://www.thenation.com/doc print.mhtml?i=20030602&s=scheer 20030520. Also, Michael Moore's well-documented section on Lynch in *Dude, Where's My Country* paints an accurate picture (pp. 80–81).

33. Goldstein, "The Shock and Awe Show."

34. "America's Army" game website: http://www.americasarmy.com. Across the top of the site is an animated panorama of hovering choppers and combat soldiers, across whom float words like "courage ... integrity ... empower yourself ... defend freedom ..."

35. Maier, p. 36.

36. Paul Wilborn, "SUV Backlash? Not

for Owners of Gas-Guzzling Hummers," *Detroit News*, January 11, 2003 [cited October 31, 2003], http://www.detnews.com/2003autoinsider/0301/11/autos-57328.htm (Oct. 31, 2003). Hummer fans have various websites (one is www.hummerteam.com) where they exchange jokes like, You know you're driving a Hummer if "you don't measure fuel efficiency by miles per gallon, but rather gallons per mile." Meanwhile, the Environment News Network has run columns with headlines like "U.S. Lawmakers Reject Higher Fuel Standards for SUV's" (www.enn.com/news). And the *Chicago Tribune* ran a three-part series on the "Death of the SuperCar"—the efficient alternative-energy model which was killed by "politics and neglect" and a "hostile auto industry." See *Chicago Tribune* Special "RedEye" Edition, December 6, 2002, cover story, p. 10.

37. Alex Moffat, "NewsFlash: H2 Gets Lousy Gas Mileage," at "ithoughtyoumightbeinterested," May 8, 2003 [cited October 31, 2003], http://www.zanthan.com/itymbi/archives/001388.html.

38. "NOW Action Alert: Speak Out Against Grand Theft Auto III" posted on *AsMaineGoes*, January 25, 2002 [cited October 26, 2003], http://www.asmainegoes.com/ubb/forum1/HTML/009958.html.

39. Maier, p. 35; Description of "N.U.D.E." (Natural Ultimate Digital Experiment) at www.xboxsolution.com.

40. "Eminem's Grammys: Should He Have Won?" at *Frontline* [cited October 26, 2003], http://www.pbs.org/wgbh/pages/frontline/shows/cool/etc/dontfwithshady.html and same site: frontline/shows/cool/etc/synopsis.html.

41. Smith, "New Phase in the War."

42. Chris Floyd, "Body Blow," posted by "womens e-news" [cited November 9, 2003], http://www.crisispapers.org/topics/women.htm.

43. "NOW and the Peace Movement," on their web site: http://www.now.org/issues/peace/index.html. Gandy's words underscore NOW's "Progressive Feminist Agenda for Peace," which includes calls to: "Expose the stifling of political dissent by the Bush administration through policies such as the Patriot Act" and "Call for an end to the U.S. campaign of militarism and corporate profit that has contributed to anti–American sentiment around the world."

44. "Legal Motions Stemming from the Peace Efforts of Three Dominican Sisters" (and other related articles) at "Sacred Earth and Space Plowshares" [cited November 6, 2003], http://www.domlife.org/2003/plowsharesupdate.html. Also, among reports on protesters arrested across the country was this one on the 700 arrested just in Chicago: Ben Jovarsky, "Taken by Surprise," *Chicago Reader*, April 4, 2003, p. 1.

45. "Legal Motions"; see also Moore's dedication in *Dude, Where's My Country* (Warner Books, 2003).

46. Chittister, "Is There Anything Left That Matters?"

47. Walker, *Sent by Earth*, pp. 18–19.

48. Ibid., pp. 19–20.

19. Suzan-Lori Parks: Putting Dirt and Deadly Games Onstage

1. Garrett, "Possession of Suzan-Lori Parks," p. 25; Suzan-Lori Parks, "Possession," in *The America Play*, pp. 3–4.

2. Miller and Cotliar, "Best in Show," pp. 143–44.

3. James Hannaham, "Bio: Suzan-Lori Parks," *Village Voice* [cited August 20, 2002], http://www.villagevoice.com/issues/9944/hannaham.shtml.

4. Savran, *Playwright's Voice*, p. 152.

5. Ibid., p. 143.

6. Garrett, p. 22.

7. Ibid.; Savran, pp. 144–45.

8. Parks, "Possession," pp. 4–5.

9. Phillips, "Our History, Her Language," p. 1. Also, in her introduction to her anthology of plays by black women (*Moon Marked and Touched by Sun*), Sydné Mahone says that a main benefit of an Ivy

League diploma is that "it almost guarantees access to the professional network already populated by fellow graduates" (p. xxvii).

10. Parks, *Imperceptible Mutabilities*, in *American Play*, pp. 25–71.

11. Savran, p. 140.

12. Parks, "Elements of Style," in *American Play*, pp. 8–9.

13. Parks, *Imperceptible Mutabilities*, in *American Play*, pp. 56–57.

14. Parks, "Elements of Style," in *American Play*, p. 6.

15. Drukman, "Suzan-Lori Parks and Liz Diamond," p. 64.

16. Kevin Kelly, "Diamond sparkles in the Director's Chair," *Boston Globe*, January 28, 1994, p. 45.

17. Garrett, "Possession of Suzan-Lori Parks," p. 24.

18. Savran, p. 160.

19. Parks, *Devotees in the Garden of Love*, in *America Play*, p. 140.

20. Savran, p. 158.

21. *Ibid.*, p. 348.

22. Robin Pogrebin, "Nothing to Prove, George Wolfe Is Liberated," *New York Times*, August 19, 2002, sec. E, p. 1.

23. Parks, *America Play*, p. 199.

24. Garrett, "Possession of Suzan-Lori Parks," p. 133.

25. *Ibid.*

26. Steven Winn, "'America' Gives History a Re-Do," *San Francisco Chronicle*, December 7, 1994 [cited May 19, 2003], http://www.brava.org/Pages/Reviews/AmPl_america.html.

27. Savran, p. 158.

28. Parks quoted in Deborah Gregory, "Suzan-Lori Parks Plays It Straight," *Essence*, February 2002, p. 80.

29. Drukman, p. 67.

30. Garrett, "Possession of Suzan-Lori Parks," p. 26.

31. Paula's comment in Vogel, letter to author, December 23, 2002.

32. Nelson Pressley, "'Blood': for Wooly, a New Dimension," *Washington Post*, final edition, January 16, 2001, sec. C, p. 1.

33. Michael Phillips, "Next Theatre's 'In the Blood' a Tragedy with Human Touch," *Chicago Tribune*, February 6, 2003, "Tempo" sec., p. 3.

34. Justin Hayford, "Symbol-Minded Message," *Chicago Reader*, February 14, 2003, sec. 1, p. 30.

35. Phillips, "Our History, Her Language," p. 1.

36. Shewey, "This Time."

37. Isherwood, "Topdog/Underdog."

38. Pochoda, "I See Thuh Black Card."

39. Matthew Murray, "Topdog/Underdog" (review), April 7, 2002, for "Talkin' Broadway" [cited July 8, 2002], http://www.allthatchat.com/world/topdogunderdog.html.

40. Brantley, "Not to Worry, Mr. Lincoln."

41. Isherwood.

42. Shewey.

43. Pochoda, p. 8.

44. Garrett, "Possession of Suzan-Lori Parks," p. 134.

45. Miller and Cotliar, "Best in Show," p. 143.

46. Brustein quoted in "Notable and Quotable," *The Wall Street Journal*, May 14, 2002, sec. D, p. 7.

47. Miller and Cotliar, "Best in Show," accompanying photo caption.

48. David Hinkle, "Fucking A" (review), March 17, 2003, for *TheaterMania.Com* [cited May 17, 2003], http:www.theatremania.com/content/news.cfm?int_news_id=3258.

49. Brantley, "A Woman Named Hester."

50. Scheck, "Fucking A" (review).

51. Gerald Rabkin, "Fucking A" (review), at *CultureVulture.net* [cited May 17, 2003], http://www.culturevulture.net/Theater5/FuckingA.htm.

52. Parks quoted in Kay Bourne, "Surrealistic Playwright Seeks to Tell of Unrecorded History," *Bay State Banner*, March 31, 1994, p. 17.

53. Steven Boone, "Topdog/Underdog," *Show Business* [cited April 9, 2002], http://www.showbusinessweekly.com/archives,136/top-dog.html.

54. Parks quoted in Phillips, "Our History, Her Language."

55. Elyse Sommers, "F***ing A—A Curtain Up Review" [cited May 17, 2003], http://www.curtainup.com/fuckinga.html.
56. Frank Scheck, "Fucking A" (review).
57. All dialogue quotes and set notations from Parks, *Topdog/Underdog*.
58. Ed Blank, "'Topdog' Draws Siblings as Prisoners of Their Own Legacy," Pittsburgh *Tribune-Review*, May 19, 2002 [cited September 15, 2003], http://www.pittsburghlive.com/x/s_71748.htm.
59. Charles Isherwood, "Topdog/Underdog" (review).
60. Michael Phillips, "'Topdog' Doesn't Soar as High as Parks' Best," *Chicago-Tribune*, September 22, 2003, sec. 5, pp. 1, 5.

20. "Also in the Winner's Circle"

1. Wilkerson, *Nine Plays*, p. xix; statistics on productions of plays by black women given by Mahone, editor, in her introduction to *Moon Marked*, pp. xv–xxvi.
2. Wilkerson, *Nine Plays*, pp. xv–xvi.
3. Angelina Grimké, "'Rachel,' The Play of the Month: The Reason and Synopsis by the Author," *The Competitor*, June 1920, p. 52.
4. Tisch Jones, introduction to *Rachel* in *Black Theatre, USA*, James V. Hatch and Ted Shine, eds. (New York: Free Press, 1996), p. 134.
5. Perkins, *Black Female Playwrights*, p. 5.
6. *Ibid.*, pp. 12–13.
7. *Ibid.*; Cheryl A. Wall, compiler, *Zora Neale Hurston* (New York: Library of America, 1995), p. 1,020.
8. "All Eyes on Zora" at Magic Negro website: http://beatsandrants.blogs.com/magic_negro/2004/04/all_eyes_on_zor.html [cited September 20, 2004].
9. Perkins and Stephens, *Strange Fruit*, pp. 5–6.
10. Lines excerpted from "A Black Woman Speaks" by Beah Richards, courtesy of Sherry Fisher Green and the Beah Richards Estate. (All rights reserved by the Estate.)

11. Phone conversation with LisaGay Hamilton, April 29, 2004.
12. Shange quoted in Mahone, p. 325.
13. Cleage, telephone interview by author.
14. *Ibid.*
15. Chill, "Pearl Cleage: *Deals with the Devil*," *Cleveland Call and Post*, July 28, 1994, http://www.fb10.uni-bremen.de/anglistik/kerkhoff/ContempDrama/Cleage.htm [cited August 27, 2002].
16. Cleage, telephone interview by author.
17. *Ibid.*
18. Rahman quoted in Mahone, p. 283.
19. Vogel, interview by author.
20. Corthron quoted in Mahone, p. 37.
21. Danitra Vance, *Live and in Color*, in Mahone, p. 396.
22. Jackson quoted in Mahone, pp. 145, 148–49. Play quote p. 165.
23. *Ibid.*, pp. 148–49.

Epilogue: Parting Thoughts on Family Flux and Cultural Flummery

1. Today's Family Help Center web site [cited August 14, 2001], www.familyhelponline.com.
2. Coontz, *Way We Never Were*, p. 21.
3. Crary, "Not Just Mom and Pop," p. 3.
4. Gilman quoted in Barbara Ehrenreich and Diedre English, *For Her Own Good* (New York: Anchor Books, 1979), p. 74. See also Woloch, *Women*, pp. 344–45.
5. Steinem, *Revolution from Within*, pp. 4–5, 57–59.
6. Coontz, p. 2.
7. Vogel, interview by author.
8. Karen Malpede, foreword to Partnow, *The Female Dramatist*, pp. ix–x.
9. Cleage, telephone interview by author.
10. Malpede, p. ix.
11. Norman quoted in Tisch Dace, "Sexism in the Theatre," *Backstage*, March 5, 1993, pp. 20, 25.
12. Cleage, telephone interview by author.

Selected Bibliography

Primary Sources

Cleage, Pearl. Telephone interview by author. January 21, 2003.
Edson, Margaret. Interview by author. New York City, May 23, 1999.
———. Letters to author. July/August 2000, November/December 2002, and June 2003.
Faludi, Susan. Address at Chicago Public Library (Main Branch), October 4, 1999.
Henley, Beth. Interview by author. Center Theater, Chicago, Ill., January 21, 1992.
———. Interview by author for doctoral dissertation. Chicago, Ill., November 14, 1990. Begun via telephone, concluded at Wisdom Bridge Theatre, Chicago.
———. Letters to author. April 1992.
———. "Playwrights Workshop." Center Theater, Chicago, Ill., January 20–24, 1992.
———. Telephone interview by author. March 12, 2003.
Norman, Marsha. Interview by author. New York City, August 6, 1991.
———. Letters to author. February 1992.
———. Phone call and e-mail exchange via agents in N.Y.C., July–August 2002.
Steinem, Gloria. Address at Loyola University, Chicago, Lakeshore Campus, October 28, 1998.
Vogel, Paula. Interview by author. Arena Stage, Washington, D.C., October 5, 1998.
———. Letters to author. December 2002.
Wasserstein, Wendy. Address at Pace University, New York City, March 2, 1992.
———. E-mail to author. March 2003.
———. "He and She." Keynote speech at Chicago Humanities Festival, Orchestra Hall, November 8, 1998.
———. Interview by author. New York City, March 2, 1992.
———. Letters to author. Fall 1992.

Books, Dissertations, and Unpublished Manuscripts

Adler, Thomas P. *Mirror on the Stage*. West Lafayette, Ind.: Purdue University Press, 1987.
Allen, Frederick Lewis. *Only Yesterday*. New York: Harper & Row, 1964.
Andreas, Carol. *Sex and Caste in America*. Englewood Cliffs, N.J.: Prentice-Hall, Inc., 1971.
Andreas, Joel. *Addicted to War*. Oakland, Calif.: AK Press, 2002, 2003.
Babcox, Deborah, and Madeline Belken, eds. *Liberation Now!* New York: Dell Publishing, 1971.
Bassnett, Susan. *Feminist Experiences*. London: Allen & Unwin, 1986.
Berger, Maurice Albert. "Mary Coyle Chase: Her Battlefield of Dreams." Ph.D. dissertation, University of Denver, 1970. Ann Arbor, Mich.: UMI, 1971.
Betsko, Kathleen, and Rachel Koenig. *Interviews with Contemporary Women Playwrights*. New York: Beech Tree Books/William Morrow, 1987.
Blum, David, and John Kobal. *A New Pictorial History of the Talkies*. New York: Perigee Books–Putnam's, 1982.
Bonin, Jane. *Major Themes in Prize-Winning American Drama*. Metuchen, N.J.: Scarecrow Press, 1975.
Brater, Enoch, ed. *Feminine Focus*. New York: Oxford University Press, 1989.
Campbell, Robert. *The Golden Years of Broadcasting: A Celebration of the First 50 Years of Radio and TV on NBC*. New York: Charles Scribner's Sons, 1976.
Chinoy, Helen Krich, and Linda Walsh Jenkins. *Women in American Theatre*. New York: Theatre Communications, 1987.
Chomsky, Noam. *Power and Terror: Post 9/11 Talks and Interviews*. New York: Seven Stories Press, 2003.
Cleage, Pearl. *Deals with the Devil and Other Reasons to Riot*. New York: Ballantine Books, 1993.
Coontz, Stephanie. *The Way We Never Were: American Families and the Nostalgia Trap*. New York: Harper Collins–Basic Books, 1992.
Corbett, Ruth. *Daddy Danced the Charleston*. Cranbury, N.J.: A.S. Barnes, 1970.
Deats, Sara Munsen, and Lagretta Tallent Lenker. *The Aching Hearth*. New York: Plenum Press, 1991.
Derleth, August. *Still Small Voice: The Biography of Zona Gale*. New York: Appleton Century, 1940.
Dorenkamp, Angela G., and John McClymer, eds. *Images of Women in American Popular Culture*. New York: Harcourt Brace, 1985.
Ehrenreich, Barbara. *The Worst Years of Our Lives: Irreverent Notes from a Decade of Greed*. New York: Harper Perennial, 1991.
Faludi, Susan. *Backlash: The Undeclared War Against American Women*. New York: Doubleday, 1992.
Ferguson, Mary Anne. *Images of Women in Literature*. 2nd ed. Boston: Houghton Mifflin, 1977.
Flexnor, Eleanor, ed. *American Playwrights, 1918–1938*. New York: Simon & Schuster, 1938.

Friday, Nancy. *My Mother/My Self.* New York: Dell Publishing, 1978.
Friedan, Betty. *The Feminine Mystique.* New York: W.W. Norton, 1963.
____. *The Feminine Mystique.* Tenth anniversary edition. New York: W.W. Norton, 1974.
Gale, Zona. *Birth.* New York: The Macmillan Co., 1918.
____. *Miss Lulu Bett.* New York: Grosset & Dunlap, 1920.
Gilligan, Carol. *In a Different Voice.* Cambridge, Mass.: Harvard University Press, 1982.
Gould, Jean. *Modern American Playwrights.* New York: Dodd, Mead, 1966.
Hagan, Kay Leigh, ed. *Women Respond to the Men's Movement.* San Francisco: Harper Collins–Pandora Press, 1992.
Harriott, Esther. *American Voices: Five Contemporary Playwrights in Essays and Interviews.* Jefferson, N.C.: McFarland, 1988.
Hohenberg, John. *The Pulitzer Prizes: A History of the Awards in Books, Drama, Music and Journalism, Based on the Private Files over Six Decades.* New York: Columbia University Press, 1974.
Huffington, Arianna. *How to Overthrow the Government.* New York: Harper Collins–Regan Books, 2001.
Jezer, Marty. *The Dark Ages: Life in the United States 1945–1960.* Boston: South End Press, 1982.
Malpede, Karen, ed. *Women in Theatre: Compassion and Hope.* New York: Drama Book Publishers, 1983.
Marshall, Richard, ed. *Great Events of the 20th Century.* Pleasantville, N.Y.: The Readers Digest Associates, 1977.
Moore, Honor, ed. *The New Women's Theatre: Ten Plays by Contemporary Women.* New York: Vintage Books, 1977.
Moore, Michael. *Dude, Where's My Country?* New York: Warner Books, 2003.
____. *Stupid White Men and Other Sorry Excuses for the State of the Nation.* New York: Harper Collins–Regan Books, 2001.
Napier, Nancy J. *Recreating Your Self.* New York: W.W. Norton, 1990.
Nathan, George Jean. *The Theatre, the Drama, the Girls.* New York: Alfred Knopf, 1921.
Partnow, Elaine T. *The Female Dramatist.* New York: Facts on File, 1998.
Perkin, Robert. *The First Hundred Years: An Informal History of Denver and the "Rocky Mountain News."* Garden City, N.Y.: Doubleday, 1959.
Peterson, Jane T., and Suzanne Bennett. *Women Playwrights of Diversity.* Westport, Conn.: Greenwood Press, 1997.
Prost, Antoine, and Gerard Vincent, eds. *A History of Private Life.* Vol. 5. Cambridge, Mass.: Belknap Press, 1991.
Riley, Jocelyn. "Zona Gale: Her Life and Writings—A Resource Guide." Madison Wisc., 1990. Privately duplicated and circulated.
Roszak, Betty, and Theodore Roszak, eds. *Masculine/Feminine.* New York: Harper & Row, 1969.
Rothe, Anna, ed. *Current Biography–1945.* New York: H. W. Wilson, 1945.
Ryan, Mary P. *Womanhood in America.* New York: New Viewpoints, 1975.
Sanger, Margaret. *Women and the New Race.* New York: Brentano's Inc., 1920.

Sarlos, Robert Karoly. *Jig Cook and the Provincetown Players.* University of Massachusetts Press, 1982.
Savran, David. *The Playwright's Voice.* New York: Theatre Communications Group, 1999.
Scanlon, Tom. *Family, Drama, and American Dreams.* Westport, Conn.: Greenwood Press, 1978.
Schneir, Miriam, ed. *Feminism: The Essential Historical Writings.* New York: Random House, 1972.
Shannon, David A. *Twentieth-Century America: The Twenties and Thirties.* Vol. 2. 3rd ed. Chicago: Rand-McNally, 1972.
Shearer, Ann. *Woman: Her Changing Image.* Rochester, Vt.: Thorson's Publishing Group, 1987.
Simonson, Harold P. *Zona Gale.* New York: Twayne Publishers, 1962.
Skolnik, Peter L. *Fads: America's Crazes, Fevers and Fancies from the 1890s to the 1970s.* New York: Thomas Y. Crowell, 1978.
Slide, Anthony, ed. *Selected Theatre Criticism.* Vol. 1, 1900–1919. Metuchen, N.J.: The Scarecrow Press, 1985.
———. *Selected Theatre Criticism.* Vol. 3, 1931–1950. Metuchen, N.J.: The Scarecrow Press, 1985.
Steinem, Gloria. *Moving Beyond Words.* New York: Simon & Schuster, 1994.
———. *Revolution from Within.* Boston: Little, Brown, 1992.
Stoltenberg, John. *Refusing to Be a Man: Essays on Sex and Justice.* New York: Meridian Press, 1990.
Swerdlow, Amy, Renate Bridenthal, Joan Kelly, and Phyllis Vine. *Families in Flux.* New York: The Feminist Press, 1989.
Toohey, John L. *A History of the Pulitzer Prize Plays.* New York: The Citadel Press, 1967.
Vidal, Gore. *Dreaming War: Blood for Oil and the Cheney-Bush Junta.* New York: Nation Books, 2002.
Walker, Alice. *Sent by Earth.* New York: Seven Stories Press, 2001.
Wasserstein, Wendy. *Bachelor Girls.* New York: Alfred A. Knopf, 1990.
———. *Shiksa Goddess (Or, How I Spent My Forties).* New York: Alfred A. Knopf, 2001.
Waterman, Arthur E. *Susan Glaspell.* New York: Twayne Publishers, 1966.
Willingham, Ralph, "'Introduce Them to Harvey': Mary Chase and the Theatre." Master's thesis, East Texas State University, 1987.
Woloch, Nancy. *Women and the American Experience.* New York: Alfred A. Knopf, 1984.

Periodical and Internet Articles

Articles Relating to Gale, Glaspell, Akins, and Their Contexts

Akins, Zoe. "Philosophy of an Adaptation." *New York Times,* January 13, 1935, pp. 1, 3.
———. "The Playwriting Passion." *Vanity Fair,* June 6, 1920, pp. 61, 106.

Atkinson, J. Brooks. "The Play." Review of *The Furies*. *New York Times*, March 8, 1928, Entertainment Section, n.p. Akins File, Archives of the New York Library for Performing Arts at Lincoln Center.
Ben-Zvi, Linda. "Susan Glaspell's Contributions to Contemporary Women Playwrights." *Feminine Focus*. Edited by Enoch Brater. New York: Oxford University Press, 1989.
Caldwell, Betty. "Winning Pulitzer Prize Makes Mary Chase's Life Dream Reality." *Rocky Mountain News*, May 8, 1945, p. 5.
Catton, Bruce. "The Restless Decade." *American Heritage*. Vol. 16, no. 5 (August 1965), pp. 4–6, 18.
Chapman, John A. "Zoe Akins—Experimenter in the Drama Laboratory." *The Spotlight*, December 24, 1921, p. 2.
"Daddy's Gone A-Hunting." Review of Akins' play. *Theatre*, November 1921, p. 315.
Inge, Benson. "The Author of Twenty Plays, Zoe Akins Adds Still Another." *New York Herald Tribune*, May 11, 1941, p. 1.
Mantle, Burns. "Declasse." Review of Akins' play. *The Green Book Magazine*, December 1919, pp. 54–56.
McCord, Bert. "Zoe Akins Has Finished Two Plays." *New York Herald Tribune*, September 5, 1943, p. 5.
Morehouse, Ward. "Broadway After Dark." *New York Evening Sun*, May 24, 1941, n.p. Akins File, Archives of the New York Library for Performing Arts at Lincoln Center.
Rapp, William. "A Self-Made Greek Hero from America." *New York Herald Tribune*, January 3, 1926, p. 3.
Reston, James B. "New York by Day and Night." *St. Paul Pioneer Press*, December 14, 1935, n.p. Akins File, Archives of the New York Library for Performing Arts at Lincoln Center.
Sumner, Keene. "The Everlasting Persistence of This Western Girl." *The American Magazine*, June 1921, pp. 34–35, 137–41.
Woollcott, Alexander. "Zowie: Or the Curse of an Akins Heart." *Vanity Fair*, July 1922, pp. 67, 101.
Yongue, Patricia Lee. "Zoe Akins." *American Women Writers*. Edited by Langdon Lynne Faust. New York: Ungar, 1988.

Articles Relating to Chase and Frings and Their Contexts

Atkinson, Brooks. "The Theatre: 'Look Homeward, Angel.'" *New York Times*, November 29, 1957.
Battelle, Phyllis. "A Write Nice Salary." *New York Journal-American*, July 9, 1955, p. 7.
Brady, Thomas. "Hollywood Digest." *New York Times*, March 19, 1950. p. 5.
Chase, Mary. "My Life with Harvey." *McCall's*, February 1951, pp. 53–57.
Cook, Joan. "Ketti Frings, Stage and Film Writer." *New York Times*, February 13, 1981, sec. A, p. 16.
Coughlin, Robert. "Changing Roles in Marriage." *Life*, December 24, 1956, pp. 110–116.

Gent, George. "Three Stars to Be in 'Angel' for C.B.S.-TV on Feb. 25." *New York Times*, January 29, 1972, n.p.
Hewes, Henry. "Broadway Postscript: Thomas Wolfe's 'Angel.'" *Saturday Review*, November 23, 1957, pp. 27–28
Melrose, Frances. "Mrs. Chase Pleased with Care of Harvey." *Rocky Mountain News*, February 28, 1977, pp. 7–9.
"PM Visits: The White Rabbit Lady," PM, November 6, 1944, p. 16. Lincoln Center Archives.
Reef, Wallis M. "She Didn't Write It for Money—She Says." *Saturday Evening Post*, September 1, 1945, p. 109.
Skinner, Cornelia Otis. "Women Are Misguided." *Life*, December 24, 1956, pp. 73–75.
Sullivan, Robert. "Mrs. Chase of Denver." *Sunday News*, November 16, 1952, p. 94.
"Wednesday Editorials: Mary Chase." *Rocky Mountain News*, October 21, 1981, p. 50.
Zolotow, Sam. "Prize Dramatist Producing Play." *New York Times*, August 4, 1961, p. L-24.

Articles Relating to Henley, Norman, Wasserstein and Their Contexts

Allen, Robert L., and Paul Kivel. "Men Challenging Men." *Ms.*, September/October 1994, pp. 50–53.
Avery, Caryl S. "Shame." *New Woman*, May 1991, pp. 48–52.
Branden, Dr. Nathaniel. "A Woman's Self-Esteem." *New Woman*, January 1993, pp. 56–58.
Burleigh, Nina. "The Wendy Chronicle." *Chicago Tribune*, October 21, 1990, sec. 6 (Tempo), pp. 1, 8.
Carter, Tom. "Humana Festival breeds success, failure." *Kentucky Enquirer*, April 3, 1988. n.p. (reproduced on press release from Tantleff Agency, N.Y., June 1991).
Cawley, Janet. "A Playwright's Birth Pangs." *Chicago Tribune* arts magazine, March 15, 1992, sec. 13, pp. 22–23.
Cocks, Jay. "How Long Till Equality?" *Time*, July 12, 1982, pp. 20–29.
Cohen, Esther. "An Interview with Wendy Wasserstein." In *Women's Studies*. Vol. 15. Edited by Wendy Martin. New York: Gordon and Breach, 1988.
Conniff, Ruth. "Interview: Susan Faludi." *The Progressive*. Vol. 57, no. 6 (June 1993), pp. 35–38.
Dace, Tish. "Sexism in the Theatre." *Backstage*, March 5, 1993.
Ehrenreich, Barbara. "Sorry, Sisters, This Is Not the Revolution." *Time* Special Issue, "Women: The Road Ahead," fall 1990, p. 15.
Gibbs, Nancy. "The Dreams of Youth." *Time* Special Issue, "Women: The Road Ahead," fall 1990, pp. 10–14.
———. "The War Against Feminism." *Time*, March 9, 1992, pp. 52–55.
———, and Jeanne McDowell. "How to Revive a Revolution." *Time*, March 9, 1992, pp. 56–57.
Gill, Brendan. "Wake of Jamie Foster." *New Yorker*, October 25, 1982, p. 161.

Gross, Amy. "Marsha Norman: Pulitzer Prize Winner." *Vogue*, July 1983, pp. 200–201, 256–58.
Haller, Scot. "Her First Play, Her First Pulitzer Prize." *Saturday Review*, November 1981, pp. 41–44.
Himes, Geoffrey. "Norman Highlights Annual Event." *The Columbia Flier*, March 31, 1988, pp. 80–81.
Hitchcock, Laura. "Hi Ho, the Passionate Life." *Performing Arts* (L.A.), July 1992, pp. 15–18.
Hoban, Phoebe. "The Family Wasserstein." *New York*, January 4, 1993, pp. 32–37.
Horwitz, Simi. "The Playwright as Woman." *Theater Week*, August 26–September 1, 1991, pp. 22–27.
Hubbard, Kim. "Bio: Wendy Wasserstein." *People*, June 25, 1990, pp. 100–106.
Jackal, Molly, and Steven Manning. "Long March to Equality." *Scholastic Update*, March 12, 1993, pp. 12–13.
Jacobs, Tom. "Control Freaks." *Variety*, August 9, 1993, p. 35.
Jacobson, Lynn. "The Heidi Mystique." *Stagebill* (Chicago), December 1991, pp. 24–26.
Jaehne, Karen. "Beth's Beauties." *Film Comment*, May/June 1989, pp. 9–16.
Kauffmann, Stanley. "Two Cheers for Two Plays." *Saturday Review*, January 1982, pp. 54–55.
Kroll, Jack. "A Modern Crisis of Faith." *Newsweek*, February 27, 1984, p. 76.
"Let's Get Real about Feminism." A debate with Gloria Steinem, bell hooks, Naomi Wolf, and Urvashi Vaid. *Ms.*, September/October 1993, pp. 34–43.
Matthews, Jack. "No Southern Comfort." *American Film*, December 1989, pp. 28–33.
McGee, Celia. "Gambling on a Garden." *New York*, April 22, 1991, pp. 65–71.
O'Haire, Patricia. "Valuing Families—and a Good Laugh." *Detroit Free Press*, December 6, 1992, p. 6-P.
Oliver, Edith. "Crimes of the Heart." *New Yorker*, January 12, 1981.
Rich, Frank. "'Firecracker'—A Beth Henley Comedy." *New York Times*, May 28, 1984, p. 11.
Rosen, Carol. "Wendy's World: An Unconventional Life." *Theater Week*, November 2, 1992, pp. 17–27.
Shepard, Alan Clarke. "Aborted Rage in Beth Henley's Women." *Modern Drama*, no. 39 (1993), pp. 96–107.
Simon, John. "The Best So Far." *New York*, November 2, 1992, pp. 100–101.
Sommer, Elyse. "Family Week." Review. *Curtain Up*, April 2000 [cited January 12, 2003], http://www.curtainup.com/familyweek.html.
Stange, Mary Zeiss. "Disarmed by Fear." *American Rifleman*, March 1992, pp. 34–37, 92.
Stone, Elizabeth. "Playwright Marsha Norman: An Optimist Writes about Suicide, Confinement, and Despair." *Ms.*, July 1983, pp. 56–59.
Stout, Kate. "Marsha Norman: Writing for the 'Least of Our Brethren.'" *Saturday Review*, September/October 1983, pp. 29–33.
Sydney, Leah. "Mission Impossible." *Culture Finder*. February 19, 1999 [cited Feb-

ruary 21, 1999], http://www.newyork.digitalcity.com/culturefinder/Henley.dci.
Walker, Beverly. "Beth Henley." *American Film*, December 1986, pp. 30–31.
Wyse, Lois. "The Way We Were." *Good Housekeeping*, April 1992, p. 252.

Articles Relating to Vogel, Edson, and Their Contexts

Albis, Theron. "In the Spotlight: Margaret Edson." *Stage and Screen*, n.d. [cited June 22, 2000]. http://www.stagenscreen.com/mybookclub/s...s/sns/Special/Authors/Margaret_Edson.htm.
Clay, Carolyn. "Donne Deal." THE BOSTON PHOENIX, January 20–27, 2000 [cited June 2, 2000]. http://www.bostonphoenix.com/archive/theatre/00/01/27/MARGARET_EDSON.htm.
Coen, Stephanie. "No Need for Gravity." *American Theatre*, April 1993, p. 26.
Drukman, Steven. "A Playwright on the Edge Turns Toward the Middle." *New York Times*, March 16, 1997, sec. C., p. 6.
Eisler, Riane. "What Do Men Really Want." In *Women Respond to the Men's Movement*. Edited by Kay Leigh Hagen. San Francisco: Harper Collins–Pandora, 1992, pp. 43–53.
Halpern, Sue. "Susan Faludi: The Mother Jones Interview." *MOJOwire* magazine, September/October 1999 [cited May 10, 2000]. http://www.motherjones.com/mother_jones/S099/Faludi.html.
Hughes, Holly. "In the Driver's Seat." *The Advocate*, January 20, 1998, p. 99.
Kelly, Jason. "Wit and Wisdom." *Georgetown Magazine*, n.d. [cited June 22, 2002]. http://www.smu.edu/~tmayo/geotownmag.htm.
Koerner, Brenden. "A Lust for Profits." *U.S. News & World Report*, March 27, 2000, pp. 36–42.
Lehrer, Jim. "Love and Knowledge." *Online Newshour*. April 14, 1999 [cited May 13, 1999]. http://www.pbs.org.newshour/bb/entertainment/jan-june99/edson_4-14.html.
Pressley, Nelson. "A Teacher's 'Wit' and Wisdom." *Washington Post*, February 27, 2000, p. G-1.
Rosenthal, Phil. "Matters of Life and Death." *Chicago Sun-Times*, March 22, 2001, p. 41.
Ruether, Rosemary Radford. "Patriarchy and the Men's Movement." In *Women Respond to the Men's Movement*. Edited by Kay Leigh Hagen. San Francisco: Harper Collins–Pandora, 1992, pp. 13–18.
Sack, Kevin. "Margaret Edson: Colors, Numbers, Letters and John Donne." *New York Times*, November 10, 1998, sec. E, p. 1.
Savran, David. "Driving Ms. Vogel." *American Theatre*, October 1998, pp. 16–18, 96–105.
Steinem, Gloria. Foreword to *Women Respond to the Men's Movement*. San Francisco: Harper Collins–Pandora, 1992, pp. v–ix.
"Women and Men, Can We Get Along?" *Utne Reader*, January/February 1993, pp. 52–76.

Selected Bibliography 327

Articles Relating to "Parks and Other Sisters," Their Contexts, and to the Epilogue

Berthelsen, Christian. "Big Banks Helped Enron, Probe Finds." *San Francisco Chronicle*, July 23, 2002, p. B-1.

Booth, Michael. "The Media Death Watch Machine: Witnessing the Pop Culture Hemorrhage." *Denver Post*, October 23, 2003, p. F-1.

Brantley, Ben. "Not to Worry, Mr. Lincoln, It's Just a Con Game." *New York Times*, April 8, 2002, sec. E, p. 1.

———. "A Woman Named Hester, Wearing a Familiar Letter." *New York Times*, March 17, 2003, sec. E, p. 1.

Brook, Dan. "Fueling the Empire." *Counterpunch*, April 17, 2003 [cited April 23, 2003]. http://www.counterpunch.org/brook04172003.html.

Chittister, Joan, OSB. "Is There Anything Left That Matters?" *Common Dreams News Center*, May 29, 2003 [cited May 29, 2003]. http://www.comdreams.org/views03/0529-10.htm.

Crary, David. "Not Just Mom and Pop." *Chicago Sun-Times*, Red-Streak Edition, August 5, 2003, p. 3.

Drukman, Steven. "Suzan-Lori Parks and Liz Diamond." *The Drama Review*, fall 1995, pp. 56–75.

Fanger, Iris. "Pulitzer Prize Winner Shakes Off Labels." *Christian Science Monitor*, April 12, 2002, p. 19.

Floyd, Chris. "Blood on the Tracks." *Counterpunch*, March 29, 2003 [cited March 31, 2003]. http://www.counterpunch.org/Floyd03292003.htm.

Garrett, Shawn-Marie. "The Possession of Suzan-Lori Parks." *American Theatre*, October 2000, pp. 22–26, 132–34.

Goldstein, Richard. "The Shock and Awe Show." *Village Voice*, March 26–April 1, 2003 [cited May 6, 2003]. http://www.villagevoice.com/issues/0313/goldstein.php.

———. "Stealth Misogyny." *Village Voice*, March 5–11, 2003, p. 43.

Heard, Linda. "Here Come the Fat Cats—Journalists Die, the Networks Lie, Iraqis Ask 'Why.'" *Counterpunch*, April 8, 2003 [cited May 10, 2003]. http://www.counterpunch.org/heard04082003.html.

———. "Repeat After Me: Iraq Is Weapons Free." COUNTERPUNCH Online, April 28, 2003. http://www.counterpunch.org/heard04282003.html (May 3, 2002).

Isherwood, Charles. "Topdog/Underdog" (review). *Variety*, August 6, 2001 [cited July 8, 2002]. http://www.findarticles.com/cf_0/m1312/11-383/77227950/print.jhtml.

Jackson, Derrick Z. "Burying the Number of Civilian Deaths in Iraq." *Chicago Tribune*, June 16, 2003, p. 15.

Krieger, David. "Bush's War on the Poor." *Counterpunch*, May 24, 2003 [cited May 29, 2003]. http://www.counterpunch.org/krieger05242003.html.

Maier, Francis X. "Why Video Games Are Great ... and Scary." *Crisis*, May 2003, pp. 35–39.

Malpede. Karen. Foreword to Elaine T. Partnow. *The Female Dramatists*. New York: Facts on File, 1998.

Matsui, Leila. "Regime Change Begins at Home." *Counterpunch*, May 5, 2003 [cited May 7, 2003]. http://www.counterpunch.org/matsui05052003.html.
Miller, Samantha, and Sharon Cotliar. "Best in Show." *People*, June 2, 2003, pp. 143–44.
Moyers, Bill. "This Is Your Story: The Progressive Story of America—Pass It On." *Common Dreams News Center*, June 10, 2003 [cited June 11, 2003]. http://www.commondreams.org/views/03/0610-11.htm.
Phillips, Michael. "Our History, Her Language." *Los Angeles Times*, July 8, 2001, Calendar Section, p. 1.
Pochoda, Elizabeth. "I See Thuh Black Card." *Nation*, May 27, 2002, p. 36.
Roy, Arundhati. "Instant-Mix Imperial Democracy: Buy One, Get One Free." *Common Dreams News Center*, May 18, 2003 [cited June 16, 2003]. http://www.commondreams.org/views/03/0518-01.html.
Schakowsky, Jan. Transcript of "Take Back America" Conference Speech, Washington, D.C., June 4, 2003 [cited June 9, 2003]. *Buzz*. http://www.buzzflash.com/contributors/03/05/05_schakowsky.htm.
Scheck, Frank. "Fucking A." Review. *Hollywood Reporter*, March 18–24, 2003, p. 20.
Shechner, Richard. "The Age of Terrorism." *The Drama Review*, summer 2002, pp. 5–6.
Shewey, Don. "This Time the Shock Is Her Turn toward Naturalism." *New York Times*, July 22, 2001, sec. 2, p. 4.
Smith, Sharon. "New Phase in the War on Women's Rights." *Counterpunch*, February 10, 2003 [cited March 25, 2003]. http://www.counterpunch.org/smith021003.html.
"The War Against Women." Editorial. *New York Times*, January 12, 2003, sec. 4, p. 14.
Wellman, David, and Charles Piller. "Anti-War Activists Join Forces; Tens of Thousands Rally in Washington, San Francisco and Elsewhere against Policy on Iraq." *Los Angeles Times*, January 19, 2003, p. A-1.
Zakaria, Fareed. "The Arrogant Empire." *Newsweek*, March 24, 2003, pp. 20–31.

PLAYS AND PLAY ANTHOLOGIES

Akins, Zoe. *The Old Maid*. From the novel by Edith Wharton. New York: Appleton-Century, Co., 1935.
Barlow, Judith. *Plays by American Women: 1900–1930*. New York: Applause Theatre Books, 1985.
Bigsby, C.W.E., ed. *Plays by Susan Glaspell*. Cambridge, MA: Cambridge University Press, 1987.
Chase, Mary Coyle. *Harvey*. New York: Dramatists Play Service, 1970.
Cleage, Pearl. *Flyin' West and Other Plays*. New York: Theatre Communications Group, 1999.
Congdon, Constance. *Tales of the Lost Formicans and Other Plays*. New York: Theatre Communications Group, 1994.
Edson, Margaret. *Wit*. New York: Dramatists Play Service, 1999.

Frank, Leah D., ed. *Facing Forward*. New York: Broadway Play Publishing, 1995.
Frings, Ketti. *Look Homeward, Angel*. New York: Samuel French, 1959.
Gale, Zona. *Miss Lulu Bett*. In *Plays by American Women: 1900–1930*. Edited by Judith E. Barlow. New York: Applause Theatre Books, 1985. [This version contains original ending.]
———. *Miss Lulu Bett*. In *The Pulitzer Prize Plays, 1918–1934*. Edited by Kathryn Coe and William H. Cordell. New York: Random House, 1935.
Glaspell, Susan. *Alison's House*. New York: Samuel French, 1930.
Hamalian, Leo, and James V. Hatch, eds. *The Roots of African-American Drama: An Anthology of Early Plays, 1858–1938*. Detroit: Wayne State University Press, 1991.
Henley, Beth. *Collected Plays*. Vol. 1. Lyme, N.H.: Smith & Kraus, 2000.
———. *Collected Plays*. Vol. 2. Lyme, N.H.: Smith & Kraus, 2000.
———. *Crimes of the Heart*. New York: Viking Press, 1982.
———. *Impossible Marriage*. New York: Dramatists Play Service, 1999.
———. *The Miss Firecracker Contest*. Garden City, N.Y.: Doubleday, 1985.
Mahone, Sydné, ed. *Moon Marked and Touched by Sun: Plays by African-American Women*. New York: Theatre Communications Group, 1994.
Moore, Honor, ed. *The New Women's Theatre: Ten Plays by Contemporary American Women*. New York: Vintage Books, 1977.
Norman, Marsha. *Four Plays*. New York: Theatre Communications Group, 1988.
———. *'Night, Mother*. New York: Dramatists Play Service, 1983.
Parks, Suzan-Lori. *The America Play and Other Works*. New York: Theatre Communication Group, 1995.
———. *The Red Letter Plays*. New York: Theatre Communications Group, 2001.
———. *Topdog/Underdog*. New York: Theatre Communications Group, 2001.
Perkins, Kathy A. *Black Female Playwrights*. Indiana University Press, 1989.
———, and Judith L. Stephens. *Strange Fruit: Plays on Lynching by American Women*. Indiana University Press, 1998.
Shange, Ntozake. *For Colored Girls Who Have Considered Suicide/When the Rainbow Is Enuf*. New York: Macmillian, 1976.
Turner, Darwin, ed. *Black Drama in America*. Washington, D.C. Howard University Press, 1994.
Vogel, Paula. *The Baltimore Waltz and Other Plays*. New York: Theatre Communications Group, 1996.
———. *How I Learned to Drive*. New York: Dramatists Play Service, 1998.
———. *The Mammary Plays*. New York: Theatre Communications Group, 1998.
Wasserstein, Wendy. *An American Daughter*. New York: Harcourt Brace, 1998.
———. *The Heidi Chronicles and Other Plays*. New York: Vintage Books, 1991.
———. *The Sisters Rosensweig*. New York: Harcourt Brace, 1993.
Wilkerson, Margaret B. *Nine Plays by Black Women*. New York: Mentor Books, 1982.

SPECIAL COLLECTIONS AND ARCHIVES

State Historical Society of Wisconsin, at University of Wisconsin, Madison. Archives, Special Zona Gale Collection.

New York Public Library for the Performing Arts, Lincoln Center, New York. Archives, Special Collection Files on: Zoe Akins, Mary Coyle Chase, Ketti Frings, Susan Glaspell.

WEB SITES

www.counterpunch.org.
www.commondreams.org.
Columbia Journalism Review—"Who Owns What?" at www.cjr.org/tools/owners/asp.
"Women of Color, Women of Words" at http://www.scils.rutgers.edu/~cybers/home.html.

Index

Actors Theatre of Louisville 145–146, 167–169, 172, 217, 263
Adler, Thomas 6–7
Advertising 84, 111, 134–135, 162
Akins, Zoe 8, 14, 60, 61–62, 65, 66–81; actress stint 66–68; Broadway successes 61, 66, 70, 74; childhood and adolescence 66–67; death 74; early years as contributing writer 67–68; Hollywood and screenplay writing 61, 71–72, 73, 74; marriage to Hugo Rumbold 71–72; poetry writing 68; Pulitzer Prize 62, 73, 75; roles for female stars 61, 67, 69–70, 74; writing philosophy 69, 72, 73, 74, 75; **writings of:** *Camille* (screenplay) 72; *Daddy's Gone A-Hunting* 70; *Declassée* 67, 69, 70, 74, 75; *The Furies* 71; *The Greeks Had a Word for It* 72; *The Happy Days* (translation) 74; *Interpretations* (poetry) 68; *The Magical City* 68; *Morning Glory* (screenplay) 61, 72; *O Evening Star* 73–74; *The Old Maid* 62, 72–73, 75–81; *Papa* 68–69; "The Playwriting Passion" 73; *Showboat* (screen adaptation of Ferber work) 71; *The Varying Shore* 71
Albee, Edward 193
Alison's House see Glaspell, Susan
Allen, Frederick Lewis 19
America's culture of violence *see* culture of violence

Anatomy is destiny (Freudian theory) 131–133

backlash (against feminism) 159, 160–164; *see also* women's movement
Backlash: The Undeclared War Against American Women (book by Faludi) 161–164, 194, 203; *see also* Faludi, Susan
Baldwin, James 260
Barlow, Judith 23, 41, 49
Barnes, Clive 148
Barrymore, Diana 74
Barrymore, Ethel 61, 67, 69, 74, 75
Behn, Aphra 4
Ben-Zvie, Linda 53
Bigsby, C. W. E. (on Glaspell) 50, 51, 54–55
birth control 20, 22, 138
A Black Woman Speaks see Richards, Beah
black women playwrights 270–271, 279–289
Blair, Emily 22
Blues for an Alabama Sky see Cleage, Pearl
Bly, Robert 209
Bogart, Anne 219
Bonin, Jane 6
Bonner, Marita 281
Bourbon at the Border see Cleage, Pearl
Bowling for Columbine (documentary by Michael Moore) 251

Boyce, Neith 48, 50
Bradshaw, John 157
Brandon, Nathaniel 128
Brecht, Bertolt 216, 220, 265, 266, 269
Breese, William (husband of Zona Gale) 26, 35, 37
Broadway (New York City) 2, 5
Broun, Heywood Hale 50, 51
Brustein, Robert 171, 268
Burnett, Frances 172–173
Bush, George W. 254, 255, 257, 292

Cage Rhythm (Kia Corthron play) 288
Caldwell, Lydy Becker (mother of Beth Henley) 142–143, 151–152
Carroll, Vinette 284
Carter, Betsy 185
Cather, Willa 68
Catton, Bruce 17, 19–20
Chalfant, Kathleen 236, 238, 239
Chapman, John 70, 97–98, 118
Chase, Mary Coyle 8, 83, 88, 89–107; childhood and adolescence 89–91; death 100; first Broadway experience 92–94; founder of Denver House of Hope 99; marriage to Robert Chase 91–92, 97–99; "Mary Chase Alley" (temporary name of Shubert Alley, Broadway theatre district, 1953) 100; as news reporter 91–92; reaction to success 98–99; response to musical of *Harvey* (*Say Hello to Harvey* by Leslie Bricusse) 100; writing for children 100; writing philosophy 95, 100; World War II years 94–95, 98; **writings of:** *The Banshee* 92; *Bernardine* 100; *Colorado Dateline* 94; *Harvey* 8, 83, 89, 95–99, 100–107; *Me, Third* 92 (as *Now You've Done It* 93); *Mrs. McThing* 99–100; *The Pooka* 96–97 (see also *Harvey*); *A Slip of a Girl* 94; *Sorority House* 94; *Too Much Business* 94
Chase, Robert (husband of Mary Coyle Chase) 91–92, 93, 96,
Chayevsky, Paddy 253
Cheney, Dick 254
Chicago Artists Renaissance 47–48
Chicago's International Congress of Women 35
Childress, Alice 271, 283–284
Chittister, Joan 257–258

Chomsky, Noam 254, 255
Civic Repertory 54
Civil Rights Act of 1964 136
Civil Rights Movement 111, 136, 137
Clark, Ramsey 254, 255
Cleage, Pearl 2, 285–287, 293–294; **writings of:** *Blues for an Alabama Sky* 286; *Bourbon at the Border* 286; *Deals with the Devil and Other Reasons to Riot* (essays) 286; *Flyin' West* 286; *I Wish I Had a Red Dress* (novel) 287; *What Looks Like Crazy on an Ordinary Day* (novel) 285, 287
Clinton, William (President) 208, 211
The Cold War 108–109
The Colored Museum (play by George C. Wolfe) 263–264
Comden, Betty 191
Commissions on Status of Women (Federal and State) 135–136
Congdon, Constance 293
consciousness-raising groups 136–137, 187, 198
consumerism 21, 62–63, 111, 134–135, 253, 256
Cook, Ellen (mother of George Cram Cook) 45, 50
Cook, George Cram (husband of Susan Glaspell) 44–54, 58
Coontz, Stephanie 130–131, 291, 292
corporate crime 253–254
Corthron, Kia 288
Coward, Noel 36, 71
created family see family, created
Crisis magazine see *NAACP Crisis* magazine
Cukor, George 74
culture of addiction in America 256
culture of violence in America 251–253, 270, 293–294

Davis, Bette 61, 73
Deals with the Devil and Other Reasons to Riot see Cleage, Pearl
Def, Mos 249, 267, 269, 277
The Depression 17, 60, 61–65, 70, 81, 88, 92, 129
Derleth, August (Gale biographer) 28, 29, 30, 32, 34, 37
Des Moines Daily News 45
Diamond, Liz 261–262, 263, 264

divorce rates, U.S. 21, 138
Dixon, Marlene 134
domestic violence 159, 209–210, 211, 220, 286
Don't Bother Me, I Can't Cope 284
Drama Critics Circle *see* New York Drama Critics Circle
DuBois, W.E.B. 280
Dude, Where's My Country? 254; *see also* Moore, Michael
Durang, Christopher 184, 188

Edson, Margaret 7, 9–10, 146, 207, 231–247, 292; association with Derek Anson Jones 233, 235, 236–237, 238, 239; childhood and adolescence 232–233; family background 232–233, 235–236; John Donne in script of *Wit* 232, 235, 241, 243, 244; Pulitzer Prize 207, 232; teaching as primary occupation 232, 235, 238, 239–240; writing philosophy 234–235, 237–238; **writings of:** *Wit* (play) 207, 231, 233, 235–236, 237, 238, 239–247; *Wit* as HBO movie adaptation by Mike Nichols 237
Ehrenreich, Barbara 41, 160, 161, 163, 308n2
Elephant (film by Van Sant) 251–252
Eminem 257
Enron Corporation scandal 253–254
Equal Opportunity Employment Commission (EEOC) 136, 137
ERA (Equal Rights Amendment) 138
The Evening Wisconsin 25

Fahrenheit 9/11 254; *see also* Moore, Michael
Faludi, Susan 161–164, 194, 210; **writings of:** *Backlash: The Undeclared War Against American Women* 161–164, 194; *Stiffed: The Betrayal of the American Man* 210
family, created (as opposed to birth family) 15, 59–60, 79, 105, 158–159, 192, 203, 218, 291, 292
family dysfunction (as dramatic theme) 6–7, 13–15, 25, 58, 182, 292–293
family myths 6–8, 13–15, 22, 38, 42, 58–60, 78–80, 88, 124–125, 130–131, 132–133, 138, 139, 181, 182, 204–206; *see also* Napier, Nancy
Farnham, Marynia 132
Fay, Frank 96–97, 98
"Fear Factor" 251, 253
Federal Theatre Project 54, 92; Federal Theatre Negro Unit 281
The Feminine Mystique see Friedan, Betty
Fires in the Mirror (Anna Deavere Smith play) 279
Flapper (1920's "New Woman") 19, 36, 42
Flyin' West see Cleage, Pearl
For Colored Girls Who Have Considered Suicide/ When the Rainbow Is Enuf 284–285
Freud, Sigmund 48, 131–133
Friday, Nancy 178–179, 182
Friedan, Betty 111–112, 129–131, 133–137, 160, 162
Frings, Ketti 3, 83, 113–126, 127; acting attempts 114; childhood and adolescence 113–114; death 119; fan magazine writing 114; marriage to Kurt Frings 114–115, 119; Pulitzer Prize 119; screenplay writing 115, 116; wartime writing 115; writing philosophy 119–120; **writings of:** *The Accused* 115–116; *Come Back Little Sheba* (screenplay adaptation of Inge play) 116; *God's Front Porch* 115; *Hold Back the Dawn* (novel and screenplay) 114–115; *The Long Dream* 119; *Look Homeward, Angel* 116–126 (teleplay version) 119; *Mr. Sycamore* 115; *The Shrike* (screen adaptation of Kramm play) 116; *Walking Happy* (book for Broadway musical) 119
Frings, Kurt (husband of Ketti Frings) 114–115, 119

Gale, Charles (Father of Zona) 25, 28–29, 35, 43
Gale, Eliza (Mother of Zona) 25, 27–28, 33
Gale, Zona 2, 7, 17, 20, 22–43, 44, 60, 80, 292; association with LaFollette family 33, 35, 36; childhood and adolescence 25–26; death 37; early writings 25–30; engagement to Ridgely

Torrence 27; essay writing 34–35; honorary doctorate degrees 35; influence on stage realism 23–24, 27; Japan, cultural ambassador to 36; Leslyn (adopted daughter) 34, 35; marriage to William Breese 26, 35; mother's influence on 27–28, 33; politics of 19, 23, 28–29, 33; Prohibition stance 28; Pulitzer Prize 32; as reporter 2, 25; roles for women 31, 32, 36; University of Wisconsin Board of Regents appointment 33; war protests 23, 28–29; Wisconsin Equal Rights Law co-drafter 33; women's rights activism 2, 23, 28, 29, 30–31, 33, 37, 41; writing philosophy 26–27, 32; **writings of:** autobiography (unfinished fragment in Derleth book) 37; *Birth* 29–30; *A Daughter of the Morning* 20, 23, 29; essays 34–35; *Faint Perfume* 32–33; *Frank Miller of Mission Inn* 36, 37; Friendship Village stories 26–27, 30, 36; *Heart's Kindred* 23, 28; *Light Woman* 36–37; *The Loves of Pelleus and Etarre* 26; *Miss Lulu Bett* (novel) 18, 30–32; *Miss Lulu Bett* (play) 2, 7, 14, 16, 30–32, 37–43; *Mister Pitt* (play adaptation of *Birth*) 33–34; *Neighbors* 24; *Papa La Fleur* 35; *Preface to a Life* 34; "What Women Won in Wisconsin" 33

Garrett, Shawn-Marie 263, 264, 265

The Gift of the Magi (O. Henry story) 220, 230, 231

Gilligan, Carol 15

Glaspell, Susan 7–8, 17, 22–24, 44–60, 292; as actress 49–51; childhood and adolescence 44–45; death 55; director of own plays 51–52; early writings 45–47; experimental nature of work 50–53; Federal Theatre Project (appointment as Midwest Director of) 54; influence on Eugene O'Neill 52–53; influence on stage realism 23–24; marriage to George Cram Cook 48–50; as news reporter 45, 49; pacifism 23; Provincetown Players (co-founder and director of, with George Cram Cook) 24, 45–55; Pulitzer Prize 54; writing methods 23, 49–50; **writings of:** *Alison's House* 7–8, 54–60; *Bernice* 51; *The Glory of the Conquered* 46; *The Inheritors* 23, 51; *Judd Rankin's Daughter* 54; "News Girl" 45; *The Outside* 50–51; *The People* 50; *The Road to the Temple* 54; *Suppressed Desires* 48–49; *Trifles* 23, 49–50; *Unveiling Brenda* 46; *The Verge* 51–53; *The Visioning* 47

Gone with the Wind (Margaret Mitchell novel, and film) 64

Gregory, Lady 4

Grimké, Angelina Weld 280, 282

gun culture, American *see* culture of violence

Hamilton, LisaGay 283

Hansberry, Lorraine 284, 285

Harding, Warren 18

Harlem Renaissance 280

Harlem Writers Workshop 284

Harvey see Chase, Mary Coyle

The Heidi Chronicles see Wasserstein, Wendy

Hellman, Lillian 5, 73, 75, 150, 174, 191

Henley, Beth 8, 127–128, 139, 140–159, 182, 217, 292; acting attempts 143; childhood and adolescence 142–143; family incorporated into work of 142, 143, 144, 145, 151–152; influence of mother 142, 150, 152; influence of Southern background 142, 144–145, 151; playwrights workshops 140–141, Pulitzer Prize 146–148; roles for women 144, 148, 149, 150–151; on sexual discrimination in theatre 144, 150; screenplay writing 143–144, 149; son (Patrick) 151; split images in plays of 142, 145, 148–149; support of other artists 150; writing philosophy 141, 142, 144, 152; **writings of:** *Abundance* 151; *Am I Blue* 143; *Control Freaks* 151; *Crimes of the Heart* (play) 127, 139, 142, 143, 144–147, 152–159, 217; (screenplay version) 146–147, 149; *The Debutante Ball* 149; *Exposed* 152; *Family Week* 152; *Impossible Marriage* 151; *Miss Firecracker* (screenplay) 149; *The Miss Firecracker Contest* (play) 148–149; *Nobody's Fool* (screenplay) 143–144, 149; *Signature* 151; *The Wake of Jamie Foster* 148

Hepburn, Katherine 61, 72
Hidden Wars of Desert Storm (documentary film) 208–209, 255
A History of Private Life 21, 86, 88, 110
Hohenberg, John 99
House Un-American Affairs Committee 109
How I Learned to Drive see Vogel, Paula
How to Overthrow the Government (book by Huffington) 254
Howard University 281, 287
Hrosvitha (tenth century playwriting nun) 4
Huffington, Arianna 254,
Hull, Josephine 97, 99
Hummer (GM vehicle) 256
Hunter, Holly 149, 151
Hurston, Zora Neale 281

I Wish I Had a Red Dress see Cleage, Pearl
In a Different Voice (book by Carol Gilligan) see Gilligan, Carol
Industrial Revolution (effects on family) 14–15
Iraq, war on 255, 256, 259
The Irish Players 48
Iron John (book by Robert Bly) 209

Jackson, Judith 288–289
Jar the Floor (Cheryl West play) 288
Johnson, Georgia Douglas 281
Jones, Derek Anson 233, 235, 236–237, 238, 239
Jones, Robert Edmond 48, 53
Jones, Tisch 280
Jory, Jon 145–146

Kennedy, Adrienne 281
King, Martin Luther, Jr. 111
King, Woodie, Jr. 285
Koenig, Rachel 10–11
Krieger, David 255, 256
Ku Klux Klan 19
Kurtz, Swoosie 189, 222

Landesman, Heidi 172
LeGallienne, Eva 34
Lewis, Sinclair 18, 30, 37
Levittown 109
Life magazine 3, 110, 113

Live and In Color (play by Danitra Vance) 288–289
Look Homeward, Angel (play) see Frings, Ketti
Look Homeward, Angel (Wolfe novel) 113, 116–118
Look magazine 110–111
lynching 280; as dramatic theme 280, 282

MacGowan, Kenneth 53, 54
Malpede, Karen 293–294
Marlowe, Julia 67
Marriage for Moderns 132
marriage for women (biases about) 6–7, 14, 19, 20, 22, 32–33, 40, 41–43, 58, 78–81, 87–88, 104, 125–126, 130, 132–133, 138–139, 162–164; see also family myths
marriage laws (restricting women) 20, 34
The Masculine Mystique (book by Andrew Kimbrell) 209
McCarthy, Joseph 109
McClintic, Guthrie 74, 100
McKinney, Cynthia 254
McLuhan, Marshall 108
Mead, Margaret 21, 132–133
Men Against Pornography 211; see also Stoltenberg, John
men's movement (of late 20th century) 209–210
military, women in 84, 85, 87
military, U.S. government spending for 255–256
Miller, Arthur 1–2, 118
Miller, Frieda 87
Miller, May 281–282
Mills, John Stuart 132
Mirror on the Stage: The Pulitzer Plays as an Approach to American Drama (book by Adler) 6–7
Miss Lulu Bett see Gale, Zona
Mitchell, Margaret 64
Modern Woman: The Lost Sex 132
The Mojo and the Sayso (play by Aishah Rahman) 287–288
Moore, Michael 251, 257, 313n20
Moorman, Jean, study of women's marriage patterns 163
Mowatt, Anna Cora 4

My Mother, My Self (book by Nancy Friday) *see* Friday, Nancy
myths, family *see* family myths

NAACP *Crisis* magazine 280–284
NAACP Drama Committee 280
Nails and Thorns (play by May Miller) 282
Napier, Nancy 13–14, 42
Nation Magazine 21, 33, 255, 267, 268
National Foundation for Women Legislators 210
National Organization for Women (NOW) 136–137, 257
National Strike of Women 137–138
New Deal (Roosevelt Administration) 62–63
New Federal Theatre 285
"New Women": (of the 1920s) 21; (of the 1930s) 64, 65
New York Drama Critics Circle 5, 73
'*Night, Mother* see Norman, Marsha
Norman, Marsha 9, 11, 13, 15, 127, 165, 166–183, 191, 193, 292, 294; association with Actors Theatre of Louisville 167–168, 171, 172, 173; childhood and adolescence 166–167; created family "matriarchy" of 166–167, 174; influence of family in work of 166–167, 170, 173, 174; Pulitzer Prize 171–172, 173; roles for women 171, 173; on sexual discrimination in theatre 173–174, 294; "solitary confinement" concept in writing 179; Tony Award (for *The Secret Garden*) 173; writing philosophy 170, 173–174, 179; **writings of:** *The Fortune Teller* (novel) 172; *Getting Out* 167–168; *The Holdup* 169; *The Last Dance* 173; *The Laundromat* (one-act from *Third and Oak*) 169; '*Night, Mother* 9, 13, 166, 169, 170, 174–183; (screen play of) 171; *Sarah and Abraham* 172; *The Secret Garden* (book of Broadway musical) 172–173; *Traveler in the Dark* 171–172; *Trudy Blue* 173
Nottage, Lynn 288
NOW *see* National Organization for Women
Nuclear Age Peace Foundation 255

Ohio Gang (Warren Harding Administration) 18, 33

The Old Maid see Akins, Zoe
O'Neill, Eugene 3, 4, 5, 6, 8, 24, 49–53; association with Provincetown Players 49–53; **plays of:** *Beyond the Horizon* 6; *Bound East for Cardiff* 49; *The Emperor Jones* 52; *The Hairy Ape* 52–53; *Long Day's Journey into Night* 112; *Mourning Becomes Electra* (trilogy) 3–4
Oscher, Paul (husband of Suzan-Lori Parks) 266–267

Parks, Rosa 111
Parks, Suzan-Lori 10, 247, 249, 251, 258, 259–278; association with Yale School of Drama/ Yale Repertory 261, 263, 264–265, 266; awards and grants 266; childhood and adolescence 259–260; marriage to Paul Oscher 266–267; Pulitzer Prize 266, 268, 270–271; "Rep & Rev" concept in writing 267; roles for women 263, 265; screenplay and teleplay writing 269–270; work with Liz Diamond 261, 262, 263, 264; work with George C. Wolfe and the Public Theatre 263–264, 266, 268; writing of first novel 270; writing philosophy 259, 261, 262, 265, 266, 268, 276; **writings of:** *The America Play* 263, 264, 266; *Devotees in the Garden of Love* 263; *Fucking A* 265, 268–269, 270; *Getting Mother's Body* (novel) 270; *Girl Six* (Spike Lee screenplay) 269; *Imperceptible Mutabilities in the Third Kingdom* 261–262; *In the Blood* 265,266, 268; *The Last Black Man in the Whole Entire World* 262–263; *The Sinner's Place* 260; *Topdog/Underdog* 10, 247, 249–250, 258, 265, 266, 267, 268, 271–278, 279; *Venus* 264–265
Pemberton, Brock (producer) 30–31, 33–34, 36–37, 54, 93, 96
Perkins, Frances (first woman U.S. Cabinet member) 63
Perry, Antoinette 92–93, 97; *see also* Tony Awards
Perseverance Theatre of Alaska 218–219, 222
"the Pill" 138; *see also* birth control

Playwrights' Theatre 50; see also Provincetown Players
Poof! (play by Lynn Nottage) 288
pornography 209–211
Prohibition 18, 28
Provincetown Players 24, 45–55
Public Theatre (Joseph Papp Public Theatre/New York Shakespeare Festival) 10, 263, 264, 285
Pulitzer Prize for Drama 1–2, 5–7, 32, 73, 112, 127, 146, 147 207, 247, 271, 278 ; history of 5–7, 297n11; see also individual playwrights

Rachel (play by Grimké) 280, 282
radio 17, 61–62, 64–65; soap opera broadcasts 61–62, 64
"rage rap" 257
Rahman, Aishah 287–288
A Raisin in the Sun 264, 284, 285
Reagan, Ronald 87, 161–162, 208, 218, 254, 257
"Red Scare" (hunt for Communists in U.S.) 18, 109
Refusing to Be a Man (book by John Stoltenberg) 209–210
Reston, James 71, 73
Revolution from Within (book by Gloria Steinem) 165, 182, 292
Richards, Beah 271, 282–283; as actress 282–283; as subject of HBO documentary *Beah: A Black Woman Speaks* 283; as writer of *A Black Woman Speaks* 282–283
Rocky Mountain News, the 91, 94, 96, 100
Roe versus Wade 138
Roosevelt, Eleanor 62–63, 65
Roosevelt, Franklin D. 62–63, 92
"Rosie the Riveter" 85, 87
Roszak, Betty 137
Roy, Arundhati 254, 255, 256
Rumbold, Hugo (husband of Zoe Akins) 71–72
Ryan, Mary P. 130–131

Sanger, Margaret 20, 286
Sarlos, Robert 50
Savran, David 218, 259, 263
Scanlon, Tom 6–7, 14–15
The Scarlet Letter (Hawthorne novel) 265–266

self-esteem *see* women and self-esteem
September 11th attacks 255
September 11th Families for Peace 255
Shange, Ntozake 271, 284–285
Shearer, Ann 111
Simonson, Harold 30, 34, 37, 41
Skolnik, Peter 64, 85, 86
Smith, Anna Deavere 279
Smith, Molly 218–219, 221–222, 223
soap operas, radio *see* radio
Spence, Eulalie 281
Steinem, Gloria 3, 160, 162, 165, 182, 209–210, 292
Stephens, Judith 282
Stiffed: The Betrayal of the American Man (book by Faludi) *see* Faludi, Susan
Still Small Voice (Derleth biography of Zona Gale) 28, 37
Stoltenberg, John 209–210, 211
Stragglers in the Dust (play by May Miller) 282
Strange Fruit: Plays on Lynching by American Women 282
Stupid White Men and Other Sorry Excuses for the State of the Nation 254; see also Moore, Michael
Susan Smith Blackburn Prize 171, 192

Tales of the Lost Formicans (play by Connie Congdon) 293
television 108, 109, 110, 112, 253
Texas Chainsaw Massacre 253
To Be Young, Gifted, and Black 284
Tony Awards (Antoinette Perry Awards) 5, 127, 173, 193
Toohey, John 32, 116
Topdog/Underdog see Parks, Suzan-Lori
Torrence, Ridgely 27–28
Triangle Shirtwaist Factory fire 20, 23, 63
Twilight, Los Angeles (play by Anna Deavere Smith) 279

Vance, Danitra 288–289
Van Sant, Gus 251–252
Vidal, Gore 254, 255
video games (in American culture of violence) 252–253, 256, 257, 294
violence in America *see* culture of violence

Vogel, Carl (brother of Paula) 213, 215, 218, 219, 222
Vogel, Paula 9, 11 207, 209–210, 212, 213–231, 288, 292; childhood and adolescence 213–215; family background 213–215; influence of Carl Vogel (brother and mentor) 213, 215, 218, 222; multiple-character roles in plays of 9, 219, 221, 222; politics of 207, 212, 213, 220, 221; Pulitzer Prize 221; roles for women 218, 222, 247; on sexual bias in theatre 215–216; university teaching positions 216, 217, 222–223; work with director Anne Bogart 219–220; work with producer/director Molly Smith 218–219, 221–222, 223; writing philosophy 216, 217, 219–220, 221, 222, 231; **writings of:** *And Baby Makes Seven* 218; *The Baltimore Waltz* 218–219, 222; *Desdemona: A Play About a Handkerchief* 216–217; *Hot 'n' Throbbing* 210, 220; *How I Learned to Drive* 9, 207, 220, 221, 223–231; *The Mineola Twins* 221–222; *The Oldest Profession* 217–218
Vonnegut, Kurt 252

Walker, Alice 254, 258, 289, 294
Warren, Mercy Otis 4
Washington Square Players 48, 52, 68
Wasserstein, Bruce (brother of Wendy Wasserstein) 185–186
Wasserstein, Lola (mother of Wendy Wasserstein) 184–185, 187–188, 190, 192
Wasserstein, Wendy 3, 5, 7, 9, 127, 183, 184–206; association with Playwrights Horizons 188, 189, 192; birth family incorporated into work of 184, 189, 190; childhood and adolescence 184–185, 187; created family in life and work of 188, 191–192, 204–205; daughter (Lucy) 195, 196; influence of women's movement on 9, 187, 188–189, 193–194, 196, 204, 205–206; Pulitzer Prize 192–192, roles for women 9, 188–189, 194; on sexual discrimination in theatre 188–189, 196; Tony Award 192–193; writing philosophy 188–189, 196, 197; **writings of:** *An American Daughter* 195–196; *Any*
Woman Can't 187–188; *Bachelor Girls* (book of essays) 196; *The Heidi Chronicles* 9, 15, 183, 197–206; *Isn't It Romantic* 190–191; *The Object of My Affection* (screenplay) 196; *Old Money* 196–197; *Pamela's First Musical* (book and stage play) 196; *Shiksa Goddess, Or How I Spent My Forties* book of essays) 196; *The Sisters Rosensweig* 194–195, 197; *Uncommon Women and Others* 188–190; *When Dinah Shore Ruled the Earth* (musical co-written with Christopher Durang) 188
Waterman, Arthur 45, 47, 52, 60
The Way We Never Were (book by Coontz) 131, 291; *see also* Coontz, Stephanie
Wedding Band (play by Alice Childress) 283–284
Wells Ida 282
West, Cheryl 288
Wharf Theatre 49; *see also* Provincetown Players
Wharton, Edith 30, 72, 78
Wilkerson, Margaret 279
Wisconson Equal Rights Amendment 33
Wit see Edson, Margaret
Wolfe, George C. 10, 263–264, 266, 268
Wolfe, Thomas 113, 116–117, 118
Woloch, Nancy 20–21, 42, 63–64, 65, 86, 87–88, 136, 138
WOMBmanWARS (play by Judith Jackson) 289
women and education 20, 110, 130, 132–133, 138
women and marriage *see* marriage for women (biases about)
women and self-esteem 128, 151, 157–158, 165, 292
Women and the American Experience (book by Woloch) 64; *see also* Woloch, Nancy
women and war 84–88, 257–258
Women Respond to the Men's Movement 209
Women's Bureau 87
women's liberation 137; *see also* women's movement
women's movement: of the early 20th

century 19–22, 33, 41–43; of the 1960s and 1970s 9, 128–139, 159, 160–165, 182, 187, 189, 193, 194, 196, 199, 201, 203, 204–206, 208, 291, 292; as presented in *The Heidi Chronicles* 197–204
women's studies programs 10, 138
Woollcott, Alexander 71, 74
World War I 18, 84, 120
World War II 61, 84–88, 94, 99, 100, 107, 108, 127, 129

The Worst Years of Our Lives (book by Barbara Ehrenreich) 160, 161, 308n2
Wright, Jeffrey 266, 267, 277

Yale Repertory (and Yale School of Drama) 188, 189, 264, 266
Yale study of women's marriage patterns (1986) 163
Yeats, William Butler 4
Your Arms Too Short to Box with God 284